Writing AIDS

BETWEEN MEN ~ BETWEEN WOMEN
LESBIAN AND GAY STUDIES
Lillian Faderman and Larry Gross, Editors

D0307983

BETWEEN MEN ~ BETWEEN WOMEN
LESBIAN AND GAY STUDIES
Lillian Faderman and Larry Gross, Editors

John Clum, *Acting Gay: Male Homosexuality in Modern Drama*

Gary David Comstock, *Violence Against Lesbians and Gay Men*

Allen Ellenzweig, *The Homoerotic Photograph: Male Images from Durieu/Delacroix to Mapplethorpe*

Lillian Faderman, *Odd Girls and Twilight Lovers: A History of Lesbian Life in Twentieth-Century America*

Richard D. Mohr, *Gays/Justice: A Study of Ethics, Society, and Law*

Sally Munt, *New Lesbian Criticism: Literary and Cultural Readings*

Judith Roof, *A Lure of Knowledge: Lesbian Sexuality and Theory*

Kath Weston, *Families We Choose: Lesbians, Gays, Kinship*

Writing AIDS

Gay Literature, Language, and Analysis

Timothy F. Murphy and Suzanne Poirier,
Editors

Columbia University Press   New York

Columbia University Press
New York   Chichester, West Sussex

Copyright © 1993 Columbia University Press
All rights reserved

Library of Congress Cataloging-in-Publication Data

Writing AIDS : gay literature, language, and analysis / Timothy F.
Murphy and Suzanne Poirier, editors.
    p.   cm. — (Between men—between women)
"Annotated bibliography of AIDS literature, 1982–91 / Franklin
Brooks and Timothy F. Murphy": p.
Includes bibliographical references and index.
ISBN 0–231–07864–1
ISBN 0–231–07865–x (pbk.)
1. Gays' writings, American—History and criticism.   2. AIDS
(Disease) in literature.   3. American literature—20th century—
History and criticism.   4. American literature—Men
authors—History and criticism.   5. Literature, Modern—20th
century—History and criticism.   6. Literature, Modern—Men
authors—History and criticism.   7. Homosexuality and literature—
History—20th century.   8. Gays' writings—History and criticism.
    I. Murphy, Timothy F., 1955–   .   II. Poirier, Suzanne.
III. Series.
PS153.G38W74   1993
810.9'356—dc20   92–20373
                                                  CIP

⊗

Casebound editions of
Columbia University Press books
are printed
on permanent and durable
acid-free paper.

Designed by Teresa Bonner
Printed in the United States of America
c 10 9 8 7 6 5 4 3
p 10 9 8 7 6 5 4 3 2 1

BETWEEN MEN ~ BETWEEN WOMEN
LESBIAN AND GAY STUDIES

Lillian Faderman and Larry Gross, Editors
Eugene F. Rice, Columbia University Advisor

Between Men ~ Between Women is a forum for current lesbian and gay scholarship in the humanities and social sciences. The series includes both books that rest within specific traditional disciplines and are substantially about gay men, bisexuals, or lesbians and books that are interdisciplinary in ways that reveal new insights into gay, bisexual, and lesbian experience, transform traditional disciplinary methods in consequence of the perspectives that experience provides, or begin to establish lesbian and gay studies as a freestanding inquiry. Established to contribute to an increased understanding of lesbians, bisexuals, and gay men, the series also aims to provide through that understanding a wider comprehension of culture in general.

Contents

Acknowledgments

The editors wish to thank our University of Illinois colleague Richard D. Mohr and Ann M. Miller of Columbia University Press for their helpful suggestions and tendance during the early stages of creating this book. We would also like to thank Brett Shingledecker and Carrie Barnett at People Like Us Books in Chicago for letting us browse at length through their bookshelves.

Writing AIDS

On Writing AIDS: Introduction

Suzanne Poirier

THE DAY before my annual summer trip home to rural Nebraska, I attended a street fair in the heart of Chicago's gay neighborhood. Same-sex and mixed-sex couples and groups idled along the street, buying beer and bratwurst from the bars and restaurants set up along the curbside, browsing among booths of crafts and trinkets, watching the antics at the dunking chair and the gay square-dance group that invited you for twenty-five cents to "two-step with a cowboy." Many booths were selling items or collecting money for various AIDS organizations and services in Chicago. I bought an ACT UP T-shirt that I threw into my suitcase before heading out of town the next morning.

As I drove across the Missouri River into Nebraska that afternoon, the local radio news broadcast a story about a woman diagnosed with AIDS, an occurrence still uncommon enough in August 1991 to be newsworthy in that part of the world. By the time I reached the rural southwestern corner of the state, local media carried no news of the epidemic at all. Nebraska has not been untouched by AIDS, even though the number of cases has not yet reached three hundred. But however small the numbers may seem beside those for New York, California, or Illinois, they are still significant figures for affected families and friends.

What struck me more, though, was the absolute silence surrounding AIDS that continued to exist in this conservative locale more than a decade into the epidemic. But why should I be surprised? Silence, I have been reminded by nearly every essay in this collection, is a difficult, often threatening barrier to break, even in the most "liberated" settings. The pride and open expressions of joy or desire that many gay men have expressed since Stonewall are still relatively new freedoms. Silence is still carefully guarded by gay men and lesbians in some communities, rigidly maintained by heterosexual men and women in others. Phillip Brian Harper ("Eloquence and Epitaph: Black Nationalism and the Homophobic Impulse in Responses to the Death of Max Robinson"), for example, writing here about the death of African-American newscaster Max Robinson, argues that "a general silence [exists] regarding the effects of the epidemic among the African-American population," with its "intersection of discursive contexts that do not allow for the expression of black male homosexuality in any recognizable form." Peter M. Bowen ("AIDS 101") writes that the notion of AIDS presents such a "threat to the imagination as well as to the bod[ies]" of his students that even in a composition course where all reading, writing, and discussions center on AIDS and the epidemic, "students' abilities to ghettoize the idea of gay sex . . . into a particularly unimaginable corridor of the imagination demonstrates to what extent this epidemic . . . could also be simply too real for words." And Sander L. Gilman ("Plague in Germany, 1939/1989: Cultural Images of Race, Space, and Disease") writes of history and culture as a silencer, because Germany's Nazi past creates a tremendous barrier to an open discourse about AIDS. "The vocabulary of difference employed in 1989 cannot abandon the imagery of 1939," Gilman says, identifying a vocabulary that links sexual difference with danger and disease and that seeks to blame identifiably different groups as threats to national (i.e., Aryan) health.

The continued silence about and resistance to homoeroticism are often exacerbated by AIDS—as is the need to break that silence. Timothy F. Murphy ("Testimony") notes the progress in awareness and circumstance that has moved gay literature "beyond the coming-out stories . . . to address the trials of ordinary human life," creating a literature that explores "relationships and families." With tragic irony, though, this progress has been achieved just in time to have to discuss relationships and families within the new realities of HIV-related illnesses and death. Gay literature almost immediately returns to a confrontation with a public mythology still committed to the belief that homosexuality = illness = death. Thus this still newly self-conscious (though hardly new) literature faces an incredible challenge. In this vein, Paula A. Treichler ("AIDS Narratives on Television: Whose Story?") debates the costs of presenting uncomfortably "conventional" characters "without too much fanfare in a prime-time television relationship" against the gains achieved in "manipulati[ng television's] own conventional elements" to enable formerly unsympathetic viewers to identify with Persons With AIDS (PWA). Many of the contributors to this collection would say that today's writers about AIDS are faced more with new responsibilities than challenges. According to John M. Clum ("'And Once I Had It All': AIDS Narratives and Memories of an American Dream"), "It is the linkings of sex = disease, homosexuality = disease, promiscuity = disease, and, finally, homosexuality = promiscuity = disease, that enchain people with AIDS and, by association, all gay men," and he praises recent writing that abjures images of passivity and wages instead a "more vital war that counters the victim mentality of many AIDS narratives."

Writing AIDS is an examination of how those equations are being rejected or rewritten in a healing way in today's writing about the epidemic in the literary presses, obituary columns, and even freshman compositions. These authors are nearly unanimous in their assertion that AIDS has irremediably changed the way that gay literature can be either written or read, whatever the reader's or writer's feelings about the epidemic or the homoerotic. Their opinions about how gay literature should be written or read, however, vary widely. Joseph Cady, for example, has characterized AIDS literature as "immersive" or "counterimmersive" (though some writing contains elements of both), looking at the direct and explicit ways through which writers present AIDS and the experiences of PWAs. Using Paul Monette's poetic and autobiographical works as a model, he praises immersive writing for its "willingness to defy the dominant culture directly and fully and its faithfulness to the emotional and social anguish of people affected by AIDS, especially to the catastrophic texture of gay men's experience under the double denial directed at them during the crisis," and he criticizes writers of the counterimmersive style, among them Andrew Holleran, because he feels that their work "exempts its audience from too close a contact with the horrors of AIDS and makes no compelling demands on the denying reader." Along these same lines, Emily Apter ("Fantom Images: Hervé Guibert and the Writing of 'sida' in France") explains that Hervé Guibert, despite heavy criticism from his friends, wrote about Michael Foucault's death from "sida" (the French acronym for AIDS) in *L'ami qui ne m'a pas sauvé la vie* because "Guibert claimed that to violate the secret (in his words an 'amorous crime') was his inevitable fate."

By contrast, James W. Jones ("Refusing the Name: The Absence of AIDS in Recent American Gay Male Fiction") argues that because "the name *AIDS* evokes certain images that circumscribe the ability to transcend the limits they impose," the word itself can make it impossible to communicate the human tragedy of AIDS to a denying, uncomfortable, or hostile audience. Refusing to name the syndrome not only allows writers "to particularize and to universalize" gay love and joy as well as suffering and grief, but disallows any credence to "efforts to marginalize gays." Jones offers Andrew Holleran and Robert Ferro as models of this defiance and concludes, "Not by ignoring its presence but by refusing the definitions American culture has loaded into AIDS these fictions also radically alter the portrayal of gays in American fiction generally." Lee Edelman ("The Mirror and the Tank: 'AIDS,' Subjectivity, and the Rhetoric of Activism"), by contrast, urges us to be cautious of all dualistic, oppositional definitions, categories, or judgments of AIDS literature, seeing such labeling as creating divisions rather than unity or even clarity. "The point," he writes, "is to focus on the logic and implications of some of the terms through which an 'AIDS activist' identity . . . is being formed—formed, to be sure, both for and by, but also, I think, in significant ways, at the expense of gay men."

Whatever their positions, however, these writers maintain that the strength of the literature they champion lies in its ability to (re)affirm gay existence, self-respect, and love, an assertion that is a central theme of the essays in *Writing AIDS*. Using Dante's *Inferno* as a prototype, James Miller ("Dante on Fire Island: Reinventing Heaven in the AIDS Elegy") describes an AIDS "elegy" that is "a kind of poetic therapy." He insists that in creating "a heaven that vibrates in the memory, that raises hope in the midst of deepening pain, [a writer] must do more than address the aching needs of the body: [he or she] should also 'emparadise the mind' (as Dante put it) with the fantastic prospect of transcendence." And Richard Dellamora ("Apocalyptic Utterance in Edmund White's 'An Oracle'") chooses to focus his analysis of Edmund White's short story "An Oracle" on Jacques Derrida's "affirmative project of deconstruction," the oracular voice in literature, a tone capable of "open[ing] upon the possibilities of personal and social renewal." Similarly, even though Michael S. Sherry ("The Language of War in AIDS Discourse") hesitates, as does Gilman, to criticize AIDS activists and political commentators for "employing a language so deeply rooted in the political culture," he still finds it hard to imagine "that alternative possibilities [are] unimaginable" and wishes for new words and metaphors that do not direct so much blame for the AIDS epidemic onto willful men and women.

The contributors differ in their estimations of the stances needed for the conceptualization and politics of AIDS, but they agree that an urgent need for thought and writing about AIDS exists in all communities. They describe this writing as taking new forms, such as Cady's descriptions of "immersive" and "counterimmersive" styles and Apter's depiction of the chaotic form taken by Guibert's writing, because he wrote *A l'ami qui ne m'a pas sauvé la vie* and *Le protocole compassionel* with the urgency of one who sees the imminence of his own death (as do a number of the authors discussed in the following pages). Apter sees this "pornography of death," with its need to "write pain so that it hurts the way pain hurts," as drawing upon the images of earlier French writing about syphilis. Gilman also sees historical connections with German literature in his comparison of Nazi and contemporary dystopias; however he notes that Germany's first AIDS novel, Peter Zingler's *Die Seuche*, written for a "liberal" (read "straight") audience, fails in its attempt to create "a utopian 'healthy' German society that would accept" PWAs—a failure that Zingler's choice of genre both predicts and abets. Other writers see other traditional literary forms, such as the obituary, the elegy, and even the oracle, taking on renewed vigor and relevance as the personal poignancy of AIDS—for those who are left (perhaps only temporarily) behind as much as for those who die—calls for more direct, personal means of expression. And still other writers study the appropriateness of nontraditional forms, such as television narratives, to convey the meanings of AIDS; Paula Treichler and John M. Clum pay particular attention to television and cinema representations of AIDS, exploring how these popular, conservative media both manipulate and fall prey to their conventions as they strive to create a broader sympathy for PWAs.

Running through nearly all these essays is the awareness that not only is AIDS writing a literary act involving conscious decisions about what to say or what not to say and how to couch what is said, but that writing about that writing is also a political act. For example, while Sander Gilman concludes his comparison of syphilis in Germany in the late 1930s and AIDS in Germany in the late 1980s with the fatalistic statement that German images of plague today must to some extent repeat the fantasies of "absolute boundaries" between health and disease that existed in 1939, he also asserts his intent to address the failure of critical discourse to recognize particular "national qualities ascribed to an illness" and the significance such differences might have on fruitful international communication about AIDS. Peter Bowen expresses similar frustration about the indelibility of cultural bias when he states that, for most of the students in his composition class, "the most confusing and contradictory lessons of AIDS have already been so thoroughly learned that they confound whatever facts an AIDS class might present," but he ends his essay with the account of a woman whose uncle had recently died of AIDS writing about the value of the class for her. Her comment helped Bowen himself "truly underst[and] the worth of this course," he concludes, a statement that justified for him the seeming ineffectualness of the course. With such a statement, though, Bowen reveals his belief that scholars need to affect the lives and thinking of the people they address in their work. Similarly, Michael Sherry explains his disappointment with the recurring use of war imagery by AIDS activists in terms of the power of culture when he says that "even the novel event had to be translated into language with imaginative signposts to the familiar," but goes on, as mentioned above, to call for a search for new metaphors.

Along these same lines, Lee Edelman analyzes the images and prejudices that would, within the gay community, fault men who do not adopt "politically correct" forms of activism. He proposes instead a new, postmodern opportunity "to challenge, as Andreas Huyssen suggests postmodernism must, 'the *ideology of the subject*' . . . by developing alternative and different notions of subjectivity" that, in turn, will generate "an activism that need not define itself against the narcissism and passivity that figure the place of gay male sexuality in the Western cultural imagination." Finally, even more forthright in their arguments are John Clum, who writes a prescription for gay AIDS literature of the 1990s when he says that "there is no need for more depictions of loss and grief" and calls instead for works of "productive anger" that will be produced by today's "younger generation of gay men who know only the Age of AIDS, the war"; Joseph Cady, who delineates what "all AIDS literature must at least minimally do to be worthy of the name"; and Phillip Harper, who writes to expose the "numerous and complex cultural factors [that] conspire to prevent such deaths from effectively galvanizing AIDS criticism in African-American communities," an exercise necessary as a first step "if we hope to stem the ravages of AIDS in the African-American community."

A final observation worth making about the essays collected here deals with privilege and the community of AIDS. The vast majority of the literature and other media discussed here is about the effect of AIDS on gay men, more particularly on gay, white men. What and how can people without HIV infections contribute to these discussions—and to the healing process that most of these writers say must take place? How can other communities of men and women affected by the epidemic broaden or contribute to the discussion and healing begun by the authors and commentators presented here?

Contributors to this collection have mentioned several groups of people who have been identified as Other by both themselves and the gay community, some of them even members of that community: gay African-Americans, "nonactivist" gays, women, (presumably) straight college students. Members of many of these groups are finding their voices and making their presence felt. Marlon Rigg's film *Tongues Untied* celebrates gay African-Americans. Recent novels by lesbian writers Sarah Shulman and Jane Rule introduce gay characters with AIDS, calling for sympathy and action from their lesbian characters. Physician Perri Klass has written a novel about a young woman physician who treats an infant with AIDS. But many novelists, journalists, and screenwriters may still see the writing of AIDS as more of an option than it seems to gay writers. I am not sure that option is as real as some of these people may think, a supposition supported by the bibliography that concludes this collection.

In a very real sense, all writing today is AIDS writing in that it must consciously choose how to respond to the epidemic, whether by direct involvement or evasion. Moreover, this involvement by an increasing diversity of writers raises the possibility of a unity of effort and concern that is encouraged or foreseen by several of the contributors to this collection. Richard Dellamora notices the brief but persistent references to friend Betty in Edmund White's "An Oracle" and comments, "Betty's presence implies the need for further micropolitical analysis: not only of the apparent necessity of the role she plays for gay men but also of reciprocity." And James Miller, looking at AIDS stories against the backdrop of Dante's *Inferno*, compares Dante's heroic ability to defy "the homophobic puritanism of his own day by daring to imagine a blessed end to the fiery isolation of the same-sex lover" with the fantasy reunion scene in the movie *Longtime Companion*, which offers "the notion of diverse sexualities working together toward a common goal of social integration." Paula Treichler ultimately is not willing to accept the limitations of primetime television because she believes that television's "failure" to "in many ways tell the story of AIDS" tells instead the story of network television's own, continuing "fearful, cautious, deadly path to self-destruction." Emily Apter sees in Guibert's *Le protocole compassionel* a unity of patient and physician, as AIDS forces new relationships: "In a sense, both are arguing that some breach in the ethics of medical distance is inevitable with this kind of illness; that doctor and patient are fatefully part of the film 'of each other's lives.'" And finally, my colleague Tim Murphy writes about testimonials to loved ones dead of AIDS, written by gay lovers and friends, parents, and wives. The need to bear witness is a common one for them, and Tim suggests that this common need and common expression carry the seeds for shared grief, understanding, and action: "The grief of the epidemic and the incentive to memorialize are no mere biological reflexes; they are an assertion against the leveling effect of death that persons are not replaceable, that death does not nullify presence."

Writing AIDS offers itself as further testimony that the personal tragedies of AIDS must not be allowed to destroy or defeat love, joy, or hope. The epidemic is not over. Much work remains to be done—in medicine, in politics, in our daily lives, and in our private and public discourse. As part of this work, *Writing AIDS* offers critical analysis that challenges us to resist easy characterizations or understandings of the epidemic and to work together to build whatever new communities of care, expression, and action are required.

The Mirror and the Tank: "AIDS," Subjectivity, and the Rhetoric of Activism

Lee Edelman

Analysis, while necessary, may also be an indefensible luxury.
—Leo Bersani

I   Writing "AIDS"

If all writing demands a subject—both insofar as it engages an economy of
reference and insofar as it posits a subject-position—it might be useful, in
order to explore some aspects of the relations between writing and
"AIDS," to consider the possibility that "AIDS" itself cannot un-
problematically function as the subject of our writing, because "AIDS" is
ideologically constructed as a form of writing itself: as an inscription of
difference whose "subject" is always the subject of ideology. "AIDS," in
the first place, and on the most literal level, lacks a coherent medical ref-
erent, remaining a signifier in search of the determinate condition or conditions it would signify. A diagnostic term describing the state in which the
immune system—compromised through HIV infection—can no longer
ward off certain officially designated opportunistic diseases, "AIDS" constitutes so unstable a signifier even in the arena of medical discourse that
on June 9, 1991, the *Boston Globe* reported:

> Officials of the Centers for Disease Control said Friday that they are con-
> sidering changing the way they define AIDS, a move that could double the
> number of Americans officially classified as suffering from the disease.
> Because AIDS causes a general devastation of the immune system, it is
> marked not by one symptom, but by dozens of infections, cancers and other
> conditions. The proposed change, which comes at the suggestion of the

Conference of State and Territorial Epidemiologists, would broaden the official classification of AIDS to encompass thousands of HIV-infected people
who have none of the conditions included in the 14-page government definition.

To this acknowledgment that even a "14-page definition" cannot secure
the referential adequacy of "AIDS" we must add the more widespread conflation, largely promulgated by journalists and politicians, of "AIDS" and
HIV seropositivity—a conflation that rhetorically identifies the effect
with the medical indicator of the putative cause as if such referential violence could, paradoxically, reinforce the coherence of "AIDS" by achiev-
ing its totalization and its ideological compaction. And if the imprecision
with which cultural "authorities" thereby encourage the public to view
"AIDS" serves the purposes of those intent on writing "AIDS" as a linear
narrative progressing ineluctably from a determinate beginning to a pre-
determined end, that fact makes it all the less likely that "AIDS" "itself"
could be our subject, since the signifier both connotes and denominates a
dense and contradictory array of medical diagnoses, social experiences,
projective fantasies, and "political" agendas.

"AIDS," then, resists our attempts to inscribe it as a manageable subject of writing—exceeding and eluding the medical, sociological, political, or literary discourses that variously attempt to confront or engage it—
to the extent that as a historical phenomenon in the so-called Western de-
mocracies it has itself taken shape (has been given shape) as that which
writes or articulates another subject altogether: a subject whose content is
suggested but not exhausted by reference to "male homosexuality." The
discursive field of "AIDS" thus unfolds as a landscape of displacements,
and given those displacements and the slipperiness of the subject, every
attempt to resist ideological enforcement in one place carries with it the
threat of resowing the seeds of ideological coercion in another. To take this
threat seriously, or to suggest that we cannot afford *not* to take this threat
seriously, does not mean that we should respond to the task of "writing
AIDS" by writing it off from the outset, or that we ought to domesticate the
intolerable losses that "AIDS" must always denote by framing "AIDS"
with the security that attends a certain sort of knowingness, as a recognizable instance of a now familiar postmodern problematic—as if "AIDS"
could be defined as *merely*, in Paula Treichler's words, an "epidemic of
signification," or as *nothing but*, in a phrase I myself used elsewhere, a
"plague of discourse."[1]

And yet, as Jeffrey Weeks acknowledges by titling an essay "Post-
Modern AIDS?," intellectual efforts to theorize the epidemic, its con-

structions, and its representations, frequently invoke, toward differing ends and with varying degrees of insight and engagement, some notion of the postmodern.[2] Roberta McGrath, for instance, observes: "HIV— which is a simulacrum of DNA—is the first human retrovirus [sic], perhaps the first post-modern disease."[3] Donna Haraway makes a similar point in "A Manifesto for Cyborgs," identifying "AIDS" with the forces of "simulation" (characteristic of what she calls the postmodern "informatics of domination") as opposed to the forces of "representation" (characteristic of the world order of industrial capitalism).[4] Remarking upon the temptation to respond to "AIDS" with global assertions that would read it as a figure for a historic shift in the cultural paradigm of "meaning," Robert Glück considers the claim that "AIDS is the disease of the Eighties. Why? Well, the destruction of the immune system is an allegory of the breakdown of 'basic structures' now experienced by our country and the West."[5] And Simon Watney affirms that the "challenge of AIDS reeducation exemplifies the insight of Ernesto Laclau and Chantal Mouffe that what is being exploded in the postmodern period, 'is the idea and the reality itself of a unique space of constitution of the political.'"[6]

Perhaps the importance of postmodernism as the framework within which these and other intellectuals have attempted to conceptualize or to respond to "AIDS" can be seen most interestingly in *AIDS Demo Graphics*, a volume in which Douglas Crimp and Adam Ralston identify the program, politics, and principles characteristic of "AIDS activist art."[7] Describing the work produced by such collectives as Gran Fury, the Silence = Death Project, and various committees from within ACT UP, Crimp and Ralston find not only "techniques of postmodernist appropriation" (18) and a "sophisticated postmodern style" (19), but also a survival of the radicalism with which, before becoming institutionalized itself, "postmodernist art advanced a political critique of art institutions" (19). One essential aspect of this critique that "AIDS activist artists" are credited with perpetuating is a challenge to the ideology whereby modernism (and the museum or literary canon as cultural establishments that both mirrored and enshrined it) affirmed an order of meaning that could be shaped, transformed, and revolutionized by the genius of the individual artist. As Crimp and Ralston observe:

> Questions of identity, authorship, and audience—and the ways in which all three are constructed through representation—have been central to postmodernist art, theory, and criticism. The significance of so-called appropriation art, in which the artist forgoes the claim to original creation by ap-

propriating already-existing images and objects, has been to show that the 'unique individual' is a kind of fiction, that our very selves are socially and historically determined through preexisting images, discourses, and events.

Young artists finding their place within the AIDS activist movement rather than the conventional art world have had reason to take these issues very seriously.   (18)

All who are interested in writing and "AIDS"—interested, that is, in how those two terms interrogate, reflect, and displace one another in the discourses through which "AIDS" is constructed—have reason to take seriously this recurrent conjunction of "AIDS" and postmodernism, to read it as gesturing toward a cultural logic centrally at stake in the conflict being waged over "AIDS" and "representation."

In this context it is not insignificant, after all, that what Fredric Jameson discusses as a crucial component of postmodernism—one that can, as he sees it, help to "explain why classical modernism is a thing of the past and why postmodernism should have taken its place"—can also illuminate the intersection of postmodernism and "AIDS": "This new component," Jameson argues, "is what is generally called 'the death of the subject.'"[8] Now to claim that we can hear in the discourse on "AIDS" reverberations of this postmodern "death of the subject" is to approach the always unstable demarcation between, on the one hand, producing a *reading* of the allegories through which the political unconscious manifests itself in the social imagination and, on the other hand, simply *producing* such potentially dangerous allegories ourselves. Yet insofar as "the death of the subject" enters popular discourse most directly through the various challenges posed to the identification of subjectivity as such with the particular subject-position associated with straight, white, middle-class men, "AIDS," which popular mythology continues to construe as largely exempting straight, white, middle-class men from its ravages, could not fail to inflect and to be inflected by the vicissitudes of "the subject" in contemporary Western culture. "AIDS," then, can be figured as a crisis in—and hence as an opportunity for—the social shaping or articulation of subjectivities because, in part, the historical context within which "AIDS" in the West achieved its "identity" allowed it to be presented as a syndrome distinctively engaging identity as an issue. In fact, whatever the direction from which we approach the subject of "AIDS," we are brought up against our own constitution as subjects of (and in) ideology and the fact that we are forced to recognize that the politics of "AIDS" as a subject of discourse is inseparable from the politics of "the subject" itself—

inseparable, that is, from the ideological construction and the cultural fantasmatics of agency.[9]

Even within those marginalized communities in which a great deal of critical energy has been expended to analyze the official representations of "AIDS," much of that energy has been directed toward prescriptions of the "proper" constitution of the discursive subject in and through what Simon Watney has called "an AIDS activist cultural practice" or "an AIDS activist aesthetic."[10] Such a practice, as he argues in an important essay, "Representing AIDS," is predicated upon "a cultural politics that is sensitive to the complex processes that produce subjectivities, and hold them in place" (190). Addressing himself to the question of photography in a way that bears extension across the spectrum of artistic modes, Watney insists that an "AIDS activist aesthetic" must counter those representational practices that depend upon a "familiar humanist pathos to stir reluctant sympathies" (179). In light of this canny observation, it may be worth considering the extent to which even the "AIDS activist aesthetic" interpellates a subject whose agency continues to be bound up problematically with the pathos of such a humanism, in that its subject continues to be caught within the falsely naturalized oppositions that give rise to our notions of sex and gender and sexuality—each of which stands in a critical relation to the conceptualization of subjectivity.[11]

My purpose, of course, is not to disable the indispensable work, including Watney's own, produced from within this activist aesthetic; rather, I want to elaborate some of the difficulties encountered in "writing AIDS" in order to hold open options for the inscription of narratives, and the interpellation of subjects, in ways that differ from those that govern so unyieldingly both the dominant discourse on "AIDS" and much of the contestatory counterdiscourse that defines itself as "activist." In the process I do not intend to suggest, as the syntax of the previous sentence may imply, any symmetry between the lethal cynicism of the government's manipulation, and even its deployment, of "AIDS," and the life-saving resistance by "AIDS activists" to the various forms that manipulation has taken. Instead, I want to examine some ways in which the overlapping crises that we experience as "AIDS" produce an oppositional political discourse that has the potential, in its necessary struggle against both the officially sanctioned representations of the epidemic and their intended constitution of a "normal" or "healthy" subjectivity, to naturalize and reposition certain aspects of the ideological structures that inform and produce those noxious representations and oppressive subjectivities in the first place.

II   Genesis and Genocide

On June 3, 1991, as journalists began to comment on the tenth anniversary of America's first official reports of what is now considered "AIDS," an editorial in New Hampshire's *Manchester Union Leader* could still insist on the truth of the genealogical narrative that has lodged itself so firmly in the Western cultural imagination that it underlies, in many cases, even the most "sophisticated" responses to the epidemic: "Homosexual intercourse is the genesis of every single case of AIDS in that every case is traceable—either directly or indirectly—to the practice. However the disease is transmitted, the sexual perversion that is anal intercourse by sodomites is the fundamental point of origin."[12] Tempting as it might be to dismiss such a statement as the ignorant, even risible, cant of a right-wing political extremist, the myth that it recirculates remains the most significant fiction our culture has produced in its efforts to understand "AIDS." Whether sublimated into the neutralizing discourse that warns of "AIDS" "spreading" from "high risk groups" to the "general population," so called, or moralized into the media's sensationalized renderings of those they insist on defining (against their always unspoken but implicit antitheses) as the epidemic's "innocent victims," the inescapability—indeed, the vitality—of a fiction that not only allows but actually *requires* the "general public" to imagine a scene (in fact, a primal scene) of anal sex between men bespeaks an imperative in the framing of "AIDS" that we ignore at our own risk.

Whatever the scientific or epidemiological "truth" about "AIDS" and HIV transmission, the logic within which "AIDS" has been made to signify in the West calls forth, as Leo Bersani observes in his provocative essay, "Is the Rectum a Grave?," the "seductive and intolerable image of a grown man, legs high in the air, unable to refuse the suicidal ecstasy of being a woman" (212). Bersani recognizes that this cultural fantasy defines gay men as a social category in terms of a particular erotic practice—sometimes described as "receptive anal intercourse," more commonly known as "getting fucked"—and that this definition allows gay men to be inscribed in the role that "properly" is inhabited by (heterosexual) women. For a man to permit himself to be so inscribed can be understood as "suicidal," then, since it connotes a willing sacrifice of the subjectivity, the disciplined self-mastery, traditionally attributed only to those who perform the "active" or penetrative—and hence "masculine"—role in the active-passive binarism that organizes "our" cultural perspective on sexual behavior.

In a phrase that registers the persistence not merely of a sexual but also of an erotic politics in the fantasmatics of subjectivity, Bersani, commenting on the Athenian belief in "a legal and moral incompatibility between sexual passivity and civic authority," draws the inevitable conclusion: *"To be penetrated is to abdicate power"* (212). David Halperin, underscoring this point, relates it to "the cultural poetics of manhood"[13] through which the political subject was called into being in the "democratizing initiative in classical Athens" (102) so as "to promote a new collective image of the citizen body as masculine and assertive, as master of its pleasures, and as perpetually on the superordinate side of a series of hierarchical and roughly congruent distinctions in status: master vs. slave, free vs. unfree, dominant vs. submissive, active vs. passive, insertive vs. receptive, customer vs. prostitute, citizen vs. non-citizen, man vs. woman" (102–3). Within this conceptual paradigm, which is, regrettably, our enduring heritage, to allow oneself to be displaced from the "superordinate side" of masculine self-assertion to the subordinate position of feminine receptivity registers as "suicidal" precisely to the extent that it signifies, and not "merely" as a figure, what could be called the "death of the subject." For given the unthinkable coincidence of power and passivity, the act by which a subject assumes the posture of an "object" constitutes the one act that a subject, *as* a subject, lacks the freedom to perform. Far from being logically inarticulable, however, that impossible performance, that confounding of the foundational distinction between activity and passivity, bears so crucially on the ideological delimitation of subjectivity itself that it appears to *demand* articulation at those moments when, as in the "crisis" that is "AIDS," "the subject" is the subject in question.

Consider again, for example, the vile mythology rehearsed by the editorial in the *Manchester Union Leader:* "Homosexual intercourse is the genesis of every single case of AIDS. . . . The sexual perversion that is anal intercourse by sodomites is the fundamental point of origin." Not surprisingly, this rabid fundamentalism of the fundament produces its genealogy of "AIDS" in the allusive penumbra cast by Genesis, the text that constitutes our cultural constitution far more than any legal document of state (as the U.S. Supreme Court all but officially announced in its decision in *Bowers v. Hardwick*). In contrast to the subject-formation related in and effected by the biblical narrative, however, the editorial's myth of the "genesis" of "AIDS" gestures toward the decomposition of the subject by proffering the act of anal intercourse—which is, in the homophobic imaginary of the West, to conjure the spectacle of gay men in the so-called "passive" or "receptive" position—as the negative counterpart of the theory that used to be packaged as "creation science." In this version of a now familiar quasi-Miltonic speculation on the origins of "AIDS," the gay male anus as the site of pleasure gives birth to "AIDS" as a figuration of death.

Significantly, this account of what gets interpreted as the definitional act of de-generation credits the anus, like the God of Genesis, with performing an act of creation ex nihilo, even if the nihilism of the anus thus threatens to annihilate all creation.[14] For if the creation of the universe recounted in Genesis provides a model for subjectivity through its image of absolute agency asserting its will through the creation and shaping of matter, the narrative that traces the origin of "AIDS" to the spontaneous emergence of a virus through an act of male-male anal sex parodically inverts that perfect congruence of self-present intention and creative act, reducing the "creator," in this case, to the condition of so much matter that finds itself subjected, in the end, to what it has "created." In the logic of this allegoresis, then, the act by which the subject renounces the autonomy that affirms his subjectivity leads directly to the "literal" realization of this symbolic gesture in the subject's death.

Moreover, just as the "passivity" identified with gay male anal intercourse results, according to this narrative, in the death of the *individual* subject, so a culture's passive acquiescence to or toleration of male-male anal sex—and thus of the category-disrupting act of passivity that male homosexuality connotes—serves as the "fundamental point of origin" for a more universal death of the subject, for the apocalyptic reversal of Genesis that radiates outward from those that Genesis, after all, enables the law to call "sodomites." As Eve Kosofsky Sedgwick importantly reminds us:

> From at least the biblical story of Sodom and Gomorrah, scenarios of same-sex desire have had a privileged, though by no means an exclusive, relation in Western culture to scenarios of both genocide and omnicide. . . . [O]ne of the few areas of agreement among modern Marxist, Nazi, and liberal capitalist ideologies is that there is a peculiarly close, though never precisely defined, affinity between same-sex desire and some historical condition of moribundity, called "decadence," to which not individuals or minorities but whole civilizations are subject.[15]

Thus at the present historical moment in which "kicking butt" is the formula of choice for asserting the value of autonomy and aggressive indominability in America, it is not merely by way of pun that gay male sexual desire, construed as anulling the subject in the pleasurable receptivity of the anus, gets fantasmatically rewritten as a fatal attraction to the end. Yet as our societal fascination with the "butt," however phobic its expression, makes clear, the violence of the assertion that "butt" must be "kicked" betrays a recognition of its demand on our attention, as if what needed to be "kicked" were not an object of scorn but a habit. Indeed, the threat of sodomitic apocalypse condensed in the *Manchester Union Leader*'s editorial invests the anus with the gravitational attraction that, astronomically speaking, it is proper to describe as a "black hole," implying that if a man's anus—or metonymically, his "butt"—is allowed to exert an attractive force on any man at all, every man will eventually collapse before (if not into) the "self"-destroying force of the "virus" that *is*, and is not merely the product of, accession, which becomes addiction, to the anus's desire.[16]

I mean to suggest, then, that the currency achieved by the scenarios of "genocide and omnicide" in the public discourse that locates the origin of "AIDS" in gay male anal sex[17] responds, by displacement, to what Michelangelo Signorile, prophetically one hopes, has described as "The Last Gasp of the White Male Heterosexuals."[18] It testifies, in other words, to the anxiety of decline and impending doom that marks, in this case, not merely a fin de siècle or millenial malaise, but, more profoundly, the deeply-rooted recognition of the imminent end of an empire, the demise of the imperial subject secure in his centrality to, his identification with, history and civilization. Given that, as Craig Owens has noted, "the representational systems of the West admit only one vision—that of the constitutive male subject—or, rather, they posit the subject of representation as absolutely centered, unitary, masculine," postmodernism in its popular version can seem to signal the fall of the West insofar as it would effect the death of the subject by, as Owens puts it, "upset[ting] the reassuring stability of that mastering position."[19]

Faced with this prospect of being toppled from the pedestal on which he has placed himself, the ideological subject as white male heterosexual elicits from "AIDS" a discourse of crisis by which he can affirm his privileged standing—for the performative effect of these representations of the apocalyptic end of the subject is to define the subject coercively as he who repudiates his end. Subtended by the always excitable fantasy of threat to this subject's agency, the originary myth linking "AIDS" to the "addictive" passivity of the anus in intercourse is mobilized largely to reaffirm, and thereby to shore against his ruins, the white male heterosexual as uniquely autonomous in his moral agency, and thus as uniquely occupying the position of the subject who, like Adam in Milton's Protestant reworking of Genesis, is in himself sufficient to stand because also free to fall.

III   Narci-schism

This fantasy of the fall or death of the (white, male, heterosexual) subject can, of course, mean different things in different discursive contexts. Reading it from within a gay-inflected psychoanalytic framework, I have argued elsewhere that it can register as "a falling *away* from the always endangered 'integrity' of maleness as culturally constructed, and thus as a falling *back* into that dreaded but seductive, maternally-identified preoedipal eros from which, on the one hand, heterosexual masculinity is imagined to have emerged, and against which, as an absolute alterity, it needs, on the other hand, to define itself."[20] Drawing upon Lacan's hypothesis of the mirror stage as both precipitate and prolepsis of the subject's self-constitution, this argument seeks to unfold the logic behind the derisive representation of gay men as narcissistically fixated and oriented toward the mother. It does so by considering the mirror stage and the castration crisis in relation to one another as the two determining moments in the formation of the heterosexual male subject that defensively *generate* the myth of that subject's uni-directional development (out of and away from identification with—and domination by—maternal power), precisely because each of those moments *refutes* such unidirectionality to the degree that its subject-shaping force depends upon its capacity to elicit *retroactively* the history from which the subject thereafter will be said to have emerged. The fact that the subject emerges, however, not from that history (whether of the "corps morcelé") or of identification with the mother who already has been "castrated") but rather from the narrative that enables him to *posit* his emergence from that history, means that the *experience* of such a history is never, properly speaking, the subject's property, and therefore that the subject can never, *as* a subject, experience it at all. To the contrary, from the perspective of the constituted subject, the possibility of experiencing what it can retroactively hypostatize as its "history" can only figure the *prospect* of the subject's dissolution. The critical moments of the mirror stage and the assumption of the castration complex, then, effect the identity of the self as (male) subject through the identification of subjectivity with autonomous control or self-mastery, the achievement of which is linked, in each case, to an assertion of distance—and difference—from the mother, who had been, until then, an imaginary mirror for what can be said to have been the subject-to-be only *after* this "mirror" is disavowed.

Jane Gallop, in a compelling analysis of this process as played out in Lacan's essay on the mirror stage, appropriately compares it to the mythology of Genesis.

The mirror stage is thus high tragedy: a brief moment of doomed glory, a paradise lost. The infant is 'decisively projected' out of this joy into the anxious defensiveness of 'history,' much as Adam and Eve are expelled from paradise into the world. Just as man and woman are already created but do not enter the human condition until expelled from Eden, so the child, although already born, does not become a self until the mirror stage. Both cases are two-part birth processes: once born into 'nature,' the second time into 'history.' When Adam and Eve eat from the tree of knowledge, they anticipate mastery. But what they actually gain is a horrified recognition of their nakedness. This resembles the movement by which the infant, having assumed by anticipation a totalized, mastered body, then retroactively perceives his inadequacy (his 'nakedness'). Lacan has written another version of the tragedy of Adam and Eve.[21]

Because the apocalyptic narratives of "AIDS" unfold in allusive relation to Genesis (as do such arguments against homosexuality as the platitudinous allegation that "God created Adam and Eve, not Adam and Steve"), the psychic stakes in the death of the (white, male, heterosexual) subject, and thus in the defensively mobilized anxiety that shapes the mythology of "AIDS," can be located not only in Lacan's psychoanalytic reinterpretation of the Fall, but also in such canonical rewritings of Genesis as the *Paradise Lost* toward which Gallop nods in the passage cited above. For Milton characterizes Adam as a free and rational moral agent, a paradigmatic subject, by framing the moment in Book 8 that might be interpreted as Adam's mirror stage in a mirroring relation to the description, in Book 4, of Eve's fascination with the image of herself in a lake.

Although Narcissus, in the Ovidian narrative from which Milton draws in this latter scene, pays for his specular fixation by "dying at life's prime,"[22] Eve escapes such a fate through the external mediation of the divine voice, a third term whose linguistic intervention both lays down and *is* the Law:

> What there thou seest fair Creature is thyself,
> With thee it came and goes; but follow me,
> And I bring thee where no shadow stays
> Thy coming, and thy soft imbraces, hee
> Whose image thou art, him thou shalt enjoy
> Inseparably thine, to him shalt bear
> Multitudes like thyself, and thence be call'd
> Mother of human Race.   (4:468–75)

Responding to this voice, Eve comes upon Adam and, judging him "less fair, / Less winning soft, less amiably mild, / Than that smooth wat'ry image" (4:478–80) of herself, turns back toward the lake before Adam persuades her that she must recognize herself in relation to him and not in terms of her shadowy reflection. If Eve, however, thus fails initially to recognize in Adam the "sympathy and love" (4:465) that she saw and was drawn to at once in her own image, Adam, in Book 8, recognizes himself immediately in Eve, or to be more exact, he immediately misrecognizes Eve as himself in a way that parallels but reverses Eve's misrecognition of her image as someone else. Describing to Raphael his first glimpse of Eve, Adam reports that he rhapsodized: "I now see / Bone of my bone, Flesh of my Flesh, my Self / Before me" (8:494–96). Raphael underscores the point that this is indeed a misrecognition when he somberly warns Adam against such a narcissistic overestimation of Eve, urging him against "attributing overmuch to things / Less excellent" (8:565–66).

Thus Adam's true constitution as a human subject takes place when he discovers his *status* as a subject in differential relation to Eve—when he learns as Raphael puts it, that Eve is "worthy well / Thy cherishing, thy honoring, and thy love, / Not thy subjection" (8:468–70); yet as Raphael goes on to suggest, the dangerously misplaced narcissism that marks this overestimation of Eve can only be controlled by encouraging Adam's "properly" narcissistic estimation of himself *in his difference from her:* "weigh with her thyself; / Then value: Oft-times nothing profits more / Than self-esteem, grounded on just and right / Well managed" (8:570–73). In effect, the text affirms Adam as subject by justifying his love for Eve not as his "Self," but as the "image" of himself, as, in this particular context, the *object* through which he can recognize (and thus attain) his rightful position as subject.[23]

Such a constitution of Adam as subject requires and exacts, however, Eve's anterior disavowal of attraction to the "wat'ry image" of *her* "Self"– requires, that is, that her narcissism be categorically separated from his. As Mary Nyquist argues, "It is not hard to see that Adam's own desire for an other self has a strong 'narcissistic' component. Yet Adam's retrospective narrative shows this narcissism being sparked, sanctioned, and then satisfied by his creator. By contrast, though in Book 4 Eve recalls experiencing a desire for an other self, this desire is clearly and unambiguously constituted by illusion, both in the sense of specular illusion and in the sense of error."[24] But Eve's "error," of course, is error only by ideological fiat of the text; she cannot, after all, see herself in Adam as he can see himself in Eve, for while she is constructed as *his* image, he is not constructed as *hers*. Only in the watery mirror can she find an image of her own, and that image reflects her "accurately"—it allows her to recognize herself—because it gives back to her the image of her status *as* image or reflection.

One might say, therefore, that Eve's narcissism, justly so called since it alludes to Narcissus, must be sacrificed to legitimize, or at least to obscure, what the text seems to want us *not* to construe as *Adam's* narcissism. The latter is honorifically represented, instead, as active engagement with otherness, as movement into and authority over a world located outside of, and defined as different from, the self. In this sense Milton's rewriting of Genesis reinforces an argument Michael Warner makes in his essay, "Homo-Narcissism; or, Heterosexuality." Meditating on the psychoanalytic pathologization of homosexuality as narcissistic (because interpreted as love of the "same"), Warner explores the logic behind the modern insistence on limiting what can be recognized as "difference" in erotic relations to the "difference" defined as gender. He contends that "the allegory of gender protects against a recognition of the role of the imaginary in the formation of the erotic. It provides reassurance that imaginary intersubjectivity has been transcended. To the extent that our culture relies on the allegorization of gender to disguise from itself its own ego erotics, it will recognize those ego erotics only in the person of the homosexual, apparently bereft of the master trope of difference."[25]

In the cultural, and thus ideological, definition of same and different, private and public, passive and active, personal and political, Eve's "ego erotics," which are assigned the position of interiority and self-involvement, are characterized pejoratively as antithetical to Adam's—much as gay sexuality is characterized, both in psychoanalytic discourse and in the cultural imagination, as narcissistic and therefore as structurally distinct from heterosexual eros. Like Adam, then, heterosexual masculinity must refuse to acknowledge the narcissism that marks the imaginary structuring of its erotic relations in order to call itself into being (as the modern *institution* of heterosexual masculinity) in the posture of mastering subject. Activity, change, sociality, civilization, life itself, from within the logic of heterosexuality—which is to say, from within the governing logic of the subject—depend upon this *imaginary* emergence from, this *imaginary* transcendence of, "imaginary intersubjectivity."

Male homosexuality in general, and its synecdoche, gay male anal sex, in particular, bear the stigma and retain the lure of such an "imaginary intersubjectivity" insofar as they seem to effect the subject's fall from master to matter: his fall *back*, in other words, from the fantasized achievement of coherence and autonomous agency to a state of mirrorlike receptivity that appears, from the vantage point of the differentiated self, as inherently "self"-negating. Were we to think of gravity, for a moment, as expressing the narcissism of matter, we might consider that the place of the anus, as the "black hole" in the mythology of "AIDS," figures the lethally disavowed narcissism that heterosexual masculinity, to define itself as such, must misread as the lethal narcissism associated with gay men—lethal because it draws the male subject back into his imaginary "history," the nonbeing that is the experientially unapproachable condition of nondifferentiation, by permitting the gay man to take himself, narcissistically, as an object, and allowing him, in consequence, as an object, to be "taken."

The popular homophobic discourse on AIDS that depends upon these apocalyptic conjunctions of narcissism, passivity, the anus, and death serves, then, to secure the ideological construction of the subject as heterosexual male in much the same way that Adam can be Adam not only on the condition that Eve *not* be Adam but also that she not, as it were, be *Steve*. Such an identity, that is, requires the ability to posit persuasively as a categorical difference what might, under a different discursive regime, be interpreted as "the same." The result, as D. A. Miller recognizes, is that "straight men unabashedly *need* gay men, whom they forcibly recruit (as the object of their blows or, in better circles, just their jokes) to enter into a polarization that exorcizes the 'woman' in man through assigning it to a class of man who may be considered no 'man' at all. Only between the woman and the homosexual together may the normal male subject imagine himself covered front and back."[26] Indeed, one might add, only *against* women and gay men may the "normal male subject" imagine himself *to be a subject* at all.

If the widespread homophobic mythology of "AIDS" constellates narcissism, passivity, and the anus as dangers against which to mobilize, and thereby reinforce, the heterosexual logic of the subject, it ought to be cause for concern when this same constellation is similarly demonized in the discourse designed to effect the constitution of an oppositional gay male subjectivity. Take, for example, a poem from Paul Monette's *Love Alone: Eighteen Elegies for Rog*, a powerful, emotionally gripping volume written in response to the "AIDS"-related death of Monette's lover, Roger Horwitz.[27] Aptly titled, "Manifesto" participates in the ongoing campaign to refashion the gay subject in terms of an "AIDS activist" identity that deploys, on occasion, as the mirror image against which it would call itself into being, a contemptuous depiction of non-"activist" gay men as narcissists addicted to pleasure, resistant to struggle, and therefore themselves responsible for the continuing devastations of "AIDS." As if invoking Genesis to achieve the genesis of a communal gay identity as warriors or resistance fighters, "Manifesto," which immediately follows a poem wherein the narrator discusses the difficulties of surviving the death of a loved one with a character called "Eve," begins by condemning, and distancing itself from, the "self-love" of a character called "Adam":

> unsolicited Adam S diagnosed 9/85
> and lucky calls to say all sickness is self-
> induced and as I start to growl oozes self-
> beatification *taking a course in miracles*
> he says and I bark my way out of his wee
> kirk and savage his name from the Rolodex
> another triumph of self-love   (1–7)

Though Monette goes on to particularize the form of this Adam's "self-love" as adherence to the "new age" anti-"AIDS" regimen with which Louise Hay is notoriously associated, these lines take aim at those responses to "AIDS" that appear to turn "inward" and toward the "self" instead of outward and toward "others"—responses that are construed as narcissistic, which is to say, as apolitical.

This familiar demonization of narcissism finds expression in familiarly phobic terms as Monette, in a bitter apostrophe, scorns this Adam's self-involvement: "deep-throat / your pale sore body lick your life like a dog's / balls" (19–21). Is it a coincidence that this "political" repudiation of narcissism (in the name of responsible activism) relies on the putatively self-evident disgust with which the reader is expected to respond to the bestializing figure of auto-fellatio, of "deep-throating" one's own body so that it turns in upon itself, both physically and emblematically, to take itself as its own object? Or that the stigmatization of narcissism so easily swallows up, as it were, the erotic practice whose intimate association with gay men has been enshrined in the denigrating epithet, "cocksucker," wielded against all who fail to embody—or at least to embody *adequately*—the active, penetrative relation of the (straight, male) subject to the world? Recapitulating the violent refusals undergirding that relation, the "activist" terms in which the "proper" gay subject is interpellated here position political engagement as the unselfish, socially conscious alternative to the self-centered and destructively hedonistic pleasures associated with a gay sexuality defined, as in the phobic discourse of the culture at large, by the mirror and the anus:

> no we need
> the living alive to bucket Ronnie's House
> with abattoirs of blood hand in hand lesions

> across America need to trainwreck the whole
> show till someone listens so no they may not
> coo in mirrors disbarring the fevered the choked
> and wasting as losers who have not learned
> like Adam the yoga with which to kiss their own
> assholes   (25–33)

The point is not to label and condemn these lines as homophobic nor to deny the importance of collective interventions to resist the political and economic profiteering that occurs at every level of the government's inadequate responses to "AIDS"; rather, it is to focus on the logic and implications of some of the terms through which an "AIDS activist" identity, here and elsewhere, is being formed—formed, to be sure, both for and by, but also, I think, in significant ways, *at the expense of* gay men.

Far from signaling opposition to the various forms of "AIDS activism," however, such a focus—though certainly susceptible to representation as narcissistic, inwardly directed, and consequently outside the field of combat—should be interpreted, as one of the forms such activism might take: a form, indeed, in which "activism" ceases to constitute itself in tendentious opposition to a "narcissism" whose stigmatization (as "passivity") uncannily reenacts the defining moment of heterosexual male subject-formation. It is true, after all, to make this point clearer, that when Larry Kramer declares that Vito Russo (who died with "AIDS"-related causes on November 7, 1990) "was killed by 25 million gay men and lesbians who for ten long years of this plague have refused to get our act together. . . . We're killing each other. Can't you see that?," he means something very different from what Patrick Buchanan means when he alleges that "homosexuals, bisexuals [and] IV drug users" with "AIDS" "have killed themselves because they could not or would not control their suicidal appetites."[28] But the difference in what we can acknowledge these two assertions to *intend* should not obscure the similarity in the ideological structures on which they rely: structures that make it easy—indeed, that attempt to make it *natural*—to represent the gay community as murderous in its attachment to "narcissistic" gratification.

While recognizing the difference in meaning that differing subject-positions thus produce, we need to remember how complicated and fissured an oppositional subject-position must be—complicated by its construction within a dominant ideology whose contradictions it may attempt to exploit, but whose logic it can never simply escape. The smoothness with which Kramer's and Buchanan's polemics come together in their depiction of gays as killers *may* signify their common need to resist what Leo Bersani has termed the "self-shattering and solipsistic *jouissance*" that is sexuality itself;[29] but it *certainly* bespeaks a political investment in a shared ideology of the subject—a subject fantasmatically brought into being through an act of self-cohesion (Kramer's "get[ing] our act together") that makes its foundational moment the primal scene of differentiation from what it reads as the torpor or passivity of its imaginary "history," the state of nonorganization to which, as Freud suggests in *Beyond the Pleasure Principle,* the death drive would have us return. Despite its merely metonymic relation to the psychoanalytic definition of the term, this is the state phobically constructed as "narcissistic" in the dominant elaboration of modern subjectivity; for narcissism, within this logic, connotes the very nondifferentiation from which the active, masculine subject, in what might be called his narci-schism, must differentiate himself.

In Monette's "Manifesto," therefore, those who are excoriated for the self-absorption that is figured as eagerness to "kiss their own / asshole" are effortlessly depicted as murderously indifferent, as people who, "even if they last forever / will only love the one poor thing themself / and bury the rest of us" (41–43). By tossing bombs at FDA labs and pelting the limousines of bureaucrats, however, the "proper" gay subject as defined by the poem, the subject the narrator implies he has become, shows his command of the aggression needed to elbow his way into the "political" world—an aggression manifest in "Manifesto" primarily through the passion with which the narrator insists on his difference from the mirror-bound narcissists reviled for a passivity defined precisely as *not* knowing the difference between their ass and their elbow. But the activist identity conceived in this way reinscribes through displacement the "self"-love that Monette so movingly evokes in his relationship with Rog, when, for example, in "The Very Same," he recalls how his lover "used to say in [his] cranked up bed / playfully astonished *But we're the same person*" (32–33). In the aftermath of Roger's death, the survival through transference of the ego erotics invested in that shared identity prompts the narrator's rejection of "self"-regard in favor of the political activism of a newly constituted communal self: "I had a self myself / once but he died when do we leave the mirror / and lie down in front of the tanks" (69–71).

Here, as in the rhetoric of "AIDS" activism more generally, the pathos that lends such urgency to the call to resist injustice readily compels assent: not simply, or even primarily, the pathos of what the media self-righteously sell to the public as the "suffering victims of AIDS," but the pathos of the political subject confronting the bad faith and the deadly contradictions of those institutions that not only shape social policy but also, and more profoundly, call forth the subject within ideology. It is all the more painful, therefore, when the rhetoric of "activists," in its resistance to the dominant discourse, redeploys the ideology of that dominant discourse in order, narcissistically, to appropriate an "activist" identity by stigmatizing as narcissistic the community, already so stigmatized, from which they emerged.

Consider, in this light, the ramifications for a self-nominated "activist" community if one were to bracket the word *sexual* in the following sentence from *Policing Desire*, Simon Watney's indispensable study of "AIDS," representation, and the media: "It is easy to detect a variety of specific defences against what are understood as 'passive' sexual acts, on the part of men whose sense of self is constructed around notions of sexual 'activity.'"[30] Watney's keen insight into such self-definition predicated on the projective expulsion of a specifically *sexual* passivity, however, does not prevent him from reinscribing a version of that projective expulsion in his own work. Examining elsewhere the ideological labor of "an AIDS activist cultural practice," he writes, "this is not for one moment to defend passivity or a retreat from active political engagement."[31] Though Watney, of course, is by no means rejecting any form of erotic experience here—least of all any form of lesbian, gay, or bisexual experience—the presupposition that passivity is "not for one moment" to be defended cannot escape ideological determination in a culture always predisposed to observe and condemn the proferred "ass" in "passive." "Passivity," after all, lies beyond the pale of defense in the rhetoric of certain "AIDS activists" because for them, as for the dominant cultural subject, it enters a fantasmatic dialectic with "activity" to describe a form of "activity" that would drain "activity" of its "proper" meaning, thereby both threatening, and defining by antithesis, the subject position they proclaim; as in the originary myth of "AIDS" rehearsed by the *Manchester Union Leader,* such "passivity" can be interpreted by some "AIDS activists" as lethal, even genocidal. "We are such passive people, we gay people," Larry Kramer laments; and addressing the Boston Lesbian and Gay Town Meeting in 1987, he declares, "I'm tired of you, by your own passivity, actively colluding in your genocide."[32]

Do I mean, then, to defend "passivity or a retreat from active political engagement"? Am I defending the "narcissism" of those gay men who refuse to "leave the mirror / and lie down in front of the tanks"? If a short answer to these questions is demanded, mine must, obviously, be yes, with the proviso that to defend those ways of responding to the epidemics that converge as "AIDS" is neither to advocate nor to encourage them for the gay community as a whole, but to accept them as part of the complex and contradictory vision—at once social, political, and erotic—that vitalizes our community. With the luxury of a less condensed reply, I would suggest that it is never, in any event, a question of leaving the mirror. It is a question, rather, of which mirror we choose to reflect the image we will recognize as ours: whether, that is, on the one hand, in our defense of an already beleaguered gay identity, we want to emulate the widespread heterosexual contempt for the image of a gay sexuality represented as passive and narcissistic in order to embrace, as our new mirror image, the power of the tanks beneath which we would lie; or whether, on the other hand, we want to refuse the "choice" ideologically imposed by such a binarism— whether we want to deny the incompatibility of passivity and power, and thereby to undertake the construction of a gay subjectivity that need not define itself against its own subset of demonized "faggots."

For those of us who are and who love gay people, it ought to be possible to affirm and participate in the work of "AIDS activism" without transforming that rubric into an identity whose exclusions uncannily mirror the exclusions of the culture at large. It ought, that is, to be possible to affirm the legitimacy and value of the innumerable ways in which lesbians, gay men, bisexuals, and their allies can participate in the continuing resistance to "AIDS" even while—indeed, even sometimes *by*–resisting the essential but sometimes too narrowly conceptualized "politics" of "activism."

Isaac Julien has commented on the fact that "the basic hidden message of safe sex in many cases is no sex—an anti-sex message in a post-sex climate";[33] and the tendency toward a similar antipleasure agenda can too easily find its way into the self-constituting rhetoric that characterizes a certain "AIDS activism." Legitimately challenging the ideological complicities of the logic with which politicians, artists, and academics have approached the representations of "AIDS," challenging especially what they see in such work as a tendency to rely on and to reinforce the values and politics of bourgeois humanism, "AIDS activists" can seem at times to demand an ascesis as fully glamorized through its relationship to "power" (and as salvific in its purificatory refusal of passivity) as the bourgeois aesthetic they rightly condemn for fixating on and oppressively enforcing the ubiquity of its own image. Ascesis, of course, has an eros of its own, but its eros is bound to the rigor with which it renounces an eros of luxury. I have tried to suggest that such ascesis is the erotic mode of the dominant subject: the civic authority of subject status is purchased through the projective refusal of the luxurious "passivity," derided as "narcissism," that signifies the erotic indulgence of the self that always threatens to undo the "self." Even in the current epidemic, gaining the power of "political" intervention by buying into the logic of ascesis that grounds the valorization of "politics" over and in opposition to the category of "pleasure," could prove a Faustian bargain for the gay community historically called into being and victimized by that logic.

The fiction of a "political activism" that would permit us to "leave the mirror," then, signals, ironically enough, the extent to which "AIDS" can be read as effecting the crisis—the marking of difference—that marks, if you will, a sort of mirror stage for the gay communities of the West. Critics of psychoanalysis in general, and of Lacanian psychoanalysis in particular, of course, have argued against the ahistorical tendency of psychoanalytic explanation: against the assumption, for instance, that the subject that emerges by way of the mirror stage must always and necessarily take shape as a subject through the sort of "narci-schism" I discussed above. In naming the overlapping "crises" called "AIDS" as the mirror stage for gay identity, I do not intend to imply that that structure compels us to generate, in an eternal return, the subject position, the identity concept, that the dominant culture has taught us. But neither do we have the option of simply asserting ex cathedra, even ex St. Patrick's Cathedral, that our subject position can be exempted from the ideological consequences—and the *historical* returns or repetitions—of its constitution within the dominant culture. To the extent that we can identify those junctures where the gay subjectivity we seek to produce recapitulates the oppressive logic of the culture that necessitated its emergence, we have the chance to displace that logic and begin to articulate the range of options for what might *become* a postmodern subject; we have the chance, in other words, to challenge, as Andreas Huyssen suggests postmodernism must, "the *ideology of the subject* (as male, white, and middle-class [and we must add, as he does not, heterosexual]) by developing alternative and different notions of subjectivity."[34]

Producing "different notions of subjectivity," however, is not the same thing as occupying a different position as a subject; though dialectically related, the latter is not simply produced by the activity of the former. Written into a discourse of power relations whose network enfolds our own discourse, making possible at once our resistances, our transformations, and our reproductions of it, we cannot act to reconstruct the social order without being ourselves the vectors through which the social order acts. Dressed in the garb of material politics, "AIDS activists" may propose, idealistically, that we can "let our discourse infect and recode the message in master discourses and knowledges (from fiction to sociology to deconstruction) rather than let this 'new' thing ["AIDS"] be treated through 'old' practices";[35] but that hope of a discourse that is "ours" and not "theirs," a hope mirrored by the binarism of "new" and "old," rests on the fantasy of a "political" subject not constituted from the outset through a subjection to language. As Diana Fuss puts it in her acute analysis of the relations among politics, identity, and subjectivity, "to see politics as a 'set of effects' rather than as the concealed motor which sets all social relations into motion would prevent us from reifying politics and mystifying its 'behind-the-scenes' operations."[36]

Because the "message in master discourses and knowledges" is never a coherent "message" at all, because the "power" of those discourses unfolds within networks of tropology, rhetoric, and grammar that never resolve into a stable conceptual field—let alone a stable conceptual field outside of which we have a place to stand in order to "infect and recode" them like some "new" organism, some "new" virus, entering the system as if created ex nihilo—we must recognize that "our" "activist" discourse is only a *mutation* of "their" "master discourses" and that its effect on them, though certain, is also always unpredictable. However appealing the assertion of a "politics" capable *simply* of reclaiming or recoding the oppressive structures of dominant culture may be—however attractive the fiction of a clear-cut distinction between the subject and object positions in any such "reappropriation"—we always have reason to question the logic of agency in such a myth of the subject and reason, therefore, to wonder, as Aretha Franklin once sang, "who's zoomin' who?"

IV   A Queerer Mirror

One way to reframe these issues is to look, as Diana Fuss enables us to formulate it, at the politics of "politics" as it is deployed in the rhetoric of "activism." "Politics," Fuss argues, "represents the aporia in much of our current political theorizing; that which signifies activism is least actively interrogated" (105). This is true, of course, in no small part because "political activism" and the theoretical interrogation sometimes dismissed from the "activist" perspective as merely "academic" are, by the political framing of such a politics, in a relation of antithesis. "The indeterminacy and confusion surrounding the sign 'politics,'" as Fuss quite rightly observes, "does not typically prevent us from frequently summoning its rhetorical power to keep 'theory' in its place" (106). That it can do so, and do

so effectively, bespeaks the extent to which "politics" designates the subject's "proper" sphere as agent and thus the extent to which the politics of
"politics" coincides with the foundational differentiation of the subject
through the exclusionary logic of active and passive, outside and inside,
public and private. In the terms of Monette's "Manifesto," this could be
phrased as the difference, itself constructed from the vantage point of
"politics," between enthrallment before the mirror and movement outward
to confront the tanks. If, however, both of these are ways of engaging and
producing a mirror image for, and as, one's self—and if, therefore, they
can be viewed as acts that, structurally, mirror one another—the difference that "politics" erects between them arises from the originary refusal
of "politics" to allow that mirrors reflect not the "sameness" of identity, but
the instability of sameness and difference that the sign "identity" always
holds in tension. For "politics," as the assertion of agency, loses the
efficacy of intervention, and thereby ceases to be what it would recognize
as "politics," insofar as it begins to reflect on the instability of the ground
on which it rests. Such reflection, after all, is the province of the "theory"
that such a "politics" works to "keep . . . in its place"; it is the hallmark,
indeed, of the mirror that "politics" becomes "politics" only by leaving.

If "AIDS," though, is viewed as the mirror in which the gay subject is
being rewritten, we may be able to displace the logic whereby "political
activism" reaffirms the discourse of coherence (including the coherence of
the self) and mastery (including the mastery of the self) in order to fantas-
ize the coincidence of agency and intention. In doing so we might try to
articulate something closer to a passive agency, an agency that acknowledges its inescapable participation in the production of social effects
while acknowledging its inability to control the effects in whose production it thereby figures.

Such a notion would require the recognition that powerfully "political"
effects can be generated even by those who would seem, from an "activist"
perspective, to be a- or antipolitical. We should remember, for example,
that the Stonewall riots, however enabled by the political organizers and
homophile societies that created a public context for claiming gay rights,
resulted from the resistance of people remote from the mainstream of gay
political "activism": those young people, transvestites, and drag queens at
the Stonewall who, as the *New York Mattachine Newsletter* observed in
1969, "[were] not welcome in, or [could] not afford, other places of homosexual social gathering."[37] The defiant luxury of their contempt for the
police who conducted what should have been a routine raid on June 27,
1969, the narcissistic splendor of their campy posturing before the law's

ascetic eye, moved the crowd to defense of their right to be "narcissistic," their right to enact what the discursive authorities could define as homosexual "passivity." Nor, as we describe the material conditions that led to the rebellion at Stonewall, should we forget the significance of elements as aleatory and apparently counterpolitical as the "self-indulgent" gay sentimentality of mourning a Judy Garland, lost to an overdose of sleeping pills, whose burial earlier that afternoon evoked a powerful emotional response in many of the drag queens and transvestites whose susceptibility to such identifications might well have been repudiated as regressive, even masochistic, by normalizing gay activists. Edmund White, describing what took place at the Stonewall Inn that Friday night, recalled in a letter written two weeks after the riots: "Someone shouted, 'Gay power,' others took up the cry—and then it dissolved into giggles. A few more prisoners—bartenders, hatcheck boys—a few more cheers, someone starts singing 'We Shall Overcome'—and then they start camping on it. A drag queen is shoved into the wagon; she hits the cop over the head with her purse. The cop clubs her. Angry stirrings in the crowd."[38] The drag queen striking the cop with her purse to defend the dignity of her narcissism before the punitive gaze of the law remains a potent image of the unexpected ways in which activism can be embodied when the dominant notions of subjectivity are challenged rather than appropriated.

Indeed, in the wake of "AIDS," some might say, such a mutation of the gay subject can already be perceived in the process by which, in certain quarters, "gay" is being rewritten as "queer." Departing from the work of "AIDS activists"—as Alexander Chee explains, "people are tired of groups with egos, processes, personality cults, and politicking"[39]— "queer nationalism" would reinvent the politics of sexuality by insisting on the fluidity of differences without the need to affirm the difference of a cordoned-off "politics" or "activism." "Rather than a strategic politics that confronts powerful institutions directly or uses lobbying and electoral campaigns to bring about change," Allen Bérubé and Jeffrey Escoffier write, queer nationalism embraces "theatrical demonstrations, infiltrations of shopping malls and straight bars, kiss-ins and be-ins."[40] Though "queer" as the endlessly mutating token of nonassimilation (and hence as the utopian badge of a would-be "authentic" position of resistance) may reflect a certain bourgeois aspiration to be always au courant, its vigorous and unmethodical dislocations of "identity" create—at the risk, to be sure, of producing a version of identity politics as postmodern commodity fetishism—a zone of possibilities in which the embodiment of the subject might be experienced otherwise.

Such specific embodiments of gay subjectivity and the pleasures that attend them are topics I do not wish to end this essay without addressing. For if the mirror has been a privileged trope for the privileging of the body and its gratifications in the history of Western gay men, it occupies a decisive place in the current narratives of "AIDS" as well. It is symptomatic, as it were, that John Weir, in *The Irreversible Decline of Eddie Socket*, recounts as follows his eponymous hero's moment of recognition: "Eddie Socket got it. AIDS. 'America is dying slowly,' he said, sitting on the lid of a toilet seat and staring into a mirror, in the bathroom just outside the doctor's office where he was diagnosed."[41]

As this suggests, the mirror is in many ways the distinctive site of the articulation of "AIDS." Reflecting the transformations the body must undergo, it also figures the discursive compulsion to reflect on the history that can seem to have led to a counternarcissistic confrontation with the body whose undoing the specular moment seems both to disclose and, causally, to explain. It readily figures, by seeming to mandate, the retroactive production of meaning that Alain Emmanuel Dreuilhe evokes in the first chapter of *Corp à corps: journal de SIDA:* "La maladie n'était prévisible que retrospectivement."[42] The mirror's rewriting of the body recurrently catalyzes, in the various discourses on "AIDS," the narrative impulse that generates "meaning" through a temporal logic of before and after that slides into a logic of cause and effect.[43] Across the spectrum of political perspectives, the "before," and thus the "cause," of "AIDS" is consistently represented as the narcissistic hedonism of a post-Stonewall generation of gay men so that "AIDS" becomes a mirror for what D. A. Miller, ventriloquizing the various homophobic dispositions of the dominant culture, unpacks as "the disease of gayness itself,"[44] the disease that exposes and abases the "irresponsibility" of gay liberation.

Commenting on this pervasive reconstruction of the past, Dreuilhe evokes the satisfactions this explanatory "history" affords the dominant subject: "D'après le cliché le plus répandu, même dans les milieux libéraux, les gays d'avant le SIDA ne pensaient qu'à faire l'amour et à danser, dépensant leur argent en futilités. Des cigales homosexuelles. La pitié de bien des hétérosexuels, aux Etats-Unis comme ailleurs, est mitigée par une vague et malsaine satisfaction qui chatouille secrètivement leur envie" (50). In the mirror of "AIDS" the erotic abandon, the luxurious collapse into the "black hole" of desire, must give way, depending on the stripe of the narrative, to death, as the recognition of the wages of sin; to monogamy, as a recognition of the immaturity of "promiscuity"; or to "activism," as a recognition of the political folly of defining gay identity through sexuality alone.

Bound by the logic of a developmental chronology that moves historically toward the disclosure of truth, these narratives, despite the significant differences in their attitudes toward sexuality, all celebrate a subject whose narci-schism eventuates in "political" authority.

But there are other ways of seeing the gay subject in the mirror that is "AIDS." In *The Motion of Light in Water,* for instance, Samuel Delaney lovingly recalls his erotic encounters with other gay men, individually and in groups, in apartments, in toilet stalls, and in trucks on New York's piers at night. In the midst of these potent memories he interrupts himself:

> What is the reason, anyone might ask, for writing such a book as this half a dozen years into the era of AIDS? Is it simply nostalgia for a medically unfeasible libertinism? Not at all. If I may indulge in my one piece of science fiction for this memoir, it is my firm suspicion, my conviction, and my hope that once the AIDS crisis is brought under control, the West will see a sexual revolution to make a laughing stock of any social movement that till now has borne the name. [45]

Delaney's memoir thus works to keep the knowledge of sexual pleasures in circulation, to counter the construction of a "politics" against, even if "only" *rhetorically* against, the body and its claims for indulgence.

Beside this "piece of science fiction," this act of imaginative activism, I would place a passage from a novel by Hervé Guibert, *A l'ami qui ne m'a pas sauvé la vie,* in which the narrator, a person with "AIDS," looks up as a medical technician draws a sample of his blood:

> Je me suis vu à cet instant par hasard dans une glace, et je me suis trouvé extraordinairement beau, alors que je n'y voyais plus qu'un squelette depuis des mois. Je venais de découvrir quelque chose: il aurait fallu que je m'habitue à ce visage décharné que le miroir chaque fois me renvoie comme ne m'appartenant plus mais déjà à mon cadavre, et il aurait fallu, comble ou interruption du narcissisme, que je réussisse à l'aimer. [46]

In the face of "AIDS," which he will not allow to usurp his own face here, the narrator insists on the necessity of learning to embrace the body anew: on the need to love, not leave, the mirror, by rediscovering the luxury of narcissism from within an experience constructed on every side as a rupture in narcissism itself. This affirmation of a self-regard that would make every mirror a stage defines, like the poses of the drag queens at Stonewall, a strategic mode of resistance not to be slighted by the discourse of "politics" as our lives are rewritten by "AIDS," a mode of resistance alert to the dangers we encounter in allowing gay politics to become a "politics" as usual.

And since the question of address must itself be addressed in the always specular fantasy that propels the use of the first person plural, let me say that the "we" to whom I refer, and to whom these remarks are largely directed, includes those lesbians, gay men, and bisexuals who are responding to the emergency in which we live by producing a variety of strategies that allow us, as part of the resistance to everything that "AIDS" has come to signify, to reinvent ourselves and our social relations, insofar as that can be done, by trying to imagine new subjectivities whose pleasures and politics no longer require conceptualization through antithesis. To be sure, in our historical moment, it is easy to gain discursive authority by defining oneself, at least rhetorically, in opposition to narcissistic indulgences, by appropriating a resolutely aggressive, outwardly focused, and thus responsibly "political" position that claims to speak both from and for a populist perspective and against the perspective of intellectuals, academics, and other "special" interests. But the oppositional "activists" who deploy such a strategy within the gay community risk writing "AIDS" as another chapter in the politics of a "politics" constituted as such through the repudiation of all that "homosexuality" signifies historically in the West.[47] In the process, such "activists" risk playing out within the ranks of the gay community a projective and only spuriously self-empowering "political" logic similar to the one Marlon Riggs has discerned in the African-American community's popular iconography of black gay men: "What strikes me as most insidious, and paradoxical, is the degree to which African American depictions of us as black gay men so keenly resonate American majority depictions of us, as black people."[48] Such internalizations of dominant logic, the pain of which Riggs knows all too well, can only result in this confirmation of dominant subjectivity.

"Activism" then? Of course "activism": the work of "AIDS activists" is saving our lives; but an "activism" that need not define itself against the "narcissism" and "passivity" that figure the place of gay male sexuality in the Western cultural imaginary. If, as Bersani persuasively puts it in the phrase that I took as my epigraph, "analysis, while necessary, may also be an indefensible luxury," we ought not to ignore the unstable relation between necessity and luxury that problematizes the question of what is defensible in the midst of an epidemic that takes as its target precisely our modes of defense. Indeed, at a moment when the "activist" interpellation of the oppositional subject invokes the logic of ascesis that underwrites the dominant subject's cultural authority, such "luxuries" as analysis and narcissism, both figured by the mirror, may themselves prove necessary as instruments of defense that can disclose the possibility of a politics in whose name the mirror need not be cracked—a politics whose lineaments no mirror as yet has ever fully shown.

NOTES

This essay has benefited from the careful readings and sound advice of Joanne Feit Diehl and Joseph Litvak. I am grateful to them both.

Epigraph from Leo Bersani, "Is the Rectum a Grave?," in Douglas Crimp, ed., *AIDS: Cultural Analysis/Cultural Activism* (Cambridge, Mass.: MIT Press, 1988), p. 199. This collection of essays was originally published as *October* 43 (Winter 1987). Where subsequent references to this work are contextually clear, page numbers will be cited in the text.

1. Paula Treichler, "AIDS, Homophobia, and Biomedical Discourse: An Epidemic of Signification," in *AIDS: Cultural Analysis/Cultural Activism*, p. 32; Lee Edelman, "The Plague of Discourse: Politics, Literary Theory, and AIDS," in Ron Butters, John Clum, and Michael Moon, eds., *Displacing Homophobia* (Durham, N.C.: Duke University Press, 1989), pp. 289–305.

2. Jeffrey Weeks, "Post-Modern AIDS?," in Tessa Boffin and Sunil Gupta, eds., *Ecstatic Antibodies: Resisting the AIDS Mythology* (London: Rivers Oram, 1990), pp. 133–41.

3. Roberta McGrath, "Dangerous Liaisons: Health, Disease, and Representation," *Ecstatic Antibodies*, p. 144.

4. Donna Haraway, "A Manifesto for Cyborgs," in Elizabeth Weed, ed., *Coming to Terms: Feminism, Theory, Politics* (New York: Routledge, 1989), p. 185.

5. Robert Glück, "HTLV-3," in John Preston, ed., *Personal Dispatches: Writers Confront AIDS* (New York: St. Martin's, 1989), p. 83.

6. Simon Watney, "The Spectacle of AIDS," *AIDS: Cultural Analysis/Cultural Activism*, p. 85.

7. Douglas Crimp and Adam Ralston, *AIDS Demo Graphics* (Seattle: Bay, 1990), p. 19. Where subsequent references to this work are contextually clear, page numbers will be cited in the text.

8. Fredric Jameson, "Postmodernism and Consumer Society," in Hal Foster, ed., *The Anti-Aesthetic: Essays on Postmodern Culture* (Port Townsend, Wash.: Bay, 1983), p. 114.

9. In the argument that follows it might be useful to bear in mind Mary Ann Doane's suggestion that "it is as though masculinity were required to effectively conceptualize access to activity or agency (whether illusory or not)" (*The Desire to Desire: The Woman's Film of the 1940s* [Bloomington: Indiana University Press, 1987], p. 8). Such a requirement derives from the cultural coincidence (which is, of course, not coincidental) of masculinity, agency, and the authority of subject status as embodiments of the principle of activity. Hence, as Teresa de Lauretis observes, "the hero, the mythical subject, is constructed as human being and as male; he is the active principle of culture, the establisher of distinction" (*Alice Doesn't: Feminism, Semiotics, Cinema* [Bloomington: Indiana University Press, 1984], p. 119).

10. Simon Watney, "Representing AIDS," *Ecstatic Antibodies*, pp. 173, 174. Where subsequent references to this work are contextually clear, page numbers will be cited in the text.

11. Judith Butler, whose work has been instrumental in helping me to think about these issues, persuasively argues that the very attempt to distinguish between sex and gender furthers the ideological project of naturalizing the body and the putative facticity of its "sex" in terms that already bear the cultural inscriptions of a "gender" that is imagined as deriving from the "naturally" sexed body in the first place. See *Gender Trouble: Feminism and the Subversion of Identity* (New York: Routledge, 1990).

12. Attributed to Jim Finnegan, this quotation is cited by Andrew Merton in "AIDS and Gay-Bashing in New Hampshire," *Boston Sunday Globe*, June 9, 1991, p. 2NH.

13. David Halperin, "The Democratic Body: Prostitution and Citizenship in Classical Athens," in *One Hundred Years of Homosexuality and Other Essays on Greek Love* (New York: Routledge, 1990), p. 95. Where subsequent references to this work are contextually clear, page numbers will be cited in the text.

14. In a recent interview, William Burroughs offers a related, though somewhat differently inflected, reading of the biblical myth parodically figured in such accounts of AIDS. "Another poll showed that an enormous number of people," he observed, "believe that homosexual intercourse can cause AIDS even if neither party had the virus! Now that's an immaculate conception!" David Ehrenstein, "Burroughs: On Tear Gas, Queers, *Naked Lunch*, and the Ginsberg Affair," *The Advocate* 581 (July 16, 1991):43.

15. Eve Kosofsky Sedgwick, *Epistemology of the Closet* (Berkeley: University of California Press, 1990), p. 128.

16. "Addiction" (understood as addiction to "drugs") and gay male sexuality are united in the popular discourse on "AIDS" not only as practices through which the body suffers "improper" penetration, but also, and more significantly, as practices that signify the renunciation of active self-mastery and control. Hence, for instance, in an article published in Jerry Falwell's *Liberty Report* and titled "Henry Waxman: The Bodyguard of Homosexuals," the unnamed author reflects on Congressman Waxman's efforts to protect the civil liberties of HIV-positive women and men: "If it were Barney Frank or Gerry Studds taking the lead in preferring megadeaths to public disapproval of sodomy, this might be easy enough to understand. But no one has ever suggested that Waxman himself is addicted to what, in a more delicate era, was known as 'unnatural vice'" (*Liberty Report: The Newspaper of the Moral Majority*, November 1987, pp. 3, 19).

17. The other frequently encountered originary myth of "AIDS," of course, plays out the racist fantasy of its dissemination from an undifferentiated "Africa," as Cindy Patton notes, where monkeys and humans live side by side and sexual relations are, in the white imaginary, fundamentally "different" (See Cindy Patton, "Inventing 'African AIDS,'" *Inventing AIDS* [New York: Routledge, 1990], pp. 77–97.) Though always widely available for activation, this fiction presents itself as a more "scientific" attempt to understand the cause of the epidemic; while frequently repeated by journalists, therefore, it does not generate the same emotional charge as does the mythic primacy of male-male anal sex, largely because the (white) Western public, generally indifferent to and ignorant of the history and experiences of Africa's nations and peoples, construes "African AIDS," with its largely "heterosexual" modes of transmission, as distinct from Western "AIDS," which, however much it may be bruited to "spread" from gay men and intravenous drug users, continues to be perceived as a disease linked *in its origins* to those identities.

18. Michelangelo Signorile, "Gossip Watch: Michelangelo the Red Queen," *Outweek* 105 (July 3, 1991):100.

19. Craig Owens, "The Discourse of Others: Feminists and Postmodernism," *The Anti-Aesthetic: Essays on Postmodern Culture*, p. 58.

20. Lee Edelman, "Imag[in]ing the Homosexual: *Laura* and the Other Face of Gender," in *Homographesis: Essays in Gay Literary and Cultural Theory* (New York: Routledge, forthcoming).

21. Jane Gallop, "Where to Begin?," *Reading Lacan* (Ithaca, N.Y.: Cornell University Press, 1985), p. 85.

22. Ovid, *The Metamorphoses*, Book 3, Horace Gregory, trans. (New York: New American Library, 1958), p. 99.

23. In a recent essay Regina Schwartz has argued that *Paradise Lost* attributes the Fall to Adam's inability properly to accept his role as subject, choosing instead to remain fixated in a specular relation to Eve: "At the core of Milton's myth of the Fall is Adam's identification with Eve, an attraction that makes him fail to embrace that 'masculine autonomy' Raphael instructs him in" ("Rethinking Voyeurism and Patriarchy: The Case of *Paradise Lost*," *Representations* 34 [Spring 1991]:99). This suggests that *Paradise Lost* could be read as a text that both produces and enforces the modern construction of a protoheterosexuality conceived as that which works against the fall *back* into a state of psychic nondifferentiation that figures, from the point of view of the subject, the Fall into mortality itself.

24. Mary Nyquist, "Gynesis, Genesis, Exegesis, and the Formation of Milton's Eve," in Marjorie Garber, ed., *Cannibals, Witches, and Divorce: Estranging the Renaissance*, Selected Papers from the English Institute, 1985 (Baltimore: Johns Hopkins University Press, 1987), p. 196.

25. Michael Warner, "Homo-Narcissism; or, Heterosexuality," in Joseph A. Boone and Michael Cadden, eds., *Engendering Men: The Question of Male Feminist Criticism* (New York: Routledge, 1990), p. 202.

26. D. A. Miller, "Anal Rope," *Representations* 32 (Fall 1990):128.

27. Paul Monette, *Love Alone: Eighteen Elegies for Rog* (New York: St. Martin's, 1988). References to poems from this volume will be given by title and line number in the text.

28. Larry Kramer, "Who Killed Vito Russo?," *Outweek* 86 (February 20, 1991):26; Patrick Buchanan, *New York Post*, June 26, 1991, cited in "Media Watch: Buchanan on Essex," *New York Native* 429 (July 8, 1991):15.

29. Leo Bersani, "Is the Rectum a Grave?," p. 222.

30. Simon Watney, *Policing Desire: Pornography, AIDS, and the Media* (Minneapolis: University of Minnesota Press, 1987), p. 49.

31. Simon Watney, "Representing AIDS," pp. 173, 189.

32. Larry Kramer, "Oh, My People," *Reports from the Holocaust: The Making of an AIDS Activist* (New York: St. Martin's, 1989), p. 191; "I Can't Believe You Want to Die," *Reports*, p. 163.

33. Issac Julien and Pratibha Parmar, "In Conversation," *Ecstatic Antibodies*, p. 100.

34. Andreas Huyssen, "Mapping the Postmodern," *New German Critique* 33 (Fall 1984):44.

35. Thomas Yingling, "Sexual Preference/Cultural Reference: The Predicament of Gay Culture Studies," *American Literary History* 3, no. 1 (Spring 1991):194.

36. Diana Fuss, "The Question of Identity Politics," *Essentially Speaking: Feminism,*

Nature, and Difference (New York: Routledge, 1989), p. 106. Where subsequent references to this work are contextually clear, page numbers will be cited in the text.

37. Donn Teal, *The Gay Militants* (New York: Stein and Day, 1971), p. 29.

38. Cited in Jonathan Ned Katz, "The Stonewall Rebellion: Edmund White Witnesses the Revolution," *The Advocate* 527 (June 20, 1989):40.

39. Alexander S. Chee, "A Queer Nationalism," *Out/Look* 11 (Winter 1991):15.

40. Allan Bérubé and Jeffrey Escoffier, "Queer/Nation," *Out/Look* 11 (Winter 1991):14.

41. John Weir, *The Irreversible Decline of Eddie Socket* (New York: Harper and Row, 1989), p. 99.

42. Alain Emmanuel Dreuilhe, *Corps à corps: journal de SIDA* (Paris: Gallimard, 1987), p. 23. Where subsequent references to this work are contextually clear, page numbers will be cited in the text.

43. From the perspective of a phobic heterosexual culture, "AIDS" inscribes the gay body as text in the latest instance of what I define elsewhere as the project of "homographesis," the disciplinary and projective fantasy that homosexuality is visibly, morphologically or semiotically, written upon the flesh so that it comes to occupy the stigmatized position of writing itself within the Western metaphysics of presence. (See Lee Edelman, "Homographesis," *The Yale Journal of Criticism* 3, no. 1 [Fall 1989]:189–207.) Harking back to the work by Oscar Wilde that most strikingly puts into play, however ironically, the homographic belief in the legibility of gay sexuality as a recognizable category of difference, Dreuilhe describes the effects of "AIDS" on his own reflected image, "J'ai pris dix ans en un an, les cernes sous mes yeux, malgré mes pratiques d'ermite, pourraient faire croire que je mène une vie de débauche, au moins que se soudain changement ne soit analogue à celui de Dorian Gray" (192).

44. D. A. Miller, "Sontag's Urbanity," *October* 49 (Summer 1989):95.

45. Samuel R. Delaney, *The Motion of Light in Water: Sex and Science Fiction Writing in the East Village, 1957–1965* (New York: New American Library, 1988), p. 175.

46. Hervé Guibert, *A l'ami qui ne m'a pas sauvé la vie* (Paris: Gallimard, 1990), p. 242.

47. This does not mean, of course, that narcissism, passivity, or luxury have any essential, trans-historical relation to the individual experiences of lesbians or gay men; but it does mean that the ideological stigmatization of those categories in order to define a realm of significant activity representative of a healthy community reproduces the exclusionary logic that constitutes "homosexuality" as a demonized category within the dominant culture of modern capitalism.

48. Marlon Riggs, "Black Macho Revisited: Reflections of a SNAP! Queen," in Essex Hemphill, ed., *Brother to Brother: New Writings by Black Gay Men*, conceived by Joseph Beam, project managed by Dorothy Beam (Boston: Alyson Publications, 1991), p. 255.

The Language of War in AIDS Discourse

Michael S. Sherry

I

The language of war was ubiquitous in the discourse on AIDS during the 1980s, as readers of this volume undoubtedly know. It was baldly evident even at the level of book titles, such as Larry Kramer's *Reports from the Holocaust* and Andrew Holleran's *Ground Zero*. It was endlessly repeated in the metaphor of a "war on AIDS." War in general, World War II in particular, and the Nazi Holocaust as that war's central tragedy have been persistently used as a metaphor for or analogue to AIDS, as models for understanding its devastation or for taking action against it.

The purpose of this essay is not to remind readers of this phenomenon, or to assess the political correctness of such language, or to retrace the ground ably covered by Susan Sontag in *AIDS and Its Metaphors*. It is less concerned with whether military metaphors for AIDS are bad, as she concludes, than it is with explaining why they exist—that is, the imaginative and political functions they serve. Given that AIDS did not involve "real" war and that alternative languages exist for its expression, why did the language of war gain such currency? This essay seeks to demystify that language and to locate it in a more general phenomenon of recent American politics—the pervasive use of war metaphors to justify and define a host of social, political, and economic crusades.

II

The language of war has been deployed in response to AIDS by such diverse parties, of such varying political strength, to such divergent purposes, and in such manifold forms that summary interpretation seems elusive. Embracing metaphors and models, casual references and elaborate analogies, the uses of war in the AIDS discourse in a broad range of fiction and nonfiction ranged from the profound to the trivial, the repellent to the inane, the charged to the innocuous. Moreover, while widespread, those uses held no monopoly on the discourse—they competed with other kinds of language, and they swelled or receded with different phases of the crisis and different forms of debate about it. But those are the characteristics of any widely used political language, and they need not prevent classification and analysis.

The most pervasive metaphor, of a "war on AIDS," emerged in the mid-1980s to galvanize collective action, especially by the federal government, against the disease. The term became commonplace in mainstream media reporting and editorial comment, among politicians and officials seeking to expand governmental action, and to a degree among gay leaders with the same goal. Thus Randy Shilts, the most noted gay journalist of AIDS, rightly described the 1988 report of the presidential commission chaired by James Watkins—notably enough, himself a retired navy admiral—as "a sweeping battle plan. . . . AIDS was war, Watkins reasoned, and in a war *somebody must be in charge;* that's how you *get things done*."[1] In the same vein, a popular magazine's profile of Watkins was titled, "Drawing the Battle Lines on AIDS."[2]

Such language above all expressed a modern liberal faith in concerted federal action, and an appropriate sense—though it was rarely articulated—that such action in modern American history had unfolded most successfully in the arena of war and military policy. That liberal faith was abundantly evident when the sociologists Charles Perrow and Mauro Guillén proposed the 1950s crash development of Polaris submarines as a model for a new program on AIDS—notably, their model was drawn from military history, not from the record of federal action against other health problems.[3] Expressing a similar outlook, the activist Larry Kramer, echoing the scientist David Baltimore, proposed the Manhattan Project that constructed America's first atomic bombs as a model for action against AIDS. Another marker of that liberal faith was the definition of what such a "war" might include. "What is needed," one review of Perrow's book maintained, "is nothing less than an all-out war on AIDS—one that attacks both sexual discrimination and poverty."[4]

That conflation of disease, discrimination, and poverty demonstrated another characteristic of the war language: its vagueness and capacity for casual slippage into a variety of meanings. The very term *war on AIDS* implied that enemies, allies, battle plans, and strategies must exist. Who, or what, was fighting whom, or what, where and how? Since the most obvious enemy—the viral agent—was faceless and invisible, it served poorly as the object of those intense emotions that war presumably arouses; it located the war within the bodies of the disease's victims, not in the arena of social and political action. A student of Lyndon Johnson's War on Poverty in the late 1960s noticed a similar problem: "poverty" was an abstraction, so the language of a "war on poverty" invited more specific identification of an enemy—perhaps those who promoted or tolerated poverty, but also the poor themselves.[5] So, too, a "war on AIDS" invited identification of enemies—faceless bureaucrats and callous politicians, but also carriers of the disease or whole groups whose members were prone to it. The war was easily reformulated to mean not only action against the disease, but war by the disease on its victims, or by those who tolerated it on those victims, or by those who transmitted it on other Americans. While the term alone hardly created such fears and fissures, it opened another channel for their vigorous expression.

For those reasons, among others, a host of other uses of war language emerged. In the well-known formulation of Patrick Buchanan, the enemy in this way was gay men themselves: "The poor homosexuals—they have declared war upon Nature, and now Nature is exacting an awful retribution."[6] A rich language for identifying the enemy emerged, however, not from the Right but from gay writers and politicians, especially those avowedly more radical or militant in the cause. They drew less on war or World War II in a generalized sense than on the Nazi Holocaust and nuclear holocaust in particular—that is, on the record or prospects of mass death or "omnicide," phenomena associated with modern warfare but not precisely equivalent to it.[7] Recent gay and lesbian politics and the Right's early response to AIDS gave point to this use of holocaust language. Such language had already been used during the 1970s—the pink triangle worn by homosexual victims of Nazism emerged as a symbol of gay militancy—prompted in part by the historical rediscovery of the mass death of gays under Nazi rule and by the more general attention given the Nazi Holocaust. In the early 1980s, proposals by conservatives and religious factions to quarantine people with AIDS and/or gay men set up a powerful resonance with the tragic record of World War II.

Thus by 1983 some activists were reminded of the incarceration of Japanese-Americans during World War II and of the "Dachau scenario," so that, Shilts writes, "it was virtually an article of faith among homosexuals that they would somehow end up in concentration camps." "Out of the Baths, Into the Ovens," read one sign in a 1984 San Francisco protest, while one gay journalist asked if government officials were now "preparing the boxcars for relocation." The Holocaust metaphor naturally invited prolific use of "fascist" and "Nazi" as well. Throughout the 1980s, those terms were applied in gay rhetoric to supposedly malign politicians, government officials, corporate leaders, or doctors, but also to supposed enemies within gay ranks themselves—gay men who supported closure of San Francisco's bathhouses were labeled "sexual fascists."[8]

The most sustained use of Holocaust metaphors and analogies came from Larry Kramer, the best-known AIDS polemicist of the decade. Kramer employed such language rather randomly early in the 1980s and systematically by its close—a trajectory suggesting that the escalation of such language was in part a response to the increasing scale of the disease and despair over it. Kramer used the Holocaust variously—as metaphor, model, analogue, and prophecy—in a fashion that was both rich and confusing, charged and strident. But above all he used the Nazi Holocaust to describe what was being done *to* gay men, less by the disease itself than by a homophobic society and its genocidal leaders. "AIDS is our holocaust and Reagan is our Hitler. New York City is our Auschwitz," he asserted in 1987. For Kramer, the Nazi Holocaust also served to illuminate what was done *by* gay men to themselves, as he decried a "participation in your own genocide" by gays analogous to the presumed complicity of Jews in their own destruction.[9]

Kramer and like-minded figures—ACT UP was the organization that most bore his imprint, its Silence = Death logo its tamest but most famous reference to the Holocaust—could not define the dominant discourse on AIDS (nor, in fact, could Patrick Buchanan). As always, that remained the province of political and cultural elites, for whom a vague war on AIDS remained the term of favor, when silence itself (as with Ronald Reagan) did not prevail. But the alternative language developed by Kramer and others was not so marginal as to be negligible. It expressed and helped define an outlook widespread in the gay community that in turn played a significant role in the politics of AIDS. Perhaps just as important, it provided a charged and sometimes skillfully publicized counterpoint to the dominant language, challenging it but also—by working within the same imaginative framework—offering testimony to its power.

If "war on AIDS" defined a dominant discourse on AIDS, and "holocaust" characterized a marginal but militant response, there was a third category of war language—one that reflected less a pointed political position than a generalized sense of the weight, terror, and random suffering of the AIDS tragedy. Not surprisingly, it appeared most often in less overtly polemical genres, especially the descriptive and fictional record that gay male writers compiled in the 1980s, where its appearance often seemed almost incidental. Thus Paul Monette, in his novel *Afterlife*, noted almost in passing that "In a jerkoff scene it was very bad form to bring up one's lover, let alone the *holocaust*," and wrote in his last sentence of the hope "only to lie like this between *the bombs*, dreaming away and not alone, because time was very short."[10] Prefacing a cycle of poems, Monette wrote of "a warrior burying a warrior."[11] Writing of his own experience with his dying lover, Monette asked, "Is this how a Jew feels when he hears 'holocaust' appropriated to some other calamity?," and he speculated that "if AIDS had struck boy scouts first rather than gay men, or St. Louis rather than Kinshasa, it would have been covered like nuclear war."[12] War metaphors were also scattered about in Shilts's journalistic account, with one section entitled "Battle Lines," another "The Butcher's Bill."[13] Bombs rate passing metaphoric mention in the film *Parting Glances*. Another film, *Longtime Companion*, concludes by equating a cure for AIDS with the end of World War II; the title of one review was, fittingly, "A People at War."[14]

In a more concerted fashion, the essayist Holleran used a holocaust metaphor, but one of nuclear, not Nazi, holocaust—of an atomic bomb that fell at the "ground zero" of Manhattan.[15] Chris Glaser converted that metaphor into an elaborate comparison of the "experience of the gay community to that of survivors of Hiroshima" in his essay, "AIDS and the A-Bomb Disease."[16] Most writers evoked World War II, the Holocaust, nuclear attack or other forms of aerial warfare, or very often a potent if indiscriminate mixture of them all—those forms of war most vividly associated in the modern imagination with mass, meaningless carnage. But sometimes it was just war in a generic sense that was summoned, or the trenches of World War I, or occasionally Third World struggles, as with references to the Vietnam War or in Emmanuel Dreuilhe's essay, "My Body, My Beirut" (a fitting metaphor for an author writing from a French as well as an American perspective).[17] These uses of war language were not confined either to gay men or to writing about them: "Fear in the Foxholes" was the imaginative title given one article about the burdens of AIDS falling on health workers. [18]

III

So varied were the sources and meanings of such war language—only cursorily sketched here—that they seem to defy a unitary explanation, other than to observe that war and mass slaughter have been so pervasive in the modern world that they naturally define the imagination. Perhaps, indeed, such language was not the lens through which divergent parties perceived the experience of AIDS, but only the sieve through which they pushed strikingly different agendas—and therefore neither reflective nor determinative of anything terribly important. Certainly those who saw a "war upon Nature" by gay men, or a war on disease and discrimination by the assertive state, or a war on people with AIDS by malign elites would have pursued their agendas without the language of war.

More important, however, than particular uses of this language was the common choice by such diverse parties of the same *kind* of language, albeit to divergent ends. How different would the political culture of AIDS have looked if other metaphors had been dominant? If, for example, a disease-related language of "plague" or images of natural disaster (earthquake, flood, etc.) had prevailed? Any language, of course, would have set up charged images and expressed political conflict, but not all in the same way. The language of war-and-holocaust highlighted human causation and the state's agency—for human responsibility and state power are central to the experience of war—and it justified extreme action to challenge or shape state power. A language of disease or natural disaster, while surely justifying state action (presumed to be the modern state's responsibility in response to epidemics or earthquakes) would not have placed people, groups, or the state in a central causative position and would have suggested an inevitability to the tragedy, its occurrence and control beyond human agency.

The historical questions raised by the use of such language are deepened because its exponents persisted in it even when it seemed forced or contradicted by other language they employed. Thus Holleran wrote that "the bomb"—of AIDS, that is—"fell without anyone's knowing the bomb had fallen," before its victims knew they were hit. But this is rather silly: bombs are noisy devices, and they hardly could explode without being noticed. Holleran persisted with his war metaphor, with its implication of human agency, even though he also placed AIDS in "that category of events—earthquakes, droughts, tidal waves, volcanic eruptions—that simply happen."[19] Similarly, Kramer pressed on with his Holocaust analogy until concluding that "Reagan is our Hitler." But Reagan as Hitler did not work well, and later he would backtrack, arguing that there can be "unintentional" holocausts, ones for which "it is not possible to locate one Hitler."[20] But his backtracking also blurred his analogy to *the* Holocaust and demonstrated the problems he was having with it. Another writer, having critically surveyed ACT UP's iconography of genocide, nonetheless described himself as "a gay man living at ground zero in one of the major AIDS war zones."[21] The confusing use of such language was hardly confined to gay polemicists. Though Buchanan's notion of gay men's war upon Nature seemed to consign them to inevitable defeat—Nature presumably had the upper hand, after all—he also revealed his fear that they would be victorious if given sufficient license to control federal policy and protect their lives. When Perrow and Guillén proposed the Polaris missile program as a model for dealing with AIDS, they offered not a word's reflection on the necessary weaknesses of any military endeavor.

What was going on, then, when various parties persisted with such metaphors and analogies even when they lost internal consistency or historical plausibility? The persistence of war language suggests that its appeal was deeply rooted and lay beyond the conscious, or at least carefully considered, purposes of the users.

There are many specific ways to understand that appeal. The politics and identities of individual writers certainly mattered—Kramer's Jewish identity self-consciously shaped his use of language, as did a well-developed tradition of linking Jews and homosexuals in both imaginative and analytic literature (a tradition with which Kramer was familiar). Many gay writers have also drawn on a long-standing imaginative tradition for understanding the Nazi Holocaust that emphasized its "unspeakable" and "indescribable" nature, so that it seemed fit to argue that "AIDS makes no sense . . . in the end you are left with a situation that is out of reach of reason or understanding."[22] Moreover, there was a long tradition before AIDS of militarizing disease, and the impulse to do so with AIDS was not uniquely American: no account of AIDS was more riddled with military metaphors and analogies than Dreuilhe's *Mortal Embrace*, which originally appeared in French. Certainly, the deep and understandable distrust of gays and lesbians towards state power was another factor. Gender may also have played a role. It was *men* who used war language most often in the politics of AIDS, and although women are not impervious to it—the lesbian activist Susie Bright lectured on "sex wars," and Andrea Dworkin penned *Letters From a War Zone*.[23] Sontag and other women, however, were more apt to criticize it, perhaps because war metaphors obviously refer to an arena of life characterized in imagination by male action and male dominance. There are, of course, other ways to inquire into the *internal* dynamics of the AIDS discourse.

But an *external* approach may be just as useful: relating the uses of war in the AIDS discourse to similar language elsewhere in American political culture. For war and holocaust as metaphors for social and political causes were widespread on the American political landscape in the 1980s. That decade had seen a "war on terrorism" and a "trade war," along with linkage in verbal and visual imagery of the Japanese economic challenge to its military challenge during World War II. The late 1980s brought a "war on drugs," complete with incessant talk of "battle plans," "fronts," "enemies," "victory," and "prisoner-of-war camps." When the Supreme Court handed down a decision on abortion services in 1989, the cover of *Ms.* magazine was emblazoned with the words, *"IT'S WAR!"* After Robert Bork's nomination for the Supreme Court was defeated, an account of his troubles was titled *Battle for Justice*, and Bork himself referred to "the war to control the legal culture." Just as some equated victims of AIDS to victims of the Holocaust, opponents of abortion had for years likened aborted fetuses to Holocaust victims. In Chicago, Mayor Richard M. Daley proclaimed a "war on rats," and in New York, Mayor David Dinkins proclaimed a "war on fear."[24] As with the war metaphor for AIDS, these other uses of war metaphors persisted despite internal inconsistencies—since, for example, the very essence of war is that it breeds fear, it is unclear how to wage a "war on fear."

It is clear that this phenomenon in political language went far beyond the AIDS discourse, and that those who used the language of war by no means had a common political purpose. Yet to a degree, they shared a common language. It may therefore be useful to examine the AIDS discourse with respect to that *common* language, rather than only for its uniqueness.

That language and its upsurge in the 1980s sprang in part from a long American tradition of antistatism—that is, of hostility toward powerful government and concerned social action. In modern American history, war as analogue and metaphor has repeatedly served to justify strong government. It has done so all the more after each major American war—the Civil War, World War I, and World War II—since victory in those wars further demonstrated the efficacy of state action. Reluctant to justify strong government in the interest of social or economic welfare—since to do so would coddle the poor, burden the taxpayer, or throttle free enterprise—Americans have repeatedly wrapped their demands for governmental action in the rhetoric of war.

Doing so, they could make a moral and political claim on resources that would be otherwise unavailable. They placed their demands in the one arena of national activity where expense is deemed incidental, partisan politics are presumably suspended, unity can be assumed or compelled, and ingrained hostilities toward taxation and centralized authority can be suspended. As the historian William Leuchtenburg once commented regarding the explosion of war language invoked to justify the New Deal, war metaphors and analogies "revealed both an impoverished tradition of reform and the reluctance of the nation to come to terms with the leviathan state. . . . The country had yet to find a way to organize collective action save in war or its surrogate."[25] Sontag has recently advanced a similar argument:

> Indeed, the transformation of warmaking into an occasion for mass ideological mobilization has made the notion of war useful as a metaphor for all sorts of ameliorative campaigns whose goals are cast as the defeat of an "enemy". . . . Abuse of the military metaphor may be inevitable in a capitalist society, a society that increasingly restricts the scope and credibility of appeals to ethical principle, in which it is thought foolish not to subject one's actions to the calculus of self-interest and profitability. Warmaking is one of the few activities that people are not supposed to view "realistically"; that is, with an eye to expense and practical outcome. In all-out war, expenditure is all-out, unprudent—war being defined as an emergency in which no sacrifice is excessive.[26]

In the 1980s, the United States still lacked "a way to organize collective action save in war or its surrogate," as Leuchtenburg put it. Such an inability has remained a persistent feature of American politics since the 1930s, as anyone will remember who lived through Lyndon Johnson's War on Poverty or Richard Nixon's war on cancer and war on smut. Indeed, most national government initiatives over the past half-century—in science and technology, in civil rights and education, in social welfare and social crusades—have been justified either by their service to national security or by a language that linked them politically to the arena of war. To be sure, those justifications often provided only cosmetic cover for political agendas quite divorced from war and national security. The persistence of those justifications nonetheless was telling. For liberals, conservatives, radicals, and reactionaries, the imperatives or language of war have served to legitimate the powerful government Americans fear to admit they want, and the huge bureaucracies they claim to hate.

Just how powerfully this distrust of government operated was suggested by more of Kramer's rhetoric: his accusation that the National Institutes of Health are "drowning in waste, fraud, corruption and mismanagement. They are, in fact, pissing one billion dollars down the toilet."[27] Drop the "pissing" from such a passage, and his rhetoric is remarkably similar to decades of conservative denunciation of national government, from Herbert Hoover through Barry Goldwater and on through Ronald Reagan and Newt Gingrich.

In the antistatist climate of American politics, then, war was repeatedly invoked to legitimate action by a government deeply distrusted. Doing so particularly made sense in the late 1980s, when Reaganism further undercut appeals for national action grounded in social justice and economic warfare. And it made sense in light of the last half-century of American history when, after all, most large-scale actions sustained successfully by national government were war-related: World War II itself, then the Cold War with its myriad programs, including the Space Race of the 1960s. It made sense, then, that new endeavors—against AIDS, against drugs, against countless other perceived threats at home or from abroad—were justified in the language of the only crusades that had proved enduring. Hence, too, advocates of national crusades invoked not only war generally, but specific models of Americans' most shining success in warfare, such as the Manhattan Project. And if models of successful action were to be drawn from wartime experience, it made sense that models of catastrophe were also drawn from wartime experience—hence the Holocaust as a model of what might be happening to gay men. Of course, when choosing historical models and metaphors, care was necessary to achieve the desired effect: the references were usually back to World War II, the war of incredible achievement and catastrophe, and rarely to the Korean or Vietnam wars, whose goals and outcomes were at best ambiguous.

The impulse to invoke war may have operated with special force for gays and lesbians confronting AIDS. Their politics had been highly localized in the 1970s, lacking a tradition of close ties with bureaucratized national government, much less trust in it. Moreover, the gay and lesbian community lacked a strong tradition of its own bureaucratic institutions. The models and metaphors of war in AIDS rhetoric served, then, to mobilize both government and the community itself. And just as that rhetoric displayed both a demand for government action and a distrust of the bureaucratic results, it displayed a demand for community organization and a distrust of the bureaucratic results. Thus Kramer (among others) hurled almost precisely the same invective of waste, fraud, and spinelessness against bureaucratized organizations like the Gay Men's Health Crisis as he did against the Food and Drug Administration or the National Institutes of Health, while alternative organizations like ACT UP thrived on an antibureaucratic and antihierarchical ethos. The use of war to summon "collective action" in the face of "an impoverished tradition of reform" operated both externally vis-à-vis national government and internally within the gay community itself.

IV

There is little to be gained by criticizing participants in the conflict over AIDS for employing a language so deeply rooted in their political culture. To a degree at least, that language was beyond their control or conscious choice. It was certainly useful for expressing searing experiences and deeply held convictions. And a political discourse stripped of metaphor and imagery would have expressed little of those experiences and convictions—it was both futile and foolish to wish for it. Yet American political culture was hardly so uniform or determinative that alternative possibilities were unimaginable. The Names Project Quilt assembled to memorialize people dead with AIDS evoked, with considerable emotional and political success, a quite different range of associations and images than talk of war and holocaust had. And at the least, the historian can hint at both the advantages and drawbacks of particular kinds of language.

It may be that war rhetoric served to mobilize gays and lesbians, government, and other parties, at the price of long-term commitment to action. Crusades in American history grounded in the metaphors and models of war—whether the war on poverty or war on cancer of the 1960s, or the war on drugs at the end of the 1980s—have tended to display a short half-life. They often bristle with activity and then flame out as quickly as they began. They then leave behind a substantial bureaucratic and legal residue, often repressive in nature, as well as frustration that ambitious goals have not been met. Talk of war, after all, presumes that victory (or defeat) will be the outcome, and in a fairly short period of time: that is the nature of most undertakings in war. As Sontag comments, the "end-of-the-world rhetoric that AIDS has evoked . . . offers a stoic, finally numbing contemplation of catastrophe," just as, Paul Boyer has argued, a similar rhetoric after the advent of atomic weapons in 1945 numbed the very citizenry whom American anti-nuclear activists hoped to arouse.[28]

A "war on AIDS" was therefore an ambiguous basis for mobilizing either government or the gay and lesbian community itself. It made sense that by 1990, Kramer himself was lecturing on "AIDS: The War is Lost." Given his model of AIDS as warfare and holocaust, Kramer had to write an ending to the story analogous to the end of World War II, when victory or unconditional surrender were the only alternatives for the combatants. That the war on AIDS, or the war by AIDS—or more accurately perhaps, the war *over* AIDS—might have a different outcome (the stalemate of the Korean war?), or that indeed war might be a metaphor of limited utility, was difficult to conceive. Much the same might be said of those commentators and politicians who by the close of the 1980s were railing against the share of the national budget seized by AIDS by what they deemed a homosexual conspiracy—they too, if with less justification or finality, seemed to be declaring defeat in their war against those who war "upon Nature."

The early 1990s hinted at a new phase to this story, for the language of war seemed to be dissipating. It was unclear whether that dissipation signified a collapse of a sense of urgency, or a translation of that urgency into more sustainable if routinized action, or some other configuration of fears and aspirations. Most likely, it did signify in part the proliferation of AIDS discourse to other parties, as both the ravages of the disease itself and the voices raised about it more evidently broadened to include women, children, inner-city blacks, and others who had not dominated the debates of the 1980s.

The American war against Iraq in 1991 also affected the use of war language in politics and culture, though in cross-cutting ways whose consequences are hard to calculate. Momentarily, it seemed to absorb or obscure such use in the mass media—like other "wars" at home, the "war on AIDS" was as eclipsed in language as it was in political agendas. But for AIDS activists, although they received little media attention, the winter of 1991 sharpened a sense of competing agendas, as they contrasted the war abroad with the neglected war against AIDS. That is, it prompted a far more pointed and conscious deployment of the war metaphor, whose earlier use had been reflexive and diffuse. Moreover, the war prompted renewal among mainstream politicians of a predictable argument: let the nation summon the same strength and unity shown in the Gulf War to address its social ills at home.[29] Now, exponents of that argument could invoke a war in their own time, not some musty if mighty experience from a half-century ago (although the dominant political equation between Hitler and Hussein indicated just how much World War II still shaped political culture).

But it was by no means clear whether such consequences would be deep or lasting, in part because American experience of the war was at once both intense and ephemeral. The very ease of victory stripped the war of that gravity of sacrifice and achievement that embeds a war in language and memory and establishes it as a model of what concerted national action can achieve. At the same time, the ambiguous outcome of the war— the villain still in power, the Kurds under assault, the Mideast still in turmoil—diminished the luster of a military victory so easily achieved. Moreover, the war's timing with respect to the AIDS debate made a difference if one assumes a limited lifespan for styles of discourse. Because the Gulf War erupted when the language of war about AIDS had run on so long and had been so reduced to cliches, its potential to regenerate that AIDS discourse was doubtful.

Meanwhile, the record of the 1980s both demands and challenges interpretation. In the business of reading language, one size does not fill all the varied uses and meanings. To shoehorn metaphors of war and holocaust for AIDS into an antistatist tradition of American politics overlooks other readings. It suggests, however, that the political language of AIDS, including that of gay men, has operated more firmly in American political traditions than is usually acknowledged—either by gay militants who trumpet the novelty of their tactics or by their opponents who regard them as alien to all that is American. As has usually been the case in American culture, even the novel event had to be translated into language with imaginative signposts to the familiar, and even those marginal to the culture must employ—albeit often in atypical ways—its language, assumptions, and methods.

NOTES

1. Randy Shilts, *And the Band Played On: Politics, People, and the AIDS Epidemic* (New York: St. Martin's, 1987), pp. 609, 610.

2. *Saturday Evening Post* (May/June 1988):50–57.

3. Charles Perrow and Mauro F. Guillén, *The AIDS Disaster: The Failure of Organizations in New York and the Nation* (New Haven: Yale University Press, 1990), pp. 181–83. For a review of this book, see *Yale Magazine* (December 1990):22.

4. On "A Manhattan Project to Deal with AIDS," see Larry Kramer, *Reports from the Holocaust: The Making of an AIDS Activist* (New York: St. Martin's, 1989), p. 189; and Larry Kramer, "A 'Manhattan Project" for AIDS," *New York Times*, July 16, 1990.

5. See David Zarefsky, *President Johnson's War on Poverty: Rhetoric and History* (Birmingham, Ala.: University of Alabama Press, 1986).

6. Buchanan's syndicated column, May 1983, quoted in Robert A. Padgug, "Gay Villain, Gay Hero: Homosexuality and the Social Construction of AIDS," in Kathy Peiss and Christine Simmons, with Robert A. Padgug, *Passion and Power: Sexuality in History* (Philadelphia: Temple University Press, 1989), p. 297.

7. One reader of an early draft of this piece objected to my identification of holocaust metaphors with war language: "The holocaust metaphors chiefly have to do with the massiveness of death, omnicide, and the like, and only indirectly with war." Yet even if the Nazi Holocaust was not directly either the cause or the product of World War II, it was too intimately associated with that war, in both historical process and American culture since the war, to see it as linked "only indirectly with war," and nuclear holocaust is unimaginable except in the context of war.

8. Quotations from Shilts, *And the Band Played On*, pp. 220, 228, 442, 447, 305.

9. Kramer, *Reports from the Holocaust*, pp. 173, 163.

10. Paul Monette, *Afterlife* (New York: Crown, 1990), pp. 51, 278; emphasis added.

11. Monette quoted in Padgug, "Gay Villain, Gay Hero," p. 310.

12. Paul Monette, *Borrowed Time* (New York: Harcourt Brace Jovanovich, 1988), pp. 85, 110.

13. Shilts, *And the Band Played On*, pp. 217, 505.

14. R. Woodward, "A People at War," *Cleveland Edition*, June 28, 1990, p. 16.

15. Andrew Holleran, *Ground Zero* (New York: Morrow, 1988).

16. Glaser essay originally appeared in the periodical *Christianity and Crisis*; the summary of it given here appeared in George S. Buse, "Chris Glaser Talks About Gays, Lesbians and Presbyterians," *Windy City Times*, November 8, 1990, p. 20.

17. See Mike Hippler, "Battlefields Revisited: AIDS and World War I," *Windy City Times*, March 16, 1989, p. 10; Michael Bronski, "Between the Lines" (review of Matthew Standler's *Landscape: Memory*), *The Guide* (October 1990):18; Emmanuel Dreuilhe, *Mortal Embrace: Living with AIDS* (New York: Hill and Wang, 1988).

18. L. Scott, "Fear in the Foxholes: Health Workers' Alarm About Telling AIDS Patients," *New York* (January 4, 1988):30–38.

19. Holleran, *Ground Zero*, pp. 22, 18.

20. Kramer, *Reports from the Holocaust*, pp. 173, 265, 270.

21. Daniel Harris, "A Blizzard of Images," (review of *AIDS Demo Graphics*, *The Nation* (December 31, 1990):851–52.

22. Quotation from Michael Bronski, "Make the AIDS Epidemic Manageable," *American Book Review* (May–June 1990):22. For the tradition in American culture of seeing the Nazi Holocaust as "unspeakable" and "indescribable," I am indebted to Lane Fenrich, "Mass Death and American Consciousness," Ph.D. diss. in progress, Northwestern University.

23. Susie Bright at the Fourth Annual Lesbian, Bisexual, and Gay Studies Con-

ference, Harvard University, October 27, 1990; Andrea Dworkin, *Letters from a War Zone: Writings, 1976–1989* (New York: Dutton, 1989).

24. On Bork, see Stanley Kutler reviewing *Battle for Justice, Chicago Tribune*, October 22, 1989, Sunday Book Review p. 3. On Daley, see "Daley Latest to Declare War on Rats," *Chicago Tribune*, April 4, 1990. On Dinkins, see "N.Y. Mayor Plans 'War on Fear,'" *Chicago Tribune*, October 3, 1990. War language in the struggles over abortion and drugs was so pervasive as to defy citation.

25. William Leuchtenburg, "The New Deal and the Analogue of War," in John Braeman, Robert H. Bremner, and Everett Walters, eds., *Change and Continuity in Twentieth-Century America* (Columbus: Ohio State University Press, 1964), p. 143.

26. Susan Sontag, *AIDS and Its Metaphors* (New York: Farrar Straus Giroux, 1989), pp. 10–11.

27. Larry Kramer, "A Call to Riot: Part II," *Outlines* (May 1990):38.

28. Sontag, *AIDS and Its Metaphors*, p. 86; Paul Boyer, *By the Bomb's Early Light: American Thought and Culture at the Dawn of the Atomic Age* (New York: Pantheon, 1985).

29. See, for example, David E. Rosenbaum, "Wanted in Home Agenda: Unity the U.S. Had in War," *New York Times*, March 20, 1991, p. 1.

Plague in Germany, 1939/1989: Cultural Images of Race, Space, and Disease

Sander L. Gilman

I

The question of the national qualities ascribed to an illness has not been widely addressed in the debates about the social construction of the idea of AIDS.[1] Indeed, there has been an assumption—in work as controversial as that of Roy Porter or Susan Sontag, or indeed in my own work—that there is a single "Western" (read "Christian" or read "medical") tradition that has determined the basic structure of the ideas of disease.[2] My intent with this study is to illustrate some of the discontinuities in such over-reaching models or, perhaps more modestly, to show the national variations on such themes. I will be looking at the cultural and social implications of "plague" in German culture under national socialism and in Germany (both East and West) in the 1980s.

My point of departure will be the cultural representation of disease.[3] I shall use two novels as my artifacts to examine the fantasies of contagion and disease within German culture of 1939 and 1989. The first is the best-selling novel by Rudolf Heinrich Daumann, *Patrouille gegen den Tod* (Patrol against Death) of 1939[4] and the second, the first "AIDS novel" in German, Peter Zingler's 1989 novel *Die Seuche* (The Plague), published half a century later.[5] These two novels reflect a basic set of attitudes in German culture concerning the relationship between ideas of space and ideas of race, between representations of the body and concepts of difference.

These concepts are, of course, Western; they use the basic paradigms of "race," of "difference," of the "normal," and of the "pathological" that are found in other Western cultures (not all of them in Europe and North America). But I would like to stress the singular construction of ideas of race and ideas of sexuality within the German context. This point was already made by my 1982 book on blacks in German culture, but it warrants a restating in this context.[6]

The texts I have selected bear striking similarities. Both Daumann and Zingler's novels are "science fiction" dystopias/utopias,[7] each set in a not too distant future that extrapolates certain qualities of a constructed present into an image of the future. They are science fiction in that they both deal with the science of medicine. Both deal with the idea of plague—indeed, both use the term "plague" (*Seuche*)—as their central metaphor. It is therefore important to examine the representation of plague in these two books in order to examine the image of the disease that is constructed in this context. Let me begin with a cursory reading of the Daumann text, to sketch the plot and to stress the construction of the representation of ideas of race, space, and disease in utopian novels as distanced in time as 1939 and 1989.

II

Rudolf Heinrich Daumann's novel begins in a research institute for tropical medicine in Hamburg in 1969—thirty years into the future from the actual publication of the novel. We are introduced to one of the new employees, an unemployed "Russian" ballerina, Maxie Perussenko. Through one of her friends she has been appointed as a factotum at the institute, and we are shown its daily routine—the counting of lice, the feeding of white mice and lab rats—through her horrified eyes. The head of the institute is the microbiologist Dr. Robert Dobbertin, but the true "hero" of the novel is his assistant, Dr. Alfried Kalsten. The laboratory is instructed to identify the nature of and, of course, find the cure for an unidentified tropical epidemic that has broken out in a mining camp at Kanda-Kanda in the Belgian Congo. Kalsten and Perussenko are sent to Africa to gather tissue samples from the victims of this disease. In Africa the reader learns the true background of the "Russian" assistant. She is really a German ballerina, the daughter of an unemployed army officer and a German countess, who has adopted a Russian identity because of the cachet associated in Germany with Russian dancers such as Pavlova. We also learn that Kalsten had refused a senior academic position because of his desire to work in the field. His banker father had offered to buy such an appointment for him by funding his own research institute.

In the Belgian Congo our protagonists experience the Africa of the European settlers who understand contagious disease as part of their experience of Africa (108). They meet Alver Reemerzijl, the Flemish physician who is in charge of the health care facilities at the mine. With him they see, and marginally interact with, a group of cannibalistic and/or marijuana-smoking natives whose hysterical fear of the disease has made them revert to the beliefs and practices of their precolonial past. Finally, flying out of the Congo with a box of infected white mice, they crash in the tropical jungle and are guided through it by a faithful native guide. During their escape and unknown to the other, Maxie and Alfried inoculate themselves with one of the strains of the disease so that their research will not be jeopardized by the death of their specimens in the jungle. This altruism causes them to admit their love for each other.[8] They return to Hamburg at the conclusion of the novel, bearing the disease within them. Kalsten, through pure intelligence, uncovers the cure for the disease and thus saves them both. At the end of the novel the cure is linked with the happy end of their relationship. The lovers find themselves at a hotel in Aswan, Egypt, and are there informed of the successful end of the epidemic but also the death, through overwork, of their Flemish counterpart, Alver Reemerzijl.

The plot for this novel is standard for the mass, "trivial" literature of the 1930s. These novels are heavily indebted to British models, such as the Tarzan novels of Edgar Rice Burroughs, as well as to the image of Africa in the extraordinarily popular novels of Karl May.[9] (The popularity of both novelists remains high in Germany today.) Within this tradition is the image of the diseased nature of the black and the need for the colonial master to serve the cause of healing.

The meaning of this topos shifted radically during the 1930s. Imperial Germany had been stripped of its African (and South Pacific) colonies as a result of the Treaty of Versailles. After 1919 the British became the main villains for the Germans in their struggle for colonial "living space." It was the British who had destroyed the careful work of the Germans in their colonies, specifically in the area of public health. The health of the natives, part of the rationale for colonial rule (a healthy native is a healthy worker), became a touchstone for the failure of colonial policy. In 1919 Hans Poeschel writes of the spread of yellow fever among the black soldiers serving in the British army in Africa during World War I:

> Hundreds of thousands of their fellow-sufferers will never see their villages again. The English neglected the obvious duty of caring for the safe and

orderly return of these tremendous armies of carriers, in the most criminal manner. The inevitable consequence was that distempers broke out everywhere—spinal meningitis, dysentery, small-pox, the sleeping sickness—and these wrought terrible havoc among our unhappy natives. The magnificent results attained by the German Administration in the sphere of hygiene may be considered as ruined for generations. [10]

After 1933, under the leadership of General Franz Ritter von Epp, the head of the Office for Colonial Politics of the Nazi Party, a conscious attempt was made to associate the British (and by extension the South African) mandates over the former German colonies with the abdication of this role in maintaining the hygiene of the natives. [11]

But after 1933 the ideological context of the term *hygiene* had taken on a different implication. [12] In the *German Colonial Yearbook* for 1940, entitled "Africa Needs Greater Germany," there is a long essay by Ernst Janisch, a state secretary in the National Biological Institute, on the abdication of racial hygiene—the need to maintain the pure race of the black inhabitants. [13] The direct accusation was that the other colonial powers, including the British and the French, permitted racial mixing, which inevitably resulted in the weakening of the pure racial qualities of the black. This charge was a mainstay of German discussions about the need for the return of the German colonies. In his broadside of 1938, H. W. Bauer asserted that the "Germans had been on the way to creating the *most valuable* type of black on the black continent" through the "cultural and hygienic care of the native population" when their colonies had been taken away from them. [14]

All these commonplaces about race and difference, about racial mixing and the degeneration of pure races are reflected in Daumann's novel. Thus in the novel it is the German pilot, Konrad Steen, who is disgusted (after the fact) by the suggestion of his Belgian acquaintance to visit a black house of prostitution (174). Indeed, the very love story between Alfried Kalsten and Maxie Perussenko that stands at the center of the book reflects the "pure racial model," for in the course of the novel the object of desire reveals herself to be a "pure" German rather than a mere Slav, and thus the relationship can be consummated.

III

The discourse about race and difference, especially in a German reading of 1939, can be more highly contextualized. The "Africa" of German fantasy, with its racial struggle played out within the strict confines of the model of colonialism, also reflects the daily preoccupation of the Germans of 1933 to 1939 with another model of race, a model in which the image of difference was not as visibly written upon the skin, but had rather to be even more carefully constructed in order to identify the Other. Daumann's novel provides an ideal image of the future of Europe, as well as its African colonies, within a very specific model of "disease and health." What I wish to examine is the idea of disease within the world that Daumann creates, its contemporary implications (i.e., readings), and its relationship to an ideal view of the future.

Daumann sees 1969 as an extension of a pre-1932 world. Real Germans, such as Maxie's former soldier father, are employed in menial jobs, or, like Maxie herself, must disguise themselves as foreigners to have any role in the cultural life of Germany. A strong Germany dominates Europe only because of its role in science. "Science" fiction becomes thus a manner of speaking about the centrality of a German identity rather than a means of escape. But this is a novel published in 1939, not in 1932. It is a novel of fulfillment, not of longing (two genres that can easily be found within the official Nazi party literature before and after the Nazi seizure of power).[15] In this rearview mirror image of the future, there is an axiom for the construction of ideas of difference and of disease. Such images are to be sought in the immediate events of the past, not in an image of the present, for specific images of the past are internalized as part of the thought collective about the origin of the present. These images are usually representations of trauma—such as the post–World War I image of the collapse of the body politic in Germany—and within the German tradition of 1939 are closely linked to the search for the origin of the collapse of that "healthy" body politic in the defeat at Versailles, in ideas of race and infection.[16]

The quality ascribed to the world of 1969 (22) that is quite missing from the world of 1939 is that the outsiders, the pollutants, are present only "outside"—in Africa, not in Europe. Thus we are confronted with an image of German science that deals with tropical medicine, but in a model of disease that has a series of very specific racial connotations. The construction of the image of the disease represented in the novel starts at its very opening, when Alfried Kalsten attempts to assuage Maxie's fears of working in the Institute by pointing out to her the ubiquitousness of infection in the "real" world outside the clinic. "Imagine," he says, "that your legs have failed and that you have to work as a bar-girl from eight in the evening to four in the morning. How do you know who is sitting near you in this shady bar? Old travelers with flattened noses, in whom the *Spirochaeta*

palladia, the white spirochaete, wends its quiet and secret path, transforming human tissue into rubber, destroying the brain and creating the
most horrible paralysis" (19). Syphilis is the model for the idea of disease
in this novel; thus the unknown disease is a "brand-new type of infectious
disease," (43) a "plague" (58) that has made "thousands of brown and
black people" in the mines unable to work (35). Indeed, at the very beginning of the novel it seems to have already killed at least two hundred, and
another six thousand are ill (58). It is no surprise that when Alfried looks
into his electron microscope the source of this mystery disease in Africa is
revealed to be a "tiny, cork-screw shaped virus-like spirochaete" (72). The
form of the disease is not overtly syphilitic, because it manifests itself as a
liver or a kidney infection, but the continual association of disease with
the "great masquerader," syphilis, is made throughout the novel. Indeed,
in explaining the virulence of this new spirochete to two friends of Maxie,
who speak in comical Bavarian dialect, Alfried states:

> "And I should be afraid for these snake-lets?" the soprano asked in-
> quisitively, as she placed a bit of eel on her dish.
> The assistant nodded his head strongly, before he supplied her with the
> necessary amount of dill sauce: "Spirochete are really dangerous, especial-
> ly the Spirochete palladia, the cause of Lues. Do you know what a Wasser-
> mann [Aquarius] is?"
> "Naturally, a sign of the Zodiac."
> "You have a pure soul! Among us bacteriologists we understand it as a
> blood sample."
> "Ah so! Parhninger, didn't you once mention a blood sample to me."
> "Keep quiet, Poderl! Mine has been negative for a long while."   (88)

Syphilis and the unknown disease found in Africa are linked through the
very word *spirochete* with its scientific province. Indeed, the discussion of
the infected specimens of liver, brought to Hamburg as tissue samples, are
immediately described as "full of unknown spirochete" (90). The disease
is thus associated throughout the novel with syphilis and, in the German
context, with a very different idea of race and disease. There was a real
fear in the 1920s and 1930s of a substantial increase in the number of
cases of syphilis and of the development of a new form of "metaLues."
Such a fear was also coupled with a sense that such an increase would
drastically effect the offspring of the present generation.[17]

But syphilis, like all stigmatizing diseases, had to be "seen"; it had to
be as evident in its signs and symptoms as the signs of "race"; it had to be
written on the skin. In the realm of German science, as in American medi-

cine during the same period,[18] syphilis was associated with a racial (as well as a pathognomonic) image of difference. And according to the first mention of syphilis in Daumann's novel (19), the sign with which it was to be identified was the shape of the nose.[19] In Germany the Jewish nose, rather than the nose of the black, was the salient sign of difference. Within the German proverbial tradition the shape and nature of the nose and that of the phallus are inexorably linked. Sexually transmitted disease, especially syphilis, was mythically associated with the Jewish (read: circumcised) penis, the physical aspect ascribed to the Jew (read: Jewish male) that in the German eye defined the Jew as readily as skin color defined the inhabitants of Africa. This in an age in which more and more German Jews (as defined racially by the Nazis) actually were uncircumcised! There was thus the need to construct another mark of difference in the concentration camps of the 1930s—the tattoo—an indelible mark upon the body that uniformly signified difference.

In Daumann's novel the Jew seems to be strangely missing. It is Jewishness, this central category of "racial" difference for the German reader and writer of 1939, that has vanished from the world of 1969. Of course, the sole exception is the name of the Jewish bacteriologist August von Wassermann, whose 1906 discovery of the serodiagnosis of syphilis led to the test that bears his name.[20] While ennobled in 1913, he remained in the anti-Semitic handbooks of the day as well as in public mind the Jew associated with syphilis.[21]

The Jew in European science and popular thought was indeed closely related to the spread and incidence of syphilis.[22] Such views had two readings. The first model saw the Jews as the carriers of sexually transmitted diseases who transmitted them to the rest of the world. This view is found in Adolf Hitler's discussion of syphilis in *Mein Kampf* (1925), the central discussion of race and disease for German culture in 1939. He links syphilis to the Jew, the prostitute, and the power of money:

> Particularly with regard to syphilis, the attitude of the nation and the state can only be designated as total capitulation. . . . The invention of a remedy of questionable character and its commercial exploitation can no longer help much against this plague. . . . The cause lies, primarily, in our prostitution of love. . . . This Jewification of our spiritual life and mammonization of our mating instinct will sooner or later destroy our entire offspring.[23]

Hitler's views also linked Jews with prostitutes and the spread of infection. Jews were the archpimps; Jews ran the brothels; but Jews also infected their prostitutes and caused the weakening of the German national fiber.[24]

Jews were also associated with the false promise of a medical cure separate from the social cures that Hitler wished to see imposed—isolation and separation of the syphilitic and his or her Jewish source from the body politic. Hitler's reference was to the belief that the specialties of dermatology and syphilology were especially dominated by Jews, who used their medical status to sell quack cures.[25]

The second model that associated Jews and syphilis postulated exactly the opposite—that Jews had a statistically lower rate of syphilitic infection, because they had become immune to it through centuries of exposure. In the medical literature of the period, reaching across all of European medicine, it was assumed that Jews had a notably lower rate of infection. In a study of the incidence of tertiary lues in the Crimea undertaken between 1904 and 1929, the Jews had the lowest consistent rate of infection.[26] In an eighteen-year longitudinal study H. Budel demonstrated the extraordinarily low rate of tertiary lues among Jews in Estonia during the prewar period.[27] All of these studies assumed that biological differences as well as the social difference of the Jews were at the root of their seeming "immunity."

Jewish scientists also had to explain the "statistical" fact of their immunity to syphilis. In a World War I study of the rate of tertiary lues, the final stage of the syphilitic infection, the Jewish physician Max Sichel attributed the relative lower incidence of infection among Jews to the sexual difference of the Jews.[28] He responded—out of necessity—with a social argument. The Jews, according to Sichel, evidenced lower incidence because of their early marriage and the patriarchal structure of the Jewish family, but also because of their much lower rate of alcoholism. They were, therefore, according to the implicit argument, more rarely exposed to infected prostitutes, whose attractiveness was always associated with the greater loss of sexual control in the inebriated male. The relationship between these two "social" diseases is made into a cause for the higher incidence among other Europeans. In 1927, H. Strauss looked at the incidence of syphilitic infection in his hospital in Berlin in order to demonstrate whether the Jews had a lower incidence but also to see (as in the infamous Tuskegee experiments among blacks in the United States) whether they had "milder" forms of the disease because of their lifestyle or background.[29] He found that Jews had indeed a much lower incidence of syphilis (while having an extraordinarily higher rate of hysteria) than the non-Jewish control group. He proposed that the disease may well have a different course in Jews than in non-Jews.

The marker for such a view of the heightened resistance to syphilis is the basic sign of difference of the Jews, the circumcised phallus. The old debates within and without the Jewish community surfaced in Germany during the 1840s. German Jews had become acculturated into German middle-class values and came to question the absolute requirement of circumcision as a sign of their Jewish identity. Led by the radical reform rabbi Samuel Holdheim and responding to a Christian tradition that denigrated circumcision, the debate was carried out as much in the scientific press as in the religious one.

There had been four traditional views of the "meaning" of circumcision after the rise of Christianity. Following the writings of Paul, the first saw circumcision as inherently symbolic and, therefore, no longer valid after the rise of Christianity (this view was espoused by Eusebius and Origen); the second saw circumcision as a form of medical prophylaxis (as in the writing of Philo but also in the work of the central German commentator of the eighteenth century, Johann David Michaelis); the third saw it as a sign of a political identity (as in the work of the early eighteenth-century theologian Johann Spencer); and the fourth saw it as a remnant of the early Jewish idol or phallus worship (as in the work of the antiquarian Georg Friedrich Daumer—this view reappears quite often in the literature on Jewish ritual murder).[30]

In the medical literature during the course of the early twentieth century, however, only two views dominated, those that bracketed the images of "health" and "disease." These views saw circumcision either as the source of disease or as a prophylaxis against disease—and in both cases syphilis plays a major role. In the first case a detailed literature discusses the transmission of syphilis to newly circumcised infants through the ritual of *metsitsah*, the sucking on the penis by the *mohel*, the ritual circumciser, in order to staunch the bleeding.[31] The opposing view, also seen as an aspect of "hygiene," the favorite word to critique or support the practice, sees circumcision as a mode of prevention that precludes the transmission of sexually transmitted diseases because of the increased capacity for cleanliness.[32] (This view is closely associated with the therapeutic use of circumcision throughout the nineteenth century as a means of "curing" the diseases caused by masturbation, with, of course, a similar split in the idea of efficacy: circumcision was either a cure for masturbation, because it eliminated the stimulation of the prepuce and deadened the sensitivity of the penis, or it was the source of Jewish male hypersexuality.)

The need to see and label the Jew at a time when Jews were becoming more and more "invisible" in Germany made the association with socially stigmatizing diseases that bore specific visible signs and symptoms especially appropriate. In the German Empire of the late nineteenth century all of the arguments placed the Jew in a special relationship to syphilis and, therefore, in a very special relationship to the healthy body politic needed to make the Jew visible. (The central medical paradigm for the establishment of the healthy state was the public health model that evolved specifically to combat the evils of sexually transmitted disease through social control.) Jews had been completely acculturated by the end of the nineteenth century and thus bore no external signs of difference (unique clothing, group language, group-specific hair or beard style). They had to bear the stigma of this special relationship to their diseased nature literally on the skin, where it could be seen.

Indeed, Jews bear the salient stigma of the black skin of the syphilitic, the syphilitic *rupia*. The Jews are black, according to nineteenth-century racial science, because they are "a mongrel race which always retains this mongrel character." That is Houston Stewart Chamberlain arguing against the "pure" nature of the Jewish race.[33] Jews had "hybridized" with blacks in Alexandrian exile. They are, in an ironic review of Chamberlain's work by the father of modern Yiddish scholarship, Nathan Birnbaum, a "bastard" race whose origin was caused by their incestuousness. But the Jews were also seen as wholly black.[34] Adam Gurowski, a Polish noble, "took every light-colored mulatto for a Jew" when he first arrived in the United States in the 1850s.[35] Jews are black because they are different, because their sexuality is different, because their sexual pathology is written upon their skin. Gurowski's "German-Jewish" contemporary, Karl Marx, associates leprosy, Jews, and syphilis in his description of his archrival Ferdinand Lassalle (in 1861): "Lazarus the leper, is the prototype of the Jews and of Lazarus-Lassalle. But in our Lazarus, the leprosy lies in the brain. His illness was originally a badly cured case of syphilis."[36] Jews = lepers = syphilitics = blacks.

By the 1930s the pathological image of the Jew was part of the general cultural vocabulary of Germany. Hitler used this image over and over in *Mein Kampf* in describing the Jew's role in German culture:

> If you cut even cautiously into such an abscess, you found, like a maggot in a rotting body, often dazzled by the sudden light—a kike! This was pestilence, spiritual pestilence, worse than the Black Death of olden times, and the people were being infected by it. (57–58)

Plague (*Seuche*) and pestilence (*Pestilenz*)—a disease from without which, like syphilis, rots the body—were the models used to identify the Jew. The syphilitic weakening of the pure race of the Germans by the Jews was likened by Hitler to the corruption of the blood of the race through another form of "mammonization," interracial marriage:

> Here we have before us the results of procreation based partly on purely social compulsion and partly on financial grounds. The one leads to a general weakening, the other to a poisoning of the blood, since every department store Jewess is considered fit to augment the offspring of His Highness—and indeed the offspring look it. In both cases complete degeneration is the consequence.   (247)

If the Germans (Aryans) are a pure race—and that is for turn-of-the-century science a positive quality—then the Jews cannot be a pure race. Their status as a mixed race became exemplified in the icon of the *Mischling* during the 1930s. The Jewishness of the *Mischling*, to use the term from racial science parallel to *Bastard* (the offspring of a black and a white race), looks and sounds degenerate. They can have "Jewish-Negroid" features.[37] And these images are often associated with the facile use of language, "the use of innumerable foreign words and newly created words to enrich the German language in sharp contrast to the necessary simplicity of the language of Germanic students."[38]

This is not to be understood as a sign of strength. In *Jewish Self-Hatred*, I have shown that there is an extensive ancient Western tradition that labels the language of the Jew as corrupt and corrupting, as the sign of the inherent difference of the Jew.[39] This tradition sees the Jew as inherently unable to have command of any cultural language, indeed not even the "holy language," Hebrew. The Jew is not only "not of our blood," as Msgr. Joseph Frings of Cologne expressed it in 1942, but also "does not speak our language."[40] The Jew's language reflects only the corruption of the Jew and his or her discourse. It is the sign of the "pathological early development" of the *Mischling*, who, as an adult, is unable to fulfill the promise of the member of a pure race. The weakness, but also the degenerate facility of the *Mischling*, is analogous to the image of the offspring of the syphilitic (an image captured for nineteenth- and early twentieth-century culture in Henrik Ibsen's play *Ghosts*). And this weakness of the race is hidden within the corrupted (and corrupting) individual. Thus Hitler's image of the *Mischling* is of the offspring of a Jewish mother and an Aryan father—hidden within the name and Germanic lineage of the child is the true corruption of the race, the maternal lineage of the Jew. And because Jews claimed their lineage through the mother (rather than through the father as in Salic law), the *Mischling* becomes the exemplary hidden Jew just waiting to corrupt the body politic.

The weakness of the offspring of Jews as well as those of syphilitics is especially evident in the nervousness of the offspring. One of the most salient signs and symptoms of this nervousness is the decay and collapse of language. But this sign is also part of the image of the black in Daumann's assumption of the general discourse of colonialism. And like the pseudo-Russian dancer, the "boy"—to use Daumann's term—is marked by a discourse of difference. The Other speaks differently, revealing him or herself in discourse. The blacks in Daumann's novel speak a mix of German, Flemish, and French, all represented in a broken grammar, a language similar in its structure to that affected by Maxie early in the novel. But unlike them she continually lapses back into "real" German. The blacks' hidden fault manifests itself in the symptom of the degeneration of language; Maxie's pure race manifests itself in her inability to maintain this sign.

Like the syphilitic marked by the collapse of language and discourse and the "hidden language of the Jew," the image of discourse is also a marker of pathological difference in this world, a signifier that links race and difference. Daumann's infected and hysteric blacks revert to the primitive religion of their forefathers, to cannibalism and drugs, to the older, pre-Christian world. For German language scholars (like the psychiatrist Richard Krafft-Ebing or the anthropologist Wilhelm Schmidt) this primitive stage was to be found frozen in the world of the Jews. For the discourse about "Jewish hysteria," as Jan Goldstein has so well shown, is already part of the medical discourse of high science in the nineteenth century.[41] By the 1930s the myth of the Jewish sacrifice of Christians—to rid themselves of specific sexually related pathologies—had reappeared.[42] The real plague among the blacks was the response to the epidemic, for "as bad as or even worse than the illness is the spiritual crisis, the fear, horror, anxiety, and doubt. . . . The best example is inner Africa today. An area almost as big as Germany can be seen as plague-ridden [*verseucht*]. . . . The quarantine [*Pestkordon*] is a paper fiction" (280). Maxie, having learned from her time in the jungle the "truth" about the world in which she now lives, observes two salient images of the syphilitic and of the Jew: first, the Jew's madness, especially apparent in the *Mischling*, and second, the impossibility of creating impermeable barriers to eliminate the disease from society.[43] By 1939 the anti-Jewish laws in Germany had excluded Jews from virtually every sphere of public life, yet the very isolation of the Jews aroused greater and greater anxiety about their presence in Germany, an anxiety that had its first major release on *Kristallnacht* in 1939. The Jews could not be kept cordoned off—they could slip through the jungle of the cities (to extend Daumann's metaphor in a viable image of the time) and continue to spread infection.

The image of the body politic and the politics of race are inexorably linked in the novel. The presence of "strange blood" in the body causes death, as we learn very early in the novel from Professor Klading's "scientific" excursus about the impossibility of putting "eel's blood" in a test rabbit (45–46). He associates this impossibility with the need for every race to be in its proper place. His "scientific" metaphor is that each race must consume its appropriate protein, seeing the primeval German diet of swine and fish as growing out of the Germans' appropriate place. This view is articulated in the concept of lebensraum (living space), the basic philosophy that underpins German rhetoric about their need for African colonies during the late 1930s and that is also closely related to specific ideas of the absolute location of race. In the work of the nineteenth-century anthropologist Friedrich Ratzel, the founder of the ecological theory of race, the Jews are seen as the one race "out of place." In the Near East they were productive (for example, creating monotheism), but in Europe they can have no real cultural meaning.[44] The association of place and race is linked in the rationale of the German in Africa or the Jew in Europe. They are presented as mirror images, for while the German in Africa "heals," the Jew in Europe "infects." No quarantine is truly successful in controlling the Jew.

The image of the plague presented in this novel is paralleled to the Black Plague, described as coming from the Middle East, and which proceeded to decimate European civilization (52–54). This image also appears, as we have seen, in *Mein Kampf*. Again the subliminal message is that disease comes from outside, from "Byzantium," or from "Kanda-Kanda," and can destroy Europe (55). The traditional association—in Hitler's presentation as well as in the "historical" studies cited in Daumann's novel[45]—is with the Jews as the "cause" of the Black Plague. These parallels between the medieval plague and a potential future one would not have been lost on the reader of 1939.

IV

In early 1989 the icon of plague in the German context should have been very different. At that time we had two clearly differentiated Germanies— the Federal Republic of Germany (FRG) and the German Democratic Republic (GDR)—each of which, in its own manner, repudiated everything about the Nazi period (at least in official rhetoric). West Berlin was a space belonging ideologically to the FRG (even though it maintained its status as a four-power city), but it was also a place always understood to be on the margin between cultures. It was a "dangerous" place, because it was neither truly "west" nor "east." The public perception of this status was radically altered after November 9, 1989. The special function that West Berlin played in fantasies about disease and its control was a reflex of that special status.

Perhaps the best place to begin with an examination of the fantasies about plague that haunt the contemporary German idea of AIDS is with a very different text from a very different world: the first gay book of belles lettres officially to appear in the GDR, Ulrich Berkes's 1987 "diary" *Eine schlimme Liebe* (An Evil Love), published by the premier publishing house of the GDR. In this text, part literary manifesto on the nature of modernism and part autobiographical catalog of the daily life of a gay poet in the GDR during 1984, there are two passing mentions of AIDS. Dated 7 April 1984 and 30 October 1984, they describe the disease first in an American context and then in an African one.[46] These fragmentary mentions of the disease are represented as but one of the building blocks in gay self-image in the GDR of 1984. But they also localize the disease as coming from "out there." The disease that by 1987 had taken a substantial hold on the imagination of German gay and straight readers is seen on the historical periphery without any seeming context.[47] While the first mention of AIDS is used to justify the practice of mutual masturbation, the second mention is reported as part of the daily "static" heard through the airwaves, which the gay individual assimilates because it relates directly to his sexuality. The USA and Africa are the "source" of AIDS for German culture.[48] (In this context one can mention the parody of the image of the African origin of AIDS in gay West German filmmaker Rosa von Praunheim's *A Virus Respects no Morals* [1986].)

While the search for a specific, localized source comes as no surprise—whether in terms of the studies of the genetics of AIDS or of the mock-epidemiological search for "Patient Zero"[49]—the implication of this localization for the 1980s in a German context must be understood, for America and Africa are not neutral spaces for the German (especially a German in the GDR) of 1984. It is this web of associations—and the absence within Berkes's text of a set of overt associations—which appears in Peter Zingler's AIDS novel (as well as elsewhere in the discourse about AIDS in Germany in the past few years), a novel written for a straight audience and published by a self-consciously liberal press (the Eichborn Verlag).

If Rudolf Heinrich Daumann's novel of 1939 deals with a heroic image of medicine, with its emphasis on high-tech research (including fantasies of laser surgery [41]) and cure, Peter Zingler's *Die Seuche*, a 1989 science fiction account of AIDS in Germany in 1999, presents the reader with the model of medicine as public health, with all of its negative associations after the Nazi period. It is this seeming rejection, but also the maintenance of parallel ideological structures, that has shaped the idea of AIDS in Germany, for the image of Nazi medicine in Germany—especially during the 1980s—was inexorably linked with social control and placed into a special category remote from "good" clinical treatment. This view had appeared in Germany as early as 1947 with the publication of Alexander Mitscherlich's studies of the physicians in the concentration camps.[50] For the German public, medicine under national socialism was tied to the icon of the concentration camps, to the annihilation of groups labeled by the society of the time as different and therefore diseased (Jews, gays, the mentally ill).[51] The immediate association between the death camps and concentration camps, between images of social control and mindless, cruel experimentation, was perhaps inevitable. Medicine as an agent of control was seen as a negative, destructive force; the image of the clinician and that of the police were one. The sense of collective responsibility of the society was here resolved as the acts of brutality in the camps became (in part) linked to the sterile and inhumane image of a science treating all human beings as if they were laboratory animals. Science fiction—or at least the fiction of futuristic medicine—became a nightmare, and the day residue in that nightmare came from the representation of the Nazi past.

Peter Zingler's AIDS novel realizes its own image of plague that resonates with this German context. The plot is set on New Year's Eve of 1999, the beginning of a "new age," and we are confronted with the scene at a border crossing from West Berlin to the FRG. The "Hiffies" (HIV-infected) are marching in a column hundreds strong out of the "AIDS-Ghetto Berlin" (5), for Berlin as of 1992 and the passage of the "Rules for the Health of the German People" (*Anordnungen zum gesundheitlichen Wohl des Deutschen Volkes* [21]) had become the largest German AIDS internment camp (*Internierungscamp*). The allies had pulled out; the only remaining inhabitants are those labeled as AIDS carriers or AIDS-infected. ("I'm proud to be in Berlin West, in Hiff-Town," [103] sings a street singer in English.) Only these, the criminals who live off the Hiffies, and the "Turks" who have nowhere else to go except back to "Istanbul" (50) remain in West Berlin. The Hiffies are shipped to West Berlin once they are found to be "positive." Even the GDR begins quietly to expel its positive cases into West Berlin (101). By 1999, four million in the FRG are in "camps," with over four hundred thousand "SSD" police in place to guard them. Of these, three million Hiffies are in West Berlin. The SSD is the *Seuchen-Sicherheitsdienst*, the Plague-Security Force, the "wasps," who are dressed in clearly identifiable black uniforms with a yellow stripe and are armed with "heavy Israeli 44 magnum automatics" (19). The border guards observe the movement of this column of the "plague-ridden" and "undertake nothing. The Hiffies can carry their viruses 'back into the Reich'" (8).

Into this world come Judith Bahl, daughter of Minister of Health Hans Kaufmann (the most important member of the cabinet), and the estranged wife of Harald Bahl, an "AIDS careerist" (20), the head of Frankfurt's city "plague-control-institute" (18). By 1999 everyone in the FRG must carry a recent HIV test result as his or her identity card, and all public facilities open only with the presentation of such an identity card. Judith is tested and is revealed to be positive. She is immediately swept off into the machinery that takes her to West Berlin.

West Berlin is a German fantasy of Alfred Döblin's Berlin of the 1920s—it is the locus of the most extraordinary excesses. Drugs of all types are openly sold on the streets (103), and sex (of all types) is the rule (173), for the inhabitants of West Berlin are beyond caring about anything except their physical pleasure (173). West Berlin has become a huge concentration camp. Indeed, the very idea of West Berlin as a camp is created in 1992, when the Bavarians reopen Dachau as an AIDS internment camp. "The other states were more discrete" (55). In West Berlin Judith arranges to meet with an escape specialist, Max Isslacker, who for fifty thousand marks has offered to help her escape from West Berlin. Max, whose tattooed body is revealed to us when he and Judith have sex (138), eventually does help her escape. She returns to Frankfurt to retrieve her daughter and flees with her to an asylum, a *Campo de Sida* in Spain. There we learn that she was indeed always negative. Her husband had rigged the test so as to claim their daughter, discredit his father-in-law, and remove his unfaithful wife.

Acquiring AIDS in this novel does not happen randomly; it has meaning. It is a disease closely linked, in the scientific discourse of the physicians and researchers in the novel, to those individuals who have already ruined their immune system through their unnatural habits and their resultant extreme use of medication. The examples cited are "homosexuals, who have to have their syphilis cured every fourteen days" by using penicillin and who "eat antibiotics as others eat peppermints," and "whores" who constantly use penicillin to cure their "professional gonorrhea" (26). These social deviants are as different from the scientists as are the inhabitants of Africa, who, according to another theory outlined in the novel, "have an immune system quite different than ours and based on their way of life. Then the whites came and introduced diseases that were unknown to them: grippe, colds, syphilis" (26). Here Africa becomes the land not of the origin of disease but of the victim. This reversal is quite different from the popular German view in 1988 that the disease was caused not only by Africans but by African black women who had sex with monkeys.[52] This is quite in line with the postwar German image of the "sexual deviancy" of the black, especially the black out of her own space, the black in Germany.[53] But where does AIDS come from in this novel? As in other images of the origins of the disease in contemporary German culture, it is American. It is Rock Hudson, "who fifteen years earlier admitted to being gay" (77), who brought the disease into German consciousness. Since then it has been an American disease.

One of the scientists, Alfred Droege, has a daughter who develops AIDS by being exposed to her father's research. Droege keeps daughter Manuela's AIDS a secret and is using every means to acquire a drug to treat her. The research centers are themselves huge concentration camps where the Hiffies serve both as the researchers and as the subjects for their own research. This is seen as an economically sound manner of using this huge interned labor pool. Supervising scientists such as Droege live in large houses and have their own laboratories. At the very end of the novel (217) the existence of the daughter is revealed to the wasps and the house is stormed, but the daughter has died from the effects of the drug, which turns everyone who takes it into a hemophiliac, a "bleeder." The image in German is even stronger: *Alle Menschen werden Bluter*, a grotesque pun on the line from Schiller's and Beethoven's "Ode to Joy": *Alle Menschen werden Brüder!*—everyone will be brothers (215). This reversal of the image of infection—"corrupt" AIDS carriers give "innocent" hemophiliacs *the* disease—becomes the leitmotiv of the novel. But such a simple reversal of stereotypes leads to the continuity of images of the locus of corruption with a very specific cultural significance.

The discourse about difference in this novel is on the surface antithetical to that in Daumann's world. It is an image of the world as a concentration camp, with all of the self-conscious evocation of the Nazi period in its response to the actual debate during the mid-1980s about the *Bundesseuchengesetze*, (Law for the Prevention and Control of Infectious Disease in Human Beings), the German law concerning contagious diseases in the FRG.[54] Already in 1984 the weekly news magazine *Der Spiegel* could write of "the plague breaking out of the gay-ghetto."[55] In an entry dated 28 August 1987 in his autobiographical account of his struggle with the social stigma of being a person with AIDS, Helmut Zander recounts the publication of an essay that revealed that a number of West German municipal officials had approved the idea for a new "AIDS-camp," the plans for which turned out to be plans for the infamous concentration camp at Sachsenhausen.[56] In Fred Breinersdorfer's 1989 novel *Quarantäne* (Quarantine), also set in "a German metropolis in the near future," this image haunts the idea of AIDS.[57] There, AIDS hospitals are the solution to the "problem of hygiene" (*Hygieneprobleme*) and are compared to the concentration camps (267). These metaphoric equations were given a "real political" dimension in the suggestion in 1987 by Peter Gauweiler, the Minister of Health of the Bavarian Republic, for the wide-scale compulsory testing of groups such as foreigners, prostitutes, drug users, prisoners, and the intimation of potential quarantine for those who tested positive.[58]

In the retelling of the plot of Peter Zingler's novel, it is evident that this construction of the idea of plague contains a series of analogues to an understanding of plague shaped by the revulsion to but also by the format of the vocabulary of disease in the Nazi period. This immediate association is reflected in the use of a vocabulary of images that has its origin in a West German understanding of the past. Indeed, the very phrase "home into the Reich" (8) with which the border guards describe the marching column of Hiffies reflects the Nazi rhetoric accompanying the Austrian Anschluss. Evoking the Nazi associations present in the late 1980s with Kurt Waldheim's Austria, in this novel the rhetoric of political space refers to an Austria of the spirit; the disease harbored in West Berlin reflects the "sick" society of the FRG.

The central fact of both novels, Daumann's from 1939 and Zingler's from 1989, is that the protagonists do not belong in the place of the novel. Daumann's scientists visit Africa and are infected. But they arrive at a cure from the African disease only when they are back in Hamburg. The disease becomes proof that they really do not belong in Africa. Judith Bahl is never positive—she belongs to none of the categories at risk—but she has had sex with a man outside of her marriage. Thus we expect her to be punished by contracting AIDS, much like the audience expectation of the eighteenth-century German tragedy that a single act of coitus must lead to pregnancy, infanticide, and suicide. She is shown as intensely heterosexual, and that category seems to be problematized by her status as a Hiffie, since she does not belong to any of the high-risk categories known to the reader in 1989. But she does not act in the light of her own knowledge of her status as a "social pollutant." Indeed, without informing him that she believes herself to be positive, she has sex with a man she knows to be negative (66). She is beyond the category of disease and, therefore, the revelation that she is truly "safe" reifies our sense that her actions are intuitively correct and that she really does not belong in this world of disease. She no more belongs in this world of disease than Maxie belongs in Africa.

The question of why she does not belong is important. It is the association of the normal—of her roles and identity as created in the novel—that saves her. Judith becomes the baseline for the healthy in contrast to the society in which she dwells. Her desire to escape from West Berlin is tied to her image as a mother. She is obsessive about returning to rescue her daughter—she is a good mother. And that, within the discourse of difference in the novel, means that she is heterosexual. The sexual contacts described in the novel, the "good" ones (mutual seductions) as well as the "bad" ones (unwanted sexual approaches or rapes), are all heterosexual. Indeed, the only overtly lesbian figure in the novels commits suicide after an attempted rape by exposing herself to freezing weather while compulsively trying to cleanse herself in a public fountain.

It is through the background given this "deviant" figure that we can begin to tie the structure of representation in Zingler even tighter to Daumann's world. For what is central about Judith is that she is not directly tied to the world of the Nazi past. All of the irony of the vocabulary of difference in the novel, all of the self-conscious evocation of the Nazi past, provides a model for difference that is tied to the idea of race. We can begin with that one image of the sexually deviant presented in the novel, the positive image of the lesbian who befriends Judith when she arrives in West Berlin but who ends in suicide. Birgit Sattler is in West Berlin because she acquired AIDS from her gay roommate (130). Her deviancy is explained by the fact that her father's health had been destroyed in a concentration camp and that she had spent her youth on the streets as a result of his early death (132). Her disease, i.e., her sexual identity, is tied to the world of gay men and is explained by her tie to the Nazi past. She is a lesbian because the Nazis destroyed her father, made him into less of a man, with the result that he could not serve her as a true parent—nor, therefore, as a model for the ideal male. Gay men are virtually invisible in the novel, and she becomes the image of the person with AIDS.

Nowhere in this novel do we in fact "see" any ill gay men any more than we "see" hoards of ill blacks in Africa. They form the frame of the novel, but we are exposed only to those deviants from the diseased norm, who, like Birgit Sattler, exhibit their deviance because of an association with the realities that lay behind the metaphors of the AIDS-Ghetto and the internment camps. The gay males, like the blacks, are the excuse for the novel, not its focus. The liberal intent of the novel is to draw the absolute boundary of difference between the sick dystopian German society that condemns people with AIDS and a utopian healthy German society that would accept them. But in creating these boundaries Zingler reverts to a historically determined model of health and illness. The association of the normal (i.e., heterosexual) with the healthy and the abnormal (i.e., the gay) with the diseased is presented here within an environmental model. This is, of course, the liberal fantasy that represses the realities of disease, realities that in German culture are associated with the oppression of Jews and gays in the Third Reich through the imposition of a medical model, and that stress the diseased nature of those exposed to the forces of evil, such as the camps. The pseudoscientific arguments about the theoretical basis of plague parallel the discussions in Daumann's book. The central difference is that they are presented ironically. But simple reversals of images lead to their structural perpetuation.

The association of the persecution of Hiffies through a future German response to AIDS is elided with the image of the persecution of the Nazi victims. And for the West German reader the representative victims of the Nazis are the Jews. This is stated quite directly in the novel in both an ironic mode and an unselfconscious one. "All human beings are brothers," but some are more human, less diseased than others. Thus we are given a long monologue by a muckraking newspaperman on the search for a new AIDS scandal. He notes that in the last issue of the newspaper there was a full column about the fact that "circumcised males are especially at risk from the plague" (141). This is ironic—and repeats quite literally the special status of the Jews as especially at risk for sexually transmitted disease, which, as we have seen, is part and parcel of the literature of the biological determinism of Jewish pathology. But it is clear that this rumor is presented in a self-undercutting mode. Zingler is presenting in this entire monologue the sort of scandal sheet stories one finds in the FRG in the *Bild-Zeitung*. It is nevertheless startling to find this repressed image from the past reappearing in the fantasized future represented in this novel, an image that never vanished altogether from German discourse. After the war Jews were accused of having imported the most horrific sexually transmitted diseases into the German-speaking world.[59] In the novel the image becomes part of the stereotypical representation of difference that is sup-

posed to characterize the horror and inflexibility of German society toward
those suffering from AIDS.

But Zingler also presents an unselfconscious association of the Jew with
disease, feeling that he is giving a positive image of the Jew. In the *Campo de
Sida* in Spain we meet the owner of the local bar, Alfons, who speaks in "an
accent which led us to believe that he was a German" (79). But he speaks
only Spanish, as he explains in "clumsy Spanish" (80), because we are
"guests, whether welcome or tolerated matters not. But we live here and live
free. One should speak the language of the country if just for this reason"
(80). Still he looks "like a vulture . . . his nose looks like a bent saber"
(80). It turns out that Alfons is a German Jew, over seventy, who had been
forced to leave Germany first with his parents under the Nazis and then fifty
years later again because his lover, with whom he had lived for thirty years,
had contracted AIDS. They fled Hamburg and opened the bar in Spain. The
lover had died two years before. Since then Alfons had "refused to speak a
word of German" (80). Most importantly: "He is not sick" (80). At the very
end of the novel we return to the *Campo de Sida* and attend Alfons's funeral:
"It is pleasing to be able to accompany some one like Alfons on his last
journey, someone who died quite naturally of old age" (215). At the cemetery "only the voice of the Rabbi could be heard" (216). After the burial
service, the crowd breaks out in lamentations while one of the participants
observes: "It is perverse . . . but I really enjoy crying at the cemetery.
Afterwards I feel relaxed and full of life" (216).

Here we have the other side of the argument—circumcised Jews (and
male Jews in this myth of the body are by definition circumcised) are immune. They do not get AIDS when they live monogamously together with
someone who has an active case. Such Jews are not perverse, they are
healthy, since they do not bear the stigma of Jewish hypersexuality. The
special discourse of the Jews, the rejection of German here for Spanish as
a sign of the necessary adaptability of the Jew, is contrasted in the novel
with the fragments of clumsy German spoken by the Turks in West Berlin.
The Turk has to speak German; the Jew adapts out of instinct. The images
are precisely those displaced from past. Indeed, there are even some
slight hints of the left anti-Semitism that constantly surfaces in the FRG
under the guise of anti-Zionism. The SSD, an acronym that immediately
recalls the Nazi SS, are armed with Israeli weapons (19). But in general the
reader in this novel, which parallels the treatment of the person with AIDS
with the Jew, is given a positive reversal of the negative stereotype of the
Jew. This reflects the image of the Jew as the agent of infection that domi-

nated Hitler's association of Jews and disease. The realities of the person
with AIDS or even the person who is HIV-positive are confused with the
attributes associated with the Jews. The Jew, who is labeled "sick," is exactly equated with the person with AIDS who is ill.[60]

In Zingler's text this association, with all of its power for the German
reader of the 1980s, whose sense of the Nazi past is limited to media
clichés, overwhelms any sense of the difference between the Jew and the
person with AIDS. The Jew thus acquires a special status in the subtextual
structure of this world of images. He is immune as the desired sign of the
ultimate reversal of the Nazi stereotype of the Jew as disease carrier or
organism, a status that is now attributed to the Hiffie, a term that replaces
"kike" in the vocabulary of difference in this text.

V

One additional observation is worth bringing forward at this point—the
way in which AIDS is not a "Jewish" disease in the FRG and the GDR but
an "American" one. Here, too, is evident the association of an intensely
negative image of America and the vicious anti-Americanism present in
both Germanies after the Vietnam War. But an older association with the
image of the pathological representation of the American and its equation
with the image of the Jew should be noted. In the nineteenth century, cities
were seen as places of disease and the Jews as the quintessential city
dwellers, the Americans of Europe. Richard von Krafft-Ebing remarked
that civilization regularly brings forth degenerate forms of sexuality because of the "more stringent demands which circumstances make upon
the nervous system," which manifest themselves in the "psychopathological or neuropathological conditions of the nation involved."[61] For him the
Jew is the ultimate city person whose sensibilities are dulled, whose sexuality is pathological, whose goals are "American."[62] The city was also
thought to trigger the weakness hidden within the corrupted individual. It
is its turbulence, its excitement, what August Forel in *The Sexual Question* (1905) calls its "Americanism," which leads to illnesses such as degenerate neurasthenia:

> Americanism.—By this term I designate an unhealthy feature of sexual
> life, common among the educated classes of the United States, and appar-
> ently originating in the greed for dollars, which is more prevalent in North
> America than anywhere else. I refer to the unnatural life which Americans
> lead, and more especially to its sexual aspect.[63]

This is an image seen by physicians of the period as "Jewish" in its dimensions. Jews "[manifest an] abnormally intensified sensuality and sexual excitement that lead to sexual errors that are of etiological significance."[64] The same unreconstructed view would be applied to gays in the 1980s. Thus, hidden within the image of the American origins of AIDS is a further association with the Jew, an association made through the image of the city (and for late nineteenth-century Germany, Berlin is the exemplary city). Berlin is the biblical Sodom and Gomorrah and, after World War II, the image of West Berlin—as can be seen in Zingler's novel—is closely associated in German fantasy with the image of the American.

But as we have seen, both sides of this issue are present within the medical discourse of the twentieth century concerning the special nature of the Jews' relationship to sexually transmitted diseases. In the dystopia of the world of plague represented in the novel, the simple reversal of images, the projection of the past and suffusing it with irony re-creates the stereotypical perception of difference. In placing Judith's misdiagnosis, a mistake—purposeful and cruel but a mistake nevertheless—at the center of this novel, Zingler undertakes the rescue of German heterosexuality as surely as Daumann rescues his protagonists. It is science—in the case of AIDS the now "accurate" AIDS test—that frees the heterosexual woman from the stigma of the disease and permits her to return to her role as mother; in the case of the African plague, it is the heroic act of the scientist who develops a cure that enables Maxie to undertake the ultimate role in German society, that of the German mother "with a little house with a red roof and a green garden, a good husband, and little children who cry 'mama' and suck on their thumbs" (168). Judith's cleanliness now parallels that of her lover Max. Although she had sex with him when she believed she was positive—and he knew he was negative—this is revealed to have been a nonpathological act even though in terms of the law on contagion in force in 1989 this would be understood as inflicting "grievous bodily harm." And indeed we knew that she was not dangerous even during the sex scene. For Max's tattoo is not a camp tattoo—it is a tattoo of Mickey Mouse (138). Here the American/Jewish danger of disease is defused and represented as an icon of childlike innocence. The private sphere in this novel is safe; danger lurks only in the public sphere, in the form of the mentality of the Nazi past. We are made to contrast Max's tattoo with the image of a bellicose, pre–World War II Germany in the pub in Frankfurt where she waits to meet Max. It is called the *Iron Cross*, and "naive paintings of tanks, war ships, and fighter planes of the Third Reich" hang on the walls (199).

The cultural image of plague in Germany in 1989 is very different from that of 1939 in trying to be an antithetical presentation of the past in its evocation of a dystopic future. And yet the romanticism of the past, of the Jew as the essential victim, moves the image into the same structure of discourse as is found under the Nazis, a discourse that creates images of the normal and the diseased with absolute boundaries. Such boundaries are to be expected in any case, but in these German texts they are constructed with an eye toward the unique German past. In Germany the evocation of a socially stigmatizing disease seems to be difficult without the evocation of past metaphors of disease and political persecution. The vocabulary of difference employed in 1989 cannot abandon the imagery of 1939, an imagery empowered by a fantasy of the past and reflecting a basic understanding of the nature of difference expressed within a vocabulary of images taken from the past.

NOTES

1. See Lynn Payer, *Medicine and Culture: Varieties of Treatment in the United States, England, West Germany, and France* (New York: Holt, 1988).

2. Roy Porter, "Ever Since Eve: The Fear of Contagion," *Times Literary Supplement*, May 27–June 2, 1988, p. 582. See Susan Sontag, *AIDS and Its Metaphors* (New York: Farrar Straus Giroux, 1989); Sander L. Gilman, *Disease and Representation: Images of Illness from Madness to AIDS* (Ithaca: Cornell University Press, 1988). On the general background of the image of the person with AIDS see Casper G. Schmidt, "The Group-Fantasy Origins of AIDS," *Journal of Psycho-history* 12 (1984): 37–78; Casper G. Schmidt, "AIDS Jokes, or Schadenfreude Around an Epidemic," *Maledicta* 8 (1984–85): 69–75; Dennis Altman, *AIDS in the Mind of America: The Social, Political, and Psychological Impact of a New Epidemic* (New York: Anchor/Doubleday, 1986); David Black, *The Plague Years: A Chronicle of AIDS, The Epidemic of Our Times* (New York: Simon & Schuster, 1986); Graham Hancock and Enver Carim, *AIDS: The Deadly Epidemic* (London: Gollanz, 1986); Richard Liebmann-Smith, *The Question of AIDS* (New York: New York Academy of Sciences, 1985); Eve K. Nichols, *Mobilizing Against AIDS: The Unfinished Story of a Virus* (Cambridge, Mass.: Harvard University Press, 1986); Lon G. Nungasser, *Epidemic of Courage: Facing AIDS in America* (New York: St. Martin's, 1986); Simon Watney, *Policing Desire: Pornography, AIDS, and the Media* (Minneapolis: University of Minnesota Press, 1987); Randy Shilts, *And the Band Played On: Politics, People, and the AIDS Epidemic* (New York: St. Martin's, 1987); Gary Alan Fine, "Welcome to the World of AIDS:

Fantasies of Female Revenge," *Western Folklore* 46 (1987): 192–97; Mirko D. Grmek, *Histoire du sida* (Paris: Payot, 1989). See George L. Mosse's brilliant study *Nationalism and Sexuality: Respectability and Abnormal Sexuality in Modern Europe* (New York: Fertig, 1985) for a sense of the national context of much of this literature.

3. See Douglas Crimp, ed., *AIDS: Cultural Analysis/Cultural Criticism* (Cambridge: MIT Press, 1989).

4. Rudolf Heinrich Daumann, *Patrouille gegen den Tod: Ein utopischer Roman* (Berlin: Schützen-Verlag, 1939). Within the first year of its publication, seventy thousand copies of this book had been sold. Where subsequent references to this work are contextually clear, page numbers will be cited in the text.

5. Peter Zingler, *Die Seuche: Roman* (Frankfurt am Main: Eichborn, 1989). (Where subsequent references to this work are contextually clear, page numbers will be cited in the text.) The German literature on AIDS is not as extensive as the Anglo-American. Of importance is the issue 94 of the *Kursbuch* (November 1988) entitled "Die Seuche."

6. Sander L. Gilman, *On Blackness Without Blacks: Essays on the Image of the Black in Germany* (Boston: Hall, 1982), pp. 119ff. See also Rosemarie K. Lester, *Trivialneger: Das Bild der Schwarzen im west-deutschen Illustrietenroman* (Stuttgart: Heinz, 1982).

7. Bernard Blanc, "Lexique à l'usage des voyageurs en S.F.," *Le Français dans le Monde* 193 (1985): 32–33, and Charles R. Saunders, "Why Blacks Don't Read Science Fiction," Tom Henighan, ed., *Brave New Universe: Testing the Values of Science in Society* (Ottawa: Tecumseh, 1980), pp. 160–68.

8. On the history of self-experimentation and the legends associated with it, see Lawrence K. Altman, *Who Goes First? The Story of Self-Experimentation in Medicine* (New York: Random House, 1987).

9. Everett Franklin Bleiler, "Edgar Rice Burroughs, 1875–1950," in Everett Franklin Bleiler, ed., *Science Fiction Writers: Critical Studies of the Major Authors from the Early Nineteenth Century to the Present Day* (New York: Scribner's, 1982), pp. 59–64; Dieter Ohlmeier, "Das psychoanalytische Interesse an literarischen Texten," in Hochen Horisch and George Christoph Tholen, eds., *Eingebildete Texte: Affairen zwischen Psychoanalyse und Literaturwissenschaft* (Munich: Fink, 1985), pp. 15–25; Gert Ueding, "Die langandauernde Krankheit des Lebens," *Jahrbuch der Karl-May-Gesselschaft* (1986): 50–68.

10. Hans Poeschel, *The Voice of German East Africa: The English in the Judgment of the Natives* (Berlin: Scherl, 1919), p. 65.

11. See Prosser Guilford and William Roger Louis, eds., *Britain and Germany in Africa: Imperial Rivalry and Colonial Rule* (New Haven: Yale University Press, 1967) and L. Smythe Barron, ed., *The Nazis in Africa* (Salisbury, N.C.: Documentary Publications, 1979).

12. See the general discussion and background in Hans-Walter Schmuhl, *Rassenhygiene, Nationalsozialismus, Euthanasie: Von der Verhütung zur Vernichtung lebensunwerten Lebens, 1890–1945* (Göttingen: Vandenhoeck & Ruprecht, 1987); Robert Proctor, *Racial Hygiene: Medicine Under the Nazis* (Cambridge, Mass.: Harvard University Press, 1988); Peter Weingart, Jürgen Kroll, and Kurt Bayertz, *Rasse, Blut und Gene: Geschichte der Eugenik und Rassenhygiene in Deutschland* (Frankfurt am Main: Suhrkamp, 1988).

13. Ernst Janisch, "Selbesbehauptung und Verpflichtung der weissen Rasse in Afrika," *Afrika braucht Gross-deutschland: Das deutsche koloniale Jarhbuch 1940* (Berlin: Süssrott [1939]), pp. 60–64.

14. G. W. Bauer, *Deutschlands Kolonialforderung und die Welt: Forderungen der deutschen Raum- und Rohstoffnot* (Leipzig: Bauer, 1938).

15. Helmut Vallery, *Führer, Volk, und Charisma: Der nationalsozialistische historische Roman* (Rugenstein: Pahl, 1980).

16. See in this context Klaus Theweileit, *Male Fantasies*, 2 vols., Stephen Conway, trans. (Minneapolis: University of Minnesota Press, 1987).

17. Max Nonne, *Syphilis und Nervensystem* (Berlin: Karger, 1921), p. 6. On the impact on various foreign countries, especially in Africa, see p. 679.

18. James H. Jones, *Bad Blood: The Tuskegee Syphilis Experiment—A Tragedy of Race and Medicine* (New York: The Free Press, 1981).

19. On the pathological meaning of the nose in German science of this period see Hans Leichner, *Die Vererbung anatomischer Variationene der Nase, ihre Nebenhöhlen, und des Gehörorgans* (Munich: Bergmann, 1928), p. 81. As important was the general discussion of "types" in medicine spinning off from Ernst Kretschmer's theory of constitution (itself in opposition to ideas of race yet incorporated in these ideas) that identify specific types—among them the types normally associated in racial science with the image of the Jew—as particularly at risk for syphilis. See Richard Stern, *Über körperliche Kennzeichen der Disposition zur Tabes* (Leipzig: Deuticke, 1912).

20. Ludwik Fleck, *Genesis and Development of a Scientific Fact*, Thaddeus J. Trenn and Robert K. Merton, eds. (Chicago: University of Chicago Press, 1979). I am indebted to Fleck's work for the basic conceptual structure presented in this essay.

21. Theodor Fritsch, *Handbuch der Judenfrage* (Leipzig: Hammer, 1935), p. 408.

22. See M. J. Guttmann, *Über den heutigen Stand der Rasse- und Krankheitsfrage der Juden* (Munich: Müller & Steinicke, 1920) and Heinrich Singer, *Allgemeine und spezielle Krankheitslehre der Juden* (Leipzig: Konegen, 1904). For a more modern analysis of the myths and realities of the diseases attributed to the Jews see Richard M. Goodman, *Genetic Disorders Among the Jewish People* (Baltimore: Johns Hopkins University Press, 1979).

23. Adolph Hitler, *Mein Kampf*, Ralph Manheim, trans. (Boston: Houghton Mifflin, 1943), p. 247.

24. Compare Edward J. Bristow, *Prostitution and Prejudice: The Jewish Fight Against White Slavery, 1870–1939* (Oxford: Clarendon, 1982). The view of the Jew as the syphilitic was not limited to the anti-Semitic fringe of the turn of the century. It possessed power even over "Jewish" writers such as Marcel Proust, whose uncomfortable relationship to his mother's Jewish identity haunted his life almost as much as did his gay identity. (Here the change and its placement within the discourse of science transcends even national distinctions. For being Jewish meant belonging to a supranational category of pathogenes, at least for those so labeled.) In Proust's *Remembrance of Things Past*, a series of novels written to recapture the world of the 1880s and 1890s, one of the central characters, Charles Swann, is a Jew who marries a courtesan. (The discussion of the images of the Jew and the homosexual is in Marcel Proust, *Cities of the Plain*, vol. 2 of *Remembrance of Things Past*, C. K. Scott Moncrieff and Terence Kilmartin, trans. [Harmondsworth: Penguin, 1986], p. 639.) This link between Jew and prostitute is mirrored in Proust's manner of representing the sexuality of the Jew. For Proust, being Jewish is analogous to being gay—it is "an incurable disease." But what marks this diseases for all to see? Proust, who discusses the signs and symptoms of syphilis with a detailed clinical knowledge in the same volume, knows precisely what marks the sexuality of the Jew upon his physiognomy. (On syphilis and Charcot see Proust, *Remembrance* 2: 1086.) It is marked upon his face as "ethnic eczema"

(Proust, *Remembrance* 1: 326). This mark upon the face is Hitler's sign of the Jew's sexual perversion. It is the infectious nature of that "incurable disease," the sexuality of the Jew, Proust's Jew fixated upon his courtesan. The Jew's sexuality, the sexuality of the polluter, is written on his face in the skin disease that announces the difference of the Jew. All of Proust's Jewish figures (including Swann and Bloch) are in some way diseased, and this image of disease always links the racial with the sexual, much as Proust's image of the homosexual links class (or at least, the nobility) with homosexuality. ("Homosexuality" is a "scientific" label for a new "disease" coined by Karoly Benkert in 1869 at the same time that the new "scientific" term for Jew hating, "anti-Semitism," was created by Wilhelm Marr.) The image of the infected and infecting Jew also had a strong political as well as personal dimension for Proust. The ability to "see" the Jew who is trying to pass as a non-Jew within French society is one of the themes of the novels, a theme that, after the Dreyfus Affair, had overt political implications. Seeing the Jew was seeing the enemy within the body politic, the force for destruction. And Proust's racial as well as sexual identity was tied to his sense of the importance of class and society in defining the individual. Thus Proust's arch-Jew Swann was visibly marked by him as the heterosexual syphilitic, as that which he was not (at least in his fantasy about his own sexual identity).

25. Fritsch, *Handbuch der Judenfrage*, pp. 406–7.

26. N. Balaban and A. Molotschek, "Progressive Paralyse bei den Bevölkerungen der Krim," *Allgemeine Zeitschrift für Psychiatrie* 94 (1931): 373–83.

27. H. Budul, "Beitrag zur vergleichenden Rassenpsychiatrie," *Monatsschrift für Psychiatrie und Neurologie* 37 (1915): 199–204.

28. Max Sichel, "Die Paralyse der Juden in sexuologischer Beleuchtung," *Zeitschrift für Sexualwissenschaft* (1919–20): 98–104.

29. H. Strauss, "Erkrankungen durch Alkohol und Syphilis bei den Juden," *Zeitschrift für Demographie und Statistik der Juden* 4 (1927): 33–39.

30. There is no comprehensive study of the German debates on circumcision. See J. Alkvist, "Geschichte der Circumcision," *Janus* 30 (1926): 86–104, 152–71.

31. On the Jewish side, see the discussion by Em. Kohn in the *Mittheilung des Ärtzlichen Vereines in Wien* 3 (1874): 169–172. On the non-Jewish side, see Dr. Klein, "Die rituelle Circumcision, eine sanitätspolizeiliche Frage," *Allgemeine Medizinische Central-Zeitung* 22 (1853): 368–69.

32. See the discussion by Dr. Bamberger, "Die Hygiene der Beschneidung," in Max Grunwald, *Die Hygiene der Juden: Im Anschluss an die internationale Hygiene-Ausstellung* (Dresden: Verlag der historischen Abteilung der internationale Hygiene-Ausstellung, 1911), pp. 103–12 (on the Jewish side) and W. Hammer, "Zur Beschneidungsfrage," *Zeitschrift füsr Bahnärzte* 1 (1916): 254 (on the non-Jewish side).

33. Houston Stewart Chamberlain, *Foundations of the Nineteenth Century*, 2 vols., John Lees trans. (London: Lane, 1910), 1: 388–89.

34. Nathan Birnbaum, "Über Houston Stewart Chamberlain," in *Ausgewählte Schriften zur jüdischen Frage* (Czernowitz: Verlag Birnbaum & Kohut, 1910), 2: 201.

35. Adam G. De Gurowski, *America and Europe* (New York: Appleton, 1857), p. 177.

36. Saul K. Padover, ed. and trans., *The Letters of Karl Marx* (Engelwood Cliffs, N.J.: Prentice-Hall, 1979), p. 459.

37. W. W. Kopp, "Beobachtung an Halbjuden in Berliner Schulen," *Volk und Rasse* 10 (1935): 392.

38. M. Lerche, "Beobachtung deutsch-jüdisher Rassenkreuzeung an Berliner Schulen," *Die medizinische Welt*, September 17, 1927, p. 1222.

39. See Sander L. Gilman, *Jewish Self-Hatred: Anti-Semitism and the Hidden Language of the Jews* (Baltimore: Johns Hopkins University Press, 1986).

40. Cited by Saul Friedländer, *Kurt Gerstein: The Ambiguity of Good*, Charles Fullman, trans. (New York: Knopf, 1969), pp. 148–49.

41. Jan Goldstein, "The Wandering Jew and the Problem of Psychiatric Anti-semitism in Fin-de-Siècle France," *Journal of Contemporary History* 20 (1985): 521–52.

42. See Sander L. Gilman, *Disease and Representation*, pp. 190–91.

43. See the discussion in Sander L. Gilman, *Difference and Pathology: Stereotypes of Sexuality, Race, and Madness* (Ithaca, N.Y.: Cornell University Press, 1986).

44. Friedrich Ratzel, *The History of Mankind*, 3 vols., A. J. Butler, trans. (London: Macmillan, 1898). See vol. 3, p. 183, on the Near East and p. 548 on Europe.

45. Daumann, *Patrouille gegen den Tod*, pp. 53–54, cites Justus Hecker, *Der schwarze Tod im 14. Jahrhundert* (Berlin: Herbig, 1832).

46. Ulrich Berkes, *Eine schlimme Liebe: Tagebuch* (Berlin: Aufbau, 1987), pp. 40–41, 214. On the background to the question of AIDS in the GDR see Günter Grau, ed., *Und diese Liebe auch: Theologische und sexualwissenschaftliche Einsichten zur Homosexualität* (Berlin: Evangelische Verlagsanstalt, 1989) as well as John Parsons, "East Germany Faces Its Past: A New Start for Socialist Sexual Politics," *Outlook* 5 (1989): 43–52.

47. See the extensive coverage in the news magazine *Der Spiegel* during 1987; for example, the cover story for February 9, 1987, pp. 30–53.

48. For a detailed overview see John Bornemann, "AIDS in the Two Berlins," in *AIDS: Cultural Analysis/Cultural Activism*, pp. 223–37.

49. On this general question see Renée Sabatier, *Blaming Others: Prejudice, Race, and Worldwide AIDS* (London: Panos, 1988). A good response to this search, in terms of Randy Shilts's discussion of "Patient Zero," is Charles L. Ortleb, "Scientist Zero," *Christopher Street*, no. 133 (1989): 8–14.

50. Alexander Mitscherlich and Fred Mielke, *Das Diktat der Menschenverachtung, Ein Dokumentation (Vom Prozess gegen 23 SS-Ärtze und deutsche Wissenschaftler)* (Heidelberg: Schneider, 1947); Alexander Mitscherlich and Fred Mielke, *Wissenschaft ohne Menschlichkeit: Medizinische und Eugenische Irrwege unter Diktatur, Burokratie, und Krieg* (Heidelberg: Schneider, 1949).

51. On the treatment of gays in the Third Reich see Richard Plant, *The Pink Triangle: The Nazi War Against Homosexuals* (New York: Holt, 1986) and Hans-Georg Stümke, *Homosexualle in Deutschland: Eine politische Geschichte* (Munich: Beck, 1989).

52. See the *Berlin Tageszeitung (TAZ)* rebuttal of this on June 6, 1989, p. 13.

53. Karin Obermeier, "Afro-German Women: Recording their Own History," *New German Critique* 46 (1989): 172–80.

54. See Wiebke Reuter-Krauss and Christoph Schmidt, *AIDS und Recht von A–Z* (Munich: dtv/Beck, 1988).

55. *Der Spiegel*, November 5, 1984, p. 100.

56. Helmut Zander, *Der Regenbogen: Tagebuch eines AIDSkranken* (Munich: Knaur, 1988), pp. 235–36.

57. Fred Breinersdorfer, *Quarantäne* (Stuttgart: Weitbrecht, 1989).

58. *Der Spiegel*, May 25, 1987, pp. 25–32.

59. Ruth Beckermann, *Unzugehoerig: Oesterreicher und Juden nach 1945* (Vienna: Lockner, 1989), p. 83.

60. This is not to confuse the fact that both Jews and gays can internalize the same sense of social difference in their confrontation with exactly such stereotypical structures. See Paul Parin, "'The Mark of Oppression': Enthnopsychoanalytische Studie über Juden und Homosexuelle in einer relative permissiven Kultur," *Psyche* 39 (1985): 193–219.

61. Richard von Krafft-Ebing, *Psychopathia Sexualis: A Medico-Forensic Study*, rev. ed., Harry E. Wedeck, trans. (New York: Putnam, 1965), p. 24.

62. Compare Otto Binswanger, *Hysterie* (Vienna: Deuticke, 1904), p. 82.

63. August Forel, *The Sexual Question: A Scientific, Psychological, Hygienic, and Sociological Study*, D. F. Marshall, trans. (New York: Physicians and Surgeons Book Co., 1925), pp. 331–32.

64. Richard von Krafft-Ebing, *Text-Book of Insanity*, Charles Gilbert Chaddock, trans. (Philadelphia: F. A. Davis, 1905), p. 143.

Fantom Images: Hervé Guibert and the Writing of "sida" in France

Emily Apter

I

The AIDS novel in France is the novel of *le sida*, spelled without capital letters. Do these differences in notation from the acronym and capitals of AIDS indicate a different cultural construction of the illness? In all probability it does, but rather than fall into the trap of making essentialist generalizations about the way this tragedy is being written country to country, I prefer to consider the work of France's premier *sida* novelist, Hervé Guibert, as an example of how the problems associated with writing AIDS are being addressed across the Atlantic. [1] From his treatment of the dawning of a *sida* consciousness in the early 1980s, to his documentation of its ravages on close circles of friends, to his own ambivalent position as voyeuristic spectator and subject of disease, Guibert has unflinchingly observed and documented. His novels are neither fiction nor pure autobiography; combining elements of both, they resemble working notebooks dispatched from the land of ghosts.

Intent on capturing the existential solitude of AIDS anguish together with the shocking propulsion of the subject into a reality composed of medicalized particulars, Guibert adopts neither a tone of politicized, uncompromising urgency nor the comforting timbre of sentimentalism. His writings stand as terrifying yet curiously understated *sida* testimonies, steeped in the French intellectual legacy of Georges Bataille, Jean-Paul

Sartre, Jean Genet, Roland Barthes, and Michel Foucault. His two most recent novels, *A l'ami qui ne m'a pas sauvé la vie* (1990) (To the friend who did not save my life) and *Le protocole compassionel* (Compassionate access), composed at breakneck speed on the winds of impending death, are blunt prose testimonies of his illness after diagnosis in 1988. The style of these narratives is first degree, first person, macabre, imbued with a private dignity of the bodily self in pain, and local—true to the milieu, at once cosmopolitan and parochial, of the Parisian intelligentsia. Guibert's characters are his friends and lovers: theater and film people, painters, photographers, writers, and doctors, interspersed with the rough trade picked up in nightclubs or encountered on the road.

Born in 1955, Guibert came of age in 1970s' Paris, the Paris of Roland Barthes and Michel Foucault. Barthes fell in love with Guibert, purportedly offering to write a preface for one of his most erotically explicit chronicles of gay life, *La Mort propagande no. 0*, in return for a sexual favor (an exchange he apparently refused). Barthes wrote a love declaration to Guibert, "Fragment pour H," which "H" later published in *L'Autre Journal*.[2] Guibert, for his part, would acknowledge the crucial influence of Barthes' *Fragments of a Lover's Discourse* on his novel about a stormy love affair entitled *Fou de Vincent* (1988) (Crazy about Vincent).

Guibert's relationship with Foucault was by his own account more serious, both in terms of the mentoring role that Foucault played in his intellectual development and in terms of their emotional involvement. The painfully hyperreal description of Foucault's 1983 death with AIDS, given by Guibert in *A l'ami qui ne m'a pas sauvé la vie*, garnered the criticism of those close to Foucault.[3] Mindful though he was of Foucault's desire for posthumous privacy,[4] Guibert claimed that to violate the secrets of Foucault's life exploits and his death with AIDS (in his words, an "amorous crime") was his inevitable fate.[5] Remaining rigorously true to his personal credo of experiential transparency in writing, committing himself to bringing the subject of AIDS out of the French closet (and the taboos associated with talking about grave illnesses are, by convention, even stronger in France than in North America), he identifies the subversive homologies between sexual violation, nosological voyeurism, and the medical rape of the subject as crucial constituents of *sida* narrative, integers of its raison d'être.

A l'ami qui ne m'a pas sauvé la vie opens with a certain defiance of the terminal logic imposed on AIDS; the force of its first sentence, "*J'ai eu le sida pendant trois mois*" ("I had AIDS for three months"), records a visitation by the grim reaper that has been foiled by the writing of this book

(ALA, 9). In this sense, though the word *sida* is immediately introduced (connoting as it does a foreclosed remediability), this book will inhabit the less fatalistic psychic zone of HIV-positivity, while eschewing false hopes of medical deliverance. Like the dysfunctional chronology in which the narrative sequences are presented, Guibert's text purposely takes us out of fixed time into that of the writing cure. The questionable asserveration, made at the end of the first section—"I was going to shake this, I was going to be, by some extraordinary chance, one of the world's first survivors of this inexorable illness"—is belied by Hervé's avowal, a mere page later, that the conditions of his book's closure are anchored in uncertainty, as wide open to imminently unforeseeable endings as the subject of the disease itself (ALA, 9–10).

The life posture of *dénégation* (avowed disavowal), with its traumatic epistemology of cynicism and suspension of disbelief, shows itself not only in Guibert's tricks with rhetorical and narratological temporality (linear sequences are shuffled and retold), but also in the way the allegory of Foucault's life and death is recounted as an exemplary credibility test. A vignette is flashed before us of the narrator and Foucault (alias Muzil, an obvious play on the Austrian author of *A Man Without Qualities*) dining together in 1981 shortly after the first news of the virus was broken by those just back from the United States. Muzil, in a fit of uncontrollable laughter, nearly falls off his chair: "A cancer that attacks only homosexuals, no, it would be too good to be true, it's enough to make one die of laughter" (ALA, 21).

In a sequence that follows shortly, inserted into a description of Muzil's sadomasochistic escapades in the leather bars of the twelfth arrondissement and the baths of San Francisco, we get a flash-forward of his apartment after his death. His widower Stéphane, wandering through emptied, disinfected rooms, comes upon a sack filled with whips, leather masks, leashes, muzzles, and handcuffs. These testaments of a secret life commemorate the uncompromising (homo)sexuality of Foucault's life and work; his insistence on celebrating the macabre solidarity that bonded men to men in the San Francisco bathhouses at the inception of the epidemic ("This floating menace has created new complicities, new forms of tenderness, new solidarities. Before, nobody exchanged a word, now, people talk to each other. Each one knows exactly why he is there."); and his obdurate refusal to read into his fatal condition a portent of gay holocaust (ALA, 30).

Did he know that he had AIDS? By all accounts he both did and did not. Didier Eribon cites Foucault's close friend and confidant Paul Veyne (whose record of a final interview with Foucault, according to Eribon, was refused publication by the journal *Critique*). Foucault allegedly said to Veyne: "I know I have *sida*, but my hysteria allows me to forget it."[6] Guibert's *récit* itself leaves a space for doubt, for patent ambiguity. In discussion from years before about the formula used by doctors to communicate the irreversibility of their patients' diseases, Muzil had said, "The doctor does not abruptly tell the truth to the patient, he offers him, through a diffuse discourse, a measure of freedom, a means of apprehending it by himself, or a way of choosing not to know if that is the option preferred" (ALA, 33). On the matter of his own interview with the doctor, Muzil elects to remain silent, leaving even his closest friends wondering how much he himself had chosen to know. Following Muzil's burial, the narrator says: "One still did not know whether Muzil had been conscious or unconscious of the nature of the illness which had killed him" (ALA, 31).

The master inventer and deconstructor of clinical discourse reserves a terrifying silence in the face of his own malady. Reduced to physical paralysis, his eyes listlessly follow the path of a tennis ball on the TV screen. When the narrator ventures a sadistic surmise—"In truth, you hope you do have *sida*"—Muzil meets his remark with a stony look that lets him know he has trespassed (ALA, 38). In the last days, seated in the hospital room in a white moleskin chair, the smell of frying fish in the air, Muzil averts his eyes and confides to Hervé that he is stricken with aphasia: "One always believes that in this kind of situation there will be something to say, and then, the situation arrives and there is nothing to say about it" (ALA, 94). By a kind of unwritten law of psychological compensation, Muzil's aphasia, his stubborn retention of the word, will be matched by the narrator's readiness to say too much, to divulge precisely what Foucault refused to let posterity know.

The ambivalent meaning of Muzil's reticence might be more fully understood in relation to the oral violation of the subject induced by medical probes and interventions. The exploratory tube thrust into Muzil's throat and lungs, miming the former pleasure of fellatio, emerges as inextricably linked to what Muzil describes as the loss of his identity in the medical maze (his own name, too well known, is purposely "lost").

Guibert amplifies and dramatizes the hurt of oral rape in *Le protocole compassionel* when he describes his own experience of the fiber-optic exam. The first one he compares to a nightmare, a horror film, the second to a drama taking place in a *salon bourgeois*, a scary fairy tale in which the pretty woman doctor turns into a toad as she approaches her quarry. The first operation raises most directly the question of medical/sexual violence in AIDS treatment. A "commando of pig-slaughterers" descends on Guibert's hapless body with the blessing of the doctor "for whom I was just a little *pédé* who was going to die anyway."[7] Rather than risk being doused with infected sputum, the doctor passes the task along to a novice, who maladroitly shoves the tube down the patient's throat into his stomach. Gagging on the instrument, the narrator rejects it in a fit of pain, much to the disgust of the doctor, who continues to bark orders at a distance. The torture is repeated, this time successfully, but the victim leaves the hospital robbed of speech, unable to say a word about the trauma.

By qualifying the doctor as a *sadique*, the narrator introduces a curious rapprochement between his medical master and his intellectual master, whose taste for sadomasochism had been alluded to in the earlier book. Guibert dares to explore the disturbing commonalities between *sida* treatments and rough gay sex—the rites of humiliation, the transgression of bodily limits, the submission to power, postures demanded and exchanged. Recalling a phrase uttered semifacetiously in a doctor's office in 1981 (well before the word *sida* had made its entrance on the French scene), Guibert's "I kiss the hands of he who delivers my condemnation" recalls the lover's assiduous pose of supplication in the sadomasochistic scene (ALA, 46). *Le protocole compassionel* could in fact be described as a tragicomic sadomasochistic version of *La Ronde*, in which doctors, visited in rapid succession and submitted to without a word, are substituted for the tricks of old.

Guibert draws out the kind of pathological *folie à deux* that installs itself in the doctor/patient power dynamic, a mimetic, mutually complementary folly that he dubs "reciprocal contagion" in a preface to a photo album of portraits of himself taken in 1980 by his intimate companion Hans Georg Berger (*L'Image de soi, ou l'injonction de son beau moment?*).[8] Photographer and model, living together in a shared delirium, creatures of each other's phantasms, dispute what belongs to neither of them (the photographed body of a healthy, curly-haired Guibert). In much the same way, doctor and patient dream each other's combat on the body of *sida*, monitoring falling T-cell counts, tracking the stigmata of Kaposi's sarcoma, directing pulmonary cleansings and oxygen injections on this "other" corpus. In *A l'ami qui ne m'a pas sauvé la vie* Guibert uses the *folie à deux* to justify the purloining of Foucault's story. "We were linked to each other by a common thanatological spell," he maintains, as if by way of underscoring that Foucault's calvary was his own, that to spy on Foucault's life was an act ratified by Hervé's own self-exposure, itself a mere extension of the "*délire*" of his more famous friend.

II

The territory of collective morbid fantasy, a *folie à deux* inclusive of all those sick with AIDS, allows the discourse of *sida* to open up into the more complex issue of how fantasmatic contagion is capable of blurring the boundaries, both mental and physical, of individual personhood. Like most serious illnesses, *sida* in this sense not only interrogates the nature of the subject as medical object, but, more hauntingly, raises the issue of disease as an affair among ghosts whereby each self, haunted and inhabited by the specter of a disappeared friend who has dissolved into the netherworld of metempsychosis, no longer knows whether it has an identity of its own.

Léon Daudet (1867–1942), avatar of right-wing ideology, homophobe, and author of a "degenerate" fiction chronicling the plight of bourgeois families struck down by hereditary illness, created (against the grain of his own work, as it were) a language of disease and sexuality, eros and pain, memory and psychosis, that seems eerily in tune with Guibert's dolorous memoir of phantoms and vanishing bodies. Haunted by his father Alphonse's grisly deterioration from syphilis, racked by the assassination (or suicide?) of his epileptic son Philippe (inheritor of the fatal family taint), Léon Daudet developed the concept of the *personimage*, defined as a "hallucinatory image" that visits the subject when his or her loved one is dead. Daudet's personimage, part and parcel of what he called *le drame intérieur*, or inner drama of mourning and pain, denoted an "emanation of the self"—a "factotum of sexual instinct," a transmissible *hérédisme*, (otherwise known in the jargon of syphilis as the microorganism of contagion: *le tréponème, la spirochète, le bacille de Koch*).[9] Daudet refers to these *tréponèmes* as the "pollen of literati," a figure of speech that seems luridly apt when one thinks of the *belle époque* literary company kept by his family, all of whom succumbed to *la grande vérole*—Flaubert, Gautier, Maupassant, Jules de Goncourt, Feydeau, and of course his dearest parent Alphonse.[10]

If I dwell for some time on the parallels between Daudet's medicophilosophical rhetoric of the pox and Guibert's hallucinatory evocations of *sida*—each rooted in the historic imaginaries of a respective fin-de-siècle pessimism—it is neither to encourage simplistic analogies between the two epidemics nor to imply that some veritable affinity exists between Daudet and Guibert as writers. Rather, I suggest that their discourses of disease and difference, of bodies erotically and socially marked, articu-

late ways in which eroticism and death collaborate on the dissolution of
the subject.

Throughout *Le protocole compassionel* Guibert's narrator is haunted by
the spectre of a dead dancer whose black-market drug ddI, believed more
powerful than AZT, was passed to him through underground channels, en-
dowing him with the gift of extended life. This image of one body as carrier
of another's lost life is a theme anticipated by Guibert in his pre-*sida* writings on photography, most of them written during the years when he
worked regularly for *Le Monde* as a photography critic. In *L'Image fantôme*
(The fantom image) he describes how the death of a person is comparable
to the loss of an archive of mental photographs, for "being" owes its survival to the willingness of memory to act as a storehouse of mnemonic representations. "Each death," Guibert writes, "provokes the destruction of a
photographic collection that will pass for the last time, one might say,
through a ray of consciousness."[11] Similarly, in Daudet's text on waking
dreams, *Le Rêve éveillé*, the narrator evokes the way in which the subject
becomes obsessed by "teaming crowds of bizarre phantasms," "reappari-
tions of beings cherished and long gone."[12] Possessed by "heredisms"
(particles of hereditary metamemory, no doubt spawned by the spiritual
table-turning seances organized by his mother Julia Allard), Daudet fash-
ions his persona as a predestined keeper of the photo album of the past:

> The wisest and most reflective, may suddenly find strange reverberations
> going right through them, the prospect of whose return (even if nothing fol-
> lows) infects them with dread and foreboding. This time, make no mistake,
> these phantoms consist of revisitations, re-apparitions of this or that ances-
> tor, loved or forgotten, known or unknown—which one might call, after my
> own neologism, heredisms. [13]

Just as family scandals are kept, like family heirlooms, locked up in vaults
for years only to be discovered and disseminated among future generations, so the secret of syphilis (telling trace of illicit sexual liaisons) is, in a
sense, forced "out" in the hereditary cycle.

Guibert's inner circle of friends will, in a somewhat comparable way,
reinforce their family ties by becoming guardians of gay secrets. At the
very end of *L'Image fantôme*, Guibert traces the destiny of the secret to its
ultimate "outing":

> —Having told you this story, I find myself feeling completely emptied
>   out. This story is my secret, you understand?
> —What about later?

—To you, I don't want to have to say, "I beg you, don't repeat it" . . .

—Yes. But now your secret has also become my secret. It has become a part of me, and I will behave toward it in the same way as I do with all my secrets. I will dispose of it when the moment comes. And it will become another's secret.

—You are right. Secrets must necessarily circulate.[14]

Secrets must indeed necessarily circulate in order to keep history, culture, and memory alive, but with the advent of fatal illness, the price paid by the self qua habitus of the personimage becomes exorbitant. One could say that HIV, with its baggage of dead souls, bears down unrelentingly on the subjectivity of those surviving with AIDS. Transmitted and introjected, like the virus itself, the ghosts of former lovers and friends settle in for the duration, crowding out the space allotted for life's ordinary preoccupations and pleasures. What the ghosts fail to claim as their personal territory, pain acquires, colonizing consciousness along with the body.

The beginning of *Le protocole compassionel* recounts this conquest of "being" by pain:

> I no longer take baths because I cannot get up out of the tub and I no longer sit cross-legged under the shower as I used to like to do, as a way of warming up to the day, because there is not enough tension in my legs and arms to allow me to disentangle myself . . . I have the sense of being a bound elephant, I have the feeling that the duvet will crush me and that my limbs are made of steel, even rest has become a nightmare, and I have no other experience of life other than this nightmare, I no longer fuck, I no longer have a single sexual thought, I can no longer masturbate, . . . my relations with friends have become a forced labor, until today I have been unable to write, I can hardly read anymore, and what you will find most astonishing is that I have at my disposal the means of committing suicide, two tubes of Digitalin are there in my open case, under my underwear.   (PC, 10–11)

Here the blunt, verbally spare tone of narration prepares the reader for the nosological realism yet to come. The narrative of *Le protocole compassionel*, like *A l'ami qui ne m'a pas sauvé la vie*, is shot through with a lexicon of technical medical terms signifying the prophylactic consciousness used to combat the physical referentiality of acute pain. While the earlier novel initiates the reader into the language of immune system breakdown, weight loss diagrams, seropositive testing and HIV treatments, the later work makes a drama out of endoscopies, rectal insertions, blood tests, chemotherapy, and administrations of the massively strong AIDS remission drug ddI ("335 milligrams of white powder made in Middlesex, England") and the antidepressant Prozac ("a daily capsule containing 20 milligrams of Fluoxétine Chlorohydrate"). These drugs *are* the constituents of "being" for the person with *sida;* as Guibert says, "It's the ddI of the dead dancer, together with Prozac, that writes this book in my place" (PC, 84). Without the compassionate dose, there is just too much pain to write the narrative of pain.

III

How does one write pain so that it hurts the way pain hurts? This was one of the central questions posed by Elaine Scarry in *The Body in Pain,* where she examined how discursive renderings of physical torture are never commensurate with its bodily endurance. But surely pain is translatable into language. [15] Gay writers, wary though they may be of misleading analogies between nineteenth-century syphilis and twentieth-century AIDS, have begun to examine some of the common ground in looking for a language of pain. Michel Tournier, for example, recently introduced the republication of Alphonse Daudet's (1840–97) "fantastic" syphilis novel of fever and contagion in the Camargue—*Le Trésor d'Arlatan* (1897)—by drawing attention to "sexual vagabondage" and physical distress enmeshed in the ideological construction of both diseases. Tournier claims that the *sida* narrative will have some catching up to do on the scale of horror produced by syphilis texts (perhaps he had not yet read Guibert's *Le protocole compassionel*), and he mentions in this regard Alphonse Daudet's harrowing journal of his illness entitled *La Doulou,* published after his death. [16] In this detailed résumé of tortures he pictures himself as a wounded Don Quixote: his bones compress him like a coat of armor, sharp rats' teeth seem to gnaw his toes, and his whole body, imaged as an anemic, wrinkled, hollowed-out carcass, becomes nothing more than a receptacle for unmitigated suffering. [17]

Daudet *père*'s chronicle of pain at the end of his life emerges in retrospect as a kind of homage to his son Léon's literary début with *Les Morticoles* (1894), a mordant satire of the medicopsychiatric profession of the late 1880s. [18] This relatively obscure medical dystopia, based on Daudet's dreadful course of study at the Faculté de Médecine under the supervision of the now-infamous choreographer of hysteria Jean-Martin Charcot, belongs to a popular fin-de-siècle genre encompassing the protofuturist works of Jules Verne and Albert Robida (*Le Vingtième siècle: Roman d'une Parisienne d'après-demain*), the negative utopianism of Gabriel de Tarde (*Fragment d'histoire future*, 1896) and the extravagant pornocracy of

Pierre Louys's *L'Ile aux dames* (circa 1912), whose title refers to the inhabitants of an island run by an oligarchy of sadistic doctors (an uncanny foreshadowing of the Nazi death camp doctors).

Like Daudet's notion of the *hérédisme* in *Le Rêve éveillé*, the *morticole* connotes a particle of death, a succubus, or atom of malevolent contagion. The hero of the story, one Félix Canelon, becomes increasingly infected the more he is inducted into the ranks of his captors. Marooned on this island of *"dégénérés"* and *"mutilés,"* he works first as a conscript in the hospitals and then moves on to more serious medical training. The twin objectives of a Morticoles medical education are the enjoyment of abjection and the endurance of disgust (what Freud would identify as the essential ingredient of perversion in his *Three Essays on the Theory of Sexuality*). Success on the final exam—"le concours du lèchement des pieds"—is contingent on licking the filthy feet of the professors without vomiting on the floor. In preparation for the exam, Canelon assists at the performance of surgical brutality that is common custom in the land:

> In the middle of an atmosphere which compounded the desire to vomit, I perceived a group of several people, propping up an ill-formed contorted body over which stood a dark little man with bright, hard eyes. Screams, interrupted only by "Oh, la, la!—Oh! how I suffer!—Oh! what pain!" were enough to rend soul and ears alike. This spectacle of horror ceased shortly. The young people fell back like a sheaf untied. "On to the next" cried the surgeon bathed in sweat. I then clearly saw the body which they had released, a large worker with a red, feverish snout, whose neck and hands were spattered with blood and pus. His eyes poured with tears and his chest heaved, still moving under his filthy undershirt, while they swathed him in cotton bandages. I watched my neighbors hardly bothered by this vision.[19]   (18)

Canelon has a weak stomach for these operations; he falls unconscious after beholding this scene, only to be castigated by his pitiless supervisors. Finally, he too becomes inured to the sight of pain, sliding from a discourse of violent medical realism into a "fantastic" mode in which visual cruelty is absorbed into *le drame intérieur* (the interior mental drama) of madness:

> After watching Dr. Malasvon's butchery, many came to relish the spectacle of gushing wounds, savoring a carnivorous pleasure. Why, after all, does every normal being tremble at the sight and smell of blood? Why does he feel that sacrilegious shiver which the perverse have converted into sexual pleasure? And why are criminals always given away by blood, its sight, its

trace, its indelibility; the bloodstain that will not disappear, clotting, hard-
ening, holding fast. I dreamed of myself on the beach of a red ocean. Crimson, heavy, rippled like silk, the waves unfurled toward me, the squinty
moon lit up a strange landscape. And, upon waking, a mute plaint, a sharp
cry signalled to me that over there the real joined my dreams.   (M, 61)

In this passage Daudet draws out the relationship between pain and
scopophilia (the love of looking). The eye is attracted to the body's indelible wounds, and what is ascribed to the "perverse" subject, namely the
extraction of *jouissance* from the spectacle of torture, is by implication applicable to everyman. The hallucinatory image of blood elides both oneiric
phantasm and contagious microbe, so that the poison coursing through the
veins of Dr. Malasvon's victims infects the viewer with a kind of psychosexual delirium.

IV

Both Daudets typified their era in their understanding of the pornography
of death. Throughout *Les Morticoles* ghoulish episodes highlight the erotic
subconscious of deathly illness. A heroic intern named Misnard courts the
negative odds of risk when he sucks the open sores of a moribund patient:

> He applied his lips to the wound . . . the patient began to breathe more
> freely, his muscles relaxed, his physiognomy expressed gratitude mixed
> with ecstasy, while the courageous intern rinsed his mouth out in the
> sink. . . . After his departure there was a concert of tender praises. One
> stared at the membranes fallen on the sheets, the drops of blood, the operat-
> ing room. Everyone felt ennobled by the beautiful image of sacrifice trium-
> phant over death.   (M, 138–139)

In Guibert's *Le protocole* there is a scene quite comparable to this one
in its conjugation of sex and death. A young delinquent lover named
Djanlouka appears out of Hervé's past on a red motorcycle and makes
a strange request. He wants to see Hervé naked, now that his body has
been wasted by AIDS. Hervé agrees, unprepared for the cruelty of
his lover's visual ravishment. Djanlouka devours his skeleton with his
eyes:

> He began to observe me from head to foot with the amazement of a young
> child, who for the first time, in a zoo, discovers the incredible existence of
> the giraffe or the elephant. One could say that he recorded every trace of
> racked flesh, that his look filmed it so as to be able to remember, to play it
> back again.   (PC, 163)

After possessing him through the gaze, Djanlouka brandishes a condom and announces that "he wants to risk death" (PC, 1963). Their lovemaking approximates a kind of reciprocal *lustmord:* Djanlouka's brutal erotic gestures express a murderous contempt, while Hervé's gentle self-offering conveys a deadly danger.

In *Le protocole compassionel*, the knowledge of impending death is sublimated into acute anxiety over symptoms of premature aging. Like Alphonse Daudet, who deplored the sight of the emaciated *"drôle de petit vieux"* (funny-looking old man) staring back at him in the mirror, we are made to feel the narrator's hurt pride at the loss of his good looks, the embarrassment of a thirty-five-year-old forced to recognize himself in the body of an old man.[20] This lobotomy of narcissism, aggravating the fear of dying young, is perhaps among the most "obscene" dimensions of AIDS self-consciousness. An episode midway in the novel, which might be dubbed the "allegory of the cave," emblematizes the person-with-*sida*'s encounter with abjection, humiliation, and outrage on learning that he is to be cheated of his life portion. While the narrator rummages in the basement for his apartment building's communal vacuum cleaner, the door slams shut accidentally, shrouding him in darkness and damp. Down with the dirt and the rats, he imagines what it will be like to be buried underground:

> I clearly envisioned my death in this basement, like an absurd vignette inlaid by destiny into another vignette, greater in misfortune, but perhaps more certain than that of the cellar from which someone would eventually rescue me, namely *sida*, which had become the running film of my life. To perish in the basement when one is stricken with *sida*, I'm the only one in the world who could finish this way, this death in my cave already belonged to my biography, in all its absurdity and horror.   (PC, 71–72)

What Guibert discovers in the cave is the Grand Guignol of his own life story. Temporarily buried alive until an old man "saves" him two hours later, he comprehends with bitter clarity the extent to which the life to which he has been returned, the life of living with *sida*, grotesquely mimes an unfinished death not unlike the panic darkness of the coffin-cave.

Le protocole compassionel ends with a scene in the office of Guibert's doctor, Claudette Demouchel, with whom he has lived a kind of Barthesian love affair, complete with rituals of courtship, seduction, fits of jealousy, lover's quarrels, peace offerings of tenderness, and exchanges of coded intimacy. When Guibert enters Claudette's office he carries a camera; he wants to film his medical examination. A private person dedicated to the confidentiality of her métier, Claudette refuses to be a party to such exhibitionism; she detests being photographed, just as she dislikes being fixed in prose on the pages of Guibert's book about AIDS. Their conversation borders on the acerbic, when, faced with Claudette's stubborn resistance to becoming part of his filmic life-writing, Hervé "pulls out his last card":

> —But you can't stop me from filming myself, it's my body not yours.
> —Yes, replies Claudette, but my body will be forced to enter into the image in order to examine you.
> —Good point.
> —And in the first place, why do you want to film this examination?
> —Because it seems to be sufficiently exceptional to merit that one leave a trace. To avoid seeing you in the picture, it is simply a question of framing.   (PC, 225)

Claudette raises the uncomfortable question of Guibert's motive in wanting to film his own wasted naked body, but in turn, he raises the question of the implication of the doctor in the patient's life and death. In a sense, both are arguing that some breach in the ethics of medical distance is inevitable with this kind of illness—that doctor and patient are fatefully part of the "film" of each other's lives.

No maudlin finale, this final episode draws together many of the thematic strands characterizing Guibert's transformation of *sida* into words: the metaphysics of disease; the psychosexual power dynamics of medical interventions; nosological voyeurism; clinical exhibitionism; the crowding out of subjectivity by ghostly personimages; the relationship between infection and hallucination, contagion and eroticism; transmission and memory; the politics of commemoration (the dispute over the right to die in secret or the politically urgent need to die publicly); and, finally, the role of film as transposing medium of self-entombment. Mediating between these overlapping themes is the filmic metaphor, a celluloid strip that imprints the ghostly trace of the personimage. We remember Guibert's encounter with the outlaw Djanlouka: his voyeuristic gaze "films" the devastated body of the *sida* lover. Similarly, during the moment of self-reckoning in the cave, Guibert conceives of his *sida* as the "running film of my life." At key moments, the "fantom image" of filmmaking returns as a figure of speech for living with *sida*. *Le protocole compassionel* ends with a displacement of the dreaded allusion to death into a cheerfully stated resolve to start making films: "Today, August 13 1990, I finished my book.

The number 13 brings good luck. There is a marked improvement in my tests, Claudette smiles (is she lying to me?). I've started to make a film. My first film" (PC, 227).

NOTES

Hervé Guibert died in Paris on December 27, 1991. I dedicate this essay to his memory.

1. For discussion of a spectrum of AIDS writing in French, see "Le sida et les lettres," *Arches* 5 (Spring 1991).

2. See "Hervé Guibert et son double," an interview between Guibert and Didier Eribon in *Le Nouvel Observateur*, July 18–24, 1991, pp. 87–89.

3. Ibid. I have also heard this criticism in conversation with critics in Paris. In *A l'ami qui ne m'a pas sauvé la vie* (Paris: Gallimard, 1990), Guibert puts the matter this way:

> From my first visit to the hospital on, I noted everything in my journal, point by point, gesture after gesture, without omitting a single word of this rarefied conversation, atrociously ordered by the situation. This journalistic activity soothed and disgusted me, I knew that Muzil would have felt so much pain if he had known that I was recording all of this like a spy, like an enemy, all these degrading little nothings, into my journal, which was perhaps destined, and this was the most abominable thing of all, to survive him, and to testify to a truth that he would have so much wished to efface from the circumference of his life so as to leave only well-polished bones, around a black diamond, lustrous and impenetrable, solidly closed on its secrets, which risked becoming his biography, a true puzzle filed henceforth with inexact details.   (pp. 97–98)

Subsequent references to this work will be cited in the text, using the abbreviation "ALA." All translations are my own, although an English translation of this text was recently published. See Guibert, *To the Friend Who Did Not Save my Life*, Linda Coverdale, trans. (London: Macmillan, 1991).

4. Didier Eribon, at the end of his biography *Michel Foucault* (Paris: Flammarion, 1986), notes Foucault's desire for privacy. Foucault insisted on destroying an autobiographical novel and a manuscript on Manet, for example.

5. In *A l'ami qui n'a pas sauvé la vie* Guibert describes the "shame and relief" that comes from writing a kind of résumé of his journal entries on Muzil's illness. He asks:

> By what right did I write all that? And vis-à-vis someone who I loved with all my heart? I felt at that moment, it was incredible, a kind of vision, or vertigo, which gave me full powers, which made me a delegate for these ignoble transcriptions, legitimizing them, because it was suddenly announced to me (through a premonition) that I was fully empowered [to write these things] [*que j'y étais pleinement habilité*] because it wasn't so much the agony of my friendship that I was in the process of describing, but the agony that awaited me, and which would be identical, it was henceforth the certainty that, beyond friendship, we were tied to each other by a common thanatological destiny [*par un sort thanatologique commun—sort* means both destiny or lot, and spell or charm].   pp. 101–102

6. In Eribon, *Michel Foucault*, p. 348.

7. Hervé Guibert, *Le protocole compassionel* (Paris: Gallimard, 1991), p. 58. Subsequent references to this work will be cited in the text, using the abbreviation "PC."

8. Hervé Guibert, *L'Image de soi, ou l'injonction de son beau moment?* (Fanlac, Périgueux: Blake, 1988), no pagination.

9. Moreau de Tours, Herbert Spencer, and Théodule Ribot were among the many theorists of heredity whose writings influenced Alphonse Daudet. For a concept of transmissible heredity akin to Daudet's "heredism" also see August Weismann's *The Germ-Plasm: A Theory of Heredity*, W. Newton Parker and Harriet Rönnfeldt, trans. (London: Scott, 1893).

10. See, Léon Daudet, *L'Hérédo: Essai sur le drame intérieur* (Paris: Nouvelle Librairie Nationale, 1906); *Devant la douleur* (Paris: Grasset, 1931); *Souvenirs littéraires* (Paris: Grasset, 1938); *Le Rêve éveillé* (Paris: Grasset, 1926); and *Fièvres de Camargue* (Paris: Gallimard, 1937).

11. Hervé Guibert, *L'Image fantôme* (Paris: Editions de Minuit, 1981), p. 144.

12. Léon Daudet, *Le Rêve éveillé*, pp. 41–42.

13. Léon Daudet, *L'Hérédo*, pp. 15–16.

14. Guibert, *L'Image fantôme*, p. 170.

15. Elaine Scarry, *The Body in Pain: The Making and Unmaking of the World* (New York: Oxford University Press, 1985).

16. Michel Tournier, "Du bon usage de la maladie," preface to Alphonse Daudet, *Le Trésor d'Arlatan* (France: Editions Viviane Hamy, 1991), pp. 14–15.

17. Alphonse Daudet, *La Doulou* (Paris: Fasquelle, 1931), pp. 25–39.

18. Daudet *fils* later gave in essay form a caustic transcription of Charcot's charlatanism in *Devant la douleur* (Paris: Grasset, 1931). For an analysis of *Les Morticoles* as a parody of Charcot's school, see Toby Gelfand, "Medical Nemesis, Paris 1894: Léon Daudet's *Les Morticoles*," *Bulletin of the History of Medicine* 60 (1986): 155–76. My thanks to Jan Goldstein for this reference.

19. Léon Daudet, *Les Morticoles* (Paris: Bibliothèque Charpentier, 1901). Subsequent references to this work will be cited in the text, using the abbreviation "M."

20. Alphonse Daudet, *La Doulou*, p. 25.

Apocalyptic Utterance in Edmund White's "An Oracle"

Richard Dellamora

I Of Oracles

Edmund White's "An Oracle" marks the course that AIDS has traced through the social forms of gay existence since 1980. Or rather, through some of these forms, since the ones that he limns are specific, dealing with upper-middle-class WASPs on the American East Coast, with painters, college professors, management consultants, and their attendants, "the joking, irresponsible, anguished half-world of the gay actor-singer-dancer-writer-waiter-model . . . who feels confident Europe is as extinct as a dead star and all the heat and life for the planet must radiate from new York"[1] (217). Marking a break within an existence that had, after Stonewall, quickly come to be taken for granted as normal, the onset of AIDS brings a forcible reminder of how recent a formation that normalcy was.

In White's short story, Ray is left at a loss after the illness and death of his lover, George: "Ray thought, 'We each need just the right weight of pettiness to serve as ballast.' George's death had tossed all the sandbags overboard and Ray had been floating higher and higher towards extinction" (222). He experiences this crisis in terms of loss of a sense of self: "'You must look out for yourself,' George had always said. But what self?" (211). Ray tries to respond, at the urging of his friend Betty, by traveling to Crete with a prominent painter and gay acquaintance, Ralph Brooks. There Ray becomes involved in sex for pay with a young Greek named

Marco, with whom he falls in love. When, at the end of the story, he proposes that they open a gay guesthouse together at Xania, Marco declines
but responds in words that may—or may not—hold a clue as to how Ray
can fashion "a new way of living" (22). A number of oracles within the
story open the prospect of establishing different relations between subjects than those that subsisted before the AIDS epidemic.

The focus of the story, though personal, is also social, since the only
way forward for Ray is to re-engage with the lives and work of others. For
him—as for White—this re-engagement requires a specifically gay sociality. Discussing the thinking that led to his decision to collaborate with
British writer Adams Mars-Jones on a book of AIDS short stories, White
comments: "We thought that fiction was the best medium for communicating what it was like actually to be living through these experiences as an
insider. We were seeing so many programs on television where experts
were discussing our problem as a medical phenomenon, even as a social
phenomenon, but always from the outside. What was being lost sight of
was that actual human beings were suffering, watching their lives crum-
ble, and having to confront very deep fears."[2] Written by a gay writer who
is HIV-positive, with a gay protagonist who is afraid to be tested for HIV
antibodies, and directed towards gay readers—White says he has Andrew
Holleran specifically in mind—"An Oracle" engages literary practice in
order to reimagine gay existence.[3] The "story about Marco" (247) that Ray
begins to write provides the text with an internal signature, since Ray's
story becomes, in effect, the one that White tells. White connects personal content with political by understanding and representing social processes "as/in narrative, as a process unfolding very local stories, which
are provisional truths."[4] By writing in an oracular mode, moreover, he
avoids making privileged claims to knowledge as he projects his readers
into an as-yet-uncharted future.

The reflections on sexual relations between men in ancient Greece that
Michel Foucault pursues in the second volume of *The History of Sexuality*,[5] and Jacques Derrida's consideration of oracle in his essay, "Of An
Apocalyptic Tone Recently Adopted in Philosophy,"[6] provide means of as-
sessing Ray's position between one existence and another yet to be envis-
aged. Foucault has traced the development in medieval and later culture
of what he calls an "individualizing power"—i.e., a power to fashion
individuals—in the Church and subsequently in the modern state.[7] In the
first volume of the *History*, Foucault argues that the formation of homosexuals has been one effect of the exercise of this power.[8] In contrast, in ancient Greek tradition he finds a technology of the self in relation to the

body and to sexual practices that is aesthetic rather than confessional in character. Foucault describes "sexual activity and sexual practices . . . problematized through practices of the self, bringing into play the criteria of an 'aesthetics of existence'" (UP, 12). In this context, the term *aesthetic* refers to a specific set of practices, especially apt for gay men, that have the potential to be articulated in resistance to an individualizing power whose forcefulness has been exacerbated in the proliferation of discourses around AIDS. While Foucault specifically rejects the use of Greek examples as an "alternative" to current gay existence, he does believe that the problematic relation between ethics and an aesthetics of existence so important in Greek thought resembles relations that demand attention in current gay self-reflection.[9] In the later volumes of *The History of Sexuality,* Foucault implicitly reads a Greek aesthetics of existence across the grain of the gay aesthetics of existence that he encountered in communities on the American East and West Coasts during his visits there in the late 1970s and early 1980s.[10] In White's story, Ray's trip to Greece, undertaken to enable him to regain a sense of self, offers an opportunity to make the contrast between these aesthetics explicit.[11]

Derrida's reflections on oracular utterance occur in a discussion of the two projects of deconstruction.[12] The first project is the analytic or "deconstructive" one, in which apparently integral entities such as the "self" are shown to be marked by internal contradictions. Analytic deconstruction disassembles the notions of unitary identity upon which appeals to self-awareness and action would otherwise all too easily be grounded. In contrast, a deconstructive approach requires its practitioners to avoid such mystification and to recognize and respect the many other differences that exist in gay and lesbian subjectivities. The demand that differences be acknowledged continues even though, in a time of "gay plague," gay "identity" is under extreme pressure. White continually undoes "gay identity" in "An Oracle" by specifying its differences. In the apocalyptic atmosphere that continues to surround many discussions of AIDS, the analytic project has a further use in subjecting to scrutiny the rhetoric of judgment, crisis, and ending that accompanies what Derrida refers to as "the apocalyptic tone."

Yet analytic deconstruction requires supplement by a second or affirmative phase that enables the subject in distress to begin to make the gains that are possible only when one begins to differ from one's customary sense of self. Derrida describes this project in terms of the ability of "the tone of another, to come at no matter what moment to interrupt a familiar tonality" and thereby to disrupt "the self-identity" of listener and speaker both (AT, 83, 84). Such utterance is, for Derrida, an oracle, which, though recognized as a linguistic fiction, is capable of generating new possibilities of meaning. In the context of the epidemic, this other is, for one, the person who has died with AIDS. The self-identity of those who remain needs to be disrupted by the oracular words of the deceased in order to enable the work of mourning to be done. Ray, who spends his time listening to messages of George's voice recorded on Betty's answering machine, is obsessed with the possibility of hearing George "interrupt a familiar tonality": "Did he love George without believing he existed? . . . [Ray] believed George still loved him, or would if God would let him speak" (224). In the oracle at the end of the story, George does speak—or, rather, his words, "Take care of yourself," return in "the tone of another," in the voice of Marco. This other tone changes the meaning of the sentence and thereby disrupts Ray's self-identity.

Derrida, always concerned about the way in which distinctions tend to become fixed categorically, is unwilling to specify who "another" might be, a reluctance that has a pragmatic basis in his concern about the projection of Others, especially of racial others.[13] His reserve, however, leaves the project of affirmative deconstruction incomplete by leaving unspoken the relevance of oracle to particular groups. By siting the possibility of oracular utterance within the history of gay existence at a moment that is fraught with suffering, confusion, and anxiety, White supplements Derrida's reflections with others that open upon the possibilities of personal and social renewal.

II   Missives

"An Oracle" begins with the following paragraph:

> After George died, Ray went through a long period of uncertainty. George's disease had lasted fifteen months and during that time Ray had stopped seeing most of his old friends. He'd even quarreled with Betty, his best friend. Although she'd sent him little cards from time to time, including the ones made by a fifty-year-old California hippie whom she represented, he hadn't responded. He'd even felt all the more offended that she'd forgotten or ignored how sickening he'd told her he thought the pastel leaves and sappy sentiments were.   (207)

With these sentences, White raises a concern about messages that recurs throughout the story, messages entailing difficulties, for instance, in their pre-scribed character. In this case "the pastel leaves and sappy sentiments" of Betty's friendship cards do not really suit the crisis that George and Ray face. There are lapses of communication: Ray is unable to communicate his irritation to Betty or at least to do so in a way that will prompt her to change her behavior. There are contingencies that further limit communication: Betty is using cards that are, apparently, her stock in trade. The use of the word *hippie* and the observation that the hippie referred to is middle-aged suggests another limit, an inability to move out of the past.

These limits do not refer simply to questions about language, self-identity, or intersubjective relations; they are immediately inscribed within and begin to describe the micropolitics of one mode of gay existence: a couple, one of whom has died (as a result of AIDS)—the withholding of the word "AIDS" here and throughout is a feature of a politics within which Ray lives—and the other of whom is beset by grief and loss. Betty, the woman who is Ray's "best friend," provides another key element in that micropolitics, since the role of the-woman-who-is-a-gay-man's-best-friend is characteristic of gay existence as represented in the story. Betty functions as a link between gay friends and with existence outside gay networks. Her presence implies the need for further analysis, not only of the apparent necessity of the role she plays for gay men but also about reciprocity. What support do Ray and Ralph provide *her* and women like her?

Later in the story, the issue of women's mourning comes to the fore when Ray becomes fascinated with an account in Loring M. Danforth's book *The Death Rituals of Rural Greece*[14] about a Greek mother's loss of her daughter. Because Ray's attempt to draw analogies between this experience and his own ignores cultural differences, his efforts produce incongruous and at times inadvertently humorous results. Nevertheless, Ray's perception of the losses faced by this and other Greek women prompts reflection about his responsibility, and that of other gay men, to women who mourn. The question is yet more apt since, like gay men in the face of AIDS, women who mourn women often find themselves in the position of needing to invent modes of expression, literary genres, and rituals to express the meaning of relationships between women that traditionally have had limited or no possibility of expression.[15]

"An Oracle" implies the need to consider such questions as well as their difficulty. The semicloseted life of Ray and George as a gay "couple" constitutes an incipient and, to a large degree, blocked social form, for which rituals of mourning are wanting.[16] However satirical White may be about what is casually referred to as a "gay lifestyle," one has to bear in mind how radically new gay existence is as a set of openly expressed social formations and that it continues to exist under duress. The very novelty of gay social forms exacerbates the disruption caused by AIDS while also inviting (indeed, almost requiring) the existence of oracular utterance—since if there is one constant in gay experience since Stonewall, it has been the need to continually adapt to quickly changing circumstances, of which AIDS presents only the most recent and the most daunting set.

In the oracle with which the story ends, the possibilities of misunderstanding and failure, personal and political, are magnified, in part because the words of the oracle, "Take care of yourself," are ones that George often repeated. The oracle raises the possibility of communication with those who have died with AIDS. But in what way can the deceased speak to those who have been left behind? Moreover, the oracle is spoken by Marco, in Ray's parlance a "hooker" (246), a term that in its very mischaracterization of the relations between well-to-do tourists and young Greek islanders indicates Ray's insensitivity to economic and other asymmetries between members of the two groups. The sender and receiver of this message are marked by differences of class, age, sexual and gender identity, language, and nationality. Will Ray see that, coming from Marco, even these familiar words must have a different meaning? Or will he regard Marco as simply the narcissistic pretext for delivering a message that Ray already knows and wishes to hear reflected back to him?

These questions are important since White is prepared to risk reaching outward to radically different experiences from a specified site of subjectivity that, to those outside, is often associated with a cultured and affluent indifference to others. White underscores the general validity of a critical assessment of Ray's lifestyle by tracing his life from boyhood on a farm in Ohio, to graduate study of Emile Durkheim's concept of anomie at the University of Chicago, to life in a gay commune in Toronto, to adjustment to corporate life in New York. Given this particular route through recent gay existence, one wonders what has happened to Ray.

III   Postmarked Greece

The shift to a Greek context provides a number of different social formations in relation to which Ray's sexuality can be interpreted: urban and rural modern Greek, Homeric, classical Athenian, Minoan, Dorian, and Hellenistic. Ray's ignorance about AIDS (for instance, his belief that the penetrator in anal intercourse is not at risk), though understandable in the early 1980s, leaves him just as unknowing about important matters as are the Greek villagers described in *The Death Rituals of Rural Greece*. More-over, Ray's and George's experiment in a durable but nonmonogamous re-lationship entails a cultivated lack of self-awareness that veils anxieties about gender inversion no less intense than those that Foucault has de-tected in classical Greek culture or that Ray finds upon arriving in Crete (UP, 18–20). As George's "doll" (218), Ray himself has been a kind of "hooker," reduced in status to the level of a high-priced commodity object ("George saw him obviously as a sort of superior home entertainment centre," 216). Within the relationship, Ray is loving, loyal, and patient but alienated, seeing himself as "impersonating George's lover" (218). White associates the relationship with Ray's loss of direction and with a thundering lack of self-knowledge on the part of George. This lack has the advantage of helping George pass for "straight" in the upper echelons of corporate America but affords no gains in awareness even in the face of illness and death. His opacity is especially marked in the phrase, "You must look out for yourself," a leitmotiv repeated with ever-varying mean-ing in the story and becoming, at last, the equivocal oracle of the story's title. George keeps using it to tell Ray he needs a job (i.e., a "well-paying" job, 211). Before he dies George finds Ray "a gig" in public relations for Amalgamated Anodynes, an irresponsible corporation that "produced a fabric for children's wear that had turned out to be flammable" (212). George himself specializes in high-priced face-lifts for corporations. White's satire of the illusion and misinformation that George and Ray pro-duce reflects their complicity in a late capitalist "we" contoured along lines of race, gender, nationality, and class.

When Ray, before leaving for Greece, gives the cat, Anna, into Betty's keeping, he thinks of George's injunction: "'You must look out for your-self,' George had said, and now he was trying" (221). In Marco, Ray seeks first a much-needed intimacy and, secondly, a chance to regain a sense of self. But the cash-nexus of the relationship enacts and parodies relations of exchange within the corporate economy and in Ray's earlier life with George. Ray's pleasurable, semiguilty fantasies about sex with Marco show that he is aware that asymmetries in the relationship do not tell in Ray's favor: "He whose conscience years of political struggle had raised now sank into the delicious guilt of Anglo fag servicing Mexican worker, of cowboy face-fucked by Indian brave, of lost tourist waylaid by wily camel boy" (239). Near the end of his stay, Ray reflects:

> When he'd first arrived in Crete he'd had the vague feeling that this holiday was merely a detour and that when he rejoined his path George would be

waiting for him. George or thoughts of George or the life George had custom-built for him, he wasn't quite sure which he meant. And yet now there was a real possibility that he might escape, start something new or transpose his old boyhood goals and values into a new key, the Dorian mode, say. Everything here seemed to be conspiring to reorient him, re-patriate him, even the way he'd become in Greece the pursuer rather than the pursued.   (247–48)

This anticipated repatriation, however, is ironic, since the patterns of sexual relation in ancient Greece indicate by contrast how unsatisfactory life with George has been. In *The History of Sexuality*, Foucault observes how the "'use of the pleasures'—*chrēsis aphrodisiōn*" is codified in classi-cal Greece so as to produce an "individual" who is "an ethical subject of sexual conduct" (UP, 32). Foucault identifies "four great axes of experi-ence" as relevant to this process. One of these axes, *dietetics*, refers to one's relation to one's body. This set of practices constitutes "a form of moderation defined by the measured and timely use of the *aphrodisia*." The second axis, termed *economics*, refers to marriage and is "a form of moderation defined not by a mutual faithfulness of marriage partners, but by a certain privilege, which the husband upholds on behalf of the lawful wife over whom he exercises his authority." The third axis, *erotics*, refers to moderation in sexual relations between men and boys. The fourth axis refers to self-conscious meditation on properly philosophic issues that arise for Plato in response to "the love of boys" (UP, 251, 252). Ray's "use of the pleasures" appears to parody the classical model. He has translated dietetics into "years of [weight] training" that "had in point of absolute fact turned him into a physical commodity" (216). "Marriage" to George in-stalled a "hierarchical structure," to use Foucault's phrase (UP, 252), in which Ray was left permanently in the role of "the looker with the brain, exactly like the starlet whom the studio hypes wearing a mortarboard and specs above her adorable snub nose and bikini" (218).

Foucault's remarks about the third axis help explain the possibilities and the limits of the Ray-Marco relation, since ethical love between a male adult and an adolescent in the ancient model excludes the exchange of money (UP, 217–19). As Ray has yet to learn, such a relationship respects "a fleeting time that leads ineluctably to an end that is near." As well, it "carries with it the ideal," if not the literal reality, "of a renunciation of all physical relations with boys" (UP, 262). On the other hand, the "black and shiny" evidence of Marco's moustache, the "first hair sprouting" on his chest, place him at the exact threshold of male love (UP, 243). The moral efficacy of the connection, however, depends on the respect that is owing to the virility of the adolescent and to his future status as a free man. It is no longer simply the problem of a man's becoming the master of his pleasure; it is a problem of knowing how one can make allowance for the other's freedom in the mastery that one exercises over oneself and in the true love that one bears for him.   (UP, 252)

This "problem" is precisely Ray's at the end of the story.

In addition to the classic model of pederastic love, other patterns of male intimacy are intimated by Ray's trip to Xania. One is the pattern of sexual and emotional ties between men that existed in Crete in pre-Greek civilization. Gay activists have exploited the cult of the Cretan bull god and the great mother goddess in Minoan culture in order to associate love between men with feminism in an alliance against patriarchy.[17] Ray affiliates Marco with this culture when he compares him with "the slim-waisted matador" (249) found in Minoan painting.[18] Yet the murals at Knossos, rediscovered in the twentieth century by the English anthropologist, Sir Arthur Evans, have been "absurdly over-restored" (235), a fact that serves as a reminder that processes of appropriation and contamination, of colonization and tourism, make impossible any exclusive affinity between Marco and his antecedents. Through his love of Marco, Ray is affiliated with the ethos of pre-Greek civilization in Crete. But countertendencies also abound. For one, when Ray invokes "the Dorian mode," he associates himself with the culture of the Dorians, a group of Greek invaders who overran Crete[19] and who, first there and later in the Peloponnesus, developed a model of pederastic relationship that became central to the formation of the soldier citizen/subject of Sparta.

White uses geographical references to associate Ray and Marco with the roles of colonizer and colonized in history. Ray, who lives on one island, Manhattan, travels to another island, Crete. White dots the story with the traces of past conquests: for example, the Turkish minaret, itself located on an island in Xania.[20] Ray and Ralph, the American with whom he travels, rent "a Venetian palace" (221), monument to four centuries of rule by the island city. Ray is also associated with imperial Rome during the Hellenistic period: "His body had acquired a certain thickness, as though the original Greek statue had been copied by a Roman" (224).

If Ray is, as I have suggested, associated with Minoan as well as Dorian and other imperial cultures, so is Marco, whose Italian name connotes the ascendancy of "the Venetian lion [of San Marco] . . . emblazoned" on the walls of Xania (227). By further associating Marco with figures of lions and cats, White draws on Minoan and Venetian referents of Marco's virility.

"Marco in his white Keds and Levi jacket came treading stealthily around the corner, noble and balanced as a lion; he winked his approval and Ray felt his own pleasure spread over his whole body like the heat of the sun" (244). These lion images imply a process of revirilization in the Ray-Marco nexus that carries negative connotations but that paradoxically is also validated as part of a return to an altered sense of self. "Cats" are "everywhere" (237) the first night that Ray follows Marco. These images, moreover, are associated with affectionate intimacy: Marco's "ass" is "hairy with nice friendly fuzz" (240).

White uses reference to a lion to register yet one other form of affiliation between men, this time in Homeric Greece. Sitting on a beach reading the *Odyssey*, Ray is moved to tears by the laments of "lion-hearted Achilles" (226) over the death of Patroclus. David Halperin has argued that the representation of this friendship in Homer celebrates a nonsexualized model of pair-bonding between male heroes.[21] The reference to Achilles, then, is a reminder of yet further diversity in the Greek imagination of male romance. Failing to recognize the cultural distance between himself and Achilles, Ray imagines Achilles' loss of Patroclus in terms of his own loss of George. Yet this distorting assimilation of heroic friendship to gay partnership is countered by an experience that results in what might be characterized as a second or minor oracle in the story. The unexpected appearance on the beach of an old herdsman and his sheep prompts Ray to see his "grief" in a new light, "as a costly gewgaw, beyond the means of the grievously hungry and hard-working world" (226) of the shepherd. Recognizing someone else's difficulty enables Ray to look at his own experience differently. This double recognition, moreover, raises a further possibility: "Maybe it was precisely his grief that joined him to this peasant" (226). I call this moment oracular because for the first time Ray's sense of self is altered by recognizing someone else's situation.

IV   Home Truths

This minor oracle invites further reflection on the ways in which "the tone of another" can "interrupt a familiar tonality" and thereby disrupt "the self-identity" of the listener. White brings this concern self-reflexively into the text by incorporating a number of passages from Danforth's book, a study of the rites of exhumation that form part of the mourning process in northern Greece. Explicit analogies between village experience and Ray's evoke the question of the relation between self and Other.

At the start of his book, Danforth tells the story of Irini, whose twenty-year-old daughter Eleni died in August 1974, in a hit-and-run accident in Thessaloniki. Eleni was a bright, attractive young woman whose parents had sent her from home at the age of twelve so she could attend high school and prepare for work as an elementary-school teacher. She was killed one month before taking up her first post (DR, 13). When Ray decides to accept an offer of a vacation in Greece, he is drawn in part by Irini's story. "It would be all new—new place, new language, no ghosts. He even liked going to the country where people expressed their grief over dying so honestly, so passionately. In that book he liked the way a mother, when she exhumed her daughter's body after three years of burial, said, 'Look what I put in and look what I took out! I put in a partridge, and I took out bones'" (DR, 65; 221).[22] Ray's interest in Irini's grief suggests theoretical questions about alterity. Do subjects—and discourses—permit the expression of difference in ways that reflexively alter those subjects and discourses? Or are such expressions always recuperated in a binary structure of signification in which the meaning of one term is subordinated to the meaning of the other?

White is familiar with such questions not only from his reading in poststructuralist theory but also from the consideration that Danforth gives them in the introduction to his book (SD, xiv, xvii–xix).[23] Danforth describes the goal of humanist anthropology as one of reducing "the distance between the anthropologist and the Other," of bridging "the gap between 'us' and 'them.'" He contends that:

> An investigation of the Other involves an exploration of the Self as well. The central problem of anthropology is thus, in Paul Ricoeur's words, "the comprehension of the self by the detour of the comprehension of the other." The anthropologist sets out to investigate the Other, only to find the Other in himself and himself in the Other. For the anthropology of death, this means that the study of 'how others die' becomes the study of 'how we die.' We must come to see in the deaths of Others our own deaths as well.   (DR, 6)

In this passage, eloquent though it is, "Others" tends to become a transparent overlay of "we." Danforth misses a key step necessary if ethnographic study is to increase self-knowledge, namely, the analysis of the investments that the ethnographer brings to his object of study. Paraphrasing Claude Lévi-Strauss, Paul de Man has argued:

> Prior to making any valid statement about a distant society, the observing subject must be as clear as possible about his attitude towards his own. He will soon discover, however, that the only way in which he can accomplish

this self-demystification is by a (comparative) study of his own social self as it engages in the observation of others, and by becoming aware of the pattern of distortions that this situation necessarily implies.[24]

In de Man's formulation, ethnography progresses not by finding us in the Other (or vice versa) but by analyzing the ethnographer's relationship to those whom he or she studies (and vice versa).

Ray's attraction to Danforth's book arises in part from the emotional deprivations of his sometimes closeted existence. (He cannot, for instance, tell his boss, Helen, about George's death.) Ray's response to the situation of the Greek women is complicated by the fact that as a gay man living in New York City, he too is in some ways not one of the we but rather an Other. Since the advent of AIDS, the tendency of gay men to be regarded as sources of contagion has exacerbated their alienation. Although Ray sometimes passes as a straight upper-middle-class WASP, his sexual difference means that in part he approaches Greece as an Other approaching an Other. His subordination as a gay man both generally and in his "wifely" relation to George intensifies his identification with the widows in Danforth's book, whom Danforth describes as experiencing a crisis of identity when they lose the male through whom their status in the village had been secured (DR, 138).

Ray shifts with considerable confusion between the positions of we and Other. In "An Oracle," the term *gay* provides a touchstone of individual and ethnic identity, but the continual variation of nominatives for subjects of male-male desire indicates continual oscillation in the significance of being such a subject. This variation amplifies once Ray is in a society where the political structure of desire between men differs from that of his own. In the course of the story, gay men are referred to as muscle queens, "lovers," pooves, boy, "the Stonewall generation," pick-ups, *poosti*, dirty old men, "girls," *putana*, transvestites, and faggots. The proliferation of terms indicates that the term *gay* refers to a subject whose meaning is continually under pressure of varying selfknowledges (and ignorances) and relations to others.

In Xania, Ray relies on a frequent visitor from the United States, a sixty-year-old Classics professor named Homer, to explain to him the construction of sexuality that permits Greek men to engage in sex for pay as long as they take the active role but which also licenses a shepherd to murder a son whom he learns "was getting fucked" (244). Homer acts as a gay ethnographer who understands the differences between sexuality at home and sexuality in Greek bar culture. Moreover, he understands the com-

patibility of sexuality at Xania with his own sexual ritual—namely, pho-
tographing the "locals" (229) in the nude. As his name wryly suggests,
Homer, whose modern Greek is patched together from an expert knowledge of ancient Greek, respects the differences between modern and ancient Greek male-male sexual practices; he is also likely aware that his
hobby is imbricated in a specifically gay tradition.[25] Of the characters in
the story, he is the one most capable of understanding male-male sexual
differences across time and space.

Barbara Godard has pointed out that translation-effects are graphic
traces of linguistic meaning that remind readers that they are reading a
text through the lenses of a language other than that in which the text was
written earlier.[26] Translation-effects are visible signs of differences in
meaning that depend on differences in language. In "An Oracle," White
both acknowledges and denies linguistic differences in ways that culmi-
nate in the open semantic structure with which the story ends. When Ray
first meets Marco, it is Marco who initiates verbal exchange: "'Ya,' he
said, that short form of *Yassou*, the all-purpose greeting" (235).[27] It is possible to hear this word as *Yeah*, Yes—that is, as an utterance with which
the Cretan elects the Manhattanite for a possible intimacy. Intimacy will
become possible, however, only if Marco can prevent Ray from sentimen-
tally misconstruing what is about to happen. "What you want?" Marco
asks, "and his faint smile suggested he already knew and that Ray's desire
was disgusting and entirely practicable" (235). Ray's answer, "You," [Ya,
You] strikes a false note because it is a pretext. What he wants at this moment is not "You" but sex.

In response, Marco "frowned angrily." Ray reads the gesture: "'Sex,'
Ray said, and this time the boy nodded. 'But money!' he threatened, rub-
bing his thumb and forefinger together." The narrator surmises that Marco's reaction occurs because "the word [you] apparently was not one of the
boy's dozen English words." But the narrator is immediately corrected.
Marco continues: "I fuck you!" (235). He does know the word *you* in the
sense of sexual object and insists on specifying the difference between
sentimental rhetoric and exchange value, a difference that is crucial for
Marco since in his sexual culture it validates his masculinity even when he
engages in sex with another man. Marco's assertion demystifies Ray's
position at the same time that it glances at a subtext of appropriation that
surfaces at the end of the story. The performative also undermines the
knowingness of the narrator in his function as ethnographer. Marco knows
more and better than the narrator, whose ignorance about self and other is
aligned, for the moment, with Ray's.

By the end of the story, Ray has fallen in love with Marco, a condition not likely to induce clarity. Paul de Man has remarked that "'Love' is a figure that disfigures, a metaphor that confers the illusion of proper meaning to a suspended, open semantic structure."[28] Ray's delusion takes the shape of the fantasy of buying a house in Xania, turning it into a guesthouse, and living there with the younger man. He finds a gay Greek journalist who agrees to translate this proposal into a letter for Marco. The expedient seems to overcome the possibility of translation-effects: Ray's meaning will be transparent to Marco because the translator is both Greek *and* gay. Along with the letter, however, Ray sends the gift of a "gold necklace, . . . the sort of sleazy bauble all the kids here were wearing" (249). It prompts semantic interference. "Kids" is condescending; and the phrase "sleazy bauble" itself, whether the narrator's or Ray's in indirect discourse, undercuts Ray's stated intentions. Is Ray attempting to buy a sleazy bauble? And is it possible for him to go Greek or for Marco to be gay in Xania, a possibility that the ethnography outlined by Homer shows to be impracticable?

For his part, Marco reads the letter silently, pauses, then returns the gift unopened. After a long silence, he says in English: "I know you love me and I love you. But Xania is no good for you. Too small. Do not rest here. You must go" (250). Marco speaks at this point with the confidence of an English native speaker, implying thereby undivulged narratives of earlier travels or contacts with anglophones, even possibly gay ones. In the sentence, Marco uses English with a difference of intonation: "I know you love me," he says; and he does know what Ray intends. His letter, written in the same grammar of possession in which George had spoken, emplots a future in which his relation with Marco will mirror the "marriage" whose ending has left Ray adrift.

Marco continues by responding, "And I love you." The predicate is the same, but the intonation is different. Love in this meaning demystifies Marco's earlier defensive positioning of himself within Greek conventions of masculinity while simultaneously suspending the chain of substitutions (George-Ray, Ray-Marco) in which Ray is caught. In Marco's words, "the possibility for the other tone, or the tone of another" becomes audible. With it occurs what Derrida refers to as the "derailment" of "the self-identity of some addressee [*destinataire*] or sender [*destinateur*]," namely Ray. With the "derailment," however, occurs "also the possibility of all emission or utterance" (AT, 83, 84), namely the possibility not only of hearing but also of speaking as another. This possibility opens the semantic structure for Ray and Marco both.

Then comes the oracular utterance: "You must look out for yourself." The imperative resembles that of "Know thyself," the inscription on the temple of Apollo at Delphi, where, according to Hellenistic accounts, the priestess of Apollo/Dionysus uttered oracles as vapor rose from the floor of the temple. In *Oedipus Rex*, the oracle speaks to the inhabitants of Thebes, another "plagued city" (266). After Marco stands and leaves, Ray is transported:

> Ray felt blown back in a wind-tunnel of grief and joy. He felt his hair streaming, his face pressed back, the fabric of his pants fluttering. In pop-song phrases he thought "this guy" had walked out on him, done him wrong, broken his heart—a heart he was happy to feel thumping again with sharp, wounded life. He was blown back on to the bed and he smiled and cried as he'd never yet allowed himself to cry over George, who'd just spoken to him through the least likely oracle.   (250)

At this moment, Ray's thinking is cast in terms of the clichés of popular song. The self, even in a moment of transformation, has to use an already given language. Yet, in challenging Ray's fantasy, Marco has opened the possibility of another meaning and prompts Ray to come to himself by completing the process of mourning denied him in New York. In the terms of Danforth's analysis of Greek ritual, the "liminal period" of mourning issues in a "conversation" in which Ray's body speaks with sobs, and George speaks by way of an echo (DR, 36, 117, 127).

In rural Greece, the exhumation of the bones of the dead confirms the mortality of the deceased while marking the return of the bereaved to the community. With this recognition, mourners are received back into the everyday life of the village—to the celebrations of rites of passage, to the bickering, to the struggles over property and sustenance. In Ray's case, the equivocal character of the oracle suspends the possibility of reunion. He invokes songs expressing the position of the wronged woman, neither the same nor decisively different. And the return to community remains outside the frame of the story, as do the referents of community, which appear to exist back in Manhattan. Hence the question of Ray's relation with Betty raised at the outset remains necessarily unanswered. Rather, a sense of apocalypse impends not only because Ray does not know what he will do but because he does not know how gays will respond to the devastating impact of AIDS; nor does he know the consequences for gays of the ways in which other communities will respond to the crisis.

Ray's reference to his trip as a "detour" (247) echoes the phrase that Danforth cites from Ricoeur about anthropology being "the comprehension of the self by the detour of the comprehension of the other" (DR, 6). White tracks the path by his use of the word "kid" and "kids," applicable to the young Cretans on *parea*, to Marco, to Ray and other adolescents of his youth near Findlay, Ohio, and, as a flattering misnomer, to Ray by older acquaintances in gay circles in New York City. Encountering the other in Marco is also an encounter with self. Finally, AIDS too is figured as "a kid": "The disease . . . seemed to him like a kid who's holding his nose underwater for an eerily long time but is bound to come crashing, gasping up for air" (219). This uncanny image suggests that like the "boyhood goals and values" that Ray would like to regain, he visualizes AIDS to be a part of himself. Looking back to his youth and forward to the prospect of untimely illness and death, Ray sees no obvious route into social existence, though White offers the possibility that Ray may turn to his long-neglected interest in writing. In contrast to the misuse of Ray's intelligence in "public relations" (211), White characterizes Ray's recuperation in terms of work: Ray thinks of Marco as a "co-worker," of "the high seriousness of the work they did together every night" (243). The achievement of intimacy leads to reflection, contemplation (another meaning of apocalypse), and writing (AT, 64). If separation is, as in Foucault's model of Greek love, necessary for Marco to come of age, writing may mark Ray's.

Had this story been written later in the 1980s, when the resilience of gay individuals and groups in the face of AIDS had become a familiar fact, White might have suggested a different route of return to self for Ray, in active participation in organized gay responses to AIDS. Ray is already an experienced care-giver as a result of George's long illness. Today many young gays know the term *intimacy* more in relation to caring for PWAs than in relation to sex. White's purpose in "An Oracle," however, is to remind his readers that sexual desire has been at the heart of the struggle for gay identity: "It is our sexuality that is contested, not the color of our hair. To build a political identity around this is therefore no mean feat" (SD, xviii–xix). In the 1983 introduction to *States of Desire*, White registers the solvent effect of both AIDS and poststructuralist theory on earlier ideas of gay identity. He also speaks of the hope, expressed in the first edition and again in 1983, that "gay men . . . will eventually lead us to a proper sense of sex as a pleasure or a kind of communication" (SD, xvii). This hope motivates his emphasis in "An Oracle" and validates his (and Ray's) use of the word *work* in relation to sexual intimacy.

Inadvertently, Derrida touches on one meaning of oracle in gay existence when he observes that the related Hebrew and Greek terms, *gala* and *apokalupto*, refer to "disclosure, discovery, uncovering, unveiling, the veil lifted from, the truth revealed about the thing: first of all, if we can say this, men's or women's genitals" (AT, 64). White's story draws to a degree on a conviction that intimacy between men can generate privileged insights into the meaning of existence. As in the case of Christian apocalypse as Derrida interprets it, the one disclosure is accompanied by another, that of divine being itself (AT, 64). In writing by subjects of masculine desire, this secondary disclosure is recognized to be figural or fictive, although gay theorists occasionally literalize the metaphor of divine presence—as when, for example, Arthur Evans, author of *The God of Ecstasy*, identifies Dionysus as "an expression of the sensual joys of life unrestrained by the state and unchanneled by the patriarchal family."[29]

White remains skeptical about this meaning of oracle (SD, xvii); none of his oracles refer to a literal unveiling of the genitals. He is more interested in the possibility that around intimacy gay men may devise new modes of sociality. By the end of the story, the oracle, "Take care of yourself," has been translated from its late capitalist meanings (look out for number one; get a good job) into a number of traditions of desire between men in Greece. In context, the most important of these is the ethical model described by Foucault, in which what mattered was "the use of pleasure" in "the care of the self." The subject stood in relation to bodily pleasures in a moral-aesthetic reflection that became a way of relating to self and other. Foucault observes that reflection and existence were usually at odds in Athenian pederasty. But the effort to bring both terms into alignment enabled a sense of self among male lovers. White's double glance, backward as well as forward, in the face of bereavement reminds gay men, in particular, of the need to continue this work.

NOTES

I have conducted workshops on White's story, along with material from Foucault and Derrida, on two occasions: in a session on theory and literary fictions of AIDS during the International Summer Institute for Semiotic and Structural Studies at the University of Toronto in June 1990; and at the University of Alberta at Edmonton in March 1991. I would like to thank Paul Brophy, Dave Pringle, Bill Whitla, and others who took part in the Toronto session and Glenn Burger, Jonathan Hart, Daphne Read, Stephen Slemon, Janice Williamson, and others who participated at Alberta.

1. Edmund White, "An Oracle," in Edmund White and Adam Mars-Jones, *The Darker Proof: Stories from a Crisis* (London: Faber and Faber, 1987). Where subsequent references to this work are contextually clear, page numbers are cited in the text.

2. Edmund White, "An Essay," *Tribe: An American Gay Journal* 1 (1990): 12.

3. Ibid.

4. Mary di Michele and Barbara Godard, "'Patterns of Their Own Particular Ceremonies': A Conversation in an Elegiac Mode," *Open Letter*, seventh series, 9 (1991): 43.

5. Michel Foucault, *The Use of Pleasure*, vol. 2 of *The History of Sexuality*, Robert Hurley, trans. (New York: Vintage, 1986). Subsequent references to this work will be cited in the text, using the abbreviation "UP."

6. Jacques Derrida, "Of an Apocalyptic Tone Recently Adopted in Philosophy," John P. Leavey, Jr., trans., *Semeia* 23 (1982): pp. 63–98. Subsequent references to this work will be cited in the text, using the abbreviation "AT."

7. Foucault says: "What I mean in fact is the development of power techniques oriented toward individuals and intended to rule them in a continuous and permanent way. If the state is the political form of a centralized and centralizing power, let us call pastorship the individualizing power" (*Politics, Philosophy, Culture: Interview and Other Writings, 1977–1984*, Alan Sheridan and others, trans., and Lawrence D. Kritzman, ed. [New York: Routledge, 1988], p. 59).

8. Michel Foucault, *An Introduction*, vol. 1 of *The History of Sexuality*, Robert Hurley, trans. (New York: Vintage, 1980), pp. 42–43.

9. Michel Foucault, "On the Genealogy of Ethics: An Overview of Work in Progress," in Paul Rabinow, ed., *The Foucault Reader* (New York: Pantheon, 1984), p. 343.

10. Foucault uses the term *Californian* to refer to a set of lifestyles of which gay lifestyles form a subset. He observes: "In the Californian cult of the self, one is supposed to discover one's true self, to separate it from that which might obscure or alienate it, to decipher its truth thanks to psychological or psychoanalytic science" (in Foucault, "Genealogy of Ethics," p. 362). The views of Arthur Evans, a gay activist in the Bay area whose writing I comment on later in the essay, fall within this sense of "Californian." Edward Said picks up the gay connotations of the term in criticism leveled at Foucault at the time of his death: "It was noticeable that he was more committed to exploring, if not indulging his appetite for travel, for different kinds of pleasure (symbolized by his frequent sojourns in California), for less and less frequent political positions" (quoted in Ed Cohen, "Foucauldian Necrologies: 'Gay' 'Politics'? Politically Gay?" *Textual Practice* 2 [1988]: 88. For a positive assessment of the importance to Foucault of California (and the existence of gay subcultures there), see Didier Eribon, *Michel Foucault*, Betsy Wing, trans. (Cambridge, Mass.: Harvard University Press, 1991), ch. 21.

11. White met Foucault in New York in 1981. After White moved to Paris in 1983, the two men became friends (letter from Edmund White to author, August 5, 1991).

12. Gayatri Chakravorty Spivak discusses the two projects in "Love Me, Love My Ombre, Elle," *diacritics* 14 (1984): 19–36.

13. I have in mind Derrida's references to fascism in Germany and Italy as well as to the concept of *Geschlecht*. See Jacques Derrida, "*Geschlecht* II: Heidegger's Hand," in John Sallis, ed., *Deconstruction and Philosophy: The Texts of Jacques Derrida* (Chicago: University of Chicago Press, 1987), pp. 69, 84.

14. Loring M. Danforth, *The Death Rituals of Rural Greece*, photography by Alexander Tsiarsas (Princeton: Princeton University Press, 1982). Subsequent references to this work will be cited in the text, using the abbreviation "DR."

15. In a special issue of *Open Letter*, dedicated to the memory of the Canadian poet Bronwen Wallace, Barbara Godard argues that the specifically male character of poetic

elegy has compelled female writers of elegy to devise new forms of writing that transgress the limits of traditional genres. Godard argues that this and analogous operations are a necessary part of the effort by women to invent connections between personal affiliations and meaning within "an affiliative secular order" (di Michele and Godard, "Patterns," p. 43).

16. The phrase "closeted gay," which has become familiar during the current debate over "outing" male homosexuals, is contradictory since the nominative, "gay," is usually predicated on the process of "coming out." The contradiction between living as a gay man and simultaneously being in the closet at work or in other contexts is, however, one that remains common in gay existence.

17. Arthur Evans, *The God of Ecstasy: Sex-Roles and the Madness of Dionysus* (New York: St. Martin's, 1988), pp. 66–68.

18. R. F. Willets, *Cretan Cults and Festivals* (London: Routledge and Kegan Paul, 1962), p. 112; Rodney Castleden, *The Knossos Labyrinth: A New View of the 'Palace of Minos' at Knossos* (New York: Routledge, 1990), ch. 10.

19. Ernst Curtius, *The History of Greece*, Adolphus William Ward, trans. (New York: Scribners, 1867), 1: 192–97.

20. Information provided by Bill Whitla.

21. David M. Halperin, *One Hundred Years of Homosexuality and Other Essays on Greek Love* (New York: Routledge, 1990), ch. 4.

22. Ray is an imperfect reader: The exhumation occurs five years after burial, not three.

23. Edmund White, *States of Desire: Travels in Gay America* (New York: Dutton, 1983). Subsequent references to this work will be cited in the text, using the abbreviation "SD."

24. Paul de Man, *Blindness and Insight: Essays in the Rhetoric of Contemporary Criticism* (New York: Oxford University Press, 1971), p. 9.

25. At the turn of the century, Baron von Gloeden, who did the same in Sicily, used the prints to promote his tourist hotel. See Tom Waugh, "Photography, Passion, and Power," *The Body Politic* (March 1984): 30.

26. See Barbara Godard, "Theorizing Feminist Discourse/Translation," *Tessera* 6 (1989): 42–53.

27. *Yassou* is a translation-effect within the passage, the rest of which is in an ethnographic mode.

28. Paul de Man, *Allegories of Reading: Figural Language in Rousseau, Nietzsche, Rilke, and Proust* (New Haven: Yale University Press, 1979), p. 198.

29. Evans, *God of Ecstasy*, p. 37.

Eloquence and Epitaph: Black Nationalism and the Homophobic Impulse in Responses to the Death of Max Robinson

Phillip Brian Harper

I Black Men and the AIDS Epidemic

From June 1981 through October 1991, 195,718 people in the United States were diagnosed as having Acquired Immune Deficiency Syndrome. Of that number, 44,330—or roughly 23 percent—occurred in males of African descent, although black males account for less than 6 percent of the total U.S. population. [1] It is common enough knowledge that black men constitute a disproportionate number of people with AIDS in this country—common in the sense that, whenever the AIDS epidemic achieves a new statistical milestone (as it did in the winter of 1991, when the number of AIDS-related deaths in the United States reached 100,000), the major media generally provide a demographic breakdown of the figures. Yet somehow the enormity of the morbidity and mortality rates for black men (like that for gay men of whatever racial identity) doesn't seem to register in the national consciousness as a cause for great concern. This is, no doubt, largely due to a general sense that the trajectory of the average African-American man's life must "naturally" be rather short, routinely subject to violent termination. And this sense, in turn, helps account for the fact that there has never been a case of AIDS that riveted public attention on the vulnerability of black men the way, for instance, the death of Rock Hudson shattered the myth of the invincible white male cultural hero.[2] This is not to say that no nationally known black male figure has died of AIDS-related causes, but rather that numerous and complex cultural factors conspire to prevent such deaths from effectively galvanizing AIDS activism in African-American communities. This essay represents an attempt to explicate several such factors that were operative in the case of one particular black man's bout with AIDS, and thus to indicate what further cultural intervention must take place if we hope to stem the ravages of AIDS in the African-American population.

II   The Sound of Silence

In December 1988, National Public Radio (NPR) broadcast a report on the death of Max Robinson, who was the first black news anchor on U.S. network television, staffing the Chicago desk of ABC's "World News Tonight" from 1978 to 1983. Robinson was one of 4,123 African-American men to die in 1988 of AIDS-related causes (of a nationwide total of 17,119 AIDS-related deaths),[3] but rather than focus on the death itself at this point, I want to examine two passages from the broadcast that, taken together, describe a problematic that characterizes AIDS in many black communities in the United States.

The first is a statement by a colleague at both ABC News and at WMAQ-TV in Chicago, where Robinson worked after leaving the network. Producer Bruce Rheins remembers being on assignment with Robinson on the streets of Chicago: "We would go out on the street a lot of times, doing a story . . . on the Southside or something . . . and I remember one time, this mother leaned down to her children, pointed, and said, 'That's Max Robinson. You learn how to speak like him.'" Immediately after this statement from Rheins, the NPR correspondent Cheryl Duvall informs us that "Robinson had denied the nature of his illness for months, but after he died . . . his friend Roger Wilkins said Robinson wanted his death to emphasize the need for AIDS awareness among black people."[4] These are the concluding words of the report, and as such they reproduce the epitaphic structure of Robinson's deathbed request, raising the question of just how well any of us is addressing the educational needs of black communities with respect to AIDS.

The juxtaposition of these two passages in the radio report is striking testimony to the power of two different phenomena that appear to be in direct contradiction. Bruce Rheins's statement underscores the im-

portance of Robinson's speech as an affirmation of black identity for the
benefit of the community from which he sprang. Cheryl Duvall's remarks,
on the other hand, implicate Robinson's denial that he had AIDS in a general silence regarding the effects of the epidemic among the African-
American population. In this essay, I will examine how speech and silence
actually interrelate to produce a discursive matrix that governs the cultural
significance of AIDS in black communities. Indeed, Max Robinson, news
anchor, inhabited a space defined by the overlap of at least two distinct
types of discourse that though often in conflict, intersect in a way that
makes discussion of Robinson's AIDS diagnosis—and of AIDS among
blacks generally—particularly difficult.

The apparent conflict between vocal affirmation and the peculiar silence effected through denial is already implicated in the nature of Max
Robinson's speech. There is a potential doubleness in the significance of
Robinson's "speaking" that the mother cited above urges upon her child as
an example to be emulated. It is clear that the reference is to Robinson's
exemplification of the articulate, authoritative presence ideally represented in the television news anchor—an exemplification noteworthy because Robinson was black. Bruce Rheins's comments illustrate this particularly well: "Max really was a symbol for a lot of people. . . . Here was
a very good-looking, well-dressed, and very obviously intelligent black
man giving the news in a straightforward fashion, and not on a black radio
station or a black TV station or on the black segment of a news report—he
was the anchorman."[5] Rheins's statement indicates the power of Robinson's verbal performance before the camera, for it is through this performance that Robinson's "intelligence," which Rheins emphasizes, is made
"obvious."

Other accounts of Robinson's tenure as a television news anchor recapitulate this reference. An article in the June 1989 issue of *Vanity Fair*
remembers Robinson for "his steely, unadorned delivery, precise diction,
and magical presence."[6] A *New York Times* obituary notes the "unforced,
authoritative manner" that characterized Robinson's on-air persona and
backs its claim with testimony from current ABC news anchor and Robinson's former colleague, Peter Jennings: "In terms of sheer performance,
Max was a penetrating communicator. He had a natural gift to look in the
camera and talk to people."[7] A 1980 *New York Times* reference asserts
that Robinson was "blessed with a commanding voice and a handsome appearance."[8] A posthumous "appreciation" in the *Boston Globe* describes
Robinson as "earnest and telegenic," noting that he "did some brilliant
reporting . . . and was a consummate newscaster."[9] James Snyder, news

director at WTOP-TV in Washington, D.C., where Robinson began his anchoring career, says that Robinson "had this terrific voice, great enunciation and phrasing. He was just a born speaker."[10] Elsewhere, Snyder succinctly summarizes Robinson's appeal, noting his "great presence on the air."[11]

All these encomia embody allusions to Robinson's verbal facility that must be understood as praise for his ability to speak articulate Received Standard English, which linguist Geneva Smitherman has identified as the dialect upon which "White America has insisted . . . as the price of admission into its economic and social mainstream."[12] The emphasis that commentators place on Robinson's "precise diction" or on his "great enunciation and phrasing" is an index of the general surprise evoked by his facility with the white bourgeois idiom considered standard in "mainstream" U.S. life, and certainly in television news. The black mother cited above surely recognizes the opportunity for social advancement inherent in this facility with standard English, and this is no doubt the benefit she has in mind for her children when she urges them to "speak like" Max Robinson.

However, although the mother's words can be interpreted as an injunction to speak "correctly," they might alternately be understood as a call for speech, per se—as encouragement to *speak out* like Max Robinson, to stand up for one's interests as a black person as Robinson did throughout his career. In this case, the import of her command is traceable to a black cultural nationalism that has waxed and waned in the U.S. since the mid-nineteenth century, but that, in the Black Power movement of the 1960s, underwent a revival that has continued to influence black cultural life in this country.[13] Geneva Smitherman notes the way this cultural nationalism has been manifested in black language and discourse, citing the movement "among writers, artists, and black intellectuals of the 1960s who deliberately wrote and rapped in the Black Idiom and sought to preserve its distinctiveness in the literature of the period" (11). Obviously, Max Robinson did not participate in this nationalistic strategy in his work as a network news anchor. Success in television newscasting, insofar as it depends upon one's conformity to models of behavior deemed acceptable by white bourgeois culture, largely precludes the possibility of one's exercising the "Black Idiom" and thereby manifesting a strong black consciousness in the broadcast context. We might say, then, that black people's successful participation in modes of discourse validated in mainstream culture—their facility with Received Standard English, for instance—actually implicates them in a profound *silence* about their African-American identity.

It is arguable, however, that Max Robinson, like all blacks who have achieved a degree of recognition in mainstream U.S. culture, actually played both sides of the behavioral dichotomy—between articulate verbal performance in the accepted standard dialect of the English language, and vocal affirmation of conscious black identity. [14] Though Robinson's performance before the cameras provided an impeccable image of bourgeois respectability that could easily be read as the erasure of consciousness of black identity, he was known for publicly affirming his interest in the sociopolitical factors that affect blacks in the United States, thus continually emphasizing his African-American identity.

For example, in February 1981, Robinson became the center of controversy when he reportedly told a college audience that the various network news departments, including ABC, discriminated against their black journalists, and that the news media in general constituted "a crooked mirror" through which "white America views itself." [15] Not only does Robinson's statement manifest semantically his consciousness of his own black identity, but the very form of the incident embodies an identifiably black cultural behavior. The allegations of network discrimination elicited a summons to the office of then-ABC News president Roone Arledge. After their meeting, Robinson said that "he had not meant to single out ABC for criticism," [16] thus performing a rhetorical backstep by which his criticism, though retracted, was effectively lodged and registered both by the public and by the network.

While this mode of protecting one's own interests is not unique to African-American culture, it does have a particular resonance within an African-American context. Specifically, Robinson's back-stepping strategy is a form of "loud-talking" or "louding"—a verbal device, common within many black-English-speaking communities, in which a person "says something of someone just loud enough for that person to hear, but indirectly, so he cannot properly respond," or so that, when the object of the remark *does* respond, "the speaker can reply to the effect, 'Oh, I wasn't talking to you.'" [17] Robinson's insistence that his remarks did not refer specifically to ABC News can be interpreted as a form of the disingenuous reply characteristic of loud-talking, thus locating his rhetorical strategy within the cultural context of black communicative patterns and underscoring his African-American identification.

Roone Arledge, in summoning Robinson to his office after the incident, made unusually explicit the suppression of African-American identity generally effected by the networks in their news productions. Such dramatic measures are not usually necessary, because potential manifestations of strong black cultural identification are normally subdued by blacks' very participation in the discursive conventions of the network newscast. [18] Thus, the more audible and insistent Max Robinson's televised performance in Received Standard English and in the white bourgeois idiom of the network newscast, the more secure the silence imposed upon the vocal black consciousness that he always threatened to display. Robinson's articulate speech before the cameras always implied a silencing of the African-American idiom.

Concomitant with the silencing in the network news context of black-affirmative discourse is the suppression of another aspect of black identity alluded to in the previous references to Max Robinson's on-camera performance. The emphasis these commentaries place on Robinson's articulateness is coupled with their simultaneous insistence on his physical attractiveness: Bruce Rheins's remarks on Robinson's "obvious intelligence" are accompanied by a reference to his "good looks"; Tony Schwartz's inventory of Robinson's assets notes both his "commanding voice" and his "handsome appearance"; Joseph Kahn's "appreciation" of Robinson cites his "brilliant reporting" as well as his "telegenic" quality. It seems impossible to comment on Robinson's success as a news anchor without noting simultaneously his verbal ability and his physical appeal.

Such commentary is not unusual in discussions of television newscasters, whose personal charms have taken on an increasing degree of importance since the early days of the medium. Indeed, Schwartz's 1980 *New York Times* article entitled "Are TV Anchormen Merely Performers?"—intended as a critique of the degree to which television news is conceived as entertainment—actually underscores the importance of a newscaster's physical attractiveness to a broadcast's success. By the late 1980s, that importance has become a truism of contemporary culture, assimilated into the popular consciousness, through the movie *Broadcast News*, for instance. [19] In the case of a black man, such as Max Robinson, however, discussions of a news anchor's "star quality" become potentially problematic and, consequently, extremely complex, because such a quality is founded upon an implicitly acknowledged "sex appeal," the concept of which has always been highly charged with respect to black men in the United States.

In the classic text on the subject, Calvin C. Hernton has argued that the black man has historically been perceived as the bearer of a bestial sexuality, as the savage "walking phallus" that poses a constant threat to an idealized white womanhood and thus to the whole social order. [20] To the extent that this is true, for white patriarchal institutions such as the mainstream media to note the physical attractiveness of any black man is for them to unleash the very beast that potentially threatens their power. Max Robinson's achievement of a professional, public position that mandates the deployment of a certain rhetoric—that of the news anchor's attractive and telegenic persona—thus also raises the problem of taming the threatening black male sexuality that that rhetoric conjures up.

This taming is once again achieved through Robinson's articulate verbal performance, references to which routinely accompany acknowledgments of his physical attractiveness. In commentary on white newscasters, paired references to their physical appeal and their rhetorical skill serve merely to defuse accusations that television journalism is superficial and image-oriented. In Robinson's case, however, the acknowledgment of his articulateness also serves to absorb the threat of his sexuality that is raised in references to his physical attractiveness. Just as Robinson's conformity to the "rules" of standard English language performance suppresses the possibility of his articulating a radical identification with African-American culture, it also, in attesting to his refinement and civility, actually *domesticates* the threatening physicality that itself *must* be alluded to in conventional liberal accounts of his performance as a news anchor. James Snyder's reference to Robinson's "great presence" is a most stunning example of such an account, for it neatly conflates and thus simultaneously acknowledges both Robinson's *physical* person (in the tradition of commentary on network news personalities) and his virtuosity in standard *verbal* performance in such a way that the latter mitigates the threat posed by the former.

Max Robinson's standard English speech, then, serves not only to suppress black culturolinguistic forms that might disrupt the white bourgeois aspect of network news but also to keep in check the black male sexuality that threatens the social order that the news media represent.[21] Ironically, in this latter function, white bourgeois discourse seems to share an objective with forms of black discourse, which themselves work to suppress certain threatening elements of black male sexuality, resulting in a strange reaction to Max Robinson's death in African-American communities.

III   Homophobia in African-American Discourse

Whether it is interpreted as a reference to his facility in Received Standard English or as a reference to his repeated attempts to vocalize the grievances of blacks against their sociopolitical status in the United States, to "speak like Max Robinson" is simultaneously to silence discussion of the various possibilities of black male sexuality. We have seen how an emphasis on Robinson's facility in white-oriented discourse defuses the threat of rampant black male sexuality that constitutes so much of the sexuopolitical structure of U.S. society. Indeed, some middle-class blacks have colluded in this defusing of black sexuality, attempting to explode whites' stereotypes of blacks as oversexed by stifling discussion of black sexuality generally.[22] At the same time, the other tradition from which Max Robinson's speech derives meaning also suppresses discussion about specific aspects of black male sexuality that are threatening to the black male image.

In her book on "the language of black America," Geneva Smitherman rather unselfconsciously cites examples of black discourse that illustrate this point. For instance, in a discussion of black musicians' adaptation of themes from the African-American oral tradition, Smitherman mentions the popular early 1960s recording of "Stagger Lee," based on a traditional narrative folk poem. The hero for whom the narrative is named is, as Smitherman puts it, "a fearless, mean dude," so that "it became widely fashionable [in black communities] to refer to oneself as 'Stag,' as in . . . 'Don't mess wif me, cause I ain't no fag, uhm Stag.'"[23] Notable here is not merely the homophobia manifested in the "rap" laid down by the black "brother" imagined to be speaking this line, but also that the rap itself, the very verbal performance, as Smitherman points out, serves as the evidence that the speaker is indeed *not* a "fag"; verbal facility becomes proof of one's conventional masculinity and thus silences discussion of one's possible homosexuality.[24]

This point touches upon a truism in studies of black discourse. Smitherman herself implies the testament to masculine prowess embodied in the black rap, explaining that, "While some raps convey social and cultural information, others are used for conquering foes and women."[25] She further acknowledges the "power" with which the spoken word is imbued in the African-American tradition (as in others), especially insofar as it is employed in masculine "image-making," through braggadocio and other highly self-assertive strategies.[26] Indeed, a whole array of these verbal strategies for establishing a strong masculine image can be identified in the contemporary phenomenon of rap music, a form indigenous to black male culture, though increasingly appropriated and transformed by members of other social groups, notably black women.[27]

If verbal facility is considered an identifying mark of masculinity in certain African-American contexts, however, this is only when it is demonstrated specifically through use of the vernacular. Indeed, a too-evident facility in the standard white idiom can quickly identify one not as a strong black man but rather as a white-identified Uncle Tom who therefore must also be weak, effeminate, and probably a "fag." This homophobic identification, reflecting as it does powerful cross-class hostilities, is certainly not unique to African-American culture. Its imbrication with questions of racial identity, however, compounds its potency in the African-American context. Simply put, within some African-American communities the "professional" or "intellectual" black male inevitably endangers his status both as black and as male whenever he shows a facility with Received Standard English—a facility upon which his very identity as a professional or an intellectual in the larger society is founded in the first place.

Max Robinson was not the first black man to face this dilemma;[28] a decade or so before he emerged on network television, a particularly influential group of black writers attempted to negotiate the problem by incorporating into their work the semantics of "street" discourse, thereby establishing an intellectual practice that was both "black" enough and virile enough to bear the weight of a stridently nationalist agenda. Thus, a strong Stagger Lee-type identification can be found in the poem "Don't Cry, Scream," by Haki Madhubuti (Don L. Lee):

> swung on a faggot who politely
> scratched his ass in my presence.
> he smiled broken teeth stained from
> his over-used tongue, fisted-face.
> teeth dropped in tune with ray
> charles singing "yesterday."[29]

Here the scornful language of the poem itself recapitulates the homophobic violence that it commemorates (or invites us to imagine as having occurred), the two together attesting to the speaker's aversion to homosexuality and, thus, to his own unquestionable masculinity.

Though it is striking, the violent hostility evident in this piece is not unusual among the revolutionist poems of the Black Arts Movement. Much of the work by the Black Arts Poets is characterized by a violent language that seems wishfully conceived of as potent and performative—as capable, in itself, of wreaking destruction upon the white establishment to which the Black Power movement is opposed.[30] What is important to note, beyond the rhetoric of violence, is the way that rhetoric is conceived as part and parcel of a black nationalism to which all sufficiently proud African-Americans must subscribe. Nikki Giovanni, for instance, urges, "Learn to kill niggers / Learn to be Black men," indicating the necessity of cathartic violence to the transformation of blacks from victims into active subjects, and illustrating the degree to which black masculinity functions as the rhetorical stake in much of the Black Arts poetry by both men and women.[31] To the extent that such rhetoric is considered integral to the cultural-nationalist strategy of Black Power politics, a violent homophobia, too, is necessarily implicated in this particular nationalistic position, which since the late 1960s has filtered throughout black communities as a major influence in African-American culture.

Consequently, Max Robinson was put in a very difficult position with respect to talking about his AIDS diagnosis. Robinson's reputation was based on his articulate outspokenness; however, as we have seen, that very well-spokenness derived its power within two different modes of discourse that, though they are sometimes at odds, both work to suppress issues of sexuality that are implied in any discussion of AIDS.[32] The white bourgeois cultural context in which Robinson derived his status as an authoritative figure in the mainstream news media must always keep a vigilant check on black male sexuality, which is perceived to be threatening generally. (It is assisted in this latter task by a moralistic black middle class that seeks to explode notions of black hypersexuality.) At the same time, the African-American cultural context to which Robinson appealed for his status as a paragon of black pride and self-determination embodies an ethic that precludes sympathetic discussion of black male homosexuality.

However rapidly the demography of AIDS in this country may be shifting as more and more people who are not gay men become infected with HIV, the historical and cultural conditions surrounding the development of the epidemic ensure its ongoing association with male homosexuality. It is thus not surprising that the latter should emerge as a topic of discussion in any consideration of Max Robinson's death. The apparent *inevitability* of that emergence (and the degree to which the association between AIDS and male homosexuality would threaten Robinson's reputation and become discursively problematic, given the contexts in which his public persona was created) is dramatically illustrated in the January 9, 1989, issue of *Jet* magazine, the black-oriented weekly. That issue of *Jet* contains an obituary of Max Robinson very similar to those in the *New York Times* and other nonblack media, noting Robinson's professional achievements and his controversial tenure at ABC News, alluding to the "tormented" nature of his life as a symbol of black success, and citing his secrecy about his AIDS diagnosis and his wish that his death be used as the occasion to educate blacks about AIDS. The *Jet* obituary also notes that "the main victims of the disease have been intravenous drug users and homosexuals," leaving open the question of Robinson's relation to either of these categories.[33]

Printed right next to Robinson's obituary in the same issue of *Jet* is a notice of another AIDS-related death, that of the popular disco singer Sylvester. Sylvester's obituary, however, offers an interesting contrast to Robinson's, for it identifies Sylvester, in its first sentence, as "the flamboyant homosexual singer whose high-pitched voice and dramatic on-stage costumes propelled him to the height of stardom on the disco music scene during the late 1970s." The piece goes on to indicate the openness with which Sylvester lived as a gay man, noting that he "first publicly acknowledged he had AIDS at the San Francisco Gay Pride March last June [1988], which he attended in a wheelchair with the People With AIDS group," and quoting his recollection of his first sexual experience, at age seven, with an adult male evangelist: "You see, I was a queen even back then, so it didn't bother me. I rather liked it."[34]

Obviously, a whole array of issues is raised by Sylvester's obituary and its juxtaposition with that of Max Robinson (not the least of which has to do with the complicated phenomenon of sex between adults and children). Most pertinent for discussion here, however, is the difference between *Jet*'s treatments of Sylvester's and Max Robinson's sexualities, and the factors that account for that difference. It is clear, I think, that Sylvester's public persona emerged from contexts different from those that produced Max Robinson. If it is true that, as *Jet* puts it, "the church was . . . the setting for Sylvester's first homosexual experience," it is also true that "Sylvester learned to sing in churches in South Los Angeles and went on to perform at gospel conventions around the state." That is to say that the church choir context in which Sylvester was groomed for a singing career has stereotypically served as a locus in which young black men both discover and sublimate their homosexuality, and also as a conduit to a world of professional entertainment generally conceived as "tolerant," if not downright encouraging, of diverse sexualities. In Sylvester's case, this was particularly true, since he was able to help create a disco culture characterized by a fusion of elements from black and gay communities and in which he and others could thrive as openly gay men. Thus, the black-church context, though ostensibly hostile to homosexuality and gay identity, nevertheless has traditionally provided a means by which black men can achieve a sense of themselves as homosexual and even, in cases such as Sylvester's, expand that sense into a gay-affirmative public persona.[35]

On the other hand, the public figure of Max Robinson, as we have seen, is cut from entirely different cloth, formed in the intersection of discursive contexts that do not allow for the expression of black male homosexuality in any recognizable form. The discursive bind constituted by Robinson's status both as a conventionally successful media personality and as exemplar of black male self-assertion and racial consciousness left him with no alternative to the manner in which he dealt with his diagnosis in the public forum—shrouding the nature of his illness in a secrecy that he intended to be broken only after his death, with the posthumous acknowledgement that he had had AIDS. Consequently, obituarists and commentators on Robinson's death are faced with the "problem" of how to address issues relating to Robinson's sexuality—to his possible *homo*sexuality—the result being a large body of wrong-minded commentary that actually hinders the educational efforts Max Robinson supposedly intended to endorse.

Because most accounts of Robinson's death do not mention the possibility of his homosexuality, it would be a mistake to think that it is not a problem to be reckoned with. On the contrary, since the discursive contexts in which Max Robinson derived his power as a public figure function to prevent discussion of black male homosexuality, the silence regarding the topic that characterizes most of the notices of Robinson's death actually marks the degree to which the possibility of black male homosexuality is worried over and considered problematic. The instances in which the possibility of Robinson's homosexuality *does* explicitly figure actually serve as proof of the anxiety that founds the more usual silence on the subject. A chronological look at a few commentaries on Robinson's death will illustrate especially how, over time, the need to quell anxiety about the possibility of Robinson's homosexuality becomes increasingly desperate and thus increasingly undermines the educational efforts that his death was supposed to occasion.

In the two weeks after Robinson died, there appeared in *Newsweek* magazine an obituary that, once again, included the obligatory references to Robinson's "commanding" on-air presence, to his attacks on racism in the media, and to the psychic "conflict" he suffered that led him to drink.[36] In addition to rehearsing this standard litany, however, the *Newsweek* obituary also emphasized that "even [Robinson's] family . . . don't know how he contracted the disease." The reference to the general ignorance as to how Robinson became infected with HIV—the virus believed to cause the suppressed immunity that underlies AIDS—leaves open the possibility that Robinson engaged in "homosexual activity" that put him at risk for infection, just as the *Jet* notice leaves unresolved the possibility that he was homosexual or an IV-drug user. Yet the invocation in the *Newsweek* piece of Robinson's "family," with all its conventional heterosexist associations, simultaneously indicates the anxiety that the possibility of Robinson's homosexuality generally produces and constitutes an attempt to redeem Robinson from the unsavory implications of his AIDS diagnosis.

The subtlety of the *Newsweek* strategy for dealing with the possibility of Robinson's homosexuality gives way to a more direct approach by Jesse Jackson, in an interview broadcast during an NPR series on AIDS and blacks. [37] Responding to charges by black AIDS activists that he missed a golden opportunity to educate blacks about AIDS by neglecting to speak out about modes of HIV transmission soon after Robinson's death, Jackson provided this statement:

> Max shared with my family and me that he had the AIDS virus, but that it did not come from homosexuality, it came from promiscuity. . . . And now we know that the number one transmission [factor] for AIDS is not sexual contact, it's drugs, and so the crises of drugs and needles and AIDS are connected, as well as AIDS and promiscuity are connected. And all we can do is keep urging people not to isolate this crisis by race, or by class, or by sexual preference, but in fact to observe the precautionary measures that have been advised, on the one hand, and keep urging more money for research immediately because it's an international health crisis and it's a killer disease. [38]

A number of things are notable about this statement. First of all, like the *Newsweek* writer, Jackson is careful to reincorporate the discussion of Robinson's AIDS diagnosis into the context of the nuclear family, emphasizing that Robinson shared his secret with Jackson *and his family* and thereby attempting to mitigate the effects of the association of AIDS with male homosexuality. Second, Jackson invokes the problematic and completely unhelpful concept of "promiscuity," wrongly opposing it to homosexuality (and thus implicitly equating it with heterosexuality) in such a way that he actually appears to be endorsing it over that less legitimate option, contrary to what he must intend to convey about the dangers of unprotected sex with multiple partners. Since he does not actually mention safer sex practices, he thereby implies that it is "promiscuity," per se that puts people at risk of contracting HIV, when it is, rather, unprotected sex with however few partners that constitutes risky behavior. Third, by identifying intravenous drug use over risky sexual behavior as the primary means of HIV transmission, Jackson shows blindness to his own insight about the interrelatedness of various factors in the phenomenon of AIDS—for unprotected sexual activity is often part and parcel of the drug culture (especially that of crack) in which transmission of HIV thrives, because sex is commonly exchanged for access to drugs in that context.[39] Finally, Jackson's sense of "all we can do" to prevent AIDS is woefully inadequate: to "urge people to observe the precautionary measures that have been advised" obviously presupposes that everyone already knows what those precautionary measures are, for Jackson himself does not outline them in his statement; to demand more money for research is crucial, but it does not enable people to protect themselves from HIV in the present; and to resist conceptualizing AIDS as endemic to one race, class, or sexual orientation is of extreme importance (though it is equally important to recognize the relative degrees of interest that different constituencies have in the epidemic), but in the context of Jackson's statement, this strategy for preventing various social groups from being stigmatized through their association with AIDS is used merely to protect Max Robinson in particular from speculation that his bout with AIDS was related to homosexual sex. Indeed, Jackson's entire statement seeks to clear Max Robinson from any suspicion of homosexuality, and his intense focus on this homophobic endeavor hinders his attempts to make factual statements about the nature of HIV transmission.

Jackson is also implicated in the third media response to Robinson's death that I want to examine, a response that, like those discussed above, represents an effort to silence discussion of the possibility of Max Robinson's homosexuality. In his June 1989 *Vanity Fair* article, Peter J. Boyer reports on the eulogy Jackson delivered at the Washington, D.C., memorial service for Max Robinson. Boyer cites Jackson's quotation of Robinson's deathbed request: "He said, 'I'm not sure and know not where [sic], but even on my dying bed . . . let my predicament be a source of education to our people.'" Boyer then asserts that "two thousand people heard Jesse Jackson keep the promise he'd made to Robinson . . . : 'It was not homosexuality,' [Jackson] told them, 'but promiscuity,'" implicitly letting people know that Robinson "got AIDS from a woman."[40] Apparently, then, the only deathbed promise Jackson kept was the one he made to ensure that people would not think Robinson was gay; no information about how HIV is transmitted or about how such transmission can be prevented has escaped his lips in connection with the death of Max Robinson, though Peter Boyer evidently has been fooled into believing that Jackson's speech constituted just such substantive information. This is not surprising, since Boyer's article is nothing more than an anxious effort to convince us of Max Robinson's heterosexuality, as if that were the crucial issue. Boyer's piece mentions Robinson's three marriages; it comments extensively on his "well-earned" reputation as an "inveterate womanizer" and emphasizes his attractiveness to women, quoting one male friend as saying, "He could walk into a room and you could just hear the panties drop," and a woman acquaintance as once telling a reporter, "Don't forget to mention he has fine thighs"; it notes that "none of Robinson's friends believe that he was a homosexual"; and it cites Robinson's own desperate attempt "to compose a list of women whom he suspected as possible sources of his disease," as though to provide written corroboration of his insistence to a friend, "But I'm not gay."

From early claims, then, that "even Robinson's family" had no idea how he contracted HIV, there developed an authoritative scenario in which Robinson's extensive heterosexual affairs were common knowledge and that posits his contraction of HIV from a female sex partner as a near certainty. It seems that, after Robinson's death, a whole propaganda machine was put into operation to establish a suitable account of his contraction of HIV and of his bout with AIDS, the net result of which was to preclude the effective AIDS education that Robinson reputedly wanted his death to occasion, as the point he supposedly intended to make became lost in a homophobic shuffle to "fix" his sexual orientation and to construe his death in inoffensive terms.

To ensure that this essay not become absorbed in that project, then, which would deter us from the more crucial task of understanding how to combat the AIDS epidemic, it is important for me to state flat out that I have no idea whether Max Robinson's sex partners were male or female or both. I explicitly acknowledge my ignorance on this matter because to do so, I think, can reopen sex in all its manifestations as a primary consideration as we review modes of HIV transmission in African-American communities. Such a move is crucial because the same homophobic impulse that informs efforts to establish Max Robinson's heterosexuality is also implicated in a general reluctance to provide detailed information about sexual transmission of HIV in black communities. Indeed, a deep silence about the details of such transmission has characterized almost all of what passes for government-sponsored AIDS education efforts throughout the United States.

IV   Sins of Omission: Inadequacy in AIDS Education Programs

Even the slickest, most visible print and television ads promoting awareness about AIDS consistently thematize a silence that has been a major obstacle to effective AIDS education in communities of color. Notices distributed around the time of Max Robinson's death used an array of celebrities—from Ruben Blades to Patti Labelle—who encouraged people to "get the facts" about AIDS, but didn't offer any, merely referring readers elsewhere for substantive information on the syndrome.[41] A bitter testimony to the inefficacy of this ad campaign is offered by a thirty-one-year-old black woman interviewed in the NPR series on AIDS and blacks. "Sandra" contracted HIV through unprotected heterosexual sex; the child conceived in that encounter died at ten months of an AIDS-related illness. In her interview, "Sandra" reflects on her lack of knowledge about AIDS at the time she became pregnant:

> I don't remember hearing anything about AIDS until either the year that I was pregnant, which would have been 1986, or the year after I had her; but I really believe it was when I was pregnant with her because I always remember saying, "I'm going to write and get that information," because the only thing that was on TV was to write or call the 1-800 number to get information, and I always wanted to call and get that pamphlet, not knowing that I was going to have firsthand information. I didn't know how it was transmitted. I didn't know that it was caused by a virus. I didn't know that [AIDS] stood for "Acquired Immune Deficiency Syndrome." I didn't know any of that.[42]

By 1986, when Sandra believes she first began even to hear about AIDS, the epidemic was at least five years old.

Even today, response to AIDS in black communities is characterized by a profound silence regarding actual sexual practices, either heterosexual or homosexual, largely because of the suppression of talk about sexuality generally and about male homosexuality in particular that is enacted in black communities through the discourses that constitute them. Additionally, this continued silence is *enabled* by the ease with which the significance of sexual transmission of HIV can be elided beneath the admittedly massive (but also, to many minds, more "acceptable") problem of IV-drug-related HIV transmission that is endemic in some black communities. George Bellinger, Jr., a "minority outreach" worker at Gay Men's Health Crisis, the New York City AIDS service organization, recounted for the NPR series "the horrible joke that used to go around [in black communities] when AIDS first started: 'There's good news and bad news. The bad news is I have AIDS, the good news is I'm an IV drug user.'"[43] This joke indicates the degree to which intravenous drug use can serve as a shield against the implications of male homosexuality that are always associated with AIDS and that hover threateningly over any discussion of sexual transmission of HIV. This phenomenon occurs even in the NPR series itself. For all its emphasis on the need for black communities to "recognize homosexuality and bisexuality" within them, and despite its inclusion of articulate black lesbians and gay men in its roster of interviewees, the radio series still elides sexual transmission of HIV beneath a focus on intravenous drug use. One segment in particular illustrates this point.

In an interview broadcast on "Morning Edition," April 4, 1989, Harold Jaffe, from the federal Centers for Disease Control, makes a crucial point regarding gay male sexual behavior in the face of the AIDS epidemic: "The studies that have come out saying gay men have made substantial changes in their behavior are true, but they're true mainly for white, middle-class, exclusively gay men." As correspondent Richard Harris reported, however, Jaffe "doesn't see that trend among black gays." Harris notes that "Jaffe has been studying syphilis rates, which are a good measure of safe sex practices." Jaffe himself proclaims his discoveries: "We find very major decreases [in the rate of syphilis] in white gay men, and either no change or even increases in Hispanic and black gay men, suggesting that they have not really gotten the same behavioral message." Harris continues: "White gay men have changed their behavior to such an extent that experts believe the disease has essentially peaked for them, so as those numbers gradually subside, minorities will make up a growing proportion of AIDS cases."

Up to this point, Harris's report has focused on important differences between the rates of syphilis and HIV transmission among gay white men and among black and Latino gay men, suggesting the inadequacy of the educational resources available to gay men of color. As his rhetoric shifts, however, to refer to the risk that *all* members of "minority" groups face, regardless of their sexual identification, the risky behaviors on which he focuses also change. After indicating the need for gay men of color to change their sexual behavior in the same way that white gay men have, and after a pause of a couple beats that would conventionally indicate the introduction of some narrative into the report to illustrate the point being made, Harris segues into a story about Rosina, a former intravenous drug user with AIDS, and to a claim that "about the only way to stop AIDS from spreading in the inner city is to help addicts get off of drugs."

Thus, Harris's early focus on AIDS among black and Latino gay men serves merely as a bridge to discussion of IV drug use as the primary factor in the spread of AIDS in communities of color. Moreover, the diversity of those communities is effaced through the conventional euphemistic reference to the "inner city"; because it disregards class differences among blacks and Latinos, this rhetoric falsely homogenizes the concerns of people of color and glosses over the complex nature of HIV transmission among them, which, just as with whites, implicates drug use *and* unprotected sexual activity as high-risk behaviors. The ease with which middle-class blacks can construe IV drug use as a problem of communities completely removed from their everyday lives (and as unrelated to high-risk sexual activity in which they may engage) makes an exclusive emphasis on IV-drug-related HIV transmission among blacks actually detrimental to effective AIDS education.

To meet the challenge that Max Robinson posed as his dying hope—efforts at *comprehensive* AIDS education in black communities—we must consider programs that utilize the logic manifested in Richard Harris's NPR report as inadequate. The inadequacy of such efforts is rooted, as I have suggested, in a reluctance to discuss issues of black sexuality that is based simultaneously on whites' stereotyped notions (often defensively adopted by blacks themselves) about the need to suppress black (male) sexuality generally, and on the strictness with which traditional forms of black discourse preclude the possibility of the discussion of black male homosexuality specifically. Indeed, these very factors necessitated Max Robinson's peculiar response to his own AIDS diagnosis—initial denial and posthumous acknowledgment.

I suggested at the beginning of this essay that Robinson's final acknowledgement of his AIDS diagnosis—in his injunction that we use his death as the occasion to increase blacks' awareness about AIDS—performs a sort of epitaphic function. As the final words of the deceased that constitute an implicit warning to others not to repeat his mistakes, Robinson's request has been promulgated through the media with such a repetitive insistence that it might as well have been literally etched in stone. The repetitive nature of the request ought itself to serve as a warning to us, however, since repetition can recapitulate the very silence that it is meant to overcome. As Debra Fried has said about the epitaph, it is both:

> silent and . . . repetitious; [it] refuses to speak, and yet keeps on saying the same thing: refusal to say anything different is tantamount to a refusal to speak. Repetition thus becomes a form of silence. . . . According to the fiction of epitaphs, death imposes on its victims an endless verbal task: to repeat without deviation or difference the answer to a question that, no matter how many times it prompts the epitaph to the same silent utterance, is never satisfactorily answered. [44]

In the case of Max Robinson's death, the pertinent question is "How can transmission of HIV and thus AIDS-related death be prevented?" The burden of response at this point is not on the deceased, however, but on us. We must formulate educational programs that offer comprehensive information on the prevention of HIV transmission. In order to do so, we must break the rules of the various discourses through which black life in the United States has traditionally been articulated. A less radical strategy cannot induce the widespread behavioral changes necessary in the face of AIDS, and our failure in this task would mean sacrificing black people to an epidemic that is enabled, paradoxically, by the very discourses that shape our lives.

NOTES

In addition to the editors of this volume, the following people assisted me in the preparation of this article by providing statistical information, directing me to source materials, or commenting on early drafts of the essay: Harold Dufour-Anderson, David Halperin, Paul Morrison, Julie Rioux, and Thom Whitaker. A slightly different version of this article appeared in Social Text *23 (1991); 68–86, and an earlier version of this paper was presented at the conference on "Nationalisms and Sexualities," held at the Center for Literary and Cultural Studies, Harvard University, June 1989.*

1. Centers for Disease Control, *HIV/AIDS Surveillance Report*, October 1991, table 5, p. 10.

2. At least not until recently. On November 7, 1991, while this volume was in preparation, black pro basketball star Earvin "Magic" Johnson announced that he is infected with HIV, thus precipitating what is arguably the most dramatic development to date in the public consciousness regarding AIDS (see the *New York Times*, November 8, 1991, pp. A1, and B11-13). As startling as Johnson's disclosure has been, however, it makes no substantive difference for the argument that I present here, largely because Johnson's status as a sports hero—which founds the tremendous impact his announcement has had—both places him outside the specific discursive context under consideration in this essay and powerfully demonstrates my implicit point about the way United States culture manages black men's physicality in order to defuse its threat to the dominant social order.

3. National Center for Health Statistics, *Health, United States, 1989* (Hyattsville, Md.: Public Health Service, 1990), table 3, p. 151.

4. From a broadcast on "All Things Considered," National Public Radio, December 20, 1988.

5. Ibid.

6. Peter J. Boyer, "The Light Goes Out," *Vanity Fair* (June 1989): 70.

7. Jeremy Gerard, "Max Robinson, 49, First Black to Anchor Network News, Dies," *New York Times*, December 21, 1988, p. D19.

8. Tony Schwartz, "Are TV Anchormen Merely Performers?" *New York Times*, July 27, 1980, sec. 2, pp. 1, 27.

9. Joseph P. Kahn, "Max Robinson: Tormented Pioneer," *Boston Globe*, December 21, 1988, pp. 65, 67.

10. Boyer, "The Light Goes Out," p. 72.

11. "Max Robinson, 49, First Black Anchor for Networks; of AIDS Complications," *Boston Globe*, December 21, 1988, p. 51.

12. Geneva Smitherman, *Talkin and Testifyin: The Language of Black America* (Boston: Houghton Mifflin, 1977), p. 12.

13. For an overview of the various black nationalist movements that have emerged in the U.S. since the late eighteenth century, see John H. Bracey, Jr., August Meier, and Elliott Rudwick, eds., *Black Nationalism in America* (Indianapolis: Bobbs-Merrill, 1970). It should be noted here that the different nationalisms (cultural, revolutionary, and economic, for instance) are not always considered as sharing a common objective. See, for example, Linda Harrison's commentary on the inadequacy of cultural nationalism with respect to a black revolutionary agenda ("On Cultural Nationalism," in Philip S. Foner, ed., *The Black Panthers Speak* [New York: Lippincott, 1970], pp. 151–53). Nevertheless, it seems to me that a generalized cultural nationalism, more than any other form, has been a pervasive influence in African-American life since the 1960s, and it is to this brand of nationalism that I allude repeatedly in this essay.

14. This dichotomy corresponds, of course, to that described by W. E. B. DuBois in his classic discussion of blacks' "double-consciousness"—the effect of their inability to reconcile their blackness and their "American" identity. See *The Souls of Black Folk* (1903; reprint, New York: Signet/New American Library, 1969), especially chapter 1, "Of Our Spiritual Strivings."

15. Tony Schwartz, "Robinson of ABC News Quoted as Saying Network Discriminates," *New York Times*, February 11, 1981, p. C21; see also Gerard, "Max Robinson," December 21, 1988.

16. Gerard, "Max Robinson," December 21, 1988.

17. Roger D. Abrahams, *Talking Black* (Rowley, Mass.: Newbury House, 1976), pp. 19, 54; see also Claudia Mitchell-Kernan, "Signifying, Loud-Talking and Marking," in Thomas Kochman, ed., *Rappin' and Stylin' Out: Communication in Urban Black America* (Urbana: University of Illinois Press, 1972), pp. 315–35.

18. An additional example of the networks' explicit suppression of African-American identity involves black newsman Ed Bradley, a correspondent on the CBS news program "60 Minutes." Bradley sent "60 Minutes" producer Don Hewitt into a panic when he decided to change his name to Shaheeb Sha Hab, thereby reflecting his allegiance with Islamic black nationalism. Hewitt was able to convince Bradley not to take this step and thus to keep black nationalist politics out of the scope of the "60 Minutes" cameras. See Don Hewitt, *Minute by Minute* (New York: Random House, 1985), p. 170.

19. This development may indicate a perverse "feminization" of the television news anchor insofar as an insistent emphasis on physical appearance to the neglect of professional accomplishment has historically characterized women's experience in the public sphere. An indication of the extent to which this tyranny of "beauty" can now shape mass cultural phenomena is provided in the field of contemporary pop music. Since the advent of music video in the 1980s, the importance of musical acts' visual appeal has increased to such a degree that models are sometimes hired to lip sync and otherwise "visualize" a song that is actually sung by someone else outside the audience's range of views; the most notorious such case involved the male duo Milli Vanilli. But the mere fact that men are increas-

ingly subject to the imperative of "sex appeal" by no means implies that they now suffer from a social oppression parallel or equal to that borne by women.

20. Calvin C. Hernton, *Sex and Racism in America* (New York: Doubleday, 1965). As support for his argument, Hernton cites numerous instances of white-perpetrated violence against black men perceived to embody a threat to white femininity. Though such instances may be much less frequent now than in 1965, a structure of sociosexual relations that confers an inordinately threatening status upon black men remains very firmly in place in the United States. Consider, for instance, the intense response to the April 1989 attack by a group of black youths on a white woman jogger in Central Park. This response, like the incident itself, was highly overdetermined and too complex to analyze here, but it culminated in a widely publicized call by real-estate magnate Donald Trump for application of the death penalty. Numerous people suggested that the intensity of the response was a function of the racial and gender identities of the parties involved and that a different configuration (white attackers or black or male victim) would not have produced the same degree of outrage or media coverage. See Craig Wolff, "Youths Rape Jogger on Central Park Road," *New York Times*, April 21, 1989, pp. B1, B3; and the full-page display ad paid for by Donald Trump, *New York Times*, May 1, 1989, p. A13. See also the daily coverage provided by the *Times* during the period framed by these two editions of the paper.

21. I want to emphasize that I consider this management of sexuality to be an operation that the culture continually performs upon each individual black male. The very appearance of a black man on the network newscast may seem to indicate that *he*, at least, has been judged safe for exposure before the bourgeois white audience, and his use of articulate and "objective" journalistic language would then serve merely as a sort of seal of his innocuousness. This could only be true, though, if the recognizably "professional" black male were generally seen as distinct from the mass of black men whose presence on U.S. streets is routinely considered a threat to the well-being of the larger community. As any of us who have been detained and questioned by white urban police for no reason can attest, however, this is not the case. Just as every black man might suddenly manifest an ideological challenge that would certainly have to be kept in check (by a Roone Arledge or a Don Hewitt, for instance, in the broadcast news context), so too does every black man represent an ongoing threat of untamed sexuality that must continually be defused. Thus Max Robinson's expert use of Received Standard English is not merely a mark of his already having been neutralized as a threat to white bourgeois interests; rather, it is itself the neutralization of the threat, continual proof against black male insurgency.

22. This phenomenon was noted in a report on the April 5, 1989, broadcast of National Public Radio's "Morning Edition." The report was part of the series "AIDS & Blacks: Breaking the Silence," broadcast on "Morning Edition" and "All Things Considered" during the week of April 3–9, 1989.

23. Smitherman, *Talkin and Testifyin*, p. 52.

24. Frequently in this essay I will use the term *homosexual* (and *homosexuality*) rather than *gay* when talking about sexual identifications within an African-American context. I do this not because I prefer the clinical connotations of *homosexual* to what I personally experience as the infinitely more liberating resonances of *gay* or *queer*, but because I want to point out the limited degree to which many men of color feel identified with these latter terms. Indeed, *gay*, especially, conjures up in the minds of many who hear it images of a population that is characteristically white, male, and financially well-off; thus it can actually efface, rather than affirm, the experiences of women and men of color. (This is why

some groups of black men who might have identified themselves as gay have chosen instead to designate themselves by terms they feel reflect a specifically Afrocentric experience. Consider the case of "Adodi," which has been used by black men in both Philadelphia and Boston. (See Elizabeth Pincus, "Black Gay Men in Boston Organize," *Gay Community News*, June 12–18, 1988, pp. 3, 9.) I use *homosexual*, then, to signal the difficulty of fairly designating any "minority" group owing to the inevitably complex and multifaceted nature of minority identity.

25. Smitherman, *Talkin and Testifyin*, p. 82.

26. Ibid., pp. 83, 97. Other researchers, too, have noted the peculiarly male-identified nature of the black "rap," among them Thomas Kochman ("'Rapping' in the Black Ghetto," *Trans-action* 6 [1969]: 26–34); Roger D. Abrahams ("Playing the Dozens," *Journal of American Folklore* 75 [1962]: 209–20); and Mitchell-Kernan, "Signifying."

27. See Lauren Berlant, "The Female Complaint," *Social Text* 19/20 (1988): 237–59.

28. Nor was he the last. My own performance in this essay (let alone in the other sites of my intellectual practice) sets me up to be targeted as too white-identified or too effete (or both) to be a "real" black man in certain contexts. The fact that I already identify *myself* as gay may mitigate my vulnerability on that score somewhat. At the same time, the fact that my work takes the form of scholarly writing that does not generally circulate outside the academy largely insulates me from charges that I am not sufficiently engaged with the day-to-day concerns of the black populace, even as it substantiates the claim. This paradox constitutes a dilemma not just for black intellectuals, certainly, but the embattled position that blacks still occupy in this country—socially, politically, economically—makes the problem especially pressing for us.

29. Don L. Lee (Haki R. Madhubuti), *Don't Cry, Scream* (Detroit: Broadside Press, 1969), pp. 27–31.

30. An effective manifesto for such a poetic practice can be seen in Imamu Amiri Baraka's "Black Art," with its call for "poems that kill." See the *Selected Poetry of Amiri Baraka/Leroi Jones* (New York: Morrow, 1979), pp. 106–7.

31. Nikki Giovanni, "The True Import of Present Dialogue: Black vs. Negro," in Dudley Randall, ed., *The Black Poets* (New York: Bantam, 1971), pp. 318–19.

32. There is an evident irony here, in that the intense masculinism of black nationalist discourse was developed as a reaction against the suppression of black manhood and black male sexuality (often taking the form of literal castration, and at any rate consistently rhetorically figured as such) enacted by the dominant white society. Of course, the emphasis on traditional masculinity is not unique to black nationalism, either in the United States or elsewhere. For an extensive discussion of the relation between European nationalist ideologies and the promulgation of a masculine ideal, see George Mosse, *Nationalism and Sexuality: Respectability and Abnormal Sexuality in Modern Europe* (Madison: University of Wisconsin Press, 1985).

33. The *Jet* obituary reflects a general journalistic ignorance of the appropriate terms to be used in reference to the AIDS epidemic. "AIDS victim," with its connotations of passivity, helplessness, and immutable doom, and its reduction of the person under discussion to a medical condition, should be rejected in favor of "person with AIDS" (PWA) or "person living with AIDS" (PLWA). Additionally, AIDS is not a "disease," it is a "syndrome"—a constellation of symptoms that indicates an underlying condition—suppressed immunity likely caused by infection with the human immunodeficiency virus (HIV).

34. "Max Robinson, First Black National TV News Anchor, Succumbs to AIDS in D.C."; "Singer Sylvester, 42, Dies of AIDS in Oakland, CA," *Jet* (January 9, 1989): 14–15, 18.

35. For some commentary on this phenomenon, see Joseph Beam, ed., *In the Life: A Black Gay Anthology* (Boston: Alyson, 1986), particularly essays by James S. Tinney ("Why a Black Gay Church?" pp. 70–86), Bernard Branner (an interview with Blackberri, "Singing for Our Lives," pp. 170–84), and Max C. Smith, ("By the Year 2000," pp. 224–29).

36. "Max Robinson: Fighting the Demons," *Newsweek* (January 2, 1989): 65.

37. "Morning Edition," April 5, 1989.

38. Among Jackson's misstatements is his reference to the "AIDS virus." There is no virus that "causes AIDS," only HIV, which produces the immunosuppression that allows the conditions that constitute AIDS to flourish. Moreover, neither HIV infection nor AIDS "comes from" either homosexuality or "promiscuity"; HIV is a virus that can merely be *transmitted* through sexual contact. It is particularly ironic, by the way, that the homophobia-informed task of legitimizing Robinson's AIDS diagnosis should be undertaken by Jackson, whose 1988 presidential campaign was characterized by support for a lesbian and gay political agenda.

39. Noted in "AIDS & Blacks," "All Things Considered," April 7, 1989.

40. Boyer, "The Light Goes Out," p. 84.

41. For an extensive analysis of this characteristic of AIDS education programs in the United States, see Douglas Crimp, "How to Have Promiscuity in an Epidemic," *AIDS: Cultural Analysis/Cultural Activism* (Cambridge, Mass.: MIT Press, 1988), pp. 237–71.

42. "All Things Considered," April 4, 1989.

43. "All Things Considered," April 3, 1989.

44. Debra Fried, "Repetition, Refrain, and Epitaph," *ELH* 53 (1986): 615–32; 620.

AIDS 101

Peter M. Bowen

I am not an expert on the topic of AIDS, but through
newspapers, TV, and magazines, I do know a little something
about this disease.

—A student

I And the Class Wrote On

AIDS classes, now installed or resisted at nearly every level of our educational system, were created to teach students about a crisis whose status as a public disaster has only recently been grasped by the media and government. Yet to some extent, AIDS is precisely what such classes cannot teach. Broadcast on the news, brought up in conversation, bursting daily on the covers of tabloids, the most confusing and contradictory lessons of AIDS have already been so thoroughly learned that they confound whatever facts an AIDS class might present. Despite rigorous educational attempts to discipline AIDS, either by offering some master narrative or by arresting certain irresponsible rumors, many students are simply overwhelmed by the enormous fears and suspicions that they bring into, and often carry out of, the classroom.[1] Indeed, as Leo Bersani observes, "an important lesson to be learned from a study of the representation of AIDS is that the messages most likely to reach their destination are messages already there."[2]

What is "already there," embedded even in the simplest "fact" about AIDS, are various preexisting cultural concepts about health, sickness, sexuality, race, drugs, etc., that have rendered this epidemic paradoxically intelligible and confusing at the same time. Intelligible because, as

Douglas Crimp has pointed out, "AIDS does not exist apart from the practices that conceptualize it, represent it, and respond to it";[3] confusing, however, since many of the social practices by and through which AIDS becomes intelligible remain mystified in the dominant media and popular imagination. While the fact that "AIDS is not a gay disease," for example, has become a cliché so widespread as to almost cover up the fact that gay men currently still suffer the greatest burdens of the epidemic, precise information about gay sexuality that would render such a fact meaningful is often left murky or simply omitted.

Even so, the increasingly large incidence of HIV transmission among college students, gay or straight, demands that something be done.[4] According to Cindy Patton, as things stand now "in most parts of the country, high-school and college students demonstrate fairly extensive knowledge about AIDS, most of which has come from the media, yet few practice safe sex."[5] While the clear solution to such a problem would be to reiterate the obvious fact that AIDS can affect anyone, the various effects that AIDS has had on most students makes this point hard to hammer home. Consequently, teaching AIDS becomes a practice of unlearning, of untangling the complicated ideological weaving of cultural misconceptions, media misrepresentation, and medical misinformation so that students can begin to recognize their relation to AIDS as both frighteningly real *and* discursively constructed.

Given the responsibility to teach a freshman composition course at Rutgers University in the last few years, I took the opportunity to teach about AIDS. As a required university course whose students were randomly selected by a computer, my writing class on AIDS guaranteed—with the class and race parameters dictated by a university context—a student composition resembling what the media so blithely term "the general population." Students did not choose to be in the class, but neither did they ordinarily leave it. Although I have taught the class six times, only two people ever left. In teaching AIDS in/as a writing class, it was not my goal to discuss medical aspects of AIDS, even though clarifying certain misconceptions necessitated discussions on matters of fact. Instead, by focusing on AIDS as a discourse, I encouraged students to rethink (and hopefully to revise) the ways in which they were already inscribed in the discourses about AIDS. This focus did not diminish the all-too-material reality of AIDS, but rather permitted students to recognize the material effect of language in their writing as well as in the various texts we considered.

Class assignments, positioned at the intersection between textual questions (vocabulary, audience, narrative, argumentation) and AIDS issues (safer sex, activist empowerment, homophobia, racism), asked students to write about AIDS, even in so simple a gesture as expressing an opinion, as a political and personal action. The first assignment, for example, asked students to identify themselves as part of a community with its own specific risk to HIV infection and then to compare and contrast safer-sex pamphlets in terms of how they constructed an audience. The second assignment asked them to consider the political force of vocabulary by discussing a single term from the ACT UP "Buzzwords Poster" in relation to issues of language.[6] The third assignment required them to analyze the logic of homophobia[7] by drawing on critical analyses of blame and homophobia.[8] A fourth assignment asked them to discuss a product of pop culture (a film, song, advertising campaign, etc.) that they felt was created either as reaction or response to the AIDS crisis. They were asked, moreover, to consider this artifact as a matter of political and moral ideology.[9] The fifth paper asked them to think about how the categories of race and gender affect our conception of AIDS.[10] The sixth assignment asked them to consider the power and limits of narrative in Randy Shilts's *And the Band Played On*.[11]

During the semester, student papers—photocopied and handed out, marked up and revised—provided the territory in which, twice a week, we as a class located and identified the various rhetorics of AIDS. While revisiting the same student papers here might seem, with all its threatening overtones, a continuation of class politics by other means, my extended textual analysis of students' work is at the same time nothing else than a continuation of the work they were required to perform. In scrutinizing their papers, in-class writings, and class discussion for any traces of the ideological constructions that have shaped the public discourse on AIDS, I am not trying to wrest from their words a confession, as if somehow my supervising role as their teacher enabled me to see right through their work to what they *really* thought. Rather, in taking their work as informed by what Simon Watney has termed, naming both the form and content of AIDS information, the "spectacle of AIDS," I reread my students' papers as refractions of the entrenched cultural fantasies continuously rerun by—for lack of a more expansive word—the media. While much of the cultural analysis of AIDS has been rightly directed at the media, I want, however, in looking the other way, to consider how the construction of AIDS within such public discourses (as the media, public health campaigns, political dialogues) are reconstructed in what and how students write about AIDS.

If in my extensive, even overextended, analysis of students' work I have failed to pay attention to the differences—of race, class, and gender, but also of religious and political leanings—between individual students, it is partially because I don't fully hold my students responsible for what they say. Nevertheless, I admit that a more thorough interrogation of the relation between students' backgrounds and their knowledge of AIDS would more precisely outline how various communities differently construct (and are constructed by) the AIDS crisis. This oversight on my part, while securing the confidentiality of my sources, reduces the entire class to the composite figure of a single student. And while I may appear to be publicly correcting this student (an intellectual discipline best left to rigorous discussions conducted in the privacy of one's own classroom), it is this imaginary student, blurred together in my bleary-eyed reading and re-reading of students' work, that in fact corrects my understanding of AIDS.

II   To Know and Not to Know

At the semester's start, I asked all students to write two one-page statements: a miniautobiography and a piece on AIDS. Photocopied and distributed to the entire class, the two pieces, sharply differentiated in both tone and intent, hung together like a diptych whose symmetry and balance remained unclear. It was only after we as a class discussed each AIDS piece individually that the relation between the two became clear. Borrowing their tone and vocabulary from yearbook descriptions and college applications, from personal ads and business résumés, the autobiographical pieces not only summed up each student's personal achievements but also confidently advertised them. The AIDS comments, however, while maintaining an air of familiarity with certain facts, remained sharply disassociated from each student's life. And thus the diptych was complete: on the one side, home, family, career; on the other, fear, disease, alienated scientific data.

The juxtaposition of these two pieces, however, revealed less some absolute difference between them than the ways in which they were dependent upon each other. The personal statements, articulated in autobiographical narratives whose lethargic unfolding from birth to college guaranteed a sense of future, maintained their familiarity at the level of the detail (the dog's name, the mother's birthplace, the writer's favorite food). But in the AIDS statements, the use of details, expressed in the innumerable facts about AIDS, ensured the reader's and writer's inability to either connect with the history of this epidemic or its future. So many details, uncontrolled by a coherent narrative, simply overwhelmed. Even the one AIDS statement that began with novelistic narrative flourish ("It was a hot summer during the month of June in 1983 when a friend called me to come over") quickly drowned in a sea of facts, so that by the end, the writer's neighborhood, her friend, and even she herself were all but completely lost. While these AIDS statements, not surprisingly, echoed the various media sources (journalism, health brochures, public service ads, etc.) from which most students had learned about AIDS, the students' tone often betrayed their confusion in trying to orchestrate these various voices into a coherent whole. Clearly this confusion arose not from any lack of facts, since their statements generously provided an almost encyclopedic array of public information about AIDS, but from an understanding of either how to coordinate the social and medical knowledge of AIDS together or how to relate such information to their own lives.

For some students, it was not simply their sense of being unaffected that justified their lack of understanding; by some intuitive reverse logic, their lack of knowledge guaranteed their safety from HIV infection:

> My knowledge of AIDS is quite narrow in my opinion. I would say that it is my own fault I know so little about AIDS. Now days [sic] there exists an abundant amount of information of AIDS and sexually transmitted diseases, however, I've been slow about obtaining the information. I know that AIDS can [be] received by anyone, but I still feel that AIDS is something that is only affecting those whom [sic] are Gay/Lesbian or drug abusers (I.V. drug users).

Linking knowledge to risk, this student, however apologetically, defended his confusion as a marker of his distance from the epidemic and the people it affects. Indeed, even the adjective that describes his knowledge ("narrow") not only justified his narrow-minded "opinion," but rezoned the epidemiological landscape of AIDS from a continuous threat to separate, "narrow" and self-contained slices-of-lifestyles. In securing his distance from the threat of HIV, the student apologetically registered his knowledge as a conflict between public information ("I know") and personal intuition ("but I still feel"), a conflict echoed in his doubled categories of risk groups. For in erroneously lumping lesbians with gay men, and in being unable to write "I.V. drug user" without also qualifying it by the term "drug abuser," the student illustrates his incomprehension of the facts about AIDS in the very gesture of naming those facts.

In reflecting—or better, refracting—the media's own doublespeak, students consistently constructed AIDS as a controversial field of knowledge split between easily knowable facts and incomprehensible practices. The facts are indeed so simple that they can be easily repeated and mechanically distributed. Exposing the assembly line nature of public AIDS education, one student explained, "I know just what every other student, educated by one health class or another, knows about AIDS." What he and "every other student" knew, however, turned out to be as much a matter of widespread myths as of medical facts. He not only knew, for example, that "AIDS attacks the immune system" or "can be contacted through sexual contact with an infected victim," but importantly that it is *not* "a homosexual disease," and can *not* be contracted "through a handshake, by sitting on a toilet seat, [or] through a sneeze or mosquito bite."

To some degree registering AIDS in the negative makes good public health sense. By recognizing the popular hysteria about AIDS that a sensational media has helped to promote, such disclaimers provide a calming reassurance that one can indeed move in the world without becoming randomly infected with HIV. But in attempting to answer questions not yet asked, in projecting the sense of a clairvoyant authority able to counter suspicions not yet formed let alone confessed, this negative construction of AIDS ultimately plants the very suspicions it wishes to dismiss. Such fears, rooted both in the hygienic paranoia attached to venereal diseases (toilet seats and handshakes) and in the fantastic imagination of the monstrous (here, the vampire shrunk to the size of a mosquito), suggest to what degree AIDS functions for these students as a threat to the imagination as well as to the body.

To extend ad infinitum such a litany of how one doesn't contract an HIV infection would ultimately imagine a world made safe again for heterosexuality. Such scrupulous reviving and sanitizing of the practices of everyday life, however, depend upon not only eliminating from discourse certain suspect practices, but also vanquishing from sight the figures of their practitioners. Unlike the utopian nostalgia of the film *Longtime Companion,* in which the crisis is eradicated by bringing back those it has made disappear—a dream fully realized in the final scene where the dead stumble out to join the living on a sunny Fire Island beach—this negative utopia eliminates those people for whom AIDS remains an everyday crisis.[12]

Rhetorically such occlusion is achieved through a mode of address that refuses to acknowledge an audience of people either living with HIV or attempting to protect themselves against infection. Indeed, how far these lists' projected audience is from the epidemic can be easily measured by the omission on student lists of practice suggestions such as "you don't get HIV by jerking off your partner or by using a clean needle while injecting drugs." By worrying instead about such clearly innocuous and domestic acts like "washing clothes" or "combing hair," these disclaimers, even as they are proffered in a rhetorical gesture of confrontation, cautiously avoid any contact with, let alone mention of, precise descriptions of safer sex or clean needle use. Instead of providing information about protection, such disclaimers offer students protection against AIDS information itself by emphatically resisting any identification with the practices that transmit HIV.

For these students, knowledge about AIDS was not only objective and universal but also had to be rigorously detached from any knowledge about themselves. As such, the controversies accompanying the people and practices culturally associated with HIV transmission became displaced onto and buried in rhetorical disclaimers that simultaneously acknowledged, but refused to name the source of, such controversy. In other places, such disclaimers were expelled more forcefully. Warning against the danger of sharing "hypodermic needles for heroine [sic] use," for example, one student felt compelled to add within the same sentence, "but I am not familiar with the drug." Knowledge about gay male sexuality was even more cautiously registered, for fear (I suspect) that too much knowledge might betray a private interest far greater than that demanded for the protection of health. For if, as Simon Watney suggests, the "homosexual body" is made visible only "upon the strictly enforced condition that any possibility of identification *with* it is scrupulously refused,"[13] any interest in fields of knowledge (AIDS, safer sex, homophobia) that must necessarily refer to that body is either carefully policed or passively accepted. Learning about AIDS became, according to one student, a forced exercise whose futility and abstraction can only be labeled academic: "I wasn't going to make an effort to become more informed, but since I'm in this class, I guess I'm going to become enlightened."

If, for the unenlightened, AIDS presents a world so imaginatively far as to be a world elsewhere, for those whose knowledge brings them close to the edge, its borders seemed still impassable. Arguing the need for open and frank discussion about AIDS, one student dramatized her point with a story involving her, her friend, and a person with AIDS.

> She [the friend] warned me not to touch or even come close to the infected individual. I could see scorn in her face. All I felt at that point was pity. Pity not for the infected person, but pity for my friend who lacked knowledge she needed to suppress the fear she was feeling. I saw how her fears could have provoked fears within me even though I knew better. Because I possessed

enough knowledge to over come [sic] all fears I willingly handed the AIDS victim the envelope and engaged in productive conversation.

Clearly recounted as an anecdote, the story nevertheless quickly re-staged itself as an allegory of enlightenment values. Here, Knowledge (played by the student) resists the wily seduction of Fear (played by the student's friend), thus enabling her both to accomplish her task (handing over the envelope) and to reap its reward (of "productive conversation"). But as sharply drawn as the characters are here—virtual cutouts of an educational scenario—the drama is blunted by the fact that the person with AIDS seems oddly out of place. [14] Both unnecessary (a third wheel in this exchange of words and nasty glances between friends) and overextended (bearing the brunt of both women's feelings), this anonymous person with AIDS becomes as abstract as the very qualities of fear, pity, and knowledge that he or she is made to objectify. To some degree, this story embodies the amorphous emotions elicited by the thought of HIV precisely in order to disembody the material reality (and threat) of a person living with AIDS. Abstract, anonymous, mute, this person with AIDS stands like a border sign marking simply the intersection between two worlds (the living and the dead), which, while perhaps conveying messages and conversation, remains separate and irreconcilable.

The moral of this story, as with the variety of facts, disclaimers, and opinions expressed in other students' writings, clearly emphasizes the power of knowledge, the need for education, and the renunciation of fear in the fight against AIDS. But such a moral, coming characteristically as the last word on the subject, produces not only a form of narrative closure, but apropos to its unspoken subject, a form of closeting, a closing off of other modes of inquiry. Indeed, if this student's valorization of knowledge rings a little hollow, it is partially because "knowledge," not unlike the figure of the person with AIDS, functions as an empty signifier similar to the mysterious, exchanged envelope and the "productive conversation" whose contents remain hermetically sealed in the very gesture of communication. The student's story totalizes knowledge—a knowledge able to "overcome all fears"—so as to render invisible the particular details of this encounter. What did the student's friend fear? What knowledge suppressed this fear? Or more to the point, what knowledge informed the friend's fear in the first place?

While within this "epidemic of signification," as Paula Treichler notes, "no clear line can be drawn between the facticity of scientific and non-scientific (mis)conceptions," [15] for this student and others, the assumption of a pure knowledge maintains a virtual *cordon sanitaire* separating the idea of AIDS and its lived reality. For the only real knowledge recovered from this encounter was that this person innocently contracted HIV "through a blood transfusion," a fact that reassures us that the student did not learn anything in her "productive conversation" that could not also be reproduced in print.

I would be a cruel schoolmaster, of course, to expect students, especially during the first week of class or even the entire freshman year, to comprehend and analyze the ideological construction of AIDS. And yet, as their statements demonstrated, they knew more than they were willing to divulge. Or rather, they knew what they should *not* divulge. For in recounting what they knew about AIDS, students outlined the epistemological structure that makes AIDS virtually unknowable to them. It is not that they did not know the publicly disseminated facts about the virus but rather that they equally knew that the carefully policed public health messages, the hushed tones of controversy in an announcer's voice, or the absence of personal statements by and for people with AIDS (especially those who contracted HIV through sex or drug injections) made clear the precarious position one assumed in talking about this subject.

III   The Classroom as Closet

Of the more than one hundred people in my class at different times, I was the only person who ever came out as gay. While people like Michael Fumento might choose to read this circumstance as further evidence of a homosexual AIDS conspiracy and against the Kinsey Report,[16] I want to consider how such invisibility makes manifest the particular forms of homophobia that exist in, even as, the walls of a classroom. It goes without saying that in discussing AIDS one would have to speak about homosexuality, but it is perhaps less clear how a student writing about AIDS would choose not to speak as a gay man or lesbian. While no students came out, there was at least one other gay man—he came out to me one night at a local gay bar—who advertised his discomfort, for those who were looking to read it, in the tension and anger that flashed across his face when other students offered their opinions about homosexuality. What I suspected he felt, what I knew I felt, even after I had come out later in the semester, was, on the one hand, a sense of being continually outside the terms of the class's discourse (as other, as deviant, as incomprehensible) and, on the other hand, a sense of always being locked inside (of myself, of my knowledge, of my secret). And in a class about AIDS, the particular proportions of the closet, this feeling of simultaneously being inside and outside, take on clinical dimensions, since the gesture of coming out posits the possibility of still more secrets (HIV-positive status, for example) being kept inside.

As Eve Kosofsky Sedgwick has explicitly diagramed, the various "epistemologically charged pairings, condensed in the figures of 'the closet' and 'coming out'," continually speak of each other so that "to discuss any of these indices in any context . . . must perhaps be to perpetuate unknowingly compulsions implicit in each."[17] The obvious placement of an HIV-positive/HIV-negative opposition on a homo/hetero axis was made clear in the class's immediate question of why I had chosen to spend an entire semester on AIDS. The question behind this question became all the more apparent as my personal answer about knowing people who had died and who were currently sick, and my professional response that I thought AIDS was intellectually challenging, did little to erase the look from their faces that I was not being forthright. My later coming out as a gay man invited the reciprocal question of whether I had AIDS—even though I had already identified myself as HIV-negative at the semester's start.[18] While these students' inquiries assumed the by-now banal but still devastating cultural conflation of homosexuality with HIV-positive status, they also assumed such categories as assumptions, that is to say, as suspicions that go without saying. Coming out when I did turned out to be a fairly redundant gesture, since a show of hands demonstrated that more than half of my students already thought of me as gay.

In effect, my being gay operated, especially after I had come out, as what D. A. Miller succinctly terms an "open secret," a secret whose knowledge is mutually silenced by agreeing "to conceal the knowledge of the knowledge."[19] Speculated on, disseminated through gossip, or hinted at in innuendo, students' knowledge of my being gay nevertheless remained a secret in student papers whose addressed audience was consistently constructed in opposition to gay men, lesbians, intravenous drug users, and more generally people with AIDS. And while such distinctions were at times overtly stated ("It is important that these changes be made within the lives of homosexuals, yet we [heterosexuals] must also follow the procedures of protection for our own good" or "Some gays may be infected just as you or I can become a carrier by being infected by other means of contact"), they appeared more pervasively in the tacit absorption of the reader and writer into such terms as "the public," "society," or simply "we."

But if homosexuality remained closeted in the classroom, so too did homophobia, which, despite its sporadic cameo appearances in class discussions and student papers, remained hidden, needing to be read be-tween the lines.[20] For even my most homophobic student, whose born-again condemnations of gay people came to me only through notes from his frustrated writing tutor, remained for the most part pleasantly stone-faced in class. Only in his initial introductory statement did this student under the cover of anonymity "come out" with his Biblical beliefs:[21]

> I believe AIDS is a plague that will be responsible for eliminating or abol-ishing a whole generation of human beings. In addition, I believe that God (Jesus Christ) will punish those who engage in premarital sex or extra-marital sex (Adultery one of the Ten Commandments) by letting them die of AIDS.

But even here, gay men, who still make up the majority of active AIDS cases, are subsumed under the categories of "those who engage in pre-marital and extramarital sex," terms that paradoxically heterosexualize homosexuality by seeing it only through an institution to which it is legally denied access. But as gay men and lesbians are buried in a language that refuses to name them, they also are recovered (and then covered over) in the biblical allusion to the demise of Sodom and Gomorrah, a story in which another whole generation of sodomites—still the name preferred by conservatives—was "abolished" by divine genocide. Quite literally pray-ing for the extermination of a whole generation, this student answers his own prayers by refusing to verbally register the very people whose disap-pearance he intends.

Most students, of course, not only recognized the existence of homosex-uals but were often cautiously sympathetic to their plight, as long as their plight was conducted in the privacy of their own homes or in newspaper columns detailing their deaths from AIDS. It was ultimately the image of homosexuality, and more specifically the image of two men or two women kissing, that provoked, along with disgust and nervous laughter, a pro-found silence.[22] But what was shocking about this kissing, an even touch-ing reminder of what homosexuals "do," was not that it was too explicit but rather that it was *not explicit enough*. For unlike the unimaginable and unspeakable images developed in the camera obscura of the closet, these photos revealed practices familiar enough to be recognizable to students as something they might do. I am not suggesting that students saw them-selves kissing people of the same sex but rather that they identified with the gesture of kissing, that nearly universal gesture of affection that sealed their fates with those of lesbians and gay men. Too familiar to provide the comfort of alienation (and too alienating to be accepted by our society's compulsory heterosexualizing gaze), these photos ruptured the safe boundaries students had built up to protect themselves from both the taint of homosexuality and the possible transmission of HIV.

While such photos threatened the comfortable distance that most students enjoyed from the AIDS crisis, more explicit photos regained that distance by providing a justifiable threat. Asked by one assignment to compare the particular rhetorical and graphic strategies deployed by safer-sex pamphlets to reach their intended audiences, one student extended his comparison to include their psychosomatic effects on him. While characterizing the "photographs of men and women close to each other, or holding hands as if they were ready to kiss" in a pamphlet, *Making Sex Safer,* as "informal, warm, [and] kind of cozy," he reserved quite a different language for "a much raunchier and graphic publication," *The Safer Sex Condom Guide for Men and Women:*

> Despite its title, I got the feeling that this publication was aimed mainly at men—homosexual men. . . . There is [a] pictogram of a man wearing tight jeans with a condom in the pocket on the front cover. This is actually quite tasteful compared to the photographs that are printed on the inside. Upon opening the pamphlet I immediately felt as though I was being attacked or raped. The first thing you notice is about a half a dozen photos of naked men putting on condoms. . . . Upon flipping the booklet over you are graced with more pictograms of gay men playing with condoms and having sex. . . . This pamphlet is aimed at uneducated homosexual men, and excludes just about everyone else from getting any useful information out of it. I guess this pamphlet has a place in society, otherwise it wouldn't be printed, but it will have no part of my life.

The shocking truth? The pamphlet, produced by the Gay Men's Health Crisis (GMHC), entails a seven-part photo series demonstrating the proper method to put on a condom. In two photos a pair of hands (definitely female in one, possibly male in another) reach out from off-frame to assist. The other images are soft-focus illustrations picturing several single men, a heterosexual Asian couple, and an unreadable image of entangled bodies cropped below the shoulders and above the knees.

Singularly homophobic, this student was not, however, alone in his condemnation. Another male student found the pamphlet's candor "uncalled for and unappealing," its tone "pornographic," and its appearance "like a sex magazine." Unconsciously restaging the 1987 congressional debate over the Helms amendment that successfully sought to restrict funds from education materials that promoted homosexual sexual activities, these students played from a script already authored by their con-

gressional elders, who had earlier lashed out against another GHMC publication, *Safer Sex Comix #4*, as "repugnant" and "demeaning."[23]

Fulfilling Senator Jesse Helms's 1987 prophecy that "if the American
people saw these books [then a comic book, now a safer-sex brochure],
they would be on the verge of revolt,"[24] these students' near-physical revulsion also rehearsed the peculairly inverted logic of homosexual panic.[25]
Naturalizing homophobia as a somatic reaction to the (re)presentation of
gay sexuality, the first student, for example, *feels* the violent threat of
being "attacked or raped" and the exclusion, along with "just about everyone else," from a publication "aimed mainly at men—homosexual men."
Taking it all too personally—every condomed cock has his name on it—
this student reacts by depersonalizing his relation to the pamphlet so
much so that he literally never sees it. Perception is rhetorically made the
responsibility of his second-person reader (i.e., "you notice," "you are
graced"). In a similar gesture, the second student, unable to swallow any
recommendation for "people to add flavor during oral sex," dismisses the
pamphlet's approach as culturally tasteless ("inappropriate," "uncalled
for") precisely in order to get rid of the bad taste these ideas have left in his
mouth.

Having "no part" of the student's life, homosexuality is thus banished
(or in the student's mind, banishes itself) to "a place in society" that, refused representation or embodiment, can only be called imaginary. After
all, the imagination, with its double operation of making things imaginary
(unrepresented, unreal) and bringing things to life (giving shape, form,
possibility), demands at once scrupulous confinement of and vigilant policing from such images. Of the numerous imagined threats posed by this
pamphlet, perhaps the most frightening is its very real threat of revealing practices that students could have—and perhaps already have—
imagined on their own. As such, the fact that this pamphlet asks "people
to use their imaginations to think of new and exciting ways to use
condoms"—not the least of which might be for anal intercourse with other
men—was delivered as perhaps the most damaging condemnation of a
safer-sex brochure.

It is perfectly understandable that within the classroom, whose institutional facade of objectivity and propriety often serves to efface individual
identity, students would choose to speak in the same moral (and moralizing) tone so often addressed to them. It is after all what the teacher wants!
But when I as their teacher spoke with the power vested in me by the university and simultaneously spoke out against certain institutionalized attitudes about sexuality, the resulting confusion often left students speech-

less. Assigned to imagine being gay for a few hours, and then to record their reactions, most students, for example, either failed to respond or responded by failing: "I tried, but I don't think I was very good"; "I found I couldn't do this assignment"; "I didn't go through the acting with completion"; "While it might be possible for me to complete this assignment, I have high moral values and will not do so." These statements, while seeming to evade the question, answer it by posing evasion as the proper response to and for homosexuality. Any attempt to comply with the classroom's order to answer the question might solicit evidence that could and would be used against students in other institutionalized contexts. Hoping to avoid incriminating herself as either a bad student or a bad citizen, one rather religious student objected by pathologizing my pedagogy: "Though the intention of the assignment may be to understand homophobia, the means are perverse."

But just as some students strategically evaded the assignment, others completed it by identifying evasion as the modus operandi of homosexuality. "It's easy to hide it," one student's narrative journey began, while another simply wished she "could just be open about who and what" she was. Devoid of any sense of pleasure, desire, or romance, these "gay" narratives construct their protagonists as guilty, shame-ridden fugitives, who, when they were not "looking over" their "shoulder" to avoid detection, were looking forward with dread and shame to the prospect of coming out to family and friends. So intensely did students connect homosexuality with concealment that at least two women came out as gay men in their journal entries. While such testimonials, which were often disqualified in the last line ("but thank God, I'm not gay"), frequently empathized with the repression of gay people, they also preserved that oppression through their specular reconstruction of the closet. While not exactly a hidden agenda, students' fantasies that lesbians and gay men constantly fear detection serves as the wish fulfillment of a certain cultural imperative that homosexuality stay in the closet. Indeed, the difficulty that one student had in imagining "what situations a homosexual finds himself in" was in no small way perpetuated by the fact that he wished that they would stay hidden: "I do not like seeing them do some of the things they do in front of me."

In a class about AIDS, the desire for evasion provided students with a powerful mechanism by which to disavow any connection with the actual means of HIV transmission. For example, in refusing to see gay people, in failing to imagine, let alone name, "those things they do in front of" or behind him or with him, this student constituted homosexuality as a series of acts so unimaginable as to be effectively unperformable. While heterosexuals seem to contract HIV through promiscuity or intravenous drug use, gay men are thought to be infected through sexual practices so fundamentally different from (hetero)sexual intercourse as to suggest a body with profoundly different sexual instrumentation. The clear danger of this "fantasized 'homosexual body'" lies, as Simon Watney reminds us, in its power to "encourage the real spread of HIV by distracting attention away from the well-proven means of blocking transmission."[26] At the same time, students' abilities to ghettoize the idea of gay sex (safe or otherwise) into a particularly unimaginable corridor of the imagination demonstrates to what extent this epidemic, and the thousands of real lives that have been lost to it, could also be simply too unreal for words.

IV   The Ideology of Choice

Midway through the semester, a student presented a newspaper photo of an AIDS poster produced by Gran Fury that featured straight, gay, and lesbian couples kissing playfully. Across the top and bottom read the message, "Kissing doesn't kill / Greed and indifference do."[27] After looking for a moment, one student asked, "What does this have to do with AIDS?", a question I bounced back to the class. Silence. "Well, then, what do greed and indifference mean here?" I pushed. One small voice piped up: "Greed refers to sexual greed, and indifference is about people who don't care how their promiscuity kills others." While shocked by this profoundly revisionist reading of the poster's intent, I thought that the student's interpretation would ignite class discussion. But there was no disagreement. Everyone in the class agreed that is what the poster meant.

Disappointed at first at not having enabled my students to comprehend the poster's implicit political critique, I quickly realized how smart my students were indeed. For considering the cannon of public-health scare tactics whose repeated bombardments, from British posters and stamp cancelations ("AIDS: DON'T DIE OF IGNORANCE") to the American television spots ("AIDS: DON'T GET IT"), have pounded home the message of personal responsibility, my students certainly got the point.[28] Students had not only taken in the message but had become quite adept at disseminating it. Through a kind of media ventriloquism, student papers, suddenly shifting from the anecdotal first person to the dogmatic second, routinely spoke in the voice of public health itself: "It takes one night of fun to ruin a whole life, so be sure not to use drugs or sleep around"; "If you are sexually active, you are [at] risk of catching AIDS"; "If you must engage in sex, use a condom."

Bolstering governmental antidrug and antisex campaigns, these messages were, of course, delivered in the authoritative tone of paternal advice, a tone that in the context of a freshman composition sounded out of
place and jarringly disruptive. Too strident not to be missed, they were at
the same time too brief to provide any real information, other than a nag-
ging reminder that you have been warned. It is perhaps, then, as a defensive reminder that people who are HIV-positive should have known better,
that these messages worked. Retroactively blaming the victim by broadcasting loud enough to carry back to the past, these messages simultaneously legitimate the innocence of those individuals (babies, hemophiliacs,
blood transfusion cases) to whom these messages are not addressed and
criminalize those people with HIV who should have listened more
carefully to information that wasn't there.

Such a concept of choice—rarely extended to include the rights of
PWAs to choose possible drug treatments, housing, employment, or even
the vocabulary used by the media to describe them—depends upon a radical dehistoricization of the AIDS crisis. Howeverful helpful such historical allusions, especially in their war-torn references to Hiroshima or the
Holocaust, are to gay writers striving to render materially real the present
horrors of AIDS,[29] it is precisely such lessons from the past, with their
conclusions that waging a "war on AIDS" means joining the ranks of those
"fighting for their lives," that many students reject. Rebutting the appropriateness of such explosive metaphors, one student insists that, while the
"victims of an atomic bomb have no choice whether or not they will be
affected by it, 'victims' of AIDS (most of the time) have the power of choice
of whether they are going to share needles or have unprotected sex." Re-
serving a temporal distinction ("most of the time") for those "victims"
whose historical blindness grants them the immunity of innocence, this
student nevertheless collapses historical differences by grammatically sit-
uating both Hiroshima and the AIDS crisis in a never-ending present
tense.

In this paradoxical economy in which choice is alternatively read as
compulsion ("if you must have sex"), historical agency is granted only by
refusing to allocate any time during which such agency could be effectively and knowledgeably exercised. Indeed, this reduction of history to a
static narrative whose characters literally embody its denouement serves
to, among other things, shift the cause of AIDS from the act of being virally
infected to the static moral condition of being someone who engages in
(criminal, addictive) drug usage or (promiscuous, transgressive) sexual
practices. As one student succinctly put it in a tone that is simultaneously

sympathetic and moralizing, "I feel that what they had done was wrong, but not enough to make them suffer." However ambiguous her sentence is in naming either the accused or their crimes, her unambiguous leveling of guilt not only criminalizes a medical condition but, more important, diagnoses those infected as both marked and criminal. For gay men, as Jeff Nunokawa has effectively demonstrated, this viral death sentence is nothing more than the logical extension of the historical construction of homosexuality itself as a lethal condition, or, if choice is to be championed, an act of suicide.[30]

To a large extent, students' ability to claim that people living with HIV choose to be infected resides in their failure to understand the history of AIDS, not only in terms of its ongoing cultural struggles, but also in the specific history of HIV inside the body. Without a doubt, the most incomprehensible, and therefore untaught, AIDS "fact" for students was the difference between HIV and AIDS, a distinction crucial for understanding the ideology of choice. To excuse this omission as a simple educational oversight would be to ignore, as Simon Watney reminds us, "the more important point that public AIDS information has successfully established a widespread 'knowledge' of the epidemic" that often promotes strategic fields of ignorance or misunderstanding.[31] In addition to a historical review of the government's general failure to provide life-saving information, a clearly elaborated explication of HIV (the potentially long window period during which it cannot be detected through testing, the possibility that someone with HIV might go years as asymptomatic) would profoundly challenge, if not thoroughly confound, students' assumptions that people consciously choose to be infected. But such a history has not been taught. And without it, emphasizing the difference between HIV and AIDS appears not only nitpicking, but, as one student protested, counterproductive to "helping those affected, or making comprehensive AIDS training programs, books, or television shows that everyone can understand" by literally confusing the issue.

What is clearly confusing about people with HIV being simultaneously infected and asymptomatic is the oxymoronic image of a healthy sick person. For in addition to raising the frightening possibility that anyone— even a freshman student—could be infected and not show it, this image complicates the rigid binary division that categorizes people as either healthy or sick, living or dying, and, to some extent, innocent or guilty. Envisioning health or illness as a continuum of symptoms rather than an absolute state demands a health care system that is not (just) focused on the search for a cure—that ideological panacea that rings through student papers with all the political evasiveness that it normally sounds in public excuses about the lack of AIDS care (i. e., "I am sorry for them, but there is no cure"). Instead, it would require a health care system intent on maintaining health by responding to the various and complex needs of people with HIV illness rather than on securing for the "general public" an absolute difference from those marked (either by disease or for death) with AIDS. With the history of people fighting to stay alive, the very existence of people with HIV healthy enough to carry on a job and even a sex life, and angry enough to demand treatment and care, fiercely questions the myth that they had irresponsibly chosen to die.

Responding to tear-jerking images of bedridden "AIDS victims" waiting to die and hair-raising stories of murderous "AIDS carriers" wanting to kill, students often inverted the empowered image of the healthy sick person into the horror of sick health or sociopathic violence. For however difficult were the clinical details of HIV for students to grasp, the idea of AIDS dementia maintained an irretractable hold on their imaginations. One student, forgoing any somatic history of HIV, rushed to detail the effects of dementia in the final stages of AIDS: "[Since] there [had] already been brain damage, such as losing the grip on reality, an AIDS victim becomes liable to do anything, including purposefully and maliciously spreading the disease among his peers." Rising out of the crypt of a hospital bed, this AIDS victim turned zombie propels the myth of Gaetan Dugas into a clinical diagnosis in which the desire to infect others becomes both the sign and production of infection. Out of his mind sick, losing his "grip on reality," the figure, nevertheless, *chooses* to "purposefully and maliciously" harm others. However absurd or paradoxical such a formulation seems, it succinctly reveals how the ideology of choice serves to pathologize people living with HIV, to perceive their actions not as choices but as symptoms (in both the psychoanalytic and medical senses of that word). Barred from a clear understanding of HIV, students thus read the vitality of people living with AIDS as nothing more than a death wish, as nothing more than the outward expression of their innermost desire to kill themselves and, perhaps, others.

V   Coda

Midway through the semester, I polled students on what they thought of the class. While most repeated the well-rehearsed, while nevertheless appreciated, compliments of class evaluation ("interesting," "eye-opening," "necessary") and some found the sustained analysis of a single subject "boring," only a few ventured to open up enough to reveal their real intimacy with the subject. Temporarily comfortable with the topic of AIDS, these students began to locate within it friends, friends of friends, distant and not-so-distant relatives, all whom they knew to be directly affected or feared to be. Their plight was perhaps best summed up by one woman's reaction to the course:

> When I walked into this class and heard that it would be about AIDS, I thought God had put me here. My uncle died of AIDS last year, and nobody in my family or my community will talk about it. This is the only place I have to talk about it.

Heart-rendering, rendering for all the portrait of a student with a heart, her words rang all the more loudly because she had rarely spoken in class. Her silence, inherited from family and neighbors, however was less—as her and others' writings had demonstrated—the absence of words than the overwhelming white noise of cultural misconceptions about AIDS and the people it has affected. While it would be overly optimistic to believe that this class could completely silence for her and others these public silences, could completely clear away the dense verbiage around AIDS so that she could hear herself think, the critical undercutting of such language nevertheless opened a space in which the discourse about AIDS became not only a topic but a topos—albeit perhaps no bigger than a classroom—in which students could begin to locate their bodies as well as their fears and prejudices.

NOTES

I would like to thank Tom Kalin and Casey Finch for their advice, assistance, and patience. I would also (of course, especially) like to thank my students.

1. In appropriating Cindy Patton's metaphor of "disciplining AIDS," I would also refer to her particular example of how ideology precedes examination in the classroom: Cindy Patton, *Inventing AIDS* (New York: Routledge, 1990), pp. 105–7.

2. Leo Bersani, "Is the Rectum a Grave?" in Douglas Crimp, ed., *AIDS: Cultural Analysis/Cultural Activism* (Cambridge, Mass.: MIT Press, 1988), p. 210. This volume originally appeared as *October* 43 (Winter 1987).

3. Douglas Crimp, *AIDS: Cultural Analysis/Cultural Activism*, p. 3.

4. See, for example, Helene D. Gayle et al., "Prevalence of the Human Immunodeficiency Virus Among University Students," *New England Journal of Medicine* 323 (1990): 1538–41. See, too, L. Biemiller, "Colleges Should Play Crucial Role in Halting Spread of AIDS Epidemic, Public Health Officials Say," *Chronicle of Higher Education*, February 11, 1987, pp. 1, 32.

5. Patton, *Inventing AIDS*, p. 109. After discussing the current problems with AIDS

education, Patton provides some extremely helpful suggestions on how to teach about AIDS (pp. 158–59).

6. Assigned texts included Edwin Diamond and Elyse Kroll, "Unsafe Sex and Unsafe Journalism," *Lears*, 1988 (July/August): 130–34; and Allan M. Brandt, "AIDS and Metaphor: Towards the Social Meaning of Epidemic Disease," *Social Research* 55 (1988): 413–32.

7. Required readings, all in Gary E. McCuen, ed., *The AIDS Crisis: Conflicting Social Values* (Hudson, Wis.: McCuen Publications, 1987), were William E. Dannemeyer, "An Informed Society's Response: The Point" (pp. 119–26); Fred Schwartz, "The Gay Lifestyle Must be Opposed" (pp. 77–83); Norman Podhoretz, "Gay Epidemic Threatens Our Health" (pp. 90–94); and Richard Restak, "Society Must Discriminate" (pp. 103–9).

8. Assigned readings in *Social Research* 55 (1988), were Dorothy Nelkin and Sander L. Gilman, "Placing Blame for Devastating Disease" (pp. 361–78) and Richard Poirier, "AIDS and the Tradition of Homophobia" (pp. 461–75).

9. The reading here was Simon Watney, "The Spectacle of AIDS," in *AIDS: Cultural Analysis/Cultural Activism*, pp. 71–86.

10. The readings here were Paula A. Treichler, "AIDS, Gender, and Biomedical Discourse: Current Contests for Meaning," in Elizabeth Fee and Daniel M. Fox, eds. *The Burdens of History* (Berkeley: University of California Press, 1988), pp. 190–266; and Harlon L. Dalton, "AIDS in Blackface," *Daedalus* 118 (1989): 205–27.

11. Randy Shilts, *And the Band Played On* (New York: St. Martin's, 1987).

12. While *Longtime Companion*'s utopian response to the AIDS crisis remains fairly nostalgic and reactionary (see Peter M. Bowen, "Island Hopping," *Outweek* 46 [May 16, 1990]: 63, 72), AIDS activist groups such as ACT UP have confronted the AIDS crisis by imagining a future with a drastically improved health care system, a more responsive drug development system, and more responsible media.

13. Watney, "The Spectacle of AIDS," p. 78.

14. In at least one educational guide for teachers dealing with AIDS (Marcia Quackenbush and Pamela Sargent, *Teaching AIDS: A Resource Guide on Acquired Immune Deficiency Syndrome* [Santa Cruz, Calif.: Network Publications, 1986], pp. 51, 56), a similarly arbitrary casting of identity takes place. Among the various case studies (short narratives with subsequent questions for class discussion), the single scenario featuring homosexuality details the plight of a gay man with visible Kaposi's sarcoma lesions being refused entrance onto a public bus. Omitting any narratives of gay sexual behavior elsewhere, the gratuitous labeling of this person with AIDS as gay serves only to confirm students' suspicions that gay men naturally have AIDS and that homosexuality can be made publicly visible only as a disease. Indeed, even the discussion questions primarily direct readers to identify with/as the "innocent" bystanders on the bus. In contrast, the safer-sex scenario involved a (never labeled straight) woman frightened to ask her "very masculine" boyfriend to use a condom.

15. Paula A. Treichler, "AIDS, Homophobia, and Biomedical Discourse: An Epidemic of Signification," in *AIDS, Cultural Activism/Cultural Criticism*, pp. 31–70.

16. For Fumento's rather essentialist and distorted perspective of the "homosexual population," see Michael Fumento, *The Myth of Heterosexual AIDS* (New York: Basic Books, 1990), pp. 205–10.

17. Eve Kosofsky Sedgwick, *Epistemology of the Closet* (Berkeley: University of California Press, 1990), pp. 72, 73.

18. Being a teacher with AIDS, Michael Lynch has written, creates a double condition

of being scrupulously scrutinized and alternatively ignored: "In a culture of identities, the textures of withholding and revealing can become all-encompassing. So can the textures of wanting to guess—and of wanting above all not to see." (Michael Lynch, "Last Onsets: Teaching with AIDS," *MLA Profession '90* [1990]: 35).

19. D. A. Miller, *The Novel and the Police* (Berkeley: University of California Press, 1988), p. 206.

20. For the various ways in which homophobia as much as homosexuality remains closeted in connotation, see D. A. Miller, "Sontag's Urbanity," *October* 49 (1989): 96.

21. Most of the initial statements were distributed unsigned. But employing the same forensic enthusiasm often used to ferret out lesbians and gay men, I was able to trace this piece back to the author by comparing typewriter characters.

22. The images that caused such controversy: A front-page photo in the student newspaper of two men kissing during National Coming Out Day, *Daily Targum*, October 15, 1990; a playful romp with two boys in a safer-sex videotape, John Greyson, *The Ads Epidemic*, 1988; lesbian and gay activists kissing after ACT UP's 1988 demonstration at New York City Hall, DIVA TV (Damned Interfering Video Activists Television), *Target City Hall*, 1989; an AIDS awareness poster showing gay, lesbian, and straight couples kissing, Gran Fury, "Kissing Doesn't Kill Poster," 1989. Greyson's *The Ads Epidemic* is included in an excellent three-volume compilation tape, *Video Against AIDS*, distributed by the Video Data Bank, 22 Warren St., New York, NY, 10007, (212) 233–3441. DIVA TV's tapes are available through ACT UP, 135 W. 29th St., New York, NY, 10001, (212) 564–2437.

23. For a comprehensive account of the original version and compromises over the Helms amendment, see Douglas Crimp, "How to Have Promiscuity in an Epidemic," in *AIDS: Cultural Analysis/Cultural Activism*, pp. 237–71.

24. Quoted in Crimp, "How to Have Promiscuity in an Epidemic," p. 260.

25. For a review of the relation between the juridical and psychological meanings of homosexual panic, see Sedgwick, *Epistemology*, pp. 19–22.

26. Watney, "The Spectacle of AIDS," p. 80.

27. This Gran Fury bus-side poster (funded by Art against AIDS, On the Road, and Creative Time) was later amended to include "CORPORATE GREED, GOVERNMENT INACTION, AND PUBLIC INDIFFERENCE MAKE AIDS A POLITICAL CRISIS," so as to avoid the very types of misreadings that my students made.

28. For an analysis of these public-health campaigns, see Simon Watney, *Policing Desire: Pornography, AIDS, and the Media* (Minneapolis: University of Minnesota Press, 1989), pp. 136–48; and Crimp, "How to Have Promiscuity in an Epidemic," pp. 266–70.

29. Larry Kramer, *Reports from the Holocaust: The Making of an AIDS Activist* (New York: St. Martin's, 1989); Andrew Holleran, *Ground Zero* (New York: Morrow, 1988). Consider also the song "Living in Wartime," music and lyrics by Michael Callen, performed by Low Life, Tops and Bottoms, Inc., BMI, used in the Testing the Limits Collective videotape, *Testing the Limits: New York* (1988).

30. Jeff Nunokawa, "'All the Sad Young Men': AIDS and the Work of Mourning," *Yale Journal of Criticism* 4 (1991): 1–12.

31. Simon Watney, "Taking Liberties: An Introduction," in Eric Carter and Simon Watney, eds., *Taking Liberties: AIDS and Cultural Politics* (London: Serpent's Tail, 1989), p. 17.

AIDS Narratives on Television: Whose Story?

Paula A. Treichler

Another friend of Molly's died. . . .She tried to think of something
else, something calming. But there was nothing else. It wasn't like
turning to another channel on the TV because AIDS was on all of
them, but only in the most idiotic terms. Everyone on television
who died of AIDS got it from a blood transfusion. Or else it was a
beautiful young white male professional with "everything to live
for," and even then the show focused on his parents and not him.
—Sarah Schulman

I

The AIDS epidemic poses problems of representation, identity, and narrative convention for network television. *An Early Frost* and *Our Sons*, two
prime-time network television dramas to date that centrally address issues
of AIDS in gay men, offer several lessons about narrative form and function provided by television in general and the AIDS epidemic in particular. It is by no means simple to determine whether, to what extent, in
which contexts, and above all for whom a particular cultural production
embodies or undermines "dominant" cultural values and positions.

II

Production creates not only an object for the subject but also a
subject for the object.
—Karl Marx

An Early Frost, a made-for-TV movie originally broadcast on NBC on November 11, 1985, was the first feature-length drama about AIDS on

network television.[1] Its protagonist is Michael Pierson, an appealing and successful young Chicago attorney whose surprise visit home for his parents' wedding anniversary opens the story and establishes the rhythms of life that AIDS will disrupt. Significantly, we meet Michael's family before we meet his lover: his parents, Nick and Kay; his grandmother, Bea; and his sister, Susan, with her husband and little boy. This scene also introduces us to the dramatic rendering on TV of Michael's first symptom of immunodeficiency: weight loss. At the dinner table, Michael is describing a momentous meeting with the head of his law firm when his grandmother passes him the potatoes:

MICHAEL: No, thanks.
BEA: You look awfully thin to me.
NICK: Everyone looks thin to you!
BEA: *You* could lose a couple of pounds.
KAY: Children, children—
MICHAEL: *Anyway*—

Resuming his story, Michael announces he's been made partner in the law firm. Amid the general congratulations, Kay says she hopes he'll leave a little time for "relaxation":

NICK: What your mother wants to know is: are you shackin' up?
MICHAEL: [very seriously] Well, I have something to tell you. [He pauses, then with a charming smile,] I'm not a monk.
KAY: What I was trying to say is—if there's anyone you ever want to bring home, she's always welcome.
NICK: She can sleep in my room.

What is absent or unspoken in these two interactions is what fills the next two hours: Michael's gayness and his illness. This is a domestic drama, a familial coming-out story, and an illness story—what television calls a "disease-of-the-week" story. *An Early Frost*'s text is marked by these genres. But it is teledrama as well as melodrama, thus marked also by television's well-established narrative conventions and uniquely overt commercial context; this format has special significance in the representation of illness because TV movies, unlike TV in general, are able to focus on problems that are complex, controversial, and difficult to solve.[2]

An Early Frost is of particular interest because it was the first television drama about AIDS: in development for some time before Rock Hudson disclosed that he had AIDS, the movie aired within weeks after Hudson's death, when AIDS was just beginning to generate its own narrative conventions and televisual agenda. AIDS was widely believed to pose great problems for coverage on television: the problem of depicting a "homosexual lifestyle," of representing homosexuality and other transgressive practices associated with HIV transmission, the bleak prognosis of AIDS, the stigma and blame attached to persons with AIDS, the baffling role of sexual difference, and the rapidly changing and often nondefinitive nature of medical information. Because actual experience was limited in 1985, *An Early Frost* provides a useful case study of the representational challenges of AIDS and how at this relatively early point in the epidemic they were handled.[3]

I should emphasize that prime-time network television, my primary focus in this essay, by no means offers the only, the best, or the most interesting video representations of the AIDS epidemic. At this point several hundred films and videos have been produced by independent film and video artists, cable stations, and educational and health care agencies; many of these can be called alternative or oppositional in form or politics to mainstream television, and I have talked about them elsewhere.[4] But different kinds of productions do different kinds of cultural work. A range of research establishes that, internationally, television is the single most important source of information about AIDS and HIV.[5] My interest here is thus in the cultural work of the prime-time popular medical drama on network TV, a form characterized by a straightforward narrative, conventional chronology, and "classical" form.

With its stunning cast, good script, accurate medical information, and unquestionably tasteful policing of desire, *An Early Frost* was widely acclaimed and not unreasonably hailed as the prototypical AIDS narrative. *Los Angeles Times* critic Howard Rosenberg wrote:

> You hesitate to use "landmark" in connection with two hours of TV. But if NBC's *Adam* marked a turning point in a campaign to alert the nation about missing children, *An Early Frost* may just as effectively define the AIDS peril for millions of Americans who inexplicably may still remain apathetic and ignorant of reality.[6]

NBC, promoting the film's subject as a vital public-health issue, mailed advance information to more than 200,000 health, educational, and social organizations, and NBC news anchor Tom Brokaw hosted a special AIDS information program afterward. The night of its premiere, *An Early Frost* captured a third of the viewing audience, beating out a controversial "Cagney and Lacey" episode as well as ABC's "Monday Night

Football," and moving thousands of viewers across the United States to call a toll-free information line after the program.[7] Despite its critics on both left and right, *An Early Frost* became the gold standard for the representation of AIDS on television, a standard most critics predicted would not be sustained: "You can bet that this will not be prime time's last word on AIDS, and that few succeeding stories on the same subject will travel such a high road."[8]

As it turned out, television studios did not flock to produce movies on AIDS. Though a few TV movies did address the epidemic, they were, as Schulman's character charges, about people who "got it from a blood transfusion"—people, as John O'Connor puts it, with "straight AIDS." Not until ABC's *Our Sons* in April 1991 did the networks try again to tell the story of a gay man with AIDS.[9] Even now, AIDS is hardly a topic TV takes for granted. Warren Littlefield, president of NBC Entertainment, commented as follows about a repeatedly postponed AIDS episode on the medical drama series "Lifestories":

> There are few things in broadcasting that we know for sure, and one of those is that when you do an episode of any series that deals with AIDS, there is going to be advertiser sensitivity to it. And if you choose to do it anyway, you better count on losing money.[10]

Describing the decision by PBS in the summer of 1991 not to air the AIDS documentary *Stop the Church* on the series "P.O.V.," Monica Collins wrote in *TV Guide* that "television has been dealing with the issues and realities of AIDS since the airing of the landmark NBC drama *An Early Frost* several years ago. But clearly the subject is still risky and potentially controversial for the medium."[11]

This is confirmed by comparing *An Early Frost* with *Our Sons*. Like the earlier film, *Our Sons* has an excellent cast, which includes Hugh Grant and Željko Ivanek as James Grant and Donald Barnes, the central male characters, and Julie Andrews and Ann-Margaret as Audrey Grant and Luanne Barnes, their mothers. As the film opens, Donald has become too sick to be cared for at home and is being taken by paramedics to the hospital; we assume this isn't the first crisis, because James knows his way around the hospital, embraces Donald without a glance at the intensive-care equipment, and falls easily into caretaking routines. Donald's first words to James, however, signal his understanding that this crisis breaks the routine: "Toto, I have the feeling we're not in Kansas anymore." The film is verbally and visually franker about the relationship between Donald and James, and more explicit about their "gayness" (the closest thing

to a Judy Garland reference in *An Early Frost* is Patti Page's voice singing
"How Much Is That Doggie in the Window?"). It also conveys more matter-
of-factly what living with AIDS entails. As James and Audrey visit Donald
in the hospital, Audrey remarks that she hasn't encountered death since
her husband died; James says, "Donald and I have been to fourteen funerals in the last eighteen months." At least some members of the audience
will share Audrey's shock as the casual statistic makes her stare at him,
aghast, suddenly understanding something of the epidemic's impact. At
the same time, the very title *Our Sons* contains its volatile topics within
familial bonds (even if maternal rather than paternal), striving to domesticate not only homosexuality and AIDS but the class difference between
the two mothers as well: when James charges Audrey with "tap
dancing"—using surface charm to evade her real feelings about the reality of his homosexuality—he might be talking about the film's own tap
dancing. Like *An Early Frost*, *Our Sons* strongly urges compassion, medical rationality, intelligence, and tolerance; it also, like *An Early Frost*,
offers viewers the family's perspectives, treats homosexuality as a
central—and legitimate—problem for the straight characters, makes little reference to AIDS as a national health care crisis, and renders the rage
and political mobilization of activist groups invisible, indeed incomprehensible.

During the 1980s, the conservative political climate produced increasingly vehement and vocal attacks on progressive, controversial television
dramas. Conservative advocacy groups organized letter-writing campaigns, product boycotts, and other protest actions. By 1991, however,
radical and progressive advocacy groups had also organized; spurred by
the AIDS epidemic, gay and lesbian activist organizations were finding
increasingly sophisticated ways to protest what they deemed negative representations of homosexuality in film and television.[12] These protests often take up Vito Russo's critique of "gay movies for straight people," that
focus on "coming out as a family problem [and] subtly say that there are no
homosexuals, only a homosexual problem." ("In *Consenting Adults*," he
writes, "we see how a handsome young jock's coming out of the closet affects his mother, his father, his sister and his college roommate. When the
latter learns of his buddy's homosexuality, he says, 'I don't believe this is
happening to me!' Such films are about the real people in our society, the
straight people. Gays are the problem they have.")[13] Or as *New York Times*
television critic John O'Connor put it, many homosexuals today "are fed
up with seeing their very existences viewed primarily as 'controversial.'
Even the occasionally more sensitive films use distancing ploys, exploring

not the lives of homosexuals but the anguished fretting of their parents or friends."[14]

On the one hand, then, television can hardly be considered a vanguard medium with respect to AIDS. On the other hand, TV looks good compared to Hollywood cinema, increasingly berated for its failure to develop films about AIDS: as of 1991, *Longtime Companion* was the only U.S. feature film on AIDS shown in theaters (I am not including films like Bill Sherwood's extraordinary *Parting Glances* of 1987 because, though AIDS is woven into its fabric, it is not "about" AIDS). Julie Lew, writing in the *New York Times*, lists several possible reasons why "the movies are ignoring AIDS": the identification of AIDS with homosexuality; the homophobia of actors, agents, producers, and audiences; Hollywood's addiction to the bottom line and therefore to upbeat endings; presumed audience intolerance for anything about AIDS; the physical unattractiveness of AIDS as a disease; and the entrenched nature of gay caricatures in film and television. Lew concludes that "AIDS offers everything a scriptwriter could wish for: drama, medical intrigue, sex, death, heroism, pathos, social conflict and immediacy. Yet to date only television has approached the topic."[15] Randy Shilts's 1987 bestseller *And the Band Played On* certainly displays these ingredients, so perhaps its problematic transition to the movies can plausibly be attributed to the reasons Lew identifies, notably, as Shilts himself puts it, Hollywood's continuing perception that "AIDS is spelled g-a-y."[16]

But an added or alternative explanation is surely not just the topic per se—AIDS, homosexuality, death—but the changes in form, genre, and ideology needed to tell the AIDS story fully—to politicize disease, to make it social and collective, to show the intrigues and bureaucratic failures of medicine, science, and public health. In American films and especially on television, this is simply not done. Of the elements of the AIDS story that Lew identifies, medical television dramas are equipped to deal with a very few indeed, only drama, death, pathos, and social conflict are staples (and social conflict only when it means interpersonal conflict). As Joseph Turow and Lisa Coe argue, it is the systemic, structural dimension of health care that figures in crises today and causes such need for a shared national agenda; yet as their study demonstrates, disease on television is virtually always something that happens to individuals—it is not socially produced and does not demand social action or policy.[17] The television medical drama, it would seem, is not *All The President's Men;* it is not even "Dallas."[18]

Medical dramas on TV are typically credited with serving a number of cultural functions: they give disease a "human face"; they portray the world of medicine and disease realistically; they educate viewers; they allow the television industry to claim that entertainment has a serious social edge; and they engage the viewer imaginatively in contemporary social and ethical issues. Like most commentary on fictional medicine in general, criticism and commentary on television medicine treats it as a representation, even a reflection, of social reality and "real" medicine. It is accordingly judged by the realism of its images of patients and healers, its medical accuracy, its authenticity, its real life therapeutic efficacy (medical dramas often provide toll-free numbers for further information), its ability to heal the wounds of ignorance, prejudice, silence. Given its concern with the real, it is ironic that such criticism continues to privilege the individual to the exclusion of the social and political. The human face of disease, even a gay face, may ultimately be more tolerable for television than its political face.[19]

This essay does not examine AIDS narratives on television strictly as representations of reality. Following Rodney Buxton in his analysis of the controversial "AIDS episode" on the series "Midnight Caller," I will argue that a television drama is always also "a discursive universe that constructs a hierarchy of meaning."[20] I want also, as Mary Poovey puts it, to "interrogate the boundary between medicine and literature," and I assume that narratives—all narratives—always and inevitably do more than "reflect" and "depict."[21] Even the most mainstream prime-time television medical narratives do not simply reinforce traditional dichotomies between the real and the fictional, the objective and the subjective, the scientific and the entertaining. Rather, to quote Poovey again, medical narratives are also "laboratories in which one can observe and learn to interpret the dynamics of meaning production."[22] Understanding their representational struggles and strategies helps us understand the same dynamics in the construction and deployment of medical meaning, including the meaning of AIDS.[23]

In the rest of this essay, I will use *An Early Frost* and *Our Sons* to talk about the problems of creating an AIDS narrative on television. As a starting point, I will use a generic definition of narrative provided by J. Hillis Miller. For Miller, a narrative—a story—requires three elements: formal structure (plot), character, and linguistic patterning.[24] In terms of form, character, and language, a number of concrete questions relate directly to the exploration of AIDS on television: How do these two films serve as prototypical AIDS dramas, and what are the differences between them? How does narrative representation facilitate or discourage identification with characters, and with which characters? What makes a given representation "positive" or "negative," and can interpretation be fully determined? What kind of cultural work do these narratives do? How do they use television codes and conventions as well as the unique constraints, possibilities, and pleasures of television? How do they display complexity, or what Turow and Coe[25] call "texture"? How is AIDS constructed: as a medical problem, as a social issue, as controversial, as sympathetic, as interesting? As a viewing experience? Through what mechanisms do these television narratives reinforce prevailing cultural values—or criticize, police, disrupt, or challenge them? Do these narratives enable us to explore alternative assumptions about the world and reality? Do these illness stories function therapeutically? Whose story do these stories tell?

III

> We tried to make a movie that hopefully we wouldn't be ashamed of in five years. We tried to make an honest depiction, something where people would say, "Hey, that's real. That's not phony, that's not TV."
> —Steve White, NBC Vice President for Movies and Miniseries

In development for two years before NBC gave permission to begin production in June 1985, *An Early Frost* "was a movie whose time almost didn't come"; it went through at least thirteen script rewrites, "some due to changing medical knowledge about AIDS, others to the network's fears about giving the appearance of either endorsing or condemning homosexuality."[26] As one producer told Jane Hall, "We wanted neither to romanticize the homosexual relationship nor hit it with a sledgehammer"; or, to put it another way, in the words of *Atlanta Journal/Constitution* editor Bill King, "the phrase 'family drama' gets quite a workout from network executives discussing *An Early Frost*. While the film is quite open in its depiction of [Aidan] Quinn's character as a homosexual, NBC is anxious that it not be seen as a 'gay' story."[27]

The scene that introduces Michael's lover, Peter, illustrates this balancing act. We know Michael is back in Chicago by the exterior shot of an urban high rise—in itself a standard piece of televisual AIDS shorthand.[28] A close-up shows him asleep in a dark bedroom. Someone enters, and a hand reaches down to tickle his ear; he swats at it.

PETER'S VOICE: Are you gonna stay in bed all day or what?

MICHAEL: What time is it?

PETER: It's eight o'clock.

MICHAEL: Why didn't you wake me?

PETER: [sits on bed, putting on socks] Well I've been trying for the last half hour.

MICHAEL: I'm gonna be late. I'm exhausted [Sits up.] Ohhh.

PETER: Well, you better start saving your strength for falling asleep on one of those beaches in Maui.

[Michael begins coughing.]

PETER: Hey, you OK? I'll tell you what—why don't you stay home today?

MICHAEL: I *can't*. Meetings . . . back to back.

We learn from this scene that Michael and Peter live together, have a domestic routine together, and indeed share the same bed, but we don't see them in it at the same time. We also learn that Michael is experiencing new symptoms, coughing, and exhaustion. As he gets up and heads for the bathroom, Peter says he has found a travel agent who has made hotel reservations in Maui. Michael now breaks the news that he can't leave because he has a trial coming up.

PETER: Michael, I've made arrangements to close the store.

MICHAEL: Well, what can I do? They just made me a partner.

PETER: [throwing his shoe in the air and catching it] O-kay! Here we go again!

If, as feminist literary critics have suggested, the real protagonist of a Victorian novel such as *Jane Eyre* is the house that the heroine gets at the end, we could argue that the real protagonist of *An Early Frost* is the American nuclear family. The scenes between Michael and Peter largely do not challenge a mom-and-pop division of labor but reproduce it, even to Peter's culinary expertise, expressive emotional life, and desire for a more open, communicative relationship. Despite the surprise element of the bedroom scene that introduces Peter as Michael's lover and the erotic symbolism of beaches on Maui, the following scene restores the interpersonal economy of a conventional heterosexual marriage. Michael is shaving at the bathroom mirror when Peter comes in with a plate of toast:

PETER: Breakfast is served.

MICHAEL: Thanks. We're almost out of shaving cream.

PETER: Oh—OK. [sits on bathroom counter] So—how'd it go with your folks?

MICHAEL: Great! I really surprised my mom.

PETER: Mmmm. That's not what I meant.

MICHAEL: [with slightly sarcastic emphasis] Well, what did you mean?
PETER: You didn't tell 'em.
MICHAEL: [still sarcastic] Yeah I told 'em—they were thrilled. Come on—
    I was there less than twenty-four hours.
PETER: How long does it take?
MICHAEL: Look, I don't have the same relationship with my parents that
    you do with yours. I don't talk about sex with them, they don't talk about
    sex with me.
PETER: Who's talking about *sex?* I'm talking about us.

As Michael silently continues to shave, Peter comes over to him and plucks something from Michael's head: "Gray hair," he says, smiling: "Time's running out." The scene invokes the formal figure of time and untimely death repeated throughout the film and embodied in the elliptical phrase "an early frost." Here it is we, the viewers, who are able to give the phrase "time's running out" ironic resonance and link it to the temporal trajectory of medical melodrama. As Judith Pastore observes, Shilts's chronology of the epidemic, using a similar strategy, "combines new journalism techniques with the bitter irony of formal tragedy. Like watching *Oedipus,* we cannot escape the knowledge eluding the actors which makes all they say and do reverberate with ominous prescience."[29] As the film unfolds, Michael does become sick and is hospitalized and diagnosed with AIDS; when Peter confesses that he has not been strictly monogamous during their two years together and therefore may be the source of the virus, Michael is angry and kicks him out of the house; Michael goes home to break the news to his family and to deal with their pain, anger, and denial. When he is hospitalized again, he makes friends with Victor, a rather flamboyant gay man with AIDS. After the crisis, Michael is back home with his folks when Peter visits and they resolve their conflict, knowing now that Michael could well have been infected before he met Peter (nothing is said about Peter's health). When Victor dies and Michael reads into the death his own fate, he tries to commit suicide; he is rescued by his father and reconciled with him. In tidying the loose ends, the story is not unconventional, but there is no deathbed scene, and, indeed, the movie ends with Michael returning to resume his life with Peter.

This bathroom scene helps establish Michael and Peter's characters and their relationship—one is closeted, the other is not, one holds a "real job," the other manages domestic arrangements (making travel arrangements, cooking, buying shaving cream), one has AIDS, the other (like women in general in AIDS discourse) is positioned as the infector whose own health as infectee is not our concern. Significantly, their limited physical contact occurs as teasing (when Peter tickles Michael's ear, a Disneylike soundtrack invokes the innocent flirtation of a bunny with a butterfly). The negation of sexuality appears to have been accomplished fairly effortlessly, yet it is actually quite skillfully orchestrated through many small moments. The larger question is precisely what is happening with sexual difference here. With Peter placed so consistently in the feminine/wife position, are conventional sexual roles reproduced and possibilities for oppositional representation negated?

While many commentators, including gay activists, can find solid evidence for answering yes and calling this yet one more gay movie for straight people, this judgment assumes we fully understand the nature of the viewing subject, how identification occurs, and how people engage with television. Surely scenes like this one require us to acknowledge the existence of several linked but not equivalent subject positions. And surely it is important that two men in a love relationship, no matter how "straight," no matter how conventional, are being shown without too much fanfare on prime-time television. Part of the pleasure of formula fiction is its manipulation of its own conventional elements; here, Ozzie and Harriet are two gay men. The politics of the relationship, its ideological conservatism, and its ultimate fate, are, of course, the price paid for the relationship's prime-time existence; yet whether or not one is willing to call this scenario progressive, the price needs to be separated from the sheer fact of representation and what it may offer different viewers.

This shaving scene is shot to complicate any unitary perspective. In the previous family scenes, we have seen Michael primarily from his mother's point of view: he first appears—to her, to the camera, and to us—when she opens the door and finds him on the front steps with a bouquet of roses. We are the mother; he is the other. In the shaving scene we begin to see from Michael's point of view, the camera behind him looking toward Peter. Yet the mirror complicates this, showing us Michael and Peter and their reflections—their relationship turned around, as it were. Drawing on long-standing visual codes, we can also see this mirrored glimpse of Michael's hidden life as a figure for his constricted vision, his concern for his image. It also, perhaps, figures the clearer vision and understanding he will ultimately (and obligatorily in such a movie) attain. Finally, the shot plays off the image—repeated with various permutations throughout the film and highlighted in promotional stills—of various family members looking out windows (notably, only the nuclear family, never Peter, appears in these publicity pictures). These window shots, paralleling the framing action of the television screen itself, also underline the metaphorical and literal importance of entrances and exits, doors, entryways, stairs, porch and patio, garden and garage, reminding us of television's theatrical—perhaps more than cinematic—origin as well as the ongoing interaction between the stage and the space of the TV within the home.[30]

When Michael subsequently repents and shows up at Peter's store to surprise him with airplane tickets to Maui, we learn that Peter sells restored objects, specializing in wholesome and innocent stuff from the 1950s—a juke box, a carousel horse. When Peter asks, "But what about your case?" and Michael responds, "It can wait a week: I - am - a - partner!" any TV fan knows that optimism like this is heading for a fall. And, sure enough, as Michael is working late at his office to prepare for the trial, he collapses and wakes up in the hospital.

I want to talk about this first hospital scene in some detail. We hear only the doctor's voice at first: "Michael? I'm Dr. Redding." Michael sits up, coughing, as the physician examines his lungs; Peter is sitting beside him.

> PETER: What's wrong with him?
> REDDING: The tests we did show that you have pneumonia.
> PETER: Pneumonia? I thought it was flu or something.
> REDDING: Are you two lovers? [Michael and Peter exchange looks] There are a lot of gay men in my practice.
> MICHAEL [answering question]: Yes.
> REDDING: How long have you been together?
> PETER: Two years. I'm Peter Hill [stands, shakes hands with physician].
> REDDING: I'm glad you're here—you should be a part of this. Michael, the type of infection you have—*Pneumocystis carinii*—doesn't usually attack someone who's otherwise healthy. So we ran some very specific tests to see if your immune system was functioning normally. The results indicate a disorder. I'm sure you've heard of acquired immune deficiency syndrome.
> MICHAEL: AIDS? Are you telling me I have AIDS?
> REDDING: We only make this diagnosis when there's the presence of an opportunistic infection like this pneumonia.
> MICHAEL: I couldn't have AIDS—it's not possible.
> REDDING: I know this is difficult.

He sits on Michael's bed and provides 1985 AIDS boilerplate: "We know a lot more than we did. . . . We've isolated the virus. . . . We're working on experimental drugs," etc. The immediate treatment plan: "We'll leave you on the IV for a week—if you're still doing well, we'll send you home on oral medication. Now try and get some rest. I'll come back and see you in a

while. [Nods to Peter.] Peter." Left alone, Michael and Peter are silent.
Flute music begins.

> PETER: I thought—I don't know what I thought. [Stands.] I'm gonna go
> talk to that doctor.
> MICHAEL: Peter. Don't leave me.

As he says this, Michael is staring out the window to our right—Peter is in
the foreground on his way out the door with his profile looking left. The
shot is held as Michael says "Don't leave me." It is ambiguous whether
Michael is talking about this moment or in general. Peter pauses, then
returns and sits down, taking Michael's hand in his two hands; Michael
curls toward him into a fetal position. Now comes a dark screen, and then
the title *An Early Frost* appears, superimposed on the signature image: in
the background, a pastoral village with a white church steeple visible
among wooded hills; in the foreground, a tree branch on which green
leaves are beginning to change color. There have been no commercials
throughout this long opening sequence of the film, thus we are fairly
caught up in the drama before the dreaded word *AIDS* occurs at last.[31]

One goal of the medical teledrama is to entertain, but as a number of
scholars demonstrate, another long-standing mission is to educate.[32] *An
Early Frost* is unusually conscientious in carrying out its pedagogic functions (as critic Howard Rosenberg commented, "This is integrity time"[33]).
Certainly *An Early Frost* escapes the charge leveled at other TV dramas of
using AIDS simply as a "plot thickener"—in other words, as just another
issue that the genre absorbs without particularizing. A noted and well-
publicized feature of the production were its "hot sets," in which the hospital setups were maintained almost up to air time so that the scenes could
be reshot with absolutely up-to-date information. Medical consultants
greatly affected ongoing script revisions—changes were made not just to
incorporate changing medical information but also to reflect growing public knowledge of the epidemic (an early version had Kay going to the library to research AIDS; the final version merely has her holding the issue
of *Newsweek* with Rock Hudson and AIDS on the cover).

The film's take-home messages about AIDS attempt to set the record
straight on contamination and casual contact, give basic biomedical AIDS
information, and suggest the risks of sexual contact. The fear of contamination, and its groundlessness, are first presented visually. A close-
up shot shows a tray of food sitting in the corridor outside Michael's hospital room. Two nurses stand in the background, looking at the tray. As Dr.

Redding approaches, we hear one of them whisper, "I don't want to go in there." As Redding picks up the tray and carries it into Michael's room, we see the "ISOLATION" sticker on the door. Redding looks back toward the nurses, his expression grim. As he tells Michael with exasperation, "You can't get AIDS just by being around someone who has it. It's only transmissible through intimate sexual contact or blood."

In interviews about his role, Aidan Quinn expressed particular outrage about the fear of people with AIDS and their isolation: "The real concern around AIDS patients is that you might give *them* something because their immune system is so low" (he donated part of his earnings from the movie to an AIDS foundation that assisted him in researching the part[34]). A number of scenes reinforce this theme. When Michael returns home, Peter stands at the sink holding a cup Michael has been drinking coffee from. Staring out the window, he begins to take a sip, then suddenly realizes what he's doing, dumps out the coffee, and rinses the cup. When friends of Michael and Peter learn of Michael's illness, they give their excuses for not coming to dinner. When Michael goes home to break the bad news, physical revulsion is his father's first negative reaction. His sister, too, won't let her son touch him and won't visit him herself because she's pregnant. Meanwhile his mother reads up on AIDS, his grandmother provides understanding and love, and in the hospital Michael gradually, if at first reluctantly, makes friends and gains support from a group of other men with AIDS, including Victor, a former chef who was fired and evicted by his roommates when he got sick. These multiple perspectives and examples provide not only a textured representation of AIDS, in Turow and Coe's sense, but also a series of lessons in the facts of transmission.[35] When Michael collapses with seizure, ambulance attendants refuse to transport him once they suspect what he has. Paul Volberding, one of the physicians consulted on the script, commented that he feared "the viewer will think that scene was made up. It's not. This has happened in San Francisco, where we pride ourselves as a model for the care of patients with AIDS."[36]

Boilerplate biomedical AIDS information constitutes a second take-home message. Here *An Early Frost* represents Western liberal humanism doing what it does best: arguing for compassion, reason, compliance with scientific authority, common sense. No one could argue with respect to AIDS that this is not crucial cultural work: "It's not a gay disease, Michael," Redding says. "It never was. The virus doesn't know or care what your sexual preference is. Gay men have been the first to get it in this country but there have been others—hemophiliacs, intravenous drug

users—and it hasn't stopped there." Further, the film even acknowledges
that a number of unanswered questions remain:

MICHAEL: [How] did I get it? I haven't had any blood transfusions lately
and haven't been with anyone except Peter.

REDDING: Has he?

MICHAEL: Of course not. We have a *relationship*.

REDDING: I'm only asking because we've discovered it's possible to be a
carrier of the disease without actually showing any of the symptoms himself.

MICHAEL: You mean you can pass it on without actually getting it?

REDDING: [nods] Michael, I'm not judging you. It's important that we know
[your sexual history] because the number of contacts would increase your
chances of being exposed to someone who—

MICHAEL: [interrupting] It was years ago! Before anyone knew about this!

REDDING: The problem is, Michael, that we don't know how long the incubation period for the disease is—it might be five years, it could be
longer. We're just not sure.

MICHAEL: You're not sure of very much, are you?

The formula for medical dramas dictates that physicians be shown to be
in control, and scriptwriters usually accede to the dictate, a practice that
downplays uncertainties, ambiguities, and incorrect interpretations. According to Howard Stein, control and containment are also at work in accounts of "real" medical cases.[37] Stein's medical ethnographies, functioning to excavate what he calls the "story behind the story" of
conventional biomedical narratives, show that the everyday discourse of
practicing physicians also works to disguise its own ambiguity and self-
questioning. The prime-time movie on American TV is likewise poorly
equipped to display subtleties, suggest ambiguities, draw fine distinctions, pose problems. Take the statement, for example, that someone can
"pass it on without actually getting it." Since one does not transmit AIDS
itself but rather a virus that destroys the immune system, and since one
does not transmit the virus without carrying it oneself, this statement is
accurate only if "it" in "pass it on" means the virus, and "it" in "not getting
it" means full-blown AIDS. Granted, this is a subtle point compared to the
crucial proven distinction between justified prudence about established
modes of transmission (sexual contact, contaminated blood) and ground-
less fears about "casual contact." Yet blurring the difference between the
virus and its later clinical manifestations makes it hard to understand the
subsequent statement that "we don't know how long the incubation period"

is. The message intended to be communicated here is no doubt that an infected person may not look sick or be sick but is still infectious to others.[38]

The take-home message about sex is even murkier, reflecting the decision "neither to romanticize the homosexual relationship nor hit it with a sledgehammer." Predictably, the movie was attacked by conservatives because it was soft on homosexuality and by activists because it was desexualized. Certainly sex is handled delicately, to say the least. In what must have been one of the most controversial and negotiated exchanges in the film, the language is almost Victorian:

> MICHAEL: What about Peter? I mean . . . when I get home?
> REDDING: Touching is fine. Hugging. But I'd be careful about being more intimate than that.

Well, we don't see much touching, let alone hugging. Indeed, when Michael comes home, he makes up a bed in the study. Peter is surprised: "But Dr. Redding said—," and Michael replies, "I know what he said. I just don't think we should take any chances." What do these cryptic exchanges mean? That Michael thinks even touching and hugging are risky? That "Dr. Redding said" something different to Peter off camera? That when he said "I'd be careful about being more intimate" he really meant "use condoms"? That he really meant abstention, so that sharing a bed is dangerous because it might lead to some kind of erotic contact? Or is it simply a device to keep the two men out of bed together? Later, after Michael has told his family that he's sick, his grandmother begins to kiss him, and he stops her; but she says, "It's a disease, not a disgrace—Come on, give your grandma a kiss." This kiss was controversial too, but the medical consensus that friendly kissing is safe prevailed.[39]

By conventional standards, *An Early Frost* was a success. Jane Hall in *People* hailed it as "a shattering AIDS TV movie [that] mirrors a family's pain," a "landmark" in dealing with the "feelings" associated with AIDS. But whose feelings? Vito Russo writes that in "*An Early Frost* we see how AIDS affects a young man's mother, father, sister, brother-in-law and grandmother. There is no consideration given to the fact that this is happening to him—not them."[40] And Jan Grover writes that

> NBC's *An Early Frost* enforced existing prejudices by returning its PWA protagonist to the bosom of his family. Evidently he lacked long-term, close-knit friends back in Manhattan [actually, Chicago]; it was only after being shorn of his sexuality and his identity as a gay man that he could be returned, neutered, to his mother and father, enfolded once again within the nuclear family, and die in peace.[41]

These critiques, uncompromisingly argued from a gay and lesbian activist position, cannot be denied. Yet it seems to me that the film may offer points of identification and perspective that require further exploration. Most obviously, *An Early Frost* deliberately avoids the traditional ending of the disease-of-the-week films, a genre that, as Howard Rosenberg describes it, is designed to produce "a torrent of teary movies about illness, each usually climaxing with a manipulative deathbed finale intended to leave viewers limp but uplifted"; it is "apparently impossible," he adds, "to be terminally afflicted these days without also being inspirational."[42] The producer of *An Early Frost* said this was precisely what they wanted to avoid, and Quinn, as Michael, said that as he learned more about real people living with AIDS, he appreciated the ending, which, without implying that Michael will get well, doesn't have him die onscreen.

I would suggest, too, that the narrative structure does other kinds of work at the ending. For example, in the scene where Michael attempts to commit suicide, he goes before dawn to the garage, closes the door, and turns on the ignition. Meanwhile his father wakes up to work out, as he does every morning. With carbon monoxide filling the garage and Nick running on his treadmill, the camera cuts back and forth between the two settings, building suspense as Michael coughs more and more, the smoke gets thicker, and Nick keeps jogging. Finally Nick goes to the kitchen, at last sees the light under the garage door, and gets Michael out in time—keeping him alive and acknowledging that he *wants* to keep him alive.

This narrative structure is such that the practiced viewer of American film and television cannot *not* want Michael to be saved. Indeed, the viewer's knowledge creates a responsibility for Michael that, for many viewers, may not have existed before and, indeed, may even now exist against their will. The narrative code, in other words, dissolves the particulars, and in this instance virtually requires the viewer to take up an engaged subject position. As in the earlier scene between Michael and Peter, one may quarrel with the ideological values ascribed to the scene—father saving son, active saving passive, straight saving gay—not to mention the macho scene that follows the rescue—first Nick sends Kay away ("Go back to the house. . . . This is between me and my son"), then goads Michael into losing his temper. 'Well, I don't give a damn what you think anymore," yells Michael, "because I'm more of a man than you'll ever be, you son of a bitch!" "That's right, that's right," croons Nick, "You go on, you call me anything you want—you hit me if you want to, as long as you don't give up." And despite Michael's return to Chicago and to Peter, heterosexuality gets the finale, with the final credits rolling against a family photo of Michael, his parents, his sister, and Bea. Nevertheless, numerous points of the narrative enable, even require, the viewer to "identify" in rather fluid and unpredictable ways. As we look more closely at the apparently conventional surface of the TV movie, we need to consider the ways that subject-positioning, critical viewing, and the legibility of television texts generate meaning for viewers at different points in their psychic, erotic, chronological, and cultural lives.

IV

> [Our Sons] is a very carefully constructed and classy
> production. . . . [It might], then, be expected to leave the gay
> community reasonably pleased. Perhaps even a little gratitude
> would be in store. Don't count on it. Many homosexuals today
> are not about to be satisfied with occasional crumbs from the
> groaning board of popular culture. They are fed up with seeing
> their very existences viewed primarily as "controversial." Even
> the occasionally more sensitive films use distancing ploys,
> exploring not the lives of homosexuals but the anguished fretting
> of their parents or friends.
> —John O'Connor, New York Times

Our Sons was broadcast as an "ABC Movie of the Week" on Sunday, May 19, 1991.[43] It is the story of two gay men, one on the verge of dying of AIDS, and how they and their mothers face and are changed by this crisis. The movie's opening credits appear against the background of the California coast, accompanied by tranquil piano music. The ocean image dissolves to a luxurious pool and a light, open, California house. An alarm clock rings; it's early. Julie Andrews as Audrey Grant reaches to turn it off, picks up her dictaphone, and begins cutting deals. This is no pastoral hometown with a white church steeple but "the coast," immediately a more urbane and sophisticated setting. And where the central metaphor of *An Early Frost* was natural, that of *Our Sons* is familial.[44]

We next see Audrey at the office making high-powered phone calls. Last on her list of tasks is "Call James." As she dials and the phone rings, we hear the prerecorded message on her son's answering machine: "Hi, you've reached James and Donald. Leave a message for either of us—we don't have secrets from each other—well, maybe one or two." In *An Early Frost*, Kay's voice on Michael's answering machine serves mainly to reinforce how little she knows about his life. *Our Sons*, aired six years later, uses the prerecorded message as a simple device to introduce "the gay relationship" and establish its openness—to all listeners, including Audrey and us. AIDS is introduced at the outset, too: as we hear Audrey leave her message, we see, in sharp contrast, the crisis taking place at James's end; rushing to get Donald into an ambulance, he simply has no time to pick up the phone. As in *An Early Frost* when Peter tells Michael teasingly that "Time's running out," our knowledge here that Donald is already seriously ill gives a twist to Audrey's plea that James call as soon as he can: "It's Monday the 23rd and counting. Have a heart."[45]

Our Sons is a coming-out story, or rather it's a road movie embedded in a medical melodrama embedded in a coming-out movie. Donald has little inclination to tell Luanne Barnes, his mother in Fayetteville, Arkansas, that he's dying: she kicked him out eleven years earlier because he was gay, and now, even if he wanted to, he's too sick to attempt a reconciliation. So James, unknown to Donald, persuades Audrey to go to Fayetteville and bring Luanne back to Donald before he dies. Luanne's refusal to fly makes the road movie necessary, giving the two women an extended opportunity to identify their class differences: in music (country & western versus classical), in personal habits (smoking versus nonsmoking), in ideology (intolerance versus tolerance of homosexuals), in hair color (blonde versus brown, a tip-off that Luanne and Audrey are the couple the film is interested in, not James and Donald).[46] Ultimately, for the sake of their sons, Audrey and Luanne not only transcend their differences but also acknowledge their similarities (for example, they find they both love jazz and that neither has a boyfriend at the moment). This in turn makes harmony possible between Luanne and Donald, who are reconciled by the time of Donald's death; between Donald and James, who have disagreed about Donald's desire to die at home (James resisting Donald's wishes as part of his own denial); and between Audrey and James, who mutually agree to try for a more honest relationship. Michael Pierson in *An Early Frost* wrestles with his father's rage and perpetual injunctions to "be a man"; in *Our Sons*, fathers are virtually erased.

So what's new? In the vision of *Our Sons*, AIDS has become routine, pervasive, and less mysterious. James is familiar with the hospital and its routines. No doctors explain "the facts of AIDS" but simply go about their business in the background, hooking up respirators, IVs, etc. Funerals are routine. When Audrey breaks the news to Luanne about Donald and starts to explain what AIDS is, Luanne comments drily: "I mean I watch TV." Whereas the producers of *An Early Frost* decided not to show Michael's health seriously deteriorate, here Donald looks very sick, very weak, and his Kaposi's sarcoma lesions are visible.[47]

When Donald tells James, "Toto, I have a feeling we're not in Kansas anymore," he acknowledges that he's seriously ill and also signals another important difference in the two movies: Michael's character was made sympathetic to a "general audience" in part by "de-gaying" him; Donald's more interesting character is self-aware, relatively campy and unconventional, and extremely funny. All three character traits—which are permitted him perhaps because progress has been made or perhaps because he dies before the movie ends—are evident as he makes offhand conversation in the hospital with Audrey:

> I gave up smoking for my health. The insurance companies should come up with a whole new concept: irony insurance. There's a fortune to be made.

"What's wrong with this picture?" Donald asks when his mother appears in his room after eleven years' estrangement. "How you been, Donnie?" asks Luanne, "I guess that's startin' out stupid." As she comes toward his bed, Donald replies, "I've been fine prior to this current nuisance." Then, "I like your outfit—très chic, Ma." Everyone gets good lines in *Our Sons*, and all get their share of irony, even when it's dark. Audrey, intensely uncomfortable with her mission in Fayetteville, obviously wishes she were anywhere but in Luanne's trailer:

> LUANNE: Want a drink?
> AUDREY: I'd *kill* for a drink.

Luanne, waiting tables after Audrey's visit and repeatedly queried about the mysterious limo that arrived at her door, finally says "I won a contest, OK?" "What for?" she's asked. She replies bitterly: "Mother of the Year."

While some reviewers complained that Luanne's Archie Bunker role was overwritten, the scriptwriters may have been trying to make her reactions complex, as Nick's, in *An Early Frost*, were not; or perhaps the critics are insulated in Los Angeles from the range of American views about AIDS. She gets other lines as well, though: "I feel like I'm in 'Dynasty'," she says, looking around Audrey's house, the house that Donald designed. And James, though in some sense the straightest of the characters, also gets opportunities to be sardonic. After Donald has been hospitalized, Audrey suggests that his mother "should be told . . . about Donald, what's happening." James bluntly interrupts: "Mother, try to stop saying that, would you—'About Donald,' 'what's happening.' Donald has AIDS. He's dying. Would you stop tap dancing."

Our Sons has little of the medical boilerplate that was centrally featured in *An Early Frost*. There is no lecture on the high-risk groups: Donald's hospital roommate is another man with AIDS; the woman caring for him tells James, "He's my husband. I've got it too." Virtually nothing is said about how Donald became infected (indeed, the line most explicit about sex is Luanne's response to hearing that when James was younger he had sexual relationships with women: "I can't understand how someone could jump the fence after tastin' normal."). In any case, the screenwriters seem more comfortable with the topic, with their own knowledge and authority. James, for example, says "Donald's dying," not "Donald's doctor says he's dying," and "He's much too sick to travel," not "They say he can't travel." He speaks with his own authority.[48]

Neither movie makes much of AIDS treatment, but there are differences. *An Early Frost* provides explicit information about the course of the disease, emphasizing the inevitability of death and futility of treatment. After the emergency room doctor tells Kay that "in my experience, I've never known anyone with AIDS to survive," she cries "But there must be something you can do! You're a *doctor!*" Though in 1985 health care professionals were becoming more skillful at treating the symptoms of AIDS and though people with AIDS and HIV infection were already trying various experimental treatments, *An Early Frost* accurately represented conventional medical wisdom: asked about a cure for AIDS, the physician replies "I wish there were. We're tying to find one. But it may take years." By 1991, many physicians had shifted their views to favor treatment, including early intervention with AZT and other drugs.

In the face of divided medical opinion, *Our Sons* is less emphatic on the treatment issue, as in the scene where Donald and James are playing cards and Donald tries to persuade James to be tested for HIV (a term the film does not use):

DONALD: When are you gonna be sensible?

JAMES: You said you wouldn't bring that up again.

DONALD: I lied. It just isn't rational not to be tested.

JAMES: If I promise to do it will you leave me alone?

DONALD: It could be negative, James.

JAMES: Yeah and what are the astronomical odds of that being true, let's find the nearest computer.

DONALD: Michael Roby died two years ago, and Peter's still testing negative.

JAMES: Peter wants to *know*, Donald.

DONALD: Yes, and if God forbid he does go positive he will have had the earliest treatment possible—as I might have had when I was still in denial mode—"*Me*—it can't happen to *me*."

JAMES: It's my choice, Donald.

DONALD: [looking at his cards] I think I'm gonna win and I haven't even started cheating yet.

This scene suggests accurately that early treatment helps. Though it doesn't get into the changing politics of testing, it does skillfully show the kind of discussion and speculation many people at risk have gone through and also shows, in James, the psychological and conversational mechanisms of what Donald calls "denial mode." The implication that treatment helps, however, is contradicted elsewhere, first by Donald's puzzling implication that seroconversion (as opposed to the appearance of symptoms) can happen even years after exposure to HIV, and again toward the end of the film, after Audrey admits she *has* been evading—"tap dancing"—the issue of James' sexuality, not communicating her resentment that, as she tells him, "you would not be marrying the girl of my dreams." She asks for a second chance at honesty between them: "I want you to be tested. Because then we'll know how much time we have to try again." Perhaps the ambiguity is for dramatic effect; perhaps it's because treatment and the prognosis for long-term management are not yet taken for granted; perhaps it attempts to reflect genuine disagreements among people working with AIDS. But still a positive HIV test is not the same as an immediate death sentence, and certainly not one with a fixed time frame.

After Donald's funeral, Audrey and James accompany Luanne (and Donald's coffin) to the airport. As they leave, Audrey gives James Donald's childhood drawing of a castle he used to tell Luanne he would build for the two of them to live in. "She wanted you to have it," says Audrey. The final shot is of Luanne's plane flying home, against the sunset. Then a white on black dedication appears:

This film is dedicated to the memory of the 108,731 people in the United States who have died of complications from AIDS.

Critics were divided on *Our Sons*. Stephen Farber saw the disparity between the film's grim subject matter and its "glossy soap operaish format" as evidence of the extreme nervousness with which television still approaches AIDS.[49] Howard Rosenberg called it ironic that an AIDS story should take the form of "a buddy movie"—"Except that the bickering buddies in this case are not the two male companions directly touched by AIDS but their mothers . . . [who] have nothing in common beyond motherhood."[50] His review stung *Our Sons* coproducer Micki Dickoff to respond that he had "missed the point" in saying that the film played "peekaboo with AIDS." "If the issue of AIDS has to be 'approached from around the corner,'" she writes, quoting Rosenberg, "or through the back door, better that way than not at all." And why assume, she continues, "the network's motive was to avoid the negative backlash of conservative pressure groups? ABC's approach to the story, by directly confronting homophobia, is more likely to offend those conservative media watchdogs and advertisers."[51] Though many gay viewers and AIDS activists disliked *Our Sons* for its focus on the mothers, Dickoff was correct that conservatives were the group most vocally outraged.

But although the broadcast of *Our Sons* was certainly a political event, the text itself does not present the collective, political, policy dimensions of the epidemic—only the closing dedication hints at such a possibility. At the same time, the narrative's conclusion reverberates with the sense that AIDS is a disease experienced by individuals and that homosexuality, inevitably, inescapably, and underlined by the absence of fathers and other straight men, has something to do with mothers. The event that most clearly resurrects and recycles this chestnut is Luanne's gift of the castle drawing to James, a gift, loaded with psychoanalytic implications, that brings almost too many meanings to the end of the film: Donald's identity, literally salvaged from Luanne's closet, is passed on to James; Luanne's defense structure is relinquished; the world of "Dynasty" is restored to those who already inhabit it; and Donald's impossible dream—to live in a castle with his mother—is transferred to his lover, who is now free to live in Donald's castle with *his* mother. Indeed, the final scene in the airport represents a kind of prime-time return of the repressed.

Perhaps the more important point, however, is that in *Our Sons*, as in *An Early Frost*, the seemingly conventional and seamless TV-movie surface gives way to a more interesting array of subject positions potentially available to the viewer. Together the two films suggest some useful ways of thinking about the format of network television dramas, the complex nature of those hypothesized figures "the character," "the viewer," and "the audience," and the legibility and intertextuality of television texts.

V

"There are eight million stories in the Naked City, but [ours] will not be one of them."
—Donald, in *Our Sons*

In this essay, I have attempted to address some of the questions I raised at the beginning: the characteristics of these two films as prototypical AIDS dramas spaced six years apart, *An Early Frost* treating AIDS as a classic disease-of-the-week, *Our Sons* treating it as a pervasive, even routine condition experienced by many; the interesting and not fully readable ways that narrative representation facilitates or discourages the viewer's identification with characters on the screen, above all challenging any simple notion of identification on the basis of demographic similarity; the specific contexts in which a given representation of gay men or people with AIDS can be—even must be—evaluated as "positive" or "negative," for example in the context of political efforts to influence television "images" or of public-health efforts to make viewers sympathetic toward people with AIDS; the problematic assumption, underlying many of these efforts, that unmediated representation can be achieved; the diverse kinds of cultural work that different AIDS narratives do; the cultural work of these mainstream, conventional dramas (in contrast to alternative and experimental videos) in creating points of identification and concern even among resistant viewers, in part by treating AIDS, despite its controversial, volatile nature and its enormous social impact in the real world, in the tradition of medical TV dramas (i.e., as a disease experienced by individuals) and by chronicling it in the established conventions of television realism; and, finally, the manipulation of television codes to tell stories about AIDS from seemingly acceptable perspectives, at the same time offering occasionally transgressive perspectives, a range of attitudes toward prevailing cultural values, and a complex and textured account of AIDS. Do these narratives enable us to explore alternative assumptions about the world and reality? Only the most subtle of footholds is offered for such an exploration. Whose story do these stories tell? This remains a difficult question.

The process of identification with a video representation is not passive, with the spectator holding a checklist on which certain features are relevant and others aren't. Take, for example, the following exchange from the first scene between Donald and Luanne:

LUANNE: You've got no accent anymore.
DONALD: No.
LUANNE: Well maybe just a smidgeon here and there—you can hardly hear it. [Long silence] I hear you've got real successful.
DONALD: Yes, I've done pretty well. Would you care for a chocolate? [Luanne refuses]
LUANNE: From drawin', more or less?
DONALD: Sorry?

LUANNE: I mean you got successful just from drawin'?
DONALD: More or less.
LUANNE: You was always drawin' when you was a kid.

In contrast to many scripts about AIDS, here the scriptwriters deliberately work to avoid heavy-handed moral judgments. This casually clever and compact exchange shows its participants in mild verbal combat, its light touch almost camouflaging Luanne's refusing the chocolate, thus failing a basic fear-of-contamination test. (Donald afterward tells James, "She wouldn't touch me, you know," and James responds, "Of course.") In television conventions, Luanne's behavior is not inevitably "negative," in part because the conversational exchange that surrounds it does not force the viewer to give it a negative interpretation, in part because it is contained by Donald and James's resigned lack of outrage. Likewise, recall the exchange between Michael and Peter in *An Early Frost:*

MICHAEL: We're almost out of shaving cream.
PETER: Oh. OK.

Whom does this exchange "represent"? Is it "negative"? If so, in what way and for whom? I suggested above that it reproduces heterosexual marriage roles, with Peter the "wife" who manages the domestic space. Is this then a "positive" representation in the eyes of Middle America? Does the straight man watching say, "I wish I had a partner like that, who'd get the shaving cream when I told him to and not give me a lot of shit like my wife does"?

Micki Dickoff, defending *Our Sons*, argues that such films have brought about "real-life reconciliations";[52] meanwhile a colleague tells me with dismay that her two sons (aged ten and twelve) made vomiting sounds during a gentle hugging scene between two gay men in *Longtime Companion*. So much for the "promotion of homosexuality" claimed by the Right! For who knows what "real audiences" really do? ("If 'the media' were so powerful, I'd be heterosexual," says Harvey Milk in the documentary about his life, *The Times of Harvey Milk*.) And what, in any case, is the relation supposed to be between television drama and real life? Does Donald's physical appearance mean he is portrayed realistically? Is his love of and quotation from old movies a stereotype? An accurate reflection of the aesthetic preferences of some gay men (though not all, including James, Michael, and Peter)? A genre-specific convention for establishing intertextuality? A gay in-joke? Moreover, a narrative's potential for indeterminability is perhaps strengthened by network television, where commercials address a different persona than do the programs, where one can always walk out, and where the picture on the screen often resembles the viewer's own living room.[53]

The AIDS teledrama embodies a tangled legacy of cinematic and televisual codes, familial and sexual metaphorical displacements, and gender and genre conventions—to the point that real life is virtually irrecoverable. At the same time, television exists within real social and historical contexts that also shape its discursive universe. As Lynn Spigel demonstrates in her wonderful essay on television in the 1950s, there was intense concern with television's potential role as an invader of the private domestic space of the home (the doors on console TVs were originally designed to provide privacy—from the television set!).[54] Given this legacy, one could argue plausibly that if AIDS has been so profoundly stigmatized, television should have been less hospitable to the epidemic than movies—which enable people to encounter it in the already contaminated space of public theaters rather than the sanctity of the home. Yet perhaps the privacy of the home is precisely where some people would prefer to learn about AIDS—not in a public theater where they might be seen, might be identified as homosexual, might share the space with homosexuals or people with AIDS, and where they can't just change the channel if they don't like it.[55] But what does this legacy really mean in the 1990s?

Rock Hudson's announcement in the summer of 1985 that he was being treated for AIDS was a turning point in the public's perception and in media coverage of the epidemic. As people talked about Hudson and AIDS, they created an interested community that had not existed before, a community which thought about AIDS as something that could happen to them or to people they knew. This was true of women as well as men: Hudson's illness was the point at which, ironically, the epidemic ceased to be seen strictly as "a gay disease." This suggests a powerful lesson about identification: we may identify with other persons not because they are demographically "like" us but because we feel we have something in common, because we have shared their experience and knowledge, laughed with them, talked with them, walked in their shoes. The narrative structures of film and television can provide this sense of shared experience; indeed, in the case of major film stars like Hudson, we may feel we know them, have even "been" them. We need therefore to think carefully about narrative form, identity, and textuality, for ultimately these characteristics may be more significant determiners of viewer response than whether a given representation is "demographically correct."[56]

In summary, questions of identity and identification appear to involve memory, the nervous system, present goals and activities, life experience, familiarity with and pleasure in the conventions of a given narrative genre, demographic and circumstantial characteristics of the human figures (including their physical appearance, political perspective, values, real-life similarities and differences—class, gender, etc.), emotional and political connections to the text, and psychic commitments. Identification can obviously also be partial, can shift in the course of a performance or text, and can piggyback on formal elements of a dramatic work: formal or technical points of identification thus include the trajectory of the drama; the structure and angle of camera shots; our knowledge, and our knowledge of the characters' knowledge; character's function in the drama (i.e., their classical dramatic positioning as protagonist, antagonist, commentator, learner); their role in producing irony, laughter, and pathos; and their ability to mark difference, to offend, to charm. Finally, the text can draw us in by virtue of its own structure and its relationship to other texts: through language, linguistic patterning, dramatic and emotive associations, use of the visual and verbal codes of television and television genres, allusion, metaphor, conversational inventiveness, and other elements of discourse.

It is in this detailed, technical sense that we can use television texts, as Poovey suggests, as "laboratories in which one can observe and learn to interpret the dynamics of meaning production." It remains to be seen whether such laboratory findings will prove directly useful in formulating our various agendas for AIDS on television—intellectual, medical, political, cultural; but they will certainly arm us with a more intelligent and nuanced understanding of all the ways that television texts produce meaning and of the diverse kinds of cultural work television narratives can do.

But this conclusion must *not* forestall critique. Yes, these made-for-television movies can be taken up and used in more diverse and progressive ways than their makers or critics may have imagined; yes, they do important cultural work for many viewers despite their limited utility for gay and AIDS activist sensibilities; yes, our critique should not be based on simplistic and unsupported assumptions about how identity and narrative form function; and yes, these cautious movies could have been much, much worse. Given the continuing urgency of the HIV/AIDS crisis in America, however, a radically different vision must accompany any generosity toward mainstream television narratives. Think, for example, of the stories that might have been told, that should have been told about gay men and this epidemic. Instead, we have two bland, humanistic, made-for-television movies. Created with better-than-average production values, resources, and good intentions, ultimately these movies are a pathetic legacy. In the last decade, more than two hundred thousand Americans were diagnosed with AIDS, more than one hundred thousand have died, infection among women and young people is growing faster than preventive behavior, people of color and gay men are continuing to become infected, the manifestations of the disease are still not fully known, the provision of drugs and treatment is still enmeshed in politics and bureaucracy, and the health care system is a disaster. Having identified the success of these two modest movies, I am even more outraged at their failure: their failure to exploit the enormous resources of narrativity demonstrated in activist and independent work, to represent the courage and dedication of the AIDS activist community, to mention the words *condom* or *safe sex* or *gay community*, to show gay men and lesbians being gay, to make manifest the shabby politics surrounding the epidemic, and to challenge the systemic inequities of the health care system. Whose story? A decade into the epidemic, the story of AIDS remains in many ways untold. Instead, AIDS narratives on television tell the story of network television, still on its fearful, cautious, deadly path to self-destruction.

NOTES

This project is supported in part by a grant from the Research Board of the University of Illinois at Urbana-Champaign. For suggestions, materials, and instructive discussions, I am indebted to Gregg Bordowitz, Jean Carlomusto, Douglas Crimp, Lisa Duggan, Jan Zita Grover, Bob Huff, Cary Nelson, Cindy Patton, Constance Penly, Suzanne Poirier, Kim Rotzoll, and Simon Watney. I am also grateful to Maria Theresa Rodriguez and Catherine Warren for research assistance.

Sarah Schulman epigraph from *People in Trouble* (New York: Penguin, 1991), pp. 72–73; Steve White epigraph is White commenting on *An Early Frost*, quoted by Bill King, "*Early Frost* Covers New Ground for Television," *Atlanta Journal/Constitution*, November 11, 1985, TV section, pp. 4–5; O'Connor epigraph from O'Connor, "Gay Images," p. 32 (cited in note 9).

1. Made for NBC Monday Night at the Movies and first broadcast on November 11, 1985, *An Early Frost* was directed by John Erman and produced by Perry Lafferty. Story by Sherman Yellin, teleplay by Daniel Lipman and Ron Cowen, music by John Kander, photography by Woody Omens. The movie stars Gena Rowlands as Kay, Ben Gazzara as Nick, Aidan Quinn as Michael, Sylvia Sidney as Bea; with D. W. Moffett as Peter, John Glover as Victor, Sydney Walsh as Susan, and Terry O'Quinn as Dr. Redding.

2. On the basis of a study of two weeks of television programming in November 1985, Joseph Turow and Lisa Coe ("Curing Television's Ills: The Portrayal of Health Care," *Journal of Communication* 35 [Autumn 1985]: 36–51) conclude that the treatment of illness on television merely exaggerates a general characteristic of TV's program formats in presenting a straightforward, short-term, single-perspective take on a problem. They call representations "textured" when they present multiple points of view and multiple discussions

of the illness by different characters, and show the illness itself as multifaceted—e.g., with both acute and chronic, and sometimes uncertain, aspects. Overall, only 5 percent of TV patients in their sample had textured medical problems; soap operas and movies were most likely to present textured representations. Turow and Coe point out a number of further ways in which the dimensions and representations of illness are influenced by program formats and constraints. For example, while the unusual or taboo illness can be treated in the expanded time offered by the TV-movie format—and provides a focal point for the network's promotional efforts—chronic illness lends itself particularly well to the continuing story lines of soap operas (and hospital sets are cheap and good for low-budget productions).

The important difference between straightforward, single-perspective treatment of AIDS and a more complex, multifaceted reporting is explored in a number of contexts: for example, nightly television news coverage in the United States (David C. Colby and Timothy E. Cook, "Epidemics and Agendas: The Politics of Nightly News Coverage of AIDS," *Journal of Health Politics, Policy, and Law* 16 [Summer 1991]: 215–49); reporting in three newspapers between 1983 and 1985 (Matthew Paul McAllister, "Medicalization in the News Media: A Comparison of AIDS Coverage in Three Newspapers," [Ph.D. diss., Institute of Communications Research, University of Illinois at Urbana-Champaign, 1989]); and media coverage of AIDS in Africa (Jenny Kitzinger and David Miller, "In Black and White: A Preliminary Report on the Role of the Media in Audience Understandings of 'African AIDS,'" working paper, AIDS Media Research Project, Glasgow, 1991).

3. Depicting the "homosexual community" on television is problematic in that it involves showing homosexuals not as single stereotypes or abstractions but as social beings—that is, as gay men and lesbians in the process of "being" (living their lives as) gay men and lesbians. Anne Karpf (*Doctoring the Media: The Reporting of Health and Medicine* [London: Routledge, 1988], pp. 135–48) and Simon Watney (*Policing Desire: Pornography, AIDS, and the Media* [Minneapolis: University of Minnesota Press, 1987]) discuss media treatment of AIDS as a classic example of a "moral panic" generated by the gay = sex = death connections. Randy Shilts (*And the Band Played On: People, Politics, and the AIDS Epidemic* [New York: St. Martin's, 1987]), James Kinsella (*Covering the Plague: AIDS and the American Media* [New Brunswick: Rutgers University Press, 1989]), and David C. Colby ("Mass Mediated Epidemic: AIDS and Television News 1981–87," paper presented at AIDS: Communication Challenges, conference held in conjunction with the annual meeting of the International Communication Association, San Francisco, May 27, 1989) discuss the reasons AIDS is deemed hard to cover and hard to show visually. Howard Rosenberg's review in the *Los Angeles Times* praised *An Early Frost* ("*Frost*—Brisk Air of Reason in Murky AIDS Arena," November 11, 1985, sec. 4, pp. 1, 9) as "a wise, honest and tender drama" that had somehow, surprisingly, remained resistant to the more typical media treatment of AIDS—which tended to be, in Rosenberg's words, "exploitive," "opportunistic," "sensational," and "obsessive" (1). "Yet even as the decade drew to a close," writes Rodney Buxton ("'After It Happened . . . ': The Battle to Present AIDS in Television Drama," *The Velvet Light Trap* 27 [Spring 1991]: 37–48), "AIDS remained a topic that television drama could only address with some difficulty" (37). The networks' reluctance to air advertising and public-service announcements about condoms is discussed from an advertising perspective by Maurine Christopher ("AIDS as TV Topic Outstrips AD Issue," *Advertising Age* 58 [February 2, 1987]: 51; and "Nets Stand Fast on Birth Control Ads," *Advertising Age* 57 [November 10, 1986]: 36). Roger Simon ("TV's Failure To Act Seriously

Sends Bad Message to Youth," *Champaign-Urbana News-Gazette*, November 19, 1991, p. A4) addresses the Fox network's decision to begin accepting such advertising in 1992.

4. Independent videos include documentaries such as *Doctors, Liars, and Women, Born in Africa, Absolutely Positive,* and *The Los Altos Story*—the first shown on *Living with AIDS* (New York cable TV), the second and third on PBS ("The AIDS Quarterly" and "P.O.V.," respectively), and the fourth on Fox; alternative and independent videos that self-consciously manipulate existing narrative genres, such as *Ojos Que No Ven, Rockville Is Burning,* and *The Pink Pimpernel;* and experimental videos that deliberately depart from conventional narrative structure, such as *Tongues Untied* (also shown on "P.O.V.," with much controversy), *Chuck Solomon: Coming of Age,* and *Danny. Paul Wynne's Journal,* though broadcast only in the San Francisco Bay area, received national attention (Howard Rosenberg, "*Wynne's Journal*—The Universal Force of AIDS," *Los Angeles Times,* June 22, 1990, F1). Taken together, these represent a range of network, cable, and independent video productions whose target audiences range from prime-time mainstream or public-television viewers to the markets of local cable outlets and specialized and alternative audiences—or a mixture of all the above. A sampling is available on the six-hour compilation *Video Against AIDS* (V-Tape in New York and Toronto, the Art Institute in Chicago). For further discussion, see Cynthia Chris, "Policing Desire," review of *Urinal* by John Greyson, *Afterimage* 17 (December 1989): 19–20; Douglas Crimp, "How to Have Promiscuity in an Epidemic," in Douglas Crimp, ed., *AIDS: Cultural Analysis/Cultural Activism* (Cambridge: MIT Press, 1988), pp. 237–71; Martha Gever, "Pictures of Sickness: Stuart Marshall's *Bright Eyes,*" in *AIDS: Cultural Analysis/Cultural Activism,* pp. 109–26; Jan Zita Grover, "Visible Lesions: Images of People with AIDS," *Afterimage* 17 (Summer 1989): 10–16; Timothy Landers, "Bodies and Anti-Bodies: A Crisis in Representation," *The Independent* 11 (January-February 1988): 18–24; Sharon Lerner, "Women . . . AIDS . . . and the Media," *PWA Coalition Newsline* 65 (May 1991): 23–24; Catherine Saalfield, "AIDS Videos by, for, and about Women," *Women, AIDS, and Activism,* The ACT UP/NY Women and AIDS Book Group (Boston: South End, 1990), pp. 281–88; Catherine Saalfield and Ray Navarro, "Not Just Black and White: AIDS, Media, and People of Color," *PWA Coalition Newsline* 65 (May 1991): 15–19; and Paula A. Treichler, "Seduced and Terrorized: AIDS on Network Television," *Artforum* 28 (October 1989): 147–51, revised for *A Leap in the Dark: AIDS, Art, and Culture,* Allan Klusacek and Ken Morrison, eds. (Montreal: Arttexte, 1992). On AIDS cinema, see Patrick Hoctel, "The Little Movie That Could," *Bay Area Reporter,* June 21, 1990, pp. 49, 55; Julie Lew, "Why the Movies Are Ignoring AIDS," *New York Times,* August 18, 1991, Arts and Entertainment section, p. 18; and Vito Russo, *The Celluloid Closet: Homosexuality in the Movies,* rev. ed. (New York: Harper & Row, 1987). Alexandra Juhasz ("From Within: Alternative AIDS Media by Women," *Praxis* 3 [1992]: 23–45) explores the unique role in the AIDS epidemic of what she classifies as "indigenous media"—film and video that is local, personal, and "speaks from the inside" (i.e., is by and about those to whom it is addressed). Lorraine Kenny's interview with the Testing the Limits Collective includes a useful discussion of conventional narrative techniques deliberately adopted by video artists for certain kinds of AIDS projects ("Testing the Limits: An Interview," *Afterimage* 17 [October 1989]: 4–7).

5. As Mim Udovitch (quoted on p. 50 of "Full Henhouse: Sitcoms and the Single Girl," *Village Voice* [October 22, 1991]: 50–51) writes, progress on prime-time network television is always relative; thus, reviewing the 1991–92 blossoming of "single girl sitcoms," with their various unconventional pregnancies and other revelations, she can write

that "I reluctantly applaud these unclosetings, compromised by the wishy-washy fairy-godmothering of their scripts as they may be." In this spirit we can acknowledge that TV does AIDS 101 rather well. Research presented at the 1989 and 1990 International Conferences on AIDS found that television was the main source of AIDS information for virtually all populations surveyed, including, in the United States, urban IV drug users (Liza Solomon et al., abstract no. FD 851 in *Abstracts*, Sixth International Conference on AIDS, AIDS in the Nineties: From Science to Policy, San Francisco, June 20–24, 1990, p. 294), sexual partners of IVDU's (Les Pappas et al., abstract no. SC 750 in *Abstracts* 3 [1990]: 276) and randomly selected respondents in the Southwest, including Black and Hispanic residents (Christine Galavotti et al., abstract no. WEP 58 in *Abstracts* Fifth International Conference on AIDS, The Scientific and Social Challenge, Montreal, June 4–9, 1989, p. 869). Outside the United States, populations studied include IV drug users in Montreal and Toronto (Janine Jason et al., abstract no. FD 852 in *Abstracts* 2 [1990]: 295); urban residents of Kinshasa, Zaire (M. Kyungu et al., abstract no. FD 846 in *Abstracts* 2 [1990]: 293); teenagers in Copenhagen (Bjarne Rasmussen et al., abstract no. SC 727 in *Abstracts* 3 [1990]: 270); the "general population" of France (Mitchell Cohen et al., abstract no. FD 847 in *Abstracts* 2 [1990]: 293); and hospital patients in Delhi (A. B. Hiramani and Neelam Sharma, abstract no. E 647 in *Abstracts* 1989, p. 910). Significantly, only one study surveyed gay men and bisexuals, reproducing an apparently pervasive inability to count these citizens among the "audience" envisioned for TV.

6. Rosenberg, *"Frost—Brisk Air,"* p. 1.

7. Morgan Gendel, "AIDS and *An Early Frost:* The Whisper Becomes a Shout," *Los Angeles Times*, November 13, 1985, sec. 6, p. 1.

8. Rosenberg, *"Frost—Brisk Air,"* p. 9.

9. In addition to prime-time dramas like *An Early Frost* and *Our Sons*, there are also docudramas like *Rock Hudson, Born in Africa*, and *The Ryan White Story*, scientific documentaries on series such as "Nova," and AIDS episodes on drama and comedy series such as "Roseanne," "Trapper John, M.D.," "thirtysomething," and "L.A. Law." AIDS episodes on "Midnight Caller" and "Miami Vice" are analyzed in depth by Rodney Buxton ("'After It Happened'") and Braddlee ("Death in Miami: AIDS, Gender, and Representation," paper presented at the annual meeting of the International Communication Association, San Francisco, May 26, 1989), respectively. John J. O'Connor discusses the controversial aspects of these shows ("Gay Images: TV's Mixed Signals," *New York Times*, May 19, 1991, sec. 2, pp. 2, 32) as well as what he calls "straight AIDS" on such shows as "DeGrassi High," "A Different World," and "First Love, Fatal Love" ("Three Shows About AIDS [Straight AIDS, That Is]," *New York Times*, April 11, 1991, sec. C, p. 15). AIDS has also been featured on daytime dramas, network and cable comedy shows, and talk shows (including the appearance of basketball superstar Magic Johnson on the "Arsenio Hall Show" in November 1991 just after he announced that he had tested positive for HIV).

10. Quoted in Steve Weinstein, "NBC Pulls AIDS-themed *Lifestories*," *Los Angeles Times*, November 20, 1990, sec. F, p. 3.

11. A number of critics keep track of TV's "flip-flops" on AIDS. Monica Collins ("PBS Flip-Flops on AIDS Shows," *TV Guide* 35 [August 31–September 6, 1991]: 27) observes that on the positive side "In the Shadow of Love: A Teen AIDS Story" aired September 18, 1991, on PBS and (in an unusual cooperative arrangement) on ABC as an Afterschool Special the next day; ABC also scheduled an eight-episode AIDS story line on "Life Goes On." Yet during the same period, the PBS series "P.O.V." showed Peter Adair's "daring" *Abso-*

lutely Positive, yet decided that the documentary *Stop the Church* "went too far" and pulled it. Steve Weinstein ("NBC Pulls AIDS-themed *Lifestories*"; and "NBC Puts Message Over Money with AIDS Show," *Los Angeles Times*, December 18, 1990, sec. F, pp. 1, 11) documents NBC's repeated postponements of the "Steven Burdick" episode on the excellent medical series "Lifestories," the account of a television news anchor who learns he is HIV positive; the network finally ran the episode many weeks after it was originally scheduled. Contradictory stances on sex are chronicled by Jon Berry ("Think Bland," *Adweek's Marketing Week* November 11, 1991, pp. 22–24); Rick DuBrow ("Is TV Too Dirty?" *The Gazette* [Montreal], November 10, 1991, sec. F, p. 2); Stephen Farber ("A Decade into the AIDS Epidemic, the TV Networks Are Still Nervous," *New York Times*, April 30, 1991, sec. C, p. 13); Rick Kogan's review of *Our Sons* ("AIDS Jitters Still Afflict Networks," *Chicago Tribune*, May 17, 1991, sec. 5, p. 1); and O'Connor ("Birds Do It, Bees Do It, So Does TV," *New York Times*, October 13, 1991, p. 29). Many critics (e.g., Howard Rosenberg, "ABC Takes Strides with 'Red, Hot'—and Bold—Special," *Los Angeles Times*, November 30, 1990, sec. F, p. 1) considered ABC's *Red, Hot, and Blue*, broadcast on December 1, 1990 (World AIDS Day), a superlative example of AIDS-related programming.

12. Joseph Turow ("Television and Institutional Power: The Case of Medicine," in Brenda Dervin et al., eds., *Rethinking Communication: Paradigm Exemplar* [Newbury Park, Cal.: Sage, 1989], 2: 454–73) provides a relevant historical account of the influences of outside institutions on early medical dramas on television, specifically the relationship between the Los Angeles County Medical Association and the American Medical Association and the programs "Medic," "Dr. Kildare," and "Ben Casey." Buxton ("'After It Happened'") analyzes the effect of diverse interest groups on a controversial AIDS episode of "Midnight Caller." Ronald Paul Hill and Andrea L. Beaver ("Advocacy Groups and Television Advertisers," *Journal of Advertising* 20 [1991]: 18–27) provide an overview of the relationship between advocacy groups and advertisers in television programming. See also Keith Alcorn ("AIDS in the Public Sphere: How a Broadcasting System in Crisis Dealt with an Epidemic," in *Taking Liberties: AIDS and Cultural Politics* [London: Serpent's Tail, 1989], pp. 193–212).

13. Russo, *The Celluloid Closet*, p. 227.

14. O'Connor "Gay Images," p. 32.

15. Lew, "Why the Movies Are Ignoring AIDS."

16. Quoted in Lew, ibid. After a feverish bidding war while it was on the best-seller list, *And the Band Played On* languished "in development" as various studios tried and failed to get the project off the ground. Rights were finally purchased by Home Box Office for development into a TV movie or miniseries. On mass-media gate-keeping processes (including shortsightedness, ambivalence, conflict of interests, and so on) affecting AIDS, sexuality, and homosexuality, see Colby and Cook, "Epidemics and Agendas"; James W. Dearing and Everett M. Rogers, "The Agenda Setting Process for the Issue of AIDS," paper presented at the annual meeting of the International Communication Association, New Orleans, May 28–June 2, 1988); Du Brow, "Is TV Too Dirty?"; Joanna Elm, "NBC Tones Down *Roe vs. Wade* TV-Movie to Avoid Angering Abortion Pressure Groups," *TV Guide* (May 13–20, 1989): 49–50; Kim Foltz, "TV, Sex, and Prevention," *Newsweek* September 9, 1985, p. 72; Judith Graham, "Ad Industry Rears up at Boycott," *Advertising Age*, July 24, 1989, p. 16, and "'New Puritanism' Colors TV Lineup," *Advertising Age*, May 29, 1989, p. 46; Aljean Harmetz, "AIDS Is Changing Hollywood Scripts and Lives," *New York*

Times, March 15, 1987, p. 20, and "Sanitizing a Hot Novel into a Lukewarm Film," *New York Times*, November 18, 1987, p. 22; Hoctel, "The Little Movie That Could"; Tom Hulce (panel presentation at SIDART, June 8, 1989, a symposium on art and culture in the AIDS epidemic, held in conjunction with the Fifth International Conference on AIDS, Montreal, June 4–9, 1989); Dirk Johnson, "Boy Meets Girl, '89, Can Be a Detective Story," *New York Times*, December 10, 1989, sec. 1, pp. 1, 27; Lorraine Kenny, "Testing the Limits: An Interview," *Afterimage* 17 (October 1989): 4–7; Allan Klusacek and Ken Morrison, eds., *A Leap in the Dark: AIDS, Art, and Activism* (Montreal: Arttexte, 1992; Russo, *The Celluloid Closet*; Michael Leahy, "Why This Young Hunk Risked Playing an AIDS Victim," *TV Guide* 34 (April 26–May 2, 1986): 34–38; Richard Lippe, "Rock Hudson: His Story," *CineAction* (Fall 1987): pp. 47–54; Susan Litwin, "Will America Be Shocked by ABC's *Rock Hudson?*" *TV Guide* 37 (January 6–12, 1990): 14–17; Elspeth Probyn, "Choosing Choice: Images of Sexuality and 'Choiceosie' in Popular Culture," in Kathy Davis and Sue Fisher, eds., *Negotiating in the Margins* (New Brunswick, N.J.: Rutgers University Press, forthcoming); Dorothy Nelkin, *Selling Science: How the Press Covers Science and Technology* (New York: Freeman, 1987); O'Connor, "Birds Do It"; Judith L. Pastore, ed., *Literary AIDS: The Responsibilities of Representation* (Urbana: University of Illinois Press, forthcoming); Planned Parenthood of America, "They did it 9,000 times on television last year. How come nobody got pregnant?" full-page advertisement, *Champaign-Urbana News-Gazette*, December 7, 1986, sec. A, p. 15); Everett M. Rogers, "Diffusion of AIDS Information Through the Electronic Media" paper presented at AIDS: Communication Challenges, San Francisco, May 27, 1989; Saalfield and Navarro, "Not Just Black and White"; and Patricia Strnad "Rakolta Seeks Allies in TV Fight," *Advertising Age*, August 6, 1990, p. 35.

17. Turow and Coe, "Curing Television's Ills."

18. "The Return of Ben Casey," a made-for-television movie broadcast in February 1988, played on the contrast between the heroic tradition of medical dramas and the faster and grittier approach of such ensemble shows as "St. Elsewhere." Vince Edwards returned to reprise his role as the arrogant, brilliant, macho male neurosurgeon of the 1961–66 series; arriving at County General, his old hospital, he finds problems everywhere and takes it upon himself to roll up his sleeves and solve them. Just like old times. But this is the late 1980s; the rules of the game (and the television show) have changed: Casey finds himself hauled up before the hospital administration for carrying inappropriate credentials, using unorthodox procedures, and committing a host of other offenses. Meanwhile the new generation of house staff treat him less like a legend than a neanderthal, and one of the women physicians has to try to fill him in on twenty years of feminism. Had the movie more consistently played with these ironic and self-conscious narrative conventions, it might well have fostered an interesting series. Instead, it was a hodgepodge that ultimately depended on an old cliché—Ben Casey *cares*—to resolve and transcend the myriad problems of contemporary medicine the show so graphically presented. For a perspective on the old and new Ben Casey, see John Stanley, "Vince Edwards at 59: A Mellowed Rogue," *San Francisco Chronicle*, Feb. 14, 1988, pp. 47, 52, and Terry Atkinson, "'Return of Ben Casey' Pilot for Possible Series Revival," *Los Angeles Times*, March 1, 1988, sec. 6, p. 10. For an overview of changes in the representation of physicians over time, see Richard Malmsheimer, *"Doctors Only": The Evolving Image of the American Physician* (New York: Greenwood Press, 1988).

19. For further critical perspectives on traditional American medicine and disease

narratives, see Philip A. Kalisch and Beatrice J. Kalisch, "When Americans Called for Dr. Kildare: Images of Physicians and Nurses in the Dr. Kildare and Dr. Gillespie Movies, 1937–1947," *Medical Heritage* 1 (September–October 1985): 348–63; Turow and Coe, "Curing Television's Ills"; Suzanne Poirier and Louis Borgenicht, "Physician-Authors— Prophets or Profiteers?" *New England Journal of Medicine* 325 (July 18, 1991): 212–14; and Mary Poovey, review of Bruce Clarke and Wendell Aycock, eds., *The Body and the Text: Comparative Essays in Literature and Medicine, Bulletin of the History of Medicine* 65 (1991): 291–92.

20. Buxton, "'After It Happened,'" p. 46.

21. Poovey, Review of *The Body and the Text*, p. 292.

22. Ibid.

23. For elaborating the idea of a discursive universe in scientific writing, I am indebted to such work in the sociology of science as Karin D. Knorr-Cetina, *The Manufacture of Knowledge: An Essay on the Constructivist and Contextual Nature of Science* (Oxford: Pergamon, 1981) and Bruno Latour and Steve Woolgar, *Laboratory Life: The Construction of Scientific Facts* (Princeton: Princeton University Press, 1986). Research in feminism and film theory usefully explores the function of identification in television narratives— and suggests that it is variable and diverse, entailing multiple transactions between what are ostensibly masculine and feminine positions. See, for example, Robert Deming, "*Kate and Allie:* 'New Women' and the Audience's Television Archive," *Camera Obscura* 16 (January 1988): 155–66; Mary Ann Doane, "The Clinical Eye: Medical Discourse in the 'Woman's Film' of the 1940s," in Susan Robin Suleiman, ed., *The Female Body in Western Culture: Contemporary Perspectives* (Cambridge, Mass.: Harvard University Press, 1986), pp. 152–74; Sandy Flitterman-Lewis, "All's Well That Doesn't End—Soap Opera and the Marriage Motif," *Camera Obscura* 16 (January 1988): 119–53; E. Ann Kaplan, ed., *Regarding Television* (Westport, Conn.: Greenwood, 1983); George Lipsitz, "The Meaning of Memory: Family, Class, and Ethnicity in Early Network Television Programs," *Camera Obscura* 16 (January 1988): 79–116; Denise Mann and Lynn Spigel, eds., "Television and the Female Consumer," special issue of *Camera Obscura* 16 (January 1988): 5–7; D. N. Rodowick, "The Difficulty of Difference," *Wide Angle* 5 (1982): 4–15; and Constance Penley, *The Future of an Illusion: Film, Feminism, and Psychoanalysis* (Minneapolis: University of Minnesota Press, 1989). With respect to AIDS, Buxton ("'After It Happened'") examines the ways the various interested parties negotiated the controversy over the "Midnight Caller" "As It Happened . . . " episode; Buxton argues that the final script's lack of closure opens up, if somewhat inadequately, its potential meanings in ways not typical of prime-time series dramas. Braddlee ("Death in Miami") looks similarly at how "God's Work," a 1989 episode on the series "Miami Vice," is "at odds with itself over the issue of sexuality and AIDS." While the overt narrative, Braddlee argues, presents the central gay character in a positive way, the show's production codes present his relationship as incomplete, his sexuality as a prison, and solitude, ultimately, as the price of virtue.

24. J. Hillis Miller ("Narrative," in Frank Lentricchia and Thomas McLaughlin, eds., *Critical Terms for Literary Study*, [Chicago: University of Chicago Press, 1990], pp. 66–79) calls this seemingly straightforward structure of narratives "by no means innocent." In somewhat more detail, his three elements include (i) an initial situation, change or reversal, and a revelation; (ii) the use of personification or some other mechanism for bringing issues "to life" through the positions of a protagonist, an antagonist, and a witness who learns; and (iii) a formal textual pattern that repeats key elements or nuclear figures—a

trope, a system of tropes, or a complex word. For this last category, Miller draws on William Empson's notion of a complex word (*The Structure of Complex Words* [Ann Arbor: University of Michigan Press, 1967]), with some modification. He suggests also that scientific and historical accounts, like fictional ones, have narrative structures that give order to phenomena, but the formal constraints and referential restraints are different—primarily in the way that science and history purport to be constrained by reality, and claim to represent events as they "really happened" or nature as it "really is." Analysts like Poovey (review of *The Body and the Text*), Latour and Woolgar (*Laboratory Life*) and Knorr-Cetina (*The Manufacture of Knowledge*) challenge the position that fictional discourse can readily be separated from scientific or historical discourse by either formal or referential criteria.

Recent work in narrative theory asks questions about the appeal of narrative structure, the role of form and representation in creating narrative pleasure, the relation of fictional narratives to "real life" and of narrative texts to each other (intertextuality), the construction of narrative meaning through form, character, and language, the purposes of narrative, and the function of narrative discourse as a staging ground for cultural struggles taking place elsewhere. As Miller notes, recent decades have generated a "swarming diversity of narrative theories" ("Narrative," p. 67). I do not have space here to enter this swarm, but interested readers may consult Miller.

25. Turow and Coe, "Curing Television's Ills."

26. Jane Hall, "A Shattering AIDS TV Movie Mirrors a Family's Pain," *People Weekly* 24 (November 18, 1985): 145. In comparison, *Roe vs. Wade*, the made-for-TV movie about the Supreme Court's decision to legalize abortion, went through seventeen rewrites before it was broadcast on May 15, 1989 (Elm, "NBC Tones Down *Roe vs. Wade*"). Like the abortion-related "Cagney and Lacey" episode originally broadcast in competition with *An Early Frost*, *Roe vs. Wade* drew much fiercer objections from conservative groups than any AIDS program to date. At least one network affiliate pulled the "Cagney and Lacey" episode in response to objections by antichoice organizations, calling it too one-sided; prolife boycott threats, likewise, caused numerous sponsors to withdraw their support from *Roe vs. Wade*. Du Brow ("Is TV Too Dirty?") comments that "One person's boundary on good taste is another person's censorship. But the question of where to draw the line has never been more difficult than it is at present." He quotes producer Steven Bochco: "The networks are all in a panic. When you cut through the bull, it's all money" (sec. F, p. 2). See also Berry ("Think Bland"), Farber ("A Decade into the AIDS Epidemic"), Harmetz ("AIDS Is Changing Hollywood" and "Sanitizing a Hot Novel"), Kogan ("AIDS Jitters"), and Strnad ("Rakolta Seeks Allies").

27. King, "*Early Frost* Covers New Ground," p. 4.

28. Colby, "Mass Mediated Epidemic."

29. Pastore, "Introduction," *Literary AIDS*.

30. Lynn Spigel, "Installing the Television Set: Popular Discourses on Television and Domestic Spaces, 1948–1955," *Camera Obscura* 16 (January 1988): 11–45.

31. According to Turow ("Television and Institutional Power"), sponsors did not regularly intervene directly in week-by-week programming, but sometimes established policies or ground rules; for example, sponsors of the "Dr. Kildare" series included a cigarette company that prohibited use of the word *cancer* and Bayer, which prohibited episodes showing overdose or death from aspirin. Hill and Beaver ("Advocacy Groups") find that although a number of companies today have developed policies or guidelines for programming and advertising on television, they note that most have none and appear to anticipate

problems in no systematic way. They conclude that a decade of deregulation has on the whole exacerbated rather than decreased such tension. (Buxton's study—"'After It Happened'"—shows that the "Midnight Caller" controversy took executives and script-writers by surprise in part because no policy existed for anticipating problems.)

32. See Turow ("Television and Institutional Power") and Kalisch and Kalisch ("When Americans Called for Dr. Kildare").

33. Rosenberg, "*Frost*—Brisk Air," p. 1.

34. Michael Hill, "*An Early Frost*, an AIDS Story," *Washington Post TV Week*, November 10–16, 1985, pp. 9–11 (quotations from p. 9).

35. A number of critics have used the example of Peter and the cup to show irrational fears of contamination. Yet isn't it a bit harsh to ask that Peter immediately adjust to living with an infectious disease, when even experienced health professionals take a bit of time to let their knowledge overcome their initial fear of contagion and to learn what is safe and what is not? And need the shot necessarily signify that Peter is contributing to the isolation that develops around the person with AIDS? Couldn't it also signify that he does not yet realize that he may be infected himself, or that it's important to avoid further exposure, or that AIDS changes an entire household? What if he had started to throw the coffee out, paused, then taken a drink? It seems to me this would also have been ambiguous, even interpreted as "a death wish" or something similar. In Schulman's novel *People in Trouble* (pp. 200–1), when this issue has become clearly coded within AIDS discourse, two women encounter an acquaintance who's afraid he's HIV positive. Afterward one woman asks the other, "Why did you drink out of his [juice] carton when he might have AIDS?" "It's a rite of passage," says the other. "People who may be HIV positive inevitably offer you a drink out of their glass. It's a test of loyalty to see if you're prejudiced or not, to see if you are informed enough to know that you can't get it that way." In *Our Sons*, James and Donald are both aware of this code.

36. Quoted by Robert Steinbrook, "Thumbs-up from Doctors," *Los Angeles Times*, November 11, 1985, sec. 1, p. 9.

37. Howard F. Stein, "The Story Behind the Clinical Story: An Inquiry into Biomedical Narrative," *Family Systems Medicine* 8 (1990): 213–27.

38. The boundary between fiction and science breaks down at the same point at which it is being reinforced. The physician, encapsulated in his two scenes, provides the core of scientific certainties the audience is intended to receive. But the core is eroded from within by the doctor's factual admission that science is "not sure of very much." See Knorr-Cetina, *The Manufacture of Knowledge*; Latour and Woolgar, *Laboratory Life*; and Ludwik Fleck, *Genesis and Development of a Scientific Fact*, Thaddeus J. Trenn and Robert K. Merton, eds., (1936; reprint, Chicago: University of Chicago Press, 1979) on the need to qualify and define statements with other statements versus shorthand strategies that enable some statements to be treated as "facts." In the feature film *Longtime Companion*, where official medicine is less prominent, theorizing takes place primarily within the affected community. The film opens in June 1981 with a series of short scenes on Fire Island and Manhattan where the repeated question is "Have you seen the *Times?*" Gay men all over New York are reading the *New York Times* article about a "rare cancer" by then seen in forty homosexual men; these readings provide the transition from one individual or group to the next and let us, the audience, eventually hear the whole article. When the first of the group of friends comes down with AIDS, it has no name yet; what's said is, "John's got something wrong with his immune system." Over the weeks, months, and years that the film covers,

we hear various theories, opinions, values put forward: "They talk about the 'rarity of the condition.'" "It's probably from using poppers." "It's from exercising too much." "It's not believed to be contagious." "I certainly don't think everyone's going to die who gets it, do you?"

39. The question of post-AIDS kissing in films has dramatically blurred the lines between the movies and real life, with a number of actors concerned about contracting HIV from on-screen kissing. The health professionals who viewed the premiere of *An Early Frost* emphasized that kissing was very unlikely to transmit HIV; but in any case, as one commented, "I always thought actors and actresses could act. Isn't there a way to fake it?" (Fannin, quoted in Steinbrook, "Thumbs-up from Doctors," p. 9). As actor Tom Hulce has observed, the representation of homosexuality is far more shocking to American audiences than the representation of gory medical details, to which they are well acclimated. What shocked them about Larry Kramer's play *The Normal Heart*, he said, "was not the medical stuff—the seizures, the lesions, and so on—they're used to medical stuff. What shocked them was seeing two men kissing" (panel presentation at SIDART).

These crossover fears recall Vito Russo's anecdote: "When the concerned mother of one young man up for a role in Arthur J. Bressan's *Abuse* asked the director if playing the part would make her son gay, he replied, 'No, and if he plays Hamlet he won't inherit Denmark, either'" (*The Celluloid Closet*, p. 302). D. W. Moffett, who played Peter in *An Early Frost*, said in interviews that he agreed with the decision to omit "kissy-poo" behavior because it would turn viewers off. The prospect of same-sex kissing may also, for an actor, embody career concerns (discomfort if he's straight, fear of exposure or rumor—or discomfort—if he's gay). *TV Guide*'s story on lead actor Aidan Quinn was titled "Why This Young Hunk Risked Playing an AIDS Victim," as though playing the role of someone with AIDS was in itself a high-risk behavior. "Back in Chicago, Quinn's home town, acquaintances couldn't understand why their gruff friend wanted to play someone so . . . unmanly, an outcast with such a vile disease. 'You gotta be courageous to play a fag, Aidan,' one told him" (Leahy, "Why This Young Hunk," p. 36). Quinn himself, however, indicates that the part helped his career by bringing him more interesting scripts with parts no longer confined to stereotypic hunks.

40. Russo, *The Celluloid Closet*, pp. 276–77.

41. See also Grover's review of *Ground Zero* by Andrew Holleran (*San Francisco Sentinel*, October 7, 1988, sec. 16, pp. 24, 34) and Landers ("Bodies and Anti-Bodies").

42. Rosenberg, "*Frost*—Brisk Air," p. 1.

43. Broadcast on ABC Movie of the Week, May 19, 1991, *Our Sons* was directed by John Erman (who also directed *An Early Frost*), produced by Phil Kleinbart, coproduced by Micki Dickoff, and written by William Hanley. Executive producers included Carla Singer, Robert Greenwald, and William Hanley; edited by Robert Florio, designed by James Hulsey, music by John Morris, and photographed by Tony Imi. Cast includes Ann-Margret as Luanne Barnes, Željko Ivanek as Donald Barnes, Julie Andrews as Audrey Grant, Hugh Grant as James Grant, and Tony Roberts as Audrey's friend Harry.

44. The metaphor of "an early frost," central to the movie's universalizing trope, arises literally in the context of gardening when Bea holds up a rose and says to Kay, "They're so beautiful this year: I hope an early frost won't nip them in the bud." Although an early frost kills not just one beautiful flower but a whole season of them, the collective potential of the metaphor is left untapped. The title and linguistic core of *Our Sons* is taken from an exchange between Luanne and Audrey:

LUANNE: How'd you get used to it? That you had a son who was one of them?
AUDREY: My son is not "one of them." Your son is not "one of them." Our sons are two of us.

45. Answering machines have multiple functions in films these days. Often they work to contrast "normal life" with a new reality or crisis (with the prerecorded message representing the earlier time of stability); in *Our Sons*, James and Donald's prerecorded message as well as Audrey's incoming call are set against the immediate crisis of Donald's health. As Timothy Murphy has suggested to me, Michael's phone arrangements in *An Early Frost* guard his gay existence against discovery; when Michael's mother calls and Peter picks up the phone, he violates the routine: technology, in other words, has for Michael been part of the closet. In other AIDS narratives, the machines function to signal that the person is still alive. Sarah Schulman writes: "I just can't imagine another one of those times when you call up an old friend and get that damn tape announcing that his number has been disconnected" (*People in Trouble*, p. 92).

46. Reviewing the small eddies of feminist currents amid the 1991–92 prime-time mainstream, Mim Udovitch writes that "the most obvious advance represented by the new . . . shows is that it is now permissible to hire three actresses for the same project without it being an absolute necessity that one be a redhead, one a blond, and one a brunette" ("Full Henhouse," p. 50). Of course, Luanne in *Our Sons* turns out to be wearing a blonde wig—the sedate head of chestnut hair underneath signals that the two women are not as different as they appear.

47. Aidan Quinn, playing Michael, initially objected to this decision; but he changed his mind as he talked to people with AIDS and their advocates and learned that many people don't look sick, and go about their lives for years. Some of the debates about visually representing the physical status of people with AIDS are discussed by Douglas Crimp ("Portraits of People with AIDS," in Lawrence Grossberg, Cary Nelson, and Paula A. Treichler, eds., *Cultural Studies*, [New York: Routledge, 1992], pp. 117–33) and by several authors in Crimp's *AIDS: Cultural Analysis/Cultural Activism*.

48. In Treichler, "How to Have Theory in an Epidemic," I discuss the evolution of AIDS treatment and AIDS treatment activism, including the resistance by many physicians and patients to the notion that AIDS can be managed as other chronic diseases are managed. In Treichler ("AIDS, HIV, and the Cultural Construction of Reality," in Gilbert Herdt and Shirley Lindenbaum, eds., *Social Analysis in the Time of AIDS* [Newbury Park, Calif.: Sage, 1992], pp. 65–98), I discuss the conceptual shift at the Montreal and San Francisco International Conferences (*Abstracts* 1989 and 1990) among front-line AIDS workers (scientists, health care professionals, patients, advocates, activists and, ultimately, media representatives) from AIDS as an acute, terminal illness to AIDS as a chronic, manageable disease. In his plenary address at San Francisco, for example, virologist Jay Levy said that it may soon be possible for people with HIV disease to think about a normal lifespan. See also ACT UP/New York Women and AIDS Book Group, *AIDS Videos* and Douglas Crimp with Adam Rolston, *AIDS Demo Graphics* (Seattle: Bay, 1990); and Elizabeth Fee and Daniel M. Fox, *AIDS: The Making of a Chronic Disease* (Berkeley: University of California Press, 1992).

49. Farber, "A Decade into the AIDS Epidemic."

50. Rosenberg, "Red, Hot and Blue."

51. Micki Dickoff, "*Our Sons* Put a Human Face on AIDS Crisis," *Los Angeles Times*, June 10, 1991, sec. F, p. 3.

52. Ibid.

53. James Hay, "Advertising as a Cultural Text: Rethinking Message Analysis in a Recombinant Culture," in Brenda Dervin et al., eds., *Rethinking Communication: Paradigm Exemplars* (Newbury Park: Sage, 1990), 2: 129–52.

54. Spigel, "Installing the Television Set."

55. Thanks to Cary Nelson for this insight. Good studies of "real" audiences that also take cultural texts seriously would help determine the range and significance of differing interpretations of AIDS texts. Most current research, involving content analysis, attitude surveys, focus groups, or textual analysis, can't really accomplish this (see several essays in Grossberg, et al., *Cultural Studies*). An exception is Kitzinger and Miller's ("In Black and White") effort to identify and interpret the diverse audience understandings of media accounts of "African AIDS."

56. Richard Meyer ("Rock Hudson's Body," in Diana Fuss, ed., *Inside/Out: Lesbian Theories, Gay Theories*, [New York: Routledge, 1991], pp. 259–88) analyzes the shock expressed by those who had to rethink their conceptions of Rock Hudson when they learned he had AIDS. "Because he has been revealed as homosexual through the spectacle of illness, Hudson is said to betray the projective fantasies of his heterosexual spectator, here a female one" (p. 279). On the representation of specific kinds of bodies on the screen, see also Saalfield and Navarro ("Not Just Black and White"). Walter Goodman ("The Story TV Can't Resist," *New York Times*, November 17, 1991, entertainment section, p. 31) predicts that, in contrast to the Rock Hudson story, which the networks approached with such nervousness (see Lippe, "Rock Hudson"; and Litwin, "Will America Be Shocked"), the case of young, blonde, and bitter Kimberly Bergalis will be "the story TV can't resist." Even more irresistible will be Magic Johnson's, whose announcement in November 1991 touched off a new explosion of projective desire. How the facts of these stories and their media constructions unfold over time will bear watching.

"And Once I Had It All": AIDS Narratives and Memories of an American Dream

John M. Clum

I   AIDS and the Dream

As it was during the Vietnam War, the most important writing during the various battles being waged in the age of AIDS is historical and political. [1] AIDS has raised so many unanswered questions that getting the facts seems paramount. Yet AIDS is the cause of thousands—millions—of personal tragedies, and more personal literary forms—the memoir, poetry, and written, staged, and filmed fictions—have focused on the effects of AIDS on individuals touched by the virus. These AIDS narratives have so far been a series of variations on a few themes. Most mainstream narratives, aimed at the popular media's mythical, cohesive, all-heterosexual audience, have usually focused on homosexual characters with AIDS but move the spotlight early in the story from the person with AIDS to his family's problems in coping with the news that he is homosexual, for homosexuality is usually equated with and presented as the cause of AIDS. However much such cultural productions claim tolerance, AIDS becomes a sign of past sexual transgressions. AIDS narratives written by gay writers have a far more complex, more troubled causality. They often focus not on coping with the disease itself, but on the character's changed relationship to their past sexual activity.

What links mainstream and gay AIDS narratives are their affluent setting and their sense that AIDS has threatened both the American dream of the good life and the sense of protection from menaces to that insular life. When AIDS comes close to heterosexuals thrown into the position of caregiver to a loved one with AIDS, it leads to emotional and spiritual crises as the linked threats of AIDS/homosexuality force people to question the assumptions of the Reagan era—that people were soundly buttressed by their affluence, freedom, technology, and carefully marketed illusions of eternal youth and health. In gay-created AIDS narratives, AIDS also transforms a world of affluence and pleasure. Paul Monette's memory in his poem "Half Life" that "once I had it all" (17)[2] refers not only to his beloved Rog, now dead from HIV-related infections, but also to the affluent world he and Rog once luxuriously shared. That world now seems invaded, compromised as AIDS throws into question the values of the 1970s, what Paul Monette calls "the time before the war."[3]

While "outside" heterosexist narratives tend to place the sexual activity which can be the mode of transmission for the AIDS virus into a murky, almost unspeakable past, a crucial issue for gay writers is how to recollect the pleasure principle that allowed urban gay communities to become a breeding ground for the AIDS virus. Even gay-authored works that critique the promiscuity of the pre-AIDS era attempt to resist self-hating explanations of AIDS.[4] In either case, a major theme of gay AIDS literature is what to do with a lost past, which was both affluent and carefree.

II   The View from Outside

Two typical outside, heterosexual AIDS narratives that seem to offer tolerance, compassion, and understanding actually reinforce aspects of the virulent AIDS mythology. In these fictions, the physical signs of AIDS not only come from the other, the homosexual, they are invasions of the ideal, affluent world of the "me generation" from someplace outside that socioeconomic location.

Early in the 1991 ABC telefilm *Our Sons* (written by William Hanley), we see the extremely successful Audrey Grant (Julie Andrews) wake up in her opulent San Diego beachfront home and begin dictating messages. This total workaholic is used to being in control professionally and emotionally. We follow Audrey to her executive office, where she dials her son James's phone number, which is eighth on her list of calls for the day. The telefilm then cuts to her son's answering machine announcing that the spacious apartment we see is the home of two men, James and Donald, who "have no secrets from each other." The camera follows handsome young

James through the large living room to a hallway where his lover Donald, who bears television's signs of AIDS—thinning, eerily orange-colored hair, an unnaturally pale complexion, and KS lesions—is being carried on a stretcher. In the ten years since his mother threw him out of their Arkansas mobile home, Donald, we discover, has become an enormously successful young California architect. James is a pianist/singer at a chic cocktail lounge.

Our Sons presents a conventional television AIDS narrative with an extremely mixed message. In a medium in which cosmetic perfection equals success and virtue, the disfigured face and frail body of the PWA is the horror usually unseen except on occasional newscasts or documentaries. Such disfiguration seems out of place on sanitized television fiction, which must be virtually indistinguishable from the commercials that pay for the program. The horror of the appearance of television's PWA contains complex codes. Donald's first line in *Our Sons*, when he is placed in his hospital bed and holds his lover's hand, is "Toto, I don't think we're in Kansas anymore." The allusion to Judy Garland codes Donald as television's generic homosexual. He bears the marks not only of the opportunistic infections and medical treatments he has endured (after all, the thinning hair and pallid complexion are as much a function of the treatments as the infections) but also the marks of his openly gay "condition." While *Our Sons* does not, as earlier telefilms about AIDS did, turn an AIDS story into a coming-out saga, it does once again link AIDS and homosexuality into one parental problem. While James's mother bravely faces the possibility that her son may be HIV-positive, she has never fully accepted his sexuality. Donald's mother, Luanne (Ann-Margret), who rejected her son because of his homosexuality, sees AIDS as its natural outcome. Both mothers spend most of their on-screen time fighting over which one has most realistically dealt with her son's sexuality. *Our Sons*, then, reinforces the notion that AIDS is ultimately equatable with if not a cause of homosexuality.

Donald comes from a working-class background far from the designer world of James and his mother (though in ten years he gained the training and connections to be a successful, fashionable southern California architect). While James's chic executive mother tries to cure Donald's brash, Southern working-class mother of her virulent bigotry, the telefilm perpetuates narrative constructions that show that affluent, handsome James is endangered, infected, by this outsider to his world.

While Donald's mother literally hates his homosexuality, James's mother has avoided dealing with James's relationship with Donald. As James describes it: "Enter Donald Barnes to share my home and hearth. . . . What could you do but distance yourself from so perversely domestic an arrangement?" The perversion here is domesticity, what British politicians refer to as a "pretended family relationship." James and Donald's home is presented as virtually windowless (disconnected from the outside world?), yet we hear a constant thunderstorm rumbling outside (in drought-plagued San Diego!) to emphasize the gay household's frailty and vulnerability to natural disaster—like lightning, flood, or nature's avenger, HIV infection.

It is worth beginning this discussion with television because there one sees most vividly how the committees of producers and writers try to accommodate their audience. The purpose of television is to make its audience feel good about itself and about television. Compassion, perhaps pity, for certain PWAs is evoked, but television is more interested in creating empathy and sympathy for their parents, those representatives of a "normal" world who suffer the invasion of homosexuality into their families. Moreover, homosexuality may be the cause of AIDS, but television must also imply causes for homosexuality. In *Our Sons*, both young men are fatherless; their mothers are tough, determined, independent women. Is the absence of a father the cause of homosexuality and thus AIDS? Is James's strong, ambivalent relationship with his tough, domineering mother the cause of his homosexuality? Does the focus on the mother's sympathetic, loving attempts to care for her son assume that fathers shouldn't have to deal with gay sons or HIV-infected sons who have obviously transgressed the Law of the Father? Causality is always assumed, even if not directly discussed, on television AIDS dramas.

The image of disfigured Donald and the presage that James will soon look like that exemplify British video artist Stuart Marshall's observations about the link of homosexuality and AIDS: "Via the relay of AIDS, the image of the gay man has been woven through with some of the most terrifying representations of degenerative disease. Death and homosexuality are now inseparably linked in the public consciousness."[5] Donald, in fact, does die in the course of the program. When James first tells his mother that Donald has AIDS and will die soon, she asks: "How long do you have?" Critic Simon Watney connects such representations, examples of what he calls "The Spectacle of AIDS," to the dominant heterosexist "truth" about homosexuality:

The spectacle of AIDS operates as a public masque in which we witness the corporal punishment of the "homosexual body," identified as the enigmatic and indecent source of an incomprehensible, voluntary resistance to the unquestionable governance of marriage, parenthood, and property.[6]

Our Sons is a version of that masque.

In Elizabeth Cox's memoir, *Thanksgiving: An AIDS Journal*, we see not only another version of the virulent coding that undergirds television AIDS narratives but a heterosexual version of the threat to the 1970s dream of affluence and pleasure. In *Thanksgiving*, AIDS has touched a seemingly ideal young American family—handsome, talented husband, beautiful wife, lovely baby. When AIDS touches their lives, it poisons the blissful innocence Elizabeth has enjoyed: "The age of innocence is over and the world seems crueler and sicker than I could ever have imagined" (59).[7] Like the typical wife/mother in television AIDS fantasies, Elizabeth finds her world poisoned by various forms of otherness that become embedded in her husband, specifically through his closeted homosexual activity and the HIV infection it makes possible.

In Cox's memoir, her handsome musician husband, Keith Avedon, a composer and arranger of music for glossy commercials, develops *Pneumocystis carinii* pneumonia while on a business trip to England. Though it is never specifically mentioned, Elizabeth is extremely lucky—she has the money to fly to London with her child to be with her husband, and her mother and his sister have the money to fly over at short notice to join her and offer support. This is a family without financial constraints.

In one revealing sequence, Elizabeth gives us the book's most horrible picture of her husband's physical condition as he recovers in a London hospital from his bout with pneumonia:

> He sat sunken into himself, his head nodding on his chest, like an old man past death, a skeleton covered with skin—a vision of Keith as he would have been at 110, an ancient Keith, a sight that must be a ghastly vision, an apparition, because my Keith is thirty-eight.   (20)

Keith's looks are gone, and so is the illusion of eternal youth. The specific numbers—110 presented as three digits, thirty-eight spelled out— suggest the importance of Keith's youth to Elizabeth. His sudden aging is something alien, horrifying. Age cannot wither Keith, but AIDS can. Like something in a 1950s horror movie, a vision of American youthfulness has been blasted in a weekend.

There must be a reason for this virus, and in outside AIDS narratives the mode of transmission is the real problem. Keith, after all, is another actor in "The Spectacle of AIDS," in which AIDS must have a behavioral cause as well as an epidemiological one. The night Elizabeth saw her suddenly aged husband, Keith's sister tells Elizabeth that "Keith has had a homosexual past" (21)—a fascinating construction. "Keith is bisexual" seems to be more accurate, but it wouldn't place Keith's present illness within the proper equation of AIDS = homosexuality = disfiguration and death. Elizabeth's first response is to identify Keith's background—his family—as the other. "Why is your family so crazy?" Elizabeth screams at Keith's sister, "Why is there nothing normal?" Elizabeth places insane, abnormal, homosexual onto the "other," Keith's troubled, artistic, half-Catholic–half-Jewish family. Narratives of causality continue to emerge, not only of the possible sexual liaisons that could have caused infection, but of the childhood traumas that could have led to the homosexual activity: "I knew it would be impossible for anyone to escape the repercussions of a childhood like Keith's. I knew that much of Keith's life was a reaction to his past" (22). Homosexual activity could not possibly have been simply the expression of a naturally occurring desire among men but must be interpreted as the outcome of childhood trauma and abuse.

Further details about Keith's past homosexual activity are couched in descriptions of a loathsome addiction and become themselves the problems Elizabeth must wrestle with: "He had been having anonymous sex with men. He couldn't help himself. He wanted to stop. It made him hate himself" (60). Elizabeth never mentions that the affairs she was having with men could have put her and her family at risk. HIV infection thus is once again connected with homosexual activity, which is a hated, fatal compulsion. Elizabeth tells us, "Keith feels guilty, marked" (51), as if only such Hester Prynne-like shame could justify and forgive him.

Throughout her memoir, Elizabeth catches herself and her husband in a double bind. On one hand, she despises intrusions of the AIDS = homosexuality equation and the causality it assumes:

> It seems that everyone I tell asks how Keith got AIDS. Why? What are they responding to, the disease or what it represents? I hate being asked how Keith got AIDS. . . . My own feeling is that nothing can explain such complete devastation of a person's life.   (50–51)

The vagueness, yet precision, of "what it represents" is fascinating. While there is denial in that euphemism, there is also a knowledge that it represents precisely homosexuality. Elizabeth seems to want to explode that equation, but she is more strongly driven to stereotypical causality, which leads her to focus on the homosexual past that is for her the cause of Keith's illness.

Elizabeth labors over her memories of the summer six years before when Keith "couldn't help" having sex with men and Elizabeth was also "staying out all night": "This is changing the way I see my past. What I thought of at the time as high-spirited recklessness I'm now being asked to see as desperation. I can't do it. It's too scary to change my memories" (61). Yet she continues to ask, "Why did he do it?" It is fascinating throughout Elizabeth's memoir to see the changes from active to passive voice and her unquestioning perpetuation of the mythology of AIDS and various mythologies of homosexuality. What is the "it" Keith did? He sullied Elizabeth's memories by spending the night with men instead of women, thus turning "carefree" sex into "desperation"? The horror isn't a virus: it is ultimately Keith's "homosexual past."

Sexual history is particularly important in AIDS literature, since a sexually transmitted disease has, for many, replaced the sex = life equation of gay liberation with the equation of sex = death[8] and the causal linking of the disease with the sexual playground of the 1970s. Gay men are sick because of sex, an unnatural causality that empowers all sorts of metaphors of disease already associated with homosexuality. Paula Treichler, in her superb essay on AIDS, homophobia, and biomedical discourse, calls AIDS "an epidemic of signification."[9] Lee Edelman goes one step further and calls it a "plague of discourse," a notion Susan Sontag also developed in *AIDS and Its Metaphors*.[10] It is the linkings of sex = disease, homosexuality = disease, promiscuity = disease, and, finally, homosexuality = promiscuity = disease that enchain people with AIDS and, by association, all gay men.

Yet Elizabeth also sees, and tries to deny, that AIDS throws her behavior into question as well. The pinpointing of that summer of sexual experimentation six years before, of testing and affirming their liberated marriage, has led both of them to this moment. "I had loved that summer while we were living it, but now it represents Keith's downfall" (61). Keith's illnesses are not only debilitation; they are also his "downfall." AIDS has also destroyed her dream world. The first sentence of the book is "There is no space in this apartment" (3), as if a limitless world of affluence and happiness has been contracted into a cell.

Space is central to such mainstream AIDS works, because AIDS came from outside the "normal" world and makes that world smaller and more vulnerable. Mainstream AIDS works therefore ask who brought this into "our" world and why. "When" becomes even more important as a question, as if AIDS were caused by not only a moment of seroconversion that must be pinpointed, but also by an era, a time of social and personal permissiveness for which one must atone. Historian Jeffrey Weeks has noted that AIDS mythology thus expresses "deeply rooted fears about the un-precedented rate of change in sexual behavior and social mores in the past two generations."[11]

In gay-created narratives, to be sure, one is still dealing with a paradise threatened by the encroachment of AIDS, with poisoning of the present by a past that seemed paradisiacal. While in mainstream narratives, "AIDS came to represent the fruits of permissiveness,"[12] gay narratives show a complex relationship to the same construction. Gay AIDS literature must deal with the past sexuality = present disease issue in a way that either breaks the chain or affirms the past in a healing way. In other words, it must avoid the self-hating causalities that poisoned Keith Avedon's sense of self and the oppressive constructions that taint his wife's journal.

III   Looking Back

At the opening of the 1990 film *Longtime Companion*, it is July 1981. A handsome, perfectly built young man jogs down a beach, stops, strips off his clothes, and runs naked into the surf in a moment of carefree isolation. This scene is followed by scenes of beautiful young men, mostly coupled, discovering through the *New York Times* that a new disease is attacking numbers of gay men. The young men we see live in roomy, expensive Man-hattan apartments and Fire Island beach houses. They are either rich or, through their beauty, charm, and availability, friends of the rich. The men work in advertising or show business. One writes episodes of a soap opera in which another stars. These men see the new "gay cancer" as something that couldn't touch them. It must be attacking men who are sleazier, more promiscuous, dirtier than they would ever be.

In *Longtime Companion* the audience sees the encroachment of AIDS on the American dream of beauty, affluence, and immortality, the dream created and sustained by the writer, actor, advertising executive, show-business lawyer, and gym worker we see in *Longtime Companion*. Fire Is-land in 1981, as it had been for years before, is the setting for the best of gay life—happiness, money, fellowship, male beauty, la dolce vita. But this isn't decadence, this is truly the American dream of television com-mercials and glossy magazine ads. Gay men in *Longtime Companion* rep-resent the leisure class, a group with which American society carries on an ardent love-hate relationship. For screenwriter Craig Lucas, director Nor-man René, and their characters, Fire Island in the days before AIDS was heaven. The AIDS-changed world the film depicts is one of fear, debilitat-ing illness, loss, anger, action—and nostalgia. In the final scene, eight years later, Willy, whose beautiful body ran into the waves at the film's opening, Fuzzy, the lover he met in Fire Island in 1981, and Fuzzy's sister Lisa walk the desolate beach of Fire Island in 1989. All are now AIDS activists. As they look longingly from the beach to the empty houses, Willy says, "I just want to be there. If they ever do fine a cure." The film cuts to the boardwalk and stairs, now filled with hundreds of men, including Willy's friends who have died in the past eight years. Willy's dream of a world without AIDS is a dream of recapturing the past, of bringing his be-loved friends back to life. It is also a dream of restoring the "carnival" of the Fire Island summers he remembers, of restoring the carefree leisure class.[13] This is one gay version of AIDS, attacked by many critics for con-fining itself to white, affluent, privileged gay men,[14] but still a leitmotiv of gay AIDS-era literature.

Willy's nostalgia is a convention of gay AIDS fiction. In a gay culture now rightfully obsessed with a plague, remembering becomes a central act, and it is how and what one remembers that defines much of AIDS literature, art, and film. That focus on memory is a central feature of the landscape of the wasteland described by AIDS-age gay writers. In this world, memory and desire take on new meaning as new links to the past must be forged, the present is sad and terrifying, and the future is drastically foreshortened. To affirm the past is to affirm the power of sexual desire; affirming the foreshortened, uncertain future is to affirm the possi-bility of love in the face of death.

Preston Wallace, the central character in the late Allen Barnett's story "Philostorgy, Now Obscure," responds to his diagnosis of full-blown AIDS by focusing on sorting and discarding memories and more tangible rem-nants of his past. As he burns his mementos he realizes, "He needed to do the same with old friends, affect their memory of him, introduce himself anew and say, 'This is me now'" (47).[15] As he looks at a letter from his first lover, Jim Stoller, Preston realizes "what Eliot had meant by mixing mem-ory and desire, a combination so intoxicating, Preston feared the room would begin to spin, that he might need help out of his clothes and into bed, and his head held if he was to sleep" (53). What Preston remembers most strongly, since "the body can recall things on its own" (52), is Jim Stoller's body, though it is ten years since he and Jim have been together. Impelled to see him once more, Preston seeks Jim out, hoping he can "arouse old feelings in Jim Stoller" (53). After Preston tells Jim he has AIDS and shares his memories of Jim, Jim offers to take Preston home to bed:

"It's too dangerous," Preston said.

"I'm not afraid of you anymore," Jim said. "And I want some say in how you remember me." (59)

Jim, living in affluence in Chicago, has not been touched by AIDS. His complacency and self-absorption lead him to misread Preston's warning of physical danger. It is Jim who should be concerned about how he remembers Preston, whose life has been foreshortened, but Jim has neither the wit nor depth to see that. For that kind of caring, Preston has his friends. He is wise enough to cherish Jim as a physical experience: "The smell of Jim was still on his beard, the taste of him under his tongue" (60).

In a world in which philostorgy, meaning natural affection, is now obscure, Barnett's story is an assertion of the power of physical desire and physical memory, reflections of the power of the body itself. Preston understands Blanche DuBois's belief that "the opposite of death is desire." Yet the allusion to Eliot's "The Wasteland" is a reminder as well that a way of life has been compromised, reduced, by AIDS.

The paradigmatic writer in this new barren land of displacement, pain, and loss is Paul Monette, whose memoir *Borrowed Time*, volume of poems *Love Alone: Eighteen Elegies for Rog*, and novel *Afterlife* define both the sweetness and the horror of what AIDS means to a gay man touched tragically by the disease. Lamenting the loss of his beloved Roger Horwitz, who fell to the "opportunistic infections" (how inopportune that word *opportunistic* is) that HIV allowed to poison his system over nineteen months of suffering, Monette, HIV-positive himself, waits for the time bomb to turn his body into another Beirut. "I don't know if I will live to finish this," Monette says on the first page of *Borrowed Time:* "All I know is this, the virus ticks in me" (BT, 1). "This" is aptly vague—is it the memoir on which he labors, an act of grief, celebration, and therapy—or is it his now incomplete and drastically curtailed life as the time bomb virus "ticks" away?

Monette's memoir is not just of him and Rog: it is a memoir of AIDS itself and how it is decimating a culture. The memoir begins, perforce, not with Rog's diagnosis, but, like *Longtime Companion*, with the insertion of AIDS into their lives: "The fact is, no one knows where to start with AIDS. Now, in the seventh year of the calamity my friends in L.A. can hardly recall what it felt like any longer, the time before the sickness" (BT, 2). The "insertion" begins with phone calls from friends telling of others sick and dying, then the friends themselves become the bravely ill others. And what is forever changed is—was—paradise, the cozy world of affluent, gay southern California, seemingly untouched by the plague riddling New York and San Francisco (though, ironically, it was in Los Angeles that a physician started drawing conclusions from the five cases of *Pneumocystis carinii* he was treating).[16] An affluent couple, lawyer and writer, beautifully, devotedly in love, in a beautiful house-cum-pool in the L.A. suburbs, wealthy enough to give to the right causes, seemed untouchable. The invasion of the home of Paul Monette and Roger Horwitz by HIV is not only an invasion of one loving couple, one household, or of gay culture; it is an invasion of the American dream itself.

The first pages of *Borrowed Time* introduce the refrain: "Equally difficult, of course, is knowing where to start" (BT, 2). The fascination of Monette's work, like so much of AIDS literature, is that every phrase becomes an omen. Why does that "of course" jump out so ominously? Monette is aware that in eschatology, language gains new power: "The world around me is defined by endings and closures—the date on the grave that follows the hyphen" (BT, 2), and for Monette, life has become circumscribed by two dates, the day Rog died, and the day of the Diagnosis, "the day we began to live on the moon" (BT, 2). Anything before March 1985 is a brief glimpse of a lost past, but even those glimpses become tainted, yellowed with what will become intimations of mortality. The past before March 1985 has been lost, as has the cozy, loving world of Rog and Paul.

What is shattered in *Borrowed Time* is a gay version of the American dream of suburban, married bliss: a beautiful house emptied of the marriage that gave it meaning, a grief-stricken man lying huddled, alone on the bed he shared with his partner. Monette and Horwitz lived the dream liberal television and filmmakers gave gay men, when they showed us at all, in the 1980s—beautiful, tasteful surroundings in which a sensitive, frightened man is bolstered by his love of a strong, brave, sweet lover/friend. The reality is more complex and tragic. Tragedy brings pain and insight: Monette, the writer of novelizations and unsold Whoppi Goldberg scripts, becomes an anguished, eloquent Jeremiah, angry at the insensitivity of many doctors, in whose cold hands people with AIDS become dependent patients,[17] angry at the disease itself, but possessed, articulate, and gifted with the ability to forge a harrowing beauty out of pain, grief, and fury. Monette becomes the bard of AIDS.

In the memoir, as in the poems, Monette begins fastidiously with details: "I sift through these details now because they are so concrete, still here in the house, evidence of all the roads of our lives in the time before the war" (BT, 25). But the "time before the war" is irretrievable, and therein lies the real pain. Not only are men lost, but a culture is waning. Monette refers to his state as "half life," because he has lost half of what made life meaningful. Searching through remnants of the past to retrieve that past, he occasionally finds Rog:

> how is it you spring full-blown
> from a thousand fragments it's like picking up
> a shard of red-black vase off a Greek hillside
> looks like part of a sandal and a girl's long hair
> in a flash the white-stone city rises entire
> around you full of just men who live to be
> 90 the buried pieces fit   (HL, 16)

As Rog emerges in Paul's imagination from concrete remnants of their past together, so does an idealized past in which men were not blasted prematurely. Now Rog is "Proof of the end / of all gentle men" (HL, 16). But Paul's "Half Life" also means that the remaining half will, like radioactive substances themselves, disintegrate. Soon he will be no more.

Paul Monette is in his mid-forties, one of a generation who "came of age" during the era of "gay liberation" that followed the 1969 Stonewall riots, a generation for whom sexual appetite could be joyfully sated. Gay men were at the vanguard of the sexual revolution, ironically supported by the protection of medicine: "Contraception and the assurance by medicine of the easy curability of sexually transmitted diseases (as of almost all infectious diseases) made it possible to regard sex as an adventure without consequences."[18] The effect of this brave new sexual world on a generation of gay men is depicted in the history of Mark in Robert Ferro's novel, *Second Son:*

> His generation had made love in great numbers, not from a sense of disobeying rules or smashing traditional morality but because moral, social reasons for abstinence no longer obtained against this sudden bursting of physical beauty and exuberance into their lives; it was the result of natural forces magnified by great numbers, into a phenomenon. Tandem notions of attachment and sex were meticulously, scrupulously disentangled. For them, as for no other generation, it could be either, instead of both or neither one.[19]

This is the past that lights the memories in AIDS literature, the unabashed enjoyment of erotic pleasure: "So many men, so little time." Even the ideal marriage of Roger and Paul involved fashioning "a sexual ethics just for us" that excluded monogamy. Although Roger "was comfortable with relative monogamy, even at a time when certain quarters of the gay world found the whole idea trivial and bourgeois," Paul "would go after a sexual encounter as if it were an ice cream cone—casual, quick, good-bye" (BT, 5). Yet Paul knows that promiscuity is not the issue: "But the disease wasn't drawn to obsessive sex or meaningless sex. Sex itself, pure and simple, was the medium and the world out there was ravenous for it" (BT, 33). But times have drastically changed: AIDS has made the sexual past fearful:

> The fear of AIDS imposes on an act whose ideal is an experience of pure presentness (and a creation of the future), a relation to the past to be ignored at one's peril. Sex no longer withdraws its partners, if only for a moment, from the social. It cannot be considered just a coupling: it is a chain, a chain of transmission, from the past.[20]

Or, as B. J., the narrator of David Feinberg's *Eighty-Sixed,* describes it: "Erica Jong's zipless fuck has gone the way of the Edsel. There is no such thing as sex without angst anymore. The specter of death cannot be ignored, forgotten" (318).[21] The past is not just the glorious memories of Whitmanesque, celebratory male coupling; it is also the possibly poisonous sexual/immunological past of you, your partner, his partners, even unto the beginning of time.

For the generation that lived through the erotic age, finding a meaningful present in an age in which sex has become not only de-eroticized but terrifying involves retrieving and affirming the past and purging it of the stigma of guilt, sin, and corruption with which AIDS and homophobia have embossed it. For men of Monette's generation, remembering is not only answering what Edmund White calls "the urge to memorialize the dead, to honor their lives,"[22] nor is it only remembering lost loves. It can also be a means of recalling the vanished past of a drastically changed society by remembering, or trying to remember, the orgiastic time before AIDS.

Some AIDS-era literature affirms the past by staying in it and ignoring the fraught present. Alan Hollinghurst's brilliant 1988 novel, *The Swimming Pool Library,* takes place in the summer of 1983, which the narrator calls "the last summer of its kind there was ever to be."[23] The novel compares the "present" experience of a young civil servant who lives for his erotic experience with those of an eighty-year-old gay man who has entrusted his memoirs to our young central character. Beginning five years before the novel's publication and moving back in time, the novel purposely ignores, and to some extent defies, AIDS. Edmund White's *The Beautiful Room Is Empty*[24] is a memoir of a young man's pre-Stonewall erotic experiences. The novel follows his own sense of the value of the past for gay men—and particular for gay writers: "There is an equally strong urge to record one's own past—one's own life—before it vanishes."[25] White's novel/memoir, a sequel to his earlier AIDS-age work, *A Boy's Own Story*, offers not only individual experience, but typical experiences for gay men of his generation who have lived through a series of rapid changes:

> To have been oppressed in the fifties, freed in the sixties, exalted in the seventies, and wiped out in the eighties is a quick itinerary for a whole culture to follow. For we are witnessing not just the death of individuals but a menace to an entire culture. All the more reason to bear witness to the cultural moment.[26]

In *The Beautiful Room Is Empty*, White, through the experience of one character, presents the early chapters of a paradigmatic history of gay men who grew up in the 1940s and 1950s, lived through the glory days, and now watch their society dwindle away in a grim performance of the "Farewell Symphony." If nothing else survives, there will at least be an imaginative record of the past in all its erotic subversiveness and subversive eroticism.

Even for some of White's characters, though, the past is not enough. Mark, the central character in White's story "Palace Days," not only partied, but made a career out of staging gay parties:

> He was the president of the Bunyonettes, a gay travel agency that arranged all-male tours. Forty gay guys would float down the Nile from Aswan to Luxor, impressing the Egyptians with their muscles and moustaches. . . . Or Mark would charter a small liner that would cruise the Caribbean and surprise the port town of Curacao when two hundred fellows, stocky, cheerful and guiltless, would ransack the outdoor clothes market looking for bits of female finery to wear to the Carmen Miranda ball scheduled for the high seas tomorrow night.   (167)[27]

AIDS imperils Mark's business and his health. He and his lover Ned flee to Europe to avoid the epidemic and to continue the party in a supposedly safe place. Europe, of course, is no escape. Mark eventually tests positive, which leads him to mourn more fervently the lost past that was, for him, home. Mark sits with Ned in a Paris theater watching a poor performance of a Balanchine ballet and remembers when "the lobby of the New York State Theater had been the drawing room of America and that we, yes, *we* Americans saw in the elaborate *enchainements* on stage a radiant vision of society" (204). But this world of elegance, unwittingly parodied by this inferior Parisian performance, is, like Balanchine himself, gone. Mark becomes homesick for a lost culture:

> His muscles registered the word "home" with a tensing, as though to push himself up out of the chair and head back towards home, to . . . stingers at the Riv and the wild nights of sex and dance, but then he relaxed back into his seat, since he knew that "home" wasn't there anymore.   (203)

Time and space are conflated into this notion of home, a place one can never be again. But the enemy is not the past. As Harvey Fierstein's Ghee proclaims in *Safe Sex*, the enemy is "now": "We can never touch as before. We can never be as before. 'Now' will always define us. Different times. Too late."[28] For young writers who came of age in the age of AIDS, there is no blissful past to remember, only a sad present.

IV   The Blank Generation

David B. Feinberg's novel *Eighty-Sixed* mixes the sadness of the age of AIDS with recollections of a brief, less-than-golden "time before the war" experienced by the younger generation of gay men who came of age after Stonewall. "Ancient History," the first of the book's two parts and written in the past tense, recounts month-by-month the sexual exploits of its narrator and central character, B. J. Rosenthal. B. J. tells the reader that "the first man I slept with demonstrated the difference between love and sex quite vividly" (17). The brief encounters of 1980 only reinforce B. J.'s first impression. Although B. J. claims both lust and love, both feelings seem destined to be aimed at "lost causes." The many sexual encounters are described in language that is far from erotic and seem to lead inevitably to venereal disease (the smorgasbord of venereal diseases of part 1 is eclipsed by AIDS in the second part). Love is nonexistent, as it inevitably would be for a man whose ambition is to "blend into a crowd of clones and disappear." Like many narrators in contemporary fiction, B. J. seems most identified with his ambition *not to feel,* for his overwhelming emotion in 1980 is a desperation not slaked by the constant, meaningless, usually pleasureless sexual activity.

Ironically, what often characterizes B. J.'s memories is his inability to remember names and sexual encounters. The first sexual encounter he describes in his book is indescribable because it has been forgotten: "Anyway, we were in the middle of some act that discretion requires I don't describe in too much detail; the fact of the matter is I don't even remember it" (4). Nor does he remember having sex with Bob Broome, whom he met

at a Juilliard concert: "What happened next I don't recall. I'm not absolutely sure what transpired" (5). Yet Bob Broome looms large in the second, present-tense, half of the novel, "Learning How to Cry," which takes
place in 1986 and centers on B.J.'s reaction to Bob's AIDS.

The news of Bob's illness throws B. J.'s memory into high gear:

> Bob. Bob. Bob. Who do I know named Bob? There's Robert Walker. Bob.
> Bob. Bob. Was he the one—? No, that's someone else. Arthur. Think. It'll
> come to me. Bob. Bob. Broome! That's it. Bob Broome. Wait a sec, he was
> the one from the Juilliard concert, wasn't he? Shit, we tricked. It must have
> been four, five years ago. What did we do?   (181)

Bob Broome may not inspire many memories, but New York City itself
evokes sad memories of past brief encounters:

> At Forty-second Street stand the twin apartment towers of Manhattan Plaza,
> grim reminders of two more miserable affairs. In the west tower resides
> Jefferson Peters, an ignoble lout who tortured me with his massive member
> and malign indifference for several months last autumn; in the east Luigi
> Porcelli, who kept his focus on the tv as I did him, watching for his alias and
> phone number to flash on the screen of the gay cable-show personals, back
> in June of '82.   (267)

The dominant features of the architectural landscape now, though, are
hospitals: "To the north, on Fifty-eighth, is Roosevelt Hospital, where
John Lennon died in 1980" (Lennon's death is the capstone of part 1), and
across the street is "St. Claire's, where Bob Broome is beginning to lose his
mind" (267). B. J. dutifully visits Bob Broome regularly and cares for him.
Yet when Bob dies, B. J. tries "to forget the Bob in the hospital and remember the Bob I knew before" (324), an impossibility, since B. J. has
virtually no memory of that Bob. Nor does B. J. have a present:

> Dave Johnson calls me and asks me what I'm doing with my time now that
> Bob has died and I don't go over to the hospital every other night. I don't
> know what to say. Maybe the worst thing is that life goes on.   (323)

There is considerable doubt whether life before AIDS was any more
meaningful for B. J. than life in the age of AIDS. Only the illness of a
former trick seems to offer structure, meaning. Like a Beckett character,
B. J. finds living painful and meaningless, especially since living now
means dealing again and again with AIDS. Bob is dead, and now Gordon,
another friend, phones to say that he has it: "'OK.' I'm practically choking. 'I'm really sorry. Stay well,' I say" (326), a nonsensical response—

"Stay well"—but what does one say? A meaningless past, a present filled with AIDS; and could the future be any different?

B. J.'s present is filled not with the numb desperation of 1980 but with choking back the tears that are certain to flow endlessly: "I am afraid that once I start crying, I will be on a jag that won't end for days. I will never stop; I will cry and cry and cry" (295). Finally, though, the tears do flow:

> It begins as a gentle rain. Just a drop, for each illness, each death. And with each passing day it gets worse. Now a downpour. Now a torrent. And there is no likelihood of its ever ending.   (326)

The tears of the "almost choking" man who has learned how to cry will only be quenched in one way: "By the time you read these words I may in all likelihood be dead" (152). The year 1986 offers a real desperation—the desperation of a man, paralyzed by loss and fear, by using his calculator to "figure the odds," who cannot even find affirmation in the memory or fantasy of a joyous, orgiastic past.

B. J. is in his early twenties in 1980 and turns thirty in 1986. He missed the real glory days celebrated by writers who came of age in the Stonewall generation. He does not have the same past to celebrate, which might account for the numbness he feels. Like chain-smoking, sex is an addiction that has ceased to offer much except the desire to have more.

John Weir's Eddie Socket, a.k.a Wallie Jeffers, is younger still, in his late twenties when he contracts and dies with AIDS. In *The Irreversible Decline of Eddie Socket*, we watch the interactions of gay men of three different decades: Eddie; the forty-five-year-old Merrit Mather; his estranged lover, thirty-six-year-old Saul Isenberg; and the young Wall Street trader, Brag Voleslavski, who, luckily, prefers masturbating on his sexual partners.

Saul and Merrit are in a state of crisis. Their friends are almost systematically dying, and their social life is composed of ominous phone calls, viewings, and funerals: "But listen, everyone does not get asked to viewings twice a week, unless they're eighty-seven or living in London in the plague of 1592, or fighting in a war. Or a New York homosexual at 6:00 A.M. this Friday, at the end of March."[29]

While Saul would like to maintain the relationship as a means of security and order in a chaotic world, Merrit has other needs: "This week he's feeling forty-five, and all his friends are dying, and he thinks he wants a virgin boy to make him feel innocent again" (22). So Merrit has a brief liaison with Eddie, then runs off to Europe with Brag Voleslavski, of whom he quickly, predictably, tires. Saul is left with memories of making love with Merrit, appropriately in a patch of pink narcissus, but AIDS encroaches even on this romantic recollection:

> I held him very tight and said that we were cosmic twins, and he said, "Saul, if I get AIDS and die, will you die, too?" And this was very early on, before we knew we couldn't take each other in our mouths, an innocent time, it's funny to think of it now as an innocent time, innocent because we believed that if we slept only with each other, we couldn't get sick.   (24)

Now Saul and Merrit have no relationship, and worse, their world is gone:

> I didn't have to end that relationship, because everybody died. Oh, Merrit didn't die, and I didn't die. But everybody else. We were just the last two remaining pieces of the puzzle. We fit together, but it didn't matter anymore; we had no context, no landscape, no frame.   (268)

Without a gay culture and society to support their life together, the relationship of Merrit and Saul becomes meaningless, and they finally, irrevocably, part, another loss in a world that is all loss: "Even grief is lost, finally, and then you mourn the loss of that" (275). Young Eddie, the representative of what Saul calls "the blank generation," dies with AIDS without ever really living. For most of the novel, Eddie seems to have nothing to lose. At the beginning, we are told, "he was still waiting for whatever miracle he thought it would take for his real life to begin" (3). Ironically, that miracle is AIDS. Miserably ill and on the run, he calls his mother from a Los Angeles phone booth and finally springs to life:

> I'm thinking that I want my life. . . . I want it whole, and I want it complete, I want its texture and its spirit. I want its internal rhythms and its external shape. I want it all at once and forever, and I want it now. I want it now that it's going, Mom, and that's the final reversal.   (192)

Eddie, who "hated men and liked dicks" (33), had little chance of being lucky in sex or in love. Sex "was either a performance or a disappointment" and "being held" was what he really wanted. Nor was there any sense of identity or belonging gained from his gayness: "There was nothing to define himself against, no lover, no family, no community, only New York, and his homosexuality, and he had not emerged in one, and he had not taken pleasure in the other" (167).

The world John Weir creates offers loss for the older generation, and, for Eddie and his peers, a tangential link to a world never really experienced. Saul works at an auction house handling the artifacts of gay celebrities who have died with AIDS. His life is a round of funerals, of loss. Merrit is insulated by his self-centeredness and will live alone, unable to sustain a relationship. Eddie is dead, but without the tragic insight that would have made death meaningful, an insight that would have come from experience, from a past:

> Because it's not convincing, not dramatically, it doesn't play for all these twenty-eight-year-olds to die. They have to learn about their lives, they have to have catharsis, something has to come from their despair, some kind of knowledge, maybe wisdom. . . . So if you're learning wisdom from a tragedy, what happens when you suffer terminal disease and death, and all you learn is that you're falling in a dream?   (199)

For a generation that knows only numbness, the generation of B. J. Rosenthal and Eddie Socket, there is no past to lament, no future to dream of, no lover to embrace. There is nothing to remember. For Saul's generation, all that is left is the possibility of memory in a lost world: "I move around the room as if to memorize the final setting, the placement of objects" (275).

Despite this overwhelming sense of loss, *The Irreversible Decline of Eddie Socket* manages to be an uplifting, touching book, an antidote to the bleakness of *Eighty-Sixed,* for it is also a celebration of the remnants of gay culture and imagination in its playfulness and sense of irony; chapter titles that echo opera, Sondheim, and Lorenz Hart lyrics; and Eddie's and Saul's camp sense of humor. In chronicling the loss of culture, the novel evokes that lost gay world and fixes it. That, too, is a crucial form of remembering. There remains, also, the voice of Saul, which contains both comic desperation and a sense of tragic insight that has come from its losses.

At the end of his poem "Half Life," Paul Monette cries, "and once I had it all" (HL, 17). That memory, for him, brings pain, when the "all" wasn't fully appreciated or acknowledged. Now there is but half life. In AIDS literature, one cry of anguish comes from the "Stonewall generation," who once thought they had found paradise, and lost it through AIDS; another comes from a sadder, younger generation experiencing pain and loss without saving memories, present love, or dreams of a future. The older generation affirms the saving possibility of love to make present and future bearable, a possibility younger gay men seem never to have believed. For both generations the urge to remember and affirm remains as a culture fights the threats from the virus and from its enemies outside. That almost obsessive focus on memory—memory of desire—is a central characteristic of gay literature in the age of AIDS as gay men fight the inroads of the virus and the oppressive constructions that could rob them of the freedom and pride gained in that now-compromised past.

V   Fighting for a Future

Sander L. Gilman has pointed out that in the popular media, pictures of people with AIDS present their subject in poses echoing the classical iconography of melancholy ("elbow on knee, head on hand, a gesture of passive submission and reflection as well as despair"):[30]

> The iconography of depression, with its emphasis on the body, stresses the age-old association of the nature of the mind (here, homosexuality as "mental illness") with the image of the body (here, homosexuality as sexual deviance). The image of the body is made to "portray" the state of mind. The person with AIDS remains the suffering, hopeless male, shown as depressed and marginal.[31]

This is also the picture many AIDS narratives have shown or described. Television's picture of the wan, sensitive young man, shoulders sagging, staring out the window, or lying inert, helpless in a bed a few sizes too large; or prose fiction's depiction of a character paralyzed into anomie by the plague, like Feinberg's B. J.; memoirs' records of the baffled voices of those witnessing the wasting away and loss of loved ones. The image is of passivity. At best, one can control how one is remembered.

Many AIDS narratives have tended to be elegiac. As mainstream narratives have equated AIDS and homosexuality, so gay AIDS narratives have, not without cause, maintained the AIDS = death equation. In a way, this tendency climaxed in the creation and display of the AIDS quilt, so movingly recorded in the television documentary, *Common Threads: Stories from the Quilt* (1989). The sight of this giant tribute to people who have died of HIV-related opportunistic infections is not only a site for celebration and grief but also an incitement to anger.

While gay fiction has in the last few years tried to incorporate the dark design of AIDS into a larger tapestry of gay life, other cultural productions have recorded the second wave of response to AIDS, that of fighting for a future for PWAs. AIDS activism is a counter to the anguished, passive responses we have seen, in which endurance is the only available sign of strength.

The counter to the melancholia of gay people with AIDS and their loved ones seen in teleplays like *Our Sons* and films like *Longtime Companion* is the productive anger at work in the 1991 documentary, *Stop the Church* (directed by Robert Hilferty), in which the viewer sees the members of ACT UP, the Women's Health Action Mobilization, and related groups plan and stage the December 1989 demonstration against Cardinal John O'Connor during a service at Saint Patrick's Cathedral in New York. The vision of Cardinal O'Connor, who has become the symbol of the unrealistic, destructive intransigence of the Catholic church on the subject of AIDS education and homosexuality, improvising a homily on the sadness of hate while AIDS activists protesting his bigotry are dragged bodily out of the cathedral, followed by the reactions of his parishioners, who share O'Connor's desire to keep his cathedral a sanctuary from reality and compassion, is chillingly powerful, and more effective as a call to arms than AIDS fictions have been. *Stop the Church* shows another, more vital war that counters the victim mentality of many AIDS narratives.

In *Stop the Church*, we see not isolated, sad young men but a supportive, productive community that has managed to have a strong impact on how AIDS is treated in this country and that wants as strong a voice in how AIDS is prevented and how the rights and dignity of people with AIDS are protected. *Stop the Church* focuses not on grief or nostalgia but on anger. It shows anger and incites anger.

One sees the same determination in Michael Callen's memoir, *Surviving AIDS*, the account of a gay man who has lived with AIDS for nine years. Callen's argument is that just as the heterosexual, heterosexist world has educated gay men into a negative self-image that has often led to self-destructive behaviors, so that world is educating people with AIDS to see themselves as hopelessly doomed by HIV infection:

> If I believed everything I was told—if I believed that tiresome boilerplate lie that AIDS is 100 percent fatal—I'd probably be dead by now. If I didn't arm myself with information—facts, statistics, and diverse views—I wouldn't be able to defend myself against the madness and gibberish that daily assault those of us who have AIDS.[32]

That daily assault is waged by editors who will not print pictures of healthy-looking people with AIDS and photographers who want picturesque shots: "When he [a *Newsweek* editor] arrived, he looked me over and then snorted contemptuously: 'Where are your lesions? I need someone with lesions!'" (56). It is also waged by the "apocalyptic" language of television reporting.

Like many earlier AIDS writers, Callen sees his condition as a byproduct of his past sexual hyperactivity. Without attacking the ethos of the 1970s, he wants to show that a host of venereal infections had already made their way into the gay community: "Unwittingly, and with the best of revolutionary intentions, a small subset of gay men managed to create disease settings equivalent to those of poor third-world nations in one of the richest nations on earth" (4). In this environment, it is not surprising that a lethal virus could be transmitted so widely.

For Callen, the issue now is not to focus on the past but to combat hopelessness and offer practical, if medically controversial, advice. Callen, for instance, argues against taking the highly toxic AZT, the drug of choice of many medical practitioners. He believes that prophylaxis against common opportunistic infections, particularly *Pneumocystis carinii* pneumonia, and avoidance of highly toxic drugs is crucial. More important, however, he says, is attitude. Central to survival is refusing "to believe AIDS is an 'automatic death sentence'" (45). Equally important, "Survivors are passionately committed to living and have a sense of 'meaningfulness and purpose in life,' of 'unmet goals.' Often the diagnosis itself enables them to find 'new meaning in life'" (45).

As the makers of *Stop the Church* celebrate political activism to end the stigmas against people with AIDS and to fight for AIDS research, education, and proper health care, so Michael Callen calls for personal activism on the part of people with AIDS as a counter to what has seemed an inevitable passivity.

Twelve years into the age of AIDS, fictions seem less important than active encounters with and vivid records of reality.[33] Few gay people have not experienced the loss and grief associated with AIDS. Few have not at least confronted for themselves the question, "to test or not to test." Recently, a gay New York theatrical producer, John Glines, proclaimed that he wouldn't produce plays about AIDS:

> One third of my audience will have AIDS and another third will have tested positive. They don't want to come to the theater at night, hear how horrible this disease is, and weep. We do that during the day. What I'm producing is entertainment for the troops during the war.[34]

There is no need for more depictions of loss and grief. There is no longer time for nostalgia for "the time before the war," which is receding farther into the past. Nor do those sagas of the encroachment of AIDS into the consumer's paradise of the Reagan era seem to fit the 1990s. There is, after all, a younger generation of gay men who know only the Age of AIDS, the war. While a *Village Voice* article once quipped that the principal theatrical event of the 1980s was the memorial service,[35] AIDS literature of the 1990s will be a record of battles waged.

NOTES

This is an expanded and revised version of an essay, "'The Time Before the War': Memory and Desire in AIDS Literature," which appeared in American Literature 62 (Winter 1990): 648–67. *An extended discussion of AIDS dramas and telefilms is contained in chapter 2 of my book* Acting Gay: Male Homosexuality in Modern Drama *(New York: Columbia University Press, 1992).*

1. I am thinking here of works like Randy Shilts's *And the Band Played On: Politics, People, and the AIDS Epidemic* (New York: St. Martin's, 1987), and the many collections of essays by AIDS scholars, such as Elizabeth Fee and Daniel M. Fox, eds., *AIDS and the Burdens of History* (Berkeley: University of California Press, 1988).

2. Paul Monette, "Half Life," *Love Alone: Eighteen Elegies for Rog,* (New York: St. Martin's, 1988). Subsequent references to this work in the text are identified by "HL" and page number

3. Paul Monette, *Borrowed Time: An AIDS Memoir* (New York: Harcourt Brace Jovanovich, 1988), p. 25. Subsequent references to this work in the text are identified by "BT" and page number.

4. Perhaps I should qualify this assertion with "for the most part." David Bergman has written a brilliant analysis of how Larry Kramer's writing reinforces the equations of heterosexist narratives ("Larry Kramer and the Rhetoric of AIDS," in David Bergman, *Gaiety Transfigured: Gay Self-Representation in American Literature* [Madison: University of Wisconsin Press, 1991], pp. 122–38). I discuss the Larry Kramer problem in my book *Acting Gay.*

5. Stuart Marshall, "Picturing Deviancy," in Tessa Boffin and Sunil Gupta, eds., *Ecstatic Antibodies: Resisting the AIDS Mythology* (London: Rivers Oram, 1990), p. 21.

6. Simon Watney, "The Spectacle of AIDS," in *AIDS: Cultural Analysis, Cultural Activism* (Cambridge: MIT Press, 1988), p. 83. This volume was originally published as *October* 43 (Winter 1987).

7. Elizabeth Cox, *Thanksgiving: An AIDS Journal* (New York: Harper & Row, 1990). Where subsequent references to this work are contextually clear, page numbers will be cited in the text.

8. My use of "equals" signs here and below not only is an echo of the AIDS activist slogan, Silence = Death but is influenced by Lee Edelman's essay, "Politics, Literary Theory, and AIDS." As Edelman puts it:

> The proliferating equations that mark the discourse on AIDS, then, suggest that in the face of the terrifying epistemological ambiguity provoked by this epidemic, in the face of so powerful a representation of the force of what we do not know, the figure of certainty, the figure of literality, is itself ideologically constructed and deployed as a defense, if not as a remedy."

(In Ronald Butters, John M. Clum, and Michael Moon, eds., *Displacing Homophobia* (Durham, N.C.: Duke University Press, 1989), p. 301.) The sex = death equation is supported by a quotation Edelman cites at the beginning of his essay: "'To die,' 'to have sex'— that coupling has always been figurative, metaphorical, sophisticated wordplay. . . . The coupling isn't figurative anymore. It's literal'" (289).

9. Paula A. Treichler, "AIDS, Gender, and Biomedical Discourse: Current Contests for Meaning," in *AIDS: The Burdens of History,* pp. 190–267.

10. Lee Edelman, "The Plague of Discourse: Political, Literary Theory, and AIDS," in

Displacing Homophobia, pp. 289–305; Susan Sontag, *AIDS and Its Metaphors* (New York: Farrar, Straus, and Giroux, 1989).

11. Jeffrey Weeks, "AIDS: The Intellectual Agenda," in Jeffrey Weeks, *Against Nature: Essays on History, Sexuality, and Identity* (London: Rivers Oram, 1991), p. 123.

12. Jeffrey Weeks, "Post-modern AIDS," in *Ecstatic Antibodies*, p. 134.

13. Bill Sherwood's film *Parting Glances* (1986), also set within an affluent, New York gay world, uses flashbacks to childlike romps around Fire Island as the central character's memory of his best friend/former lover's pre-AIDS freedom and exuberance. The film ends on a desolate Fire Island beach.

14. Vincent Canby of the *New York Times* attacked Lucas and René "for making a film that unwittingly trivializes its own middle-class characters by failing to see them as anything but rather superficial and parochial stereotypes" (May 11, 1990, sec. C, p. 16). In a later column, he attacked the film for not being "unruly" enough, essentially for presenting characters who were too well adjusted (*New York Times*, June 24, 1991, sec. 2, pp. 1, 18–19). Canby misses the point. Lucas and René have purposely set their AIDS stories within and against the soap-opera world their characters create. For once, a film is inhabited by beautiful, well-adjusted gay people for whom homosexuality is not a problem. It is a cosmetically perfect fantasy world—gay men deserve to see that once in a while—but it is also just that fantasy, that gay version of the American dream, that AIDS has destroyed.

15. Allen Barnett, "Philostorgy, Now Obscure," in *The Body and Its Dangers and Other Stories* (New York: St. Martin's, 1990). Where subsequent references to this work are contextually clear, page numbers will be cited in the text.

16. Shilts, *And the Band Played On*. While recent critics have attacked Shilts's book, it is still the best history of AIDS and the beginnings of AIDS activism up to 1985. For examples of critiques of Shilts, see Jeff Nunokawa, "'All the Sad Young Men': AIDS and the Work of Mourning," in Diana Fuss, ed., *inside/out: Lesbian Theories and Gay Theories* (New York: Routledge, 1991), pp. 311–23.

17. In December 1989, the American Medical Association defeated an effort to add "sexual orientation" to its antidiscrimination policy, though it earlier recommended that medical schools and hospitals implement policies of antidiscrimination toward medical students and residents. The gist of this Catch-22 is that hospitals should allow gay students and residents, but these benighted souls will never be able to join their professional association as openly gay men and lesbians. One delegate said the resolution was defeated because of "uninformed and misguided" delegates who "over-reacted" for "illogical reasons" (*Washington Blade*, December 22, 1989, p. 6). These "uninformed and misguided" people are those on whom AIDS patients are dependent for their relative well-being.

18. Sontag, *AIDS and Its Metaphors*, p. 72.

19. Robert Ferro, *Second Son* (New York: Crown, 1988), pp. 89–90.

20. Sontag, *AIDS and Its Metaphors*, pp. 72–73.

21. David B. Feinberg, *Eighty-Sixed* (New York: Viking Penguin, 1989). Where subsequent references to this work are contextually clear, page numbers will be cited in the text.

22. Edmund White, "Esthetics and Loss," in John Preston, ed., *Personal Dispatches: Writers Confront AIDS* (New York: St. Martin's, 1989), p. 150.

23. Alan Hollinghurst, *The Swimming Pool Library* (London: Chatto & Windus, 1988), p. 3.

24. Edmund White, *The Beautiful Room Is Empty* (New York: Knopf, 1988).

25. White, "Esthetics and Loss," p. 151.

26. Ibid.

27. Edmund White, "Palace Days," in Edmund White and Adam Mars-Jones, *The Darker Proof: Stories from a Crisis* (London: Faber and Faber, 1987). Where subsequent references to this work are contextually clear, page numbers will be cited in the text.

28. Harvey Fierstein, *Safe Sex* (New York: Atheneum, 1988), pp. 57–58.

29. John Weir, *The Irreversible Decline of Eddie Socket* (New York: Harper & Row, 1989), p. 23. Where subsequent references to this work are contextually clear, page numbers will be cited in the text.

30. Sander L. Gilman, "AIDS and Syphilis: The Iconography of Disease," in Douglas Crimp, ed., *AIDS: Cultural Analysis/Cultural Activism* (Cambridge, Mass.: MIT Press, 1988), p. 95.

31. Ibid., p. 99.

32. Michael Callen, *Surviving AIDS* (New York: Harper, 1990), p. 11.

33. David B. Feinberg's novel, *Spontaneous Combustion* (New York: Viking, 1991), the sequel to *Eighty-Sixed*, covers the years 1985–90, in a fictional account of an HIV-positive gay man's movement through "psychological paralysis" to living a representative life of an HIV-positive person: engaging in AIDS activism, monitoring his health and taking medication, and looking for a supportive partner. Feinberg's book is funny, but his "emotionally barren" protagonist, B. J. Rosenthal, is incapable of commitment to person or cause. It is typical of B. J. that his participation in the ACT UP St. Patrick's Cathedral protest is not out of commitment, but because "all of my friends were either inside at the demo or outside screaming their lungs out; there was nobody left to see a movie with, and moreover, there was nothing particularly interesting on television that afternoon" (184). After seeing *Stop the Church* and reading accounts of the important work of AIDS activists, Feinberg's protagonist seems too glib for comfort. The end of the novel is B. J.'s vision of the future, "After the Cure," and his return to his pre-AIDS lifestyle with no awareness that he found it unfulfilling the first time around. Unlike the powerful conclusion of *Eighty-Sixed*, *Spontaneous Combustion* ends with a punch line.

34. Quoted in Michael LaSalle, "Broadway Loses Talent to AIDS," *The Advocate* 591 (October 8, 1991): 72.

35. "Principal dramatic form of the decade (owing to AIDS): the memorial service" (Michael Feingold, in "Theater: The Best of the 90's," *Village Voice*, January 2, 1990, p. 93).

Refusing the Name: The Absence of AIDS in Recent American Gay Male Fiction

James W. Jones

I

The application of a name carries with it cultural connotations. "AIDS" especially conveys cultural biases and stigmas, since the majority of those who now have the syndrome in the United States and Western Europe are either gay males or intravenous drug users—two groups already stigmatized by definitions of sexual "normalcy" and of narcotic legality. The act of naming imprints values upon the body of the named. As Susan Sontag has shown in her works *Illness as Metaphor* and *AIDS and Its Metaphors*, each culture interprets disease according to its view of the group or the individual who is diseased. AIDS has particular meanings within the United States because American culture needs to punish groups of persons who "choose" to engage in culturally proscribed behaviors. AIDS acquires meaning because it still largely affects people who are socially marginalized, and thus it evokes questions of stereotyping, scapegoating, retribution for "unnatural" lives, and the pathology of proscribed sex.[1] Thus, certain meanings of AIDS permit the further marginalization of gay men, drug users, and prostitutes, to name but three groups.

AIDS has particular meaning for gay male American authors especially, because of the ways they are directly affected by it. Either they themselves have the syndrome or HIV infection (Robert Ferro and Sam D'Alle-sandro, for example, have died with it), or they accompany friends and lovers through the paths of the disease(s) and the social reactions to AIDS. I sketch here only briefly and in broad strokes some chief aspects of the way American authors writing about gay men are influenced by the health crisis, and the way they respond to the public discourses about AIDS in the United States, especially those that configure AIDS as morally synonymous with homosexuality.

According to a pervasive and powerful interpretation, AIDS is acquired because one is a certain kind of person, namely one who refuses to obey social, legal, religious, or moral restrictions on behavior. People with AIDS are often divided into two groups: innocent victims ("innocent" because they have broken no rule) and those deserving the disease. Even methods of education and treatment reinforce this division. For example, as Deb Whippen describes it, "heteroAIDS" mandates the use of a condom for heterosexual intercourse, but "homoAIDS" demands that all gay sex cease.[2] Stephen Johnson, who has done statistical research on the attitudes of American fundamentalists toward people with AIDS, explains "that homosexuals, and by association AIDS victims, may serve as scapegoats for conservative fundamentalists, so that they might blame someone for the moral decay they see all around them."[3] Richard Poirier observes "that the designation of the virus as the primary cause of the disease . . . has created an opportunity for a most primitive designation of homosexuality as the criminal mode of its transmission."[4] Thus, "the need to eradicate homosexuality, even as homosexuals lie dying, takes precedence over the need to eradicate disease. . . . AIDS has become the metaphor for the *sin* of homosexuality and, more generally I think, the *sin* of sexual pleasure."[5]

Such a description of AIDS is clearly just one aspect of the discourses about the epidemic in America. Another, the "enlightened" or "liberal" discourse, maintains that AIDS is an "equal opportunity destroyer." This discourse seems to break the links established between morality and disease but in fact reinforces it for gays, precisely because the discourse aims at keeping the majority (i.e., heterosexuals) healthy and confining HIV to "risk groups" of the socially marginalized and politically disenfranchised. And thus again does AIDS = homosexuality.[6] This point has been made a number of times: "What distinguishes AIDS as it has been constructed in the United States from other diseases is the centrality of sexuality, specifically homosexuality, to its etiology and spread."[7] The packaging of AIDS ostensibly aims at controlling contagion. In fact, it also, often overtly (as in William F. Buckley's call for tattooing gays on the buttocks), more often covertly (as in repeated denials of federal funding for publishing "safe sex" educational materials that use "explicit" language), seeks to reinforce the link between disease and homosexuality, so that homosexuality becomes the death that aberrance calls upon itself.

Gay men recognized early on that "in this country, how we think about disease determines who lives and who dies."[8] They have therefore fought to create a counterdiscourse to defend against efforts to cordon off the sick by labeling them and to empower those living "at risk." Thus, one finds competing terms such as "Persons with AIDS" used to supplant the unfortunate and common term of "AIDS victims." Drug companies and the medical establishment develop new modes of profit and control while activist groups such as ACT UP seek to redistribute power by creating new processes of social empowerment. The discourses compete over the questions of who will be the subjects and who the objects of their speech: who may say "I," and who will become the "they" whom the "I" regulates.

AIDS continues to exist as a developing social construction.[9] In it, as Deb Whippen writes, fact and fiction clearly (at least to the constructors and the constructed) intersect. The "fact" of HIV infection, or of certain "opportunistic" diseases, is given meaning through an interpretation that is in many cases itself *fictive*. She describes how the homophobia of scientists determined what questions they asked about the "facts" of the epidemic, and how this made them see what they wanted to find: a "lifestyle" and not a virus.[10] The effect of such psychological blinders occurs often, but the public discourses on AIDS often cloak their speech in the authenticity and validity of science, making the facts they proclaim appear to be the truth—whereas they clearly are someone's fictions.[11] Estimates of numbers of infected persons and prognostications of numbers of sick, for example, are accepted as inevitable truths, whereas these numbers are speculative. But from them one is expected to deduce the fact that HIV = AIDS = death. The facts of modes of transmission make "unprotected" anal and, to some "experts," oral sex probably lethal. But the description of such modes of transmission can be—and has been—used to titillate and to stir up disgust on the part of nongays, thus creating an often equally lethal fiction for gays who are the recipients of this homophobia based on fact. These facts also turn all sex outside of the proscribed limits of monogamous heterosexual marriage into anonymous sex behind which, as Allan Brandt shows,[12] stands the deathly specter of homosexual sex. What the cultural crisis of AIDS makes quite evident is that the distinction between fact and fiction has become extremely blurred and has been in many instances completely erased. In the end, many facts of the epidemic have been shown to be merely convenient fictions to describe a threatening reality/morality.

II

Is it possible, however, to break the equation in which AIDS = homosexuality = general moral decay = death? Literature presents one way to do so. Many authors have created stories in which gay men have AIDS; yet, surprisingly, the name *AIDS* is not often mentioned. Instead, narrators and characters speak of "my terrible news," "it," "this horrible disease," "my illness." But the various illnesses that afflict these characters or their context make it clear that the unnamed disease is AIDS. For example, in Robert Ferro's novel *Second Son,* Mark develops purplish lesions, and his lover, Bill, becomes ill with pneumonia. Neither illness is named, but the symptoms and treatments mark them as those two common diseases, Kaposi's sarcoma and *Pneumocystis carinii* pneumonia, that among others signify AIDS. The symptomatology of AIDS traces itself throughout the stories: weight loss, diarrhea, night sweats, cytomegalovirus, dementia. The reactions to illness in oneself and in others make it possible to understand that AIDS is what is meant. "The test," "immune systems," guilt about past anonymous sex, and the "plague" make up the semiotics of this language of indirection, which, because the characters are gay men living in the present and because the signs placed into the text are found in everyday discourses of AIDS, is easily decoded.

The name *AIDS* evokes certain images that circumscribe the ability to transcend the limits they impose. By refusing to utter or write the name *AIDS* in these stories, as in the case of *Second Son,* the author pushes the disease to the edge of fiction; it is the effects upon the lives of individuals and the life of the community that form the centers of these stories, rather than the disease itself and its public mythology. In Susan Sontag's short story "The Way We Live Now," many friends, women and men, talk to each other about their mutual friend, a gay man with AIDS. Each friend is named, but the name of the man with AIDS is never given. The story consists of a series of paragraphs that use indirect discourse to report on the man's pneumonia and on his friends' reaction and accommodations to it. Sontag is concerned with the ways in which AIDS is changing relationships and behavior between friends: They vie to spend time with him and arrange their schedules to suit him, which may just be "a way of our trying to define ourselves more firmly and irrevocably as the well, those who aren't ill, who aren't going to fall ill."[13] As one of them says, "Even *we* are all side effects" (45). Yet, he, the friend with AIDS, is able to say the name of the disease, an act that is a sign of health, "a sign that one has accepted being who one is, mortal, vulnerable, not exempt" (60). His friends, however, cannot. They view themselves as exempt because of good health, even when one of them, Max, another gay man, suddenly falls ill and is put on a respirator. They are the ones who declare that "the way he had lived until now" is finished. The incessant chatter of the story expresses the overwhelming flood of news about AIDS and friends with AIDS that is the lived reality for gay men and their friends today, as well as the inability of many of these friends to come to terms with it. As Michael Bronski observes: "It is impossible to be a gay male today and not think of AIDS all the time."[14]

And it is impossible to read a piece of fiction about gay men in the present and not assume AIDS is going to make its presence felt one way or another. Writings by and about gay men must henceforth assume that the reader bears in mind precisely that culturally determined equation of homosexuality = AIDS. That is why the name does not need to be invoked specifically and yet the reader can be expected to be able to decode the signs that signify AIDS within the text. That is also why readers can understand the significance of *refusing* to use that name. Only where the name is expected can its absence be made significant. What will become evident in the following is the nature of that significance.[15]

III

Sontag's story demonstrates one way in which, as Paula Treichler describes it, AIDS has become an epidemic of signification.[16] The unnamed thing that remains always the Other for these friends retains a power of signification that their chatter cannot mute, much less break. Here the equation merely restates its meaning (homosexuality = AIDS = death), and not naming AIDS becomes merely another capitulation to the signification a homophobic culture has already ascribed to AIDS.

The focus is quite different in Andrew Holleran's "Friends at Evening," in which several men gather to talk about a friend with AIDS, a friend who has already died. Four friends meet to go to his funeral, and the story centers on the effect of AIDS upon the gay community in general as represented in this group: Mister Lark, Ned, Curtis, and the first-person narrator (who mostly reports what the others say and do). The effect of AIDS upon the gay community, in Holleran's view, has been the end of a gay identity that drew men together in sexual community. Louis died because, as Ned puts it, "he came into his penis" and "realized the value of what he had" (101).[17] That is, he pursued his identity sexually. Ned now feels guilty about his own promiscuity; he has retreated to Ohio to nurse his invalid father and believes gays should have known better. Mister Lark berates such remorse as the misplaced angst of middle age: "The virus is merely a tragic accident that has nothing to do with either Africa, or our sex lives. . . . It does not invalidate the thing which still persists in the midst of all this horror—I mean . . . the incalculable, the divine, the overwhelming, godlike beauty of the . . . male body" (110).

Mister Lark continues to find beauty and inspiration in men, but only because he never has sex with them. For the others, sex has become dangerous and lethal, and this danger has shaken the foundations of gay identity. Ned has given up sex; he can conjure a romantic fantasy only by setting it in a place he believes untouched by AIDS: "Budapest, in a light snow" (113). A stranger calls Mister Lark on a pay phone and wants him to watch while the stranger exhibits himself and masturbates in his apartment window above. Sex separated by a street and a sheet of glass, love in a city imagined from films and novels—this is what Holleran suggests gay erotic possibility and, thus, identity threatens to become.

AIDS has sundered the gay community in Holleran's story. Louis has died, Ned lives in Ohio, Curtis is being evicted from his apartment. The old gay life that has a history in these men's friendships and loves, that even has a literary tradition in the story's title, taken from Walt Whitman, appears at an end. It appears to be in the evening of its existence, and what it will become remains unclear. At the time of writing this story, Holleran was very pessimistic about the future of gay community and identity. As a gay man writing for gay men, he faced the dilemma: "How could one write truthfully of the horror when part of one's audience was experiencing that horror?"[18] In particular, he did not see how literature could help define the future: "Literature could not heal or explain this catastrophe. . . . Someday writing about this plague may be read with pleasure, by people for whom it is a distant catastrophe, but I suspect the best writing will be nothing more, nor less, than a lament: 'We are as wanton flies [sic] to the gods; they kill us for their sport.'"[19]

Despite the melancholy tone of this story and the pessimistic attitude of these statements, there is something nonetheless in Holleran's writing that affirms a gay spirit, a refusal to concede desire altogether in the face of disease. At the story's conclusion, the friends climb into a cab to go to Louis's funeral, a moment in which it seems "as if one renews one's life each time a meter switches on" (113), and Mister Lark strikes up a conversation with the Argentinean cab driver. The possibility inherent in simply *being* gay opens itself even in the darkness.

In three other short stories, the unspoken disease is the silence that continually speaks. In so doing, its language alters forever the lives of those who hear it. Sam D'Allesandro's "Nothing Ever Just Disappears" provides an interior monologue by "S" about his lover "J" in which he describes how they met and became involved and what has happened to him since J's death. Through a spare language full of unstated meanings, D'Allesandro shows how love develops incongruously, in spurts. His simple, short sentences take the reader swiftly through the prose sections: "Here's what I found out that afternoon: He was a painter. He was a waiter. He was thirty. It was enough to know" (126–27).[20] The conversations he relates, on the other hand, contain inscrutable exchanges that ask to be explained: "'Your way is not bad. I do the same thing. We're not the same.' 'No, we're not.' 'Maybe you're right.'" (127).

A break in the story (not the first) after their relationship has been established separates S's and J's lives before and after AIDS. The next sentence comes as a shock then: "When the time came I wasn't waiting for him to die" (130). D'Allesandro provides none of the usual signs that other stories use to indicate that death has been caused by AIDS, though he does supply a possible hint early in the third section of the story, when S tells how J "said a lot of things that I didn't exactly understand, or that seemed to carry connotations other than those most obvious" (126). At J's hospital bedside the narrator mentions "tubes that sucked at his arms like hungry little snakes, trying to put life back in" (130) and doctors discussing J "like some kind of textbook experiment" (130). But the fact of one gay man writing about the death of his lover at this time in history forces us, whether we want to or not, to fill that break in the text with the name *AIDS*, especially when the author does *not* fill that break with another cause of death.

D'Allesandro's silence about the cause of the death, even about the course of the disease, makes us focus on the effect J's death has upon his lover. His repetition of certain sentences and phrases makes us ask what they mean, leading us to interpret them according to our experience of love, of gay love, of gay love in the age of AIDS. When D'Allesandro states, before we know that J dies, "there is such a thing as the tyranny of fate" (130), the sentence's meaning is vague; but when he repeats it after his lover's death, we can read this as a response to the argument that AIDS is a just punishment for an unnatural life. In the final paragraphs, S's incantation of "Everything's OK" and "I'm OK" become a mantra, a chant to free himself of the past while continually invoking it. He knows he can never leave that past because it is always the present, in some form, because "nothing ever just disappears," not J, not their love, and not AIDS, whether spoken or not.

An unspoken name also shapes the lives of gay men in Edmund White's "Palace Days." Mark and Ned, lovers who no longer have sex with each other, have left New York for Paris. Their relationship began in 1981, a time "when the official line had been 'Limit the number of your partners. Know their names'" (134).[21] In Europe, where the effects of and consciousness about AIDS developed somewhat later than in the United States, they attempt to continue the hedonism they had enjoyed on the other side of the Atlantic. They believe themselves protected by their relationship and their life made secure by the money flowing from their gay tour business. Using their pet name for one another, they ask: "'Aren't we cosy here, Peters?' That was their word for happy: 'cosy'" (137). As the ravages of the epidemic became more clear, it also meant "free of disease."

As time passes and the disease draws nearer, Mark begins to fear their dependence upon outsiders for sex. He wonders whether "they might already be harboring this lazy seed, this century plant of death" (141). Nonetheless, Mark becomes involved with a health-conscious German, Hajo, and they are "passionate but cautious," not exchanging "those fluids that had once been the gush of life but that now seemed the liquid drained off a fatal infection" (151). When Mark confesses that he had been promiscuous, Hajo demands more and more precautions be used in what little sex they do have. Their relationship ends as their friends begin to die in the United States and as Mark's supply of money dwindles. Mark eventually tests positive. White does not specify what the test is, but the entire context and discourse of the story make this abundantly clear. He returns to Ned, who has enjoyed his own affairs, and "they both expected to die" (155). Reunited with his lover with whom he shares everything except sex, Mark realizes "Ned was the only home he had" (167). The unspoken disease shapes desire and destroys life, but in White's story it also creates a community of love and of strength.

That silence about AIDS does literally speak in another story by Edmund White, "An Oracle." Ray's lover, George, has died of AIDS before the story begins. The reader can interpret "George's disease" as AIDS through such signs as "the virus," the "blood test,"[22] and a dentist's refusal to treat George. The impact of AIDS upon the sexual relationships of gay men today makes itself evident in the relationship Ray forms with a young Greek man, Marco. No longer is it possible to take part in the Greek tradition or to lose oneself in the Greek history of homosexuality. Now, it is the younger man wearing a condom who sodomizes the older partner. Ray further breaks the tradition by falling in love with Marco. When he offers to quit his life in New York and move to Greece, a more circumspect Marco replies, "I won't see you again. You must look out for yourself."[23] And yet something in that Greek past of men loving men still lives today. George, to whom Ray has clung even since his death, seems to have used Marco as an oracle through which to set Ray free.

IV

Robert Ferro's *Second Son* and Christopher Davis's *Valley of the Shadow* provide further evidence of how not naming the disease enables the authors to push AIDS, as culturally defined and defining, to the edge of the work and place the relationships of gay men affected by the epidemic at the center. Ferro's novel focuses on the relationships of its central character, Mark Valerian, the second son, to his family and to Bill Mackey, the lover he finds in the course of the novel. Like his mother who recently died, Mark seeks to hold the family together by hanging on to the family's summer home. His father and older brother do not understand why he will not agree to sell the house when the family business desperately needs money.

At the beginning of the relationship, both lovers have Kaposi's sarcoma but are relatively healthy. When Bill becomes ill with pneumonia, the feeling grows that something must be done—about their health (even though Bill recovers and Mark's health remains stable) and about the house. Letters from Mark's friend Matthew, an author, describe a possible way out of this dilemma. The "Lambda Project," a group of gay men searching for a haven, has discovered beings from the planet Sirius (which the Sirians call "Splendora"), who are willing to help them emigrate; AIDS seems not to present a problem there; it may be that the Sirians have a cure or that the escape itself represents a cure. The reality of this is never entirely assured, however, especially since it may just be a product of Matthew's fantasy. Bill is willing to believe the emigration can happen, and

Mark slowly accepts it as a possibility. Before they must decide whether to go, there is time to take one more measure. Mark enters a drug protocol, which he had previously refused to do. Should it fail or should their illnesses get worse, then they can seize this last chance.

Ferro slowly makes it clear that Mark is sick: he is "ill, dying perhaps" (4)[24] and then "apparently dying" (18) of "the medical thing" later referred to as "It" (71). His illness is linked to his "inverted sexuality" and to the distance he now feels from desire for men. Handsome men, his erotic ideals and masturbatory fantasies, exist at first only on the other side of panes of glass in his bedroom or in taxicabs. Descriptions of Mark's lesions, theories as to the etiology of "the disease" (germ warfare, infected plasma in gamma globulin shots for hepatitis B, something in the pools at gay bathhouses [75]), as well as descriptions of the social responses to this disease (the search for a vaccine, the attitude of letting the sick die off and seeking to protect the healthy [28]) all make it evident that AIDS is the subject not being named outright. It is not named because the family does not want to hear it, and Mark does not want to invite its presence by invoking it. Perhaps most importantly for the structure of this novel, AIDS is not named because its reality would undermine the elements of fantasy in the possibility of Splendora and in the metaphor of a haven and safe vessel that the house, built in the form of a ship, represents.

Letters, mostly from Matthew to Mark, maintain a fantasy element that deprives AIDS of its power to define reality. They evade its power by using a premodern literary form largely associated with women, and they also maintain a kind of gay identity by employing camp humor. Matthew and Mark close their letters with remarks that might be made by the women whose names they sign ("[Mrs.] Edward R. Murrow," "Mark's teacher [Mrs.]," "[Mrs.] Neil Armstrong").

Fantasy provides the realm where the tyranny of "science" can—if anywhere—perhaps be overthrown. A clairvoyant in Rome tells Mark that radiation will cure him, that his disease is not fatal. The love he shares with Bill reinvigorates and renews him. Emigration to another planet represents a possibility for survival (just as the drug protocol does). All these nonrational elements offer other answers to the lockstep equation that determines so much of our concept of AIDS in reality, as well as the possibility that love—in particular and, here, of necessity, between two men who have AIDS—may break that equation.

Valley of the Shadow by Christopher Davis is another novel that places relationships rather than disease at its center. A memory book written by the narrator, Andy, in the first person as a way to take control of his disease, it is by his own description, "a story of just one gay man who enjoyed life, who enjoyed being gay, who loved his lover as much as one man can love another, and who will die before he is thirty" (199).[25] As a student at Columbia University, Andy meets Ted, who leads him into an assured, political gay identity and who becomes his lover. Their stormy relationship ends, however, and Andy immerses himself in the wide variety of gay erotic experiences available in New York. Some years after their breakup, Andy meets Ted by chance and notices he is wearing makeup—to hide the lesions on his face. Andy forces Ted, who is alone and without money, to move in with him, and the two build a new relationship as loving friends. Three weeks after Ted's death, Andy is himself diagnosed with pneumonia, and within a short time he dies. He writes about the loving support of his family and friends. The novel concludes with his obituary.

As with Ferro's novel, hints are given from the beginning that the main character is gay and ill. These two pieces of information ("I no longer have the strength," "I would masturbate, and when I had I usually thought about boys" [4,5]) become linked in the story. Moreover, because they are also linked in the extratextual discourse of AIDS, the reader deciphers the following remarks as referring to AIDS: "[Ted] always looked so good, not at the end, of course" (21); "I am not ashamed of the kind of sex I had" (23). Without the extratextual discourse of AIDS, such remarks could refer to any sort of death from disease or even old age, for the sex is not explicitly linked to death. But the relationship that exists inside that discourse (AIDS = homosexuality) determines as well as enables this reading—and writing—about gay men with AIDS.

In this novel, the narrator *does* at one point name AIDS as his disease. In a defiant, angry statement Andy declares: "I *have* AIDS, I *am* dying, and the result *will be* death" (137). But that single sentence is the only identification of AIDS as his disease. The term is also mentioned three other times: in reference to Ted, to a gay man who is alone and embittered because of his illness, and to an acquaintance from the small town in which Andy and his family celebrate holidays. Perhaps these direct mentions of AIDS ought to disqualify this novel from consideration here. They are, however, isolated, and only a single direct mention is made late in the novel with respect to the illness of the narrator. Indeed, once may be more than enough where AIDS is concerned, but throughout the novel Andy typically mentions not AIDS but "this horrible disease" or "this damned disease."

Davis employs the term AIDS sparingly and instead chooses euphemisms and metaphors for two significant reasons. He wants to resist the popular conception, even among gay people, that AIDS is a gay disease, that it somehow punishes gays justly for their unjust desires:

> "Why is it so much a part of *gay* life!" I cried, and Teddy held my hand and told me that it was important to remember that this damned disease is just a virus. It is not our *fault* that it infects us; it is just an organism that happens to flourish in the free-sex culture we developed. That does not mean that our culture was wrong; it only means that some insidious little organism has, in some kind of perverse Darwinist survival-of-the-fittest way, found us a physical medium in which to thrive.   (182)[26]

Deconstructing that mythology strips the power from discourses of stereotyping and scapegoating. Secondly, Davis refuses to characterize AIDS as a disease with a name and a process proceeding inevitably to death because he refuses to portray these gay men with AIDS as victims. Again, he is responding to the image, evoked under the popular discourse, of people with AIDS as powerless over the destiny of their lives. Andy's telling of his story is an act of empowerment. He refuses to speak of AIDS and instead describes the joys of being gay and loving men and the sorrow of dying.

The form of Davis's novel is perfectly suited to these intents. The first-person narrator of this fictional autobiography draws the reader into the text, creating a familiarity with this fearful Other, be it AIDS or homosexuality. It evokes identification with the narrator and makes his life, his love, and his death sympathetic and understandable. The politics of *Valley of the Shadow* refute popular (mis)conceptions of gay men with AIDS in that Andy feels no remorse for his sexual life. On the contrary, he maintains a vigorous erotic life until he becomes too sick to do so. In the novel, gay men create their own families, and, while some families of blood break all ties with their gay sons because of AIDS, Andy's family stands by him.[27]

While Ferro uses fantasy or nonrational elements to counteract the oppressive reality of the disease, Davis explores the intricacies of memory in order to evade the determining grip of AIDS. Memories reshaped by what has been learned and what has occurred since then form the basis of the novel. The process of memory, obstructed by the dementia that sometimes accompanies AIDS, provides a style that acts as a metaphor for the disease itself. The obituary that ends this memory book is like a wall the reader strikes, leaving him/her with the imprint of the memory of this text and the need to react to it.

Refusing to name enables all these authors to particularize and to universalize the effects of AIDS upon those characters and their communities. Because of the discourse on AIDS outside the text, both possibilities occur: it is necessary to demystify AIDS by individualizing it, and it is necessary to demonstrate the commonality of experiences and the possibility of community in the face of a disease that often isolates the diseased. [28] These works use the space created by not naming to make readers familiar with the feelings and experiences of people with AIDS, which are both individual to these particular characters and also representative of the ways gay men and their lovers, friends, and family are responding to AIDS. An exception to this intertwining of individualization and universalization is Susan Sontag's "The Way We Live Now." The secondhand reports of what the gay man's friends say about him focus the story upon the diversity of responses among the *healthy*, linking them within a common experience and separating them from the sick individual. Of course, that is exactly Sontag's point: the way we (or at least a good number of us) live now is shaped by our responses to those with AIDS, responses that draw ever more sharply the division between health and illness. [29]

V

In demonstrating the universality of AIDS as it affects gay men, these stories combat efforts to marginalize gays further because of their sexuality or their erotic practices. They draw new lines around a gay identity that is threatened by a society that would like to use AIDS as an excuse to erase the existence of gays. Because of this process of particularization and universalization, individual gay characters or the interplay between several gay characters speaks for common gay experience at this point in time. The contradictory opinions of Ned and Mister Lark as to the "reasons" for AIDS among gays are an example in point. This division of opinion occurs even in such disparate forms as the interior monologue of "Nothing Ever Just Disappears," the third-person narrative of *Second Son,* and the first-person "autobiography" of *Valley of the Shadow.* In the two novels, the individuality of each man's disease and of his reactions to being ill are depicted along with the commonality of the diseases and their symptomatology.

Falling in and being in love are described as experiences shared by all, experienced in the same way whether gay or straight. In "Nothing Ever Just Disappears" S describes his relationship with J: "Let's just say things were fine. Some usual things happened, some unusual. That's normal" (130). Andy in *Valley of the Shadow* addresses the reader: "In Love. I know that sounds foolish and trite and sentimental and banal and like a horrible cliché, but when you are experiencing this, and every person—man or woman, gay or straight—has, I hope, experienced it at least once, it does not seem banal or trite or any of the other disparaging things: It is wonderful" (24). What makes these loves unique, however, is precisely the facts that the men in love *are* gay and that, through sexual contact with other men, they have become infected. Through the love relationships in these three works, the individuals (gay men with AIDS and a gay man whose lover dies of AIDS) are set within a common framework of experience with only individual permutations. In depicting the relationships in this way, the stories create for them a universality available to the reader.

The "gay space" that critic Jacob Stockinger mentioned over a decade ago in "Homotextuality: A Proposal"[30] requires a new definition because of AIDS. The division between interior and exterior has long been central to gay texts, but now its meanings vary. Interiors confine the disease and the diseased in White's "Palace Days," forcing gay men to come to terms with it; even the walled city of West Berlin becomes such an interior, "an emblem of their endangered, quarantined happiness" (151). With D'Allesandro, the interiority of the monologue form itself contains both the sense of refuge S had found in his relationship with J ("In his apartment I always became very relaxed. I didn't do a lot of thinking there. When I entered I stopped making plans" [127]) and the emptiness he feels.

Interior space in *Second Son* supplies safe haven from the threats of AIDS. But the defenses are breached. Rome falls under the radioactive cloud from Chernobyl. The cabin's lack of heat intensifies Bill's pneumonia. The family home, built in the form of a ship, seems ready to depart at the order of its owner, but its safety is threatened by the mortgage his family has taken upon it. That space is complemented by the expanse of the heavens, which represent a possible salvation, even a return to a home never seen but long felt: "For it seemed that what they would do together— what would be done to them in the hospital—was a kind of trip, a voyage home. As with Matthew, the ship had become their metaphor, something to look for by day over the horizon, by night among the stars" (214–15). Even space, too, is compromised: earlier, Matthew had written about the explosion of the Challenger and the uncertainty of future space travel.

Without benefit of social approval and example, gay men must create their own homes and their own communities to overcome their exile from the community of the majority, an exile whose borders have been drawn tighter with the advent of AIDS. Paul Monette describes the situation as he and his lover experienced it: "It begins in a country beyond tears. Once you have your arms around your friend with his terrible news, your eyes are too shut to cry."[31] Robert Ferro writes of Mark as an exile continually seeking admittance to his own family: "It was not that it didn't exist, this idea of family, but that it did not seem to exist always, and never as Mark saw it; or if it did, which he saw it did, it was really only among each of them and for their very own. Meaning that he was not a member, in each case, of *their very own*" (24). In this regard, *Second Son* does not permit the resolution found in the TV drama *An Early Frost* (1985). Whereas the family in the latter rethinks its attitudes toward the gay son because of his AIDS, here the gay son rethinks his attitude toward his family because of his illness.[32] Gay men and heterosexual women bridge the exile of many of these men with AIDS, but the links are tenuous. The friends die; the women are involved with their own families. The gay men are left, like Mark and Bill or Ned and Mark, to make their own "home" with each other.

Christopher Davis's novel presents yet another view. Andy has never had to struggle for acceptance from his family, and although he works in a conservative business, he never mentions having faced discrimination. But precisely that economic status and social integration enable Davis to infuse *AIDS* with his own meanings. Because the characters here do not have to deal with jobs, rent, disapproving parents, and fearful friends, Davis can focus upon the relationship between AIDS and gays in terms of the influence AIDS has on gay identity and gay community. Although there are family tensions around Mark's sexuality, the gay characters in Ferro's novel similarly do not face difficulties with money or jobs, with the mundane necessities of life beyond that so crucial: health. As Richard Goldstein writes, because they are simultaneously privileged and oppressed, they are "therefore acutely aware of the gap between perception and power"[33] that AIDS has widened. AIDS does not succeed in destroying identity and community; on the contrary, gays themselves redefine identity and expand community.

Not naming AIDS represents a process of empowerment for these gay authors. By refusing to succumb to AIDS they are able to define death *and* life. While the numbing chatter of the friends in "The Way We Live Now" reflects their inability to affect the disease itself or its effects on them, most of the other stories and novels reflect attempts to define death on gay men's terms, that is, not as the end of gay identity or gay community but as leading both in new directions. The definitions vary among the stories. The pessimism of Holleran's "Friends at Evening" is tempered by the optimism of Mister Lark's desire to meet new men. Gay eroticism takes new forms, but it never disappears, not even in White's melancholy "Running on Empty." As George Stambolian writes, "It is death that has had the most troubled history in gay fiction."[34] The response of these writers to that awfully troubled present is to state plainly and boldly "that the gay community exists and will survive."[35]

These fictions about gay men with AIDS find ways for gays to create new spaces, new interiors and exteriors, according to their own definitions; thus, they continue to explore the homosexual space Stockinger described. Not by ignoring its presence, but by refusing the definitions American culture has loaded into AIDS, these fictions also radically alter the portrayal of gays in American fiction generally. The homosexual male character in American literature had until only very recently been defined according to the medical-psychological discourse that created the very category of "the homosexual" in the late nineteenth and early twentieth centuries. His assigned lot remained unhappiness, suffering, and death (ideally by his own hand). These were the necessary corollaries of the equation homosexuality = illness.[36] With the gay liberation movement of the 1970s, that equation was broken, and a much wider variety of gay realities, experiences, and lives found expression within American literature.

AIDS elicited, however, a forceful restatement of the link that never entirely disappeared in American culture: homosexuality = illness. And since illness = AIDS, it follows as a matter of course that homosexuality = AIDS. While other works within the growing genre of AIDS literature may indeed ultimately reinforce that link, the works discussed here break that chain of signification and continue the project of gay liberation by moving the representation of gays within literature onto radically different avenues by defusing the power of oppressive discourse, by refusing the name.[37] While the gay character in American fiction until the 1970s was defined by a majority, nongay, homophobic society within a literature written primarily for members of that society, these characters can discover methods of empowerment within a minority, gay society. These stories build on the achievements of a gay liberation tradition created over the past two decades, refusing to cede the power gained in moving from a discourse of disease to a discourse of desire, from being the objects of speech to the subjects of speaking.

The gay men depicted in AIDS literature are often indeed physically ill, and their illness has indeed followed the physical love of men. But that illness does not throw these gay characters back into the arms of physicians waiting to cure them of their "real" illness (homosexuality) or to attend them as they experience the just reward of their aberrance (death). Instead, they turn to the welcoming arms of other gay men and of nongay friends to find new kinds of gay community and gay identity. To refuse to name is to resist a power that seeks to strengthen and protect itself by classifying and by excluding. That refusal has become a dynamic theme within the literary response to AIDS. It empowers both sick and healthy to move beyond the language of AIDS and to speak to one another with the words of their shared humanity.

NOTES

1. For excellent analyses of these cultural processes see Sander L. Gilman's pathbreaking works *Disease and Pathology: Stereotypes of Sexuality, Race, and Madness* (Ithaca, N.Y.: Cornell University Press, 1985) and *Disease and Representation: Images of Illness from Madness to AIDS* (Ithaca, N.Y.: Cornell University Press, 1988).

2. Deb Whippen, "Science Fictions: The Making of a Medical Model for AIDS," *Radical America* 20 (November-December 1986):50–51.

3. Stephen D. Johnson, "Factors Related to Intolerance of AIDS Victims," *Journal for the Scientific Study of Religion* 26 (1987):109.

4. Richard Poirier, "AIDS and Traditions of Homophobia," *Social Research* 55 (1988):463.

5. Ibid., p. 464.

6. See Susan Sontag's analysis of the phrase "equal opportunity destroyer" as affirming what it intends to deny, in *AIDS and Its Metaphors* (New York: Farrar, Straus, and Giroux, 1989), pp. 82–83.

7. Robert Padgug, "More Than the Story of a Virus: Gay History, Gay Communities, and AIDS," *Radical America* 21 (March-April 1987):36. See also Allan Brandt, "AIDS and Metaphor: Toward the Social Meaning of Epidemic Disease," *Social Research* 55 (1988):413–32; Dennis Altman, *AIDS in the Mind of America: The Social, Political, and Psychological Impact of a New Epidemic* (Garden City, N.Y.: Anchor, 1986), especially chapter 3, "The Conceptualization of AIDS"; and Cindy Patton, *Sex and Germs: The Politics of AIDS* (Boston: South End, 1985).

8. Evelynn Hammonds, "Race, Sex, AIDS: The Construction of 'Other'," *Radical America* 20 (November-December 1986):29.

9. Excellent analyses of the construction of discourses of AIDS can be found in the following: Paula Treichler, "AIDS, Homophobia, and Biomedical Discourse: An Epidemic of Signification," in Douglas Crimp, ed., *AIDS: Cultural Analysis/Cultural Activism* (Cambridge, Mass: MIT Press, 1988), pp. 31–70; Allan M. Brandt, "AIDS: From Social History to Social Policy," in Elizabeth Fee and Daniel M. Fox, eds., *AIDS: The Burdens of History* (Berkeley: University of California Press, 1988), pp. 147–71; and Simon Watney, *Policing Desire: Pornography, AIDS, and the Media* (Minneapolis: University of Minnesota Press, 1987).

10. Whippen, "Science Fictions," p. 40.

11. See Sontag, *AIDS and Its Metaphors*, pp. 28ff.

12. Brandt deciphers C. Everett Koop's oft-quoted dictum: "When you have sex with someone, you're really having sex with all of their partners for perhaps as long as the last ten years." "It suggests," Brandt explains, "every *single* sexual encounter is a promiscu-

ous encounter. . . . No matter how well known a partner may be, the relationship is *anonymous*." The discourse on AIDS has assigned meanings of promiscuity and anonymity to the realm of homosexual sex. Therefore, "the metaphor implies to heterosexuals that if they are having sex with their partner's (heterosexual) partners, they are in fact engaging in homosexual acts. In this view, every sexual act becomes a homosexual encounter" (Brandt, "AIDS and Metaphor," pp. 430–31).

13. Susan Sontag, "The Way We Live Now," *The New Yorker* 24 (November 1986):45. Where subsequent references to this work are contextually clear, page numbers will be cited in the text.

14. Michael Bronski, "Death and the Erotic Imagination," *Radical America* 21 (March-April 1987):60.

15. This process of redefining by not naming has also been used outside prose texts. A recent modern-dress production of *La Traviata* by Opera New England replaced Violetta's tuberculosis with AIDS. Not a word of the libretto was changed in director Esquire Jauchem's production; the term was mentioned only in the program notes. Here "Violetta dies of pneumonia as a consequence of AIDS," enabling viewers at last "to understand what the stakes of the drama are," according to Michael Bronski ("The Ultimate Incurable Romantic," *The Advocate* [September 12, 1989]:54–55). Alfredo's "risk," his father's objections to his son's relationship with Violetta, and Violetta's own social role take on new meanings for an audience that decodes that unnamed disease as AIDS.

16. See Paula A. Treichler, "AIDS, Homophobia, and Biomedical Discourse: An Epidemic of Signification," pp. 31–70.

17. Andrew Holleran, "Friends at Evening," in George Stambolian, ed., *Men on Men: Best New Gay Fiction* (New York: New American Library, 1986). Where subsequent references to this work are contextually clear, page numbers will be cited in the text.

18. Andrew Holleran, *Ground Zero* (New York: Morrow, 1988), p. 15.

19. Holleran, *Ground Zero*, pp. 16, 18.

20. Sam D'Allesandro, "Nothing Ever Just Disappears," in *Men on Men*. Where subsequent references to this work are contextually clear, page numbers will be cited in the text.

21. Edmund White, "Palace Days," in Edmund White and Adam Mars-Jones, *The Darker Proof: Stories from a Crisis* (New York: New American Library, 1988). Where subsequent references to this work are contextually clear, page numbers will be cited in the text.

22. Edmund White, "An Oracle," in *The Darker Proof*, p. 169.

23. Ibid., p. 209.

24. Robert Ferro, *Second Son* (New York: Crown Publishers, 1988). Where subsequent references to this work are contextually clear, page numbers will be cited in the text.

25. Christopher Davis, *Valley of the Shadow* (New York: St. Martin's, 1988). Where subsequent references to this work are contextually clear, page numbers will be cited in the text.

26. Each of these works explicitly repudiates the myth that being gay is the "cause" of AIDS. In this essay "The Absence of Anger" Andrew Holleran says,

Nothing is so difficult for the human mind to accept as the fact that much suffering in life is random, meaningless, and in a sense completely trivial: the wrong place at the wrong time. Once the plague established itself, gay men in doctors' offices all over Manhattan were weeping over their pasts. AIDS had simply tapped into the remorse, the conviction ('I have been unlucky in life') harbored by homosexuals who may not even suspect they have these feelings. Echoing Pat Buchanan, they say, 'If only I had not been homosexual, this never would have happened.' Strictly true, perhaps. But their being homosexual did not cause the illness; the virus simply exploited their homosexuality. But like someone whose child is injured on a hike they took them on, they blame themselves for ever having gone walking.   (*Ground Zero*, p. 199)

27. See, for example, Paul Reed, *Facing It* (San Francisco: Gay Sunshine, 1984).

28. Susan Sontag states: "AIDS is understood in a premodern way, as a disease incurred by people both as individuals and as members of a 'risk group'—that neutral-sounding, bureaucratic category which also revives the archaic idea of a tainted community that illness has judged." (*AIDS and Its Metaphors*, p. 46).

29. That not all silence is refusal and thus empowering can also be seen in stories by Christopher Davis and Edmund White in which fear is the cause of not naming AIDS. Christopher Davis's "The Boys in the Bars" (1987) describes the friendships that the main character, Gene, has with several men over a long period of time. When one particular friend, Peter, reappears at the end of the story after a long absence, we suddenly learn that Gene has AIDS, a fact he has hidden from everyone. The story concludes with Gene leading Peter "into the bright sunlight . . . to tell him my terrible news" (*Men on Men 2: Best New Gay Fiction* [New York: New American Library, 1988], p. 337). In Edmund White's "Running on Empty" (1988), Luke is frightened and surprised by his sickness: "It was a gay disease and he scarcely thought of himself as gay" (*The Darker Proof*, p. 217). The illness undermines his life and his identity. The family, to which he belongs but which also exiles him, comes together to tend the family graveyard. One of his aunts invites him to pick a spot for his grave. This double ostracism of himself from his family because of his illness and of himself from any gay community because of his view of his sexuality stifles the relationships in the story.

30. Jacob Stockinger, "Homotextuality: A Proposal," in Louie Crew, ed., *The Gay Academic* (Palm Springs, Cal.: ETC Publications, 1978), pp. 143–51.

31. Paul Monette, *Borrowed Time: An AIDS Memoir* (New York: Harcourt Brace Jovanovich, 1988), p. 77.

32. See discussion of this in Richard Goldstein's review of the novel: "Till Death Do Us Part: Love and Loyalty in the Age of AIDS," *Voice Literary Supplement*, June 1988, pp. 11–12.

33. Ibid., p. 12.

34. Stambolian, *Men on Men*, p. 9.

35. Ibid.

36. For a history of the gay character in American fiction, see Roger Austen, *Playing the Game: The Homosexual Novel in America* (Indianapolis: Bobbs-Merrill, 1977) and James Levin, *The Gay Novel* (New York: Irvington Publishers, 1983).

37. For discussion of works within the AIDS literature, see Douglas Crimp, "How to Have Promiscuity in an Epidemic," in *AIDS: Cultural Analysis/Cultural Activism*, pp. 237–71; K. McQueen and D. Fassler, "Children's Books About AIDS," *Children's Literature in Education* 20 (1989):183–90; G. Newtown, "Sex, Death, and the Drama of AIDS," *Antioch Review* 47 (1989):209–22; Shaun O'Connell, "The Big One: Literature Discovers AIDS," in Padraig O'Malley, ed., *The AIDS Epidemic: Private Rights and Public Interest* (Boston: Beacon, 1989), pp. 485–506.

Immersive and Counterimmersive Writing About AIDS: The Achievement of Paul Monette's *Love Alone*

Joseph Cady

I

The profound denial that has dominated worldwide cultural reaction to AIDS has spurred two distinct responses in the growing body of literature about the epidemic. One, which I call "immersive" AIDS writing, is frankly, though not exclusively, concerned with that denial and confronts it squarely in an effort to undo it. Though immersive AIDS writings go to various lengths in that attempt, central to all of them are prolonged moments when the reader is thrust into a direct imaginative confrontation with the special horrors of AIDS and is required to deal with them with no relief or buffer provided by the writer. The other, which I call "counterimmersive" AIDS writing, also recognizes the dreadfulness of the disease, as all AIDS literature must at least minimally do to be worthy of the name, and also indicates the problem of denial in the larger society. But, in context, its stance toward that denial seems ultimately deferential. Counterimmersive AIDS writing typically focuses on characters or speakers who are in various degrees of denial about AIDS themselves, and it customarily treats its readers the way its characters handle their disturbing contact with AIDS, protecting them from too jarring a confrontation with the subject through a variety of distancing devices. A quantity of counterimmersive AIDS writings might cumulatively have some discomfiting effect, but individual counterimmersive texts characteristically do nothing to dislodge whatever impulse their audience may have to deny the disease.

In this essay I want to illustrate and analyze these kinds of writing about AIDS, partly to help establish the beginnings of a critical framework and vocabulary for AIDS literature and partly because these terms could also be useful in describing social and personal responses to AIDS. I take my examples from gay male writing about AIDS, chiefly by American authors, and work mostly by close reading of a few representative texts. As is well known, homosexual men were the group first struck in full force by AIDS and still make up the overwhelming majority of diagnosed AIDS cases in the United States.[1] For those reasons, and because as social outcasts even before AIDS appeared they had nothing left to lose in taking up the stigmatized subject, gay men have produced most of the AIDS literature to date.

In addition, gay men have experienced a unique double measure of denial under AIDS. Like all other groups affected by the disease, they have felt the denial directed at AIDS as an especially terrible medical condition—e.g., its seemingly mysterious onset and ungovernable course, its particularly horrible bodily wastage, and the fact that so far the disease has inevitably proved fatal. But homosexuals were already categorically denied (i.e., deemed less than fully human) by culture before AIDS because of their unique stereotype as entirely "untouchable" and "unspeakable" (in contrast even to the most socially disapproved of the other AIDS risk groups defined by the Centers for Disease Control— poor black and Hispanic IV drug users, whose "saving" heterosexuality keeps them within the bounds, if still near the edges, of the assumed human community).[2] Since gay men in the AIDS epidemic thus face a unique double degree of cultural disavowal, their writing about AIDS provides the fullest arena for seeing the influence and effects of the widespread denial of the disease.

II

Paul Monette's writing offers a classic example of immersive AIDS writing. A poet, novelist, and screenwriter who has lived in Los Angeles since 1977, Monette lost his lover of twelve years, Roger Horwitz, to AIDS in October 1986. Two years afterward Monette published two companion volumes about Roger's illness and death and the personal and social havoc of AIDS: *Love Alone: Eighteen Elegies for Rog,* a set of long poems narrated by Paul and often directly addressed to Rog, and *Borrowed Time: An AIDS Memoir*, a finalist for the National Book Critics' Circle award for the best work of general nonfiction of that year. Since then he has also published two novels in which AIDS is a major concern: *Afterlife* (1990), about three Los Angeles "AIDS widowers" who met while their lovers lay dying in the same hospital, and *Halfway Home* (1991), about a gay man with AIDS and his heterosexual brother who had earlier rejected him.

In *Love Alone* the experience of AIDS is one of near-total "wreckage" (to adapt a term from "Three Rings," the eleventh poem in the book, in which Monette compares the effect of the disease to "a car wreck" [33]).[3] This devastation is of course partly medical—Rog and other people with AIDS have been struck by a physically horrendous disease that is also, at this early stage in the epidemic, seemingly inexplicable and uncontrollable (Rog was diagnosed in March 1985). However, for Rog, Paul, and other gay men this havoc is multiplied by the special cultural situation of homosexuals mentioned above. AIDS is unthinkable enough simply because of its fearsome physical effects. But it has become doubly so at this early point in the crisis because it seems only to be afflicting the already untouchable and unspeakable homosexual population. The results are a compounded cultural denial of the disease and a near-total isolation for the affected gay male community, which has been left to suffer AIDS almost entirely alone and left almost entirely to its own resources to seek treatment for it.[4]

From the very first in *Love Alone*, Monette indicates his concern with this denial—he states in the preface that he wants the poems "to allow no escape" (p. xii). His primary target in the book is what might be called the denying reader, whom he seeks to shock and unsettle out of his or her insensibility to AIDS. (There is of course a paradox to this feature of immersive AIDS writing, for, strictly speaking, a denying reader might avoid AIDS literature in the first place; in real terms, it is perhaps best to think of this reader as someone who has come in contact with the subject for some reason but is still unwilling to confront its painful features and implications.) In this aspect of *Love Alone*, Monette effectively follows Kafka's maxim that "A book should serve as the ax for the frozen sea within us" and Tillie Olsen's outlook in her collection *Tell Me A Riddle*, "Better immersion than to live untouched."[5] Monette has a second audience in mind in *Love Alone* as well, another feature typical of immersive AIDS writing. This is the population of all people affected by AIDS, but especially his doubly beset community of fellow gay men, reeling from the compound assault of AIDS and their long-standing oppression as essentially untouchable anyway. In one tradition of classic plague literature, Monette wants *Love Alone* also to be a work of confirmation, witness, and encouragement for this suffering audience, heartening readers affected by AIDS with evidence that their experience is shared and will not go undocumented.

Love Alone's immersion of its audience in the catastrophe of AIDS is accomplished in part simply by its special content, by the ways in which Monette directly and repeatedly records the medical, social, and human perils of the disease. For example, the book features harrowing specifics about AIDS and its treatment, from a portrayal of Rog's growing blindness in the third poem, "Your Sightless Days" (*"How are you* jerks would ask *Read Job* you'd say" [7]), to attacks in the twelfth and fourteenth poems, "Current Status 1/22/87" and "Manifesto," on the medical establishment and on what might be called the "New Age AIDS healing establishment" personified by Louise Hay and her followers. Monette sees both as sharing a similar icy abstractness and detachment, the "nerdy white-coat . . . / . . . test-givers" of "Current Status" (34–35) and "Lady Hay" of "Manifesto," whom he describes as proclaiming that "all sickness is self- / induced . . . / every sucker in the ICU's to blame" (40).

Most notably, *Love Alone* is dominated by explicit, intense, and unembarrassed statements of painful personal feeling, which, in both their frequency and intimacy, are perhaps the book's most powerful literal representations of the devastation of AIDS. For example, in the ninth poem, "The Very Same," Monette compares all the poems to "blood-cries" (21), and he repeatedly speaks in the language of extremity in depicting the ruin AIDS has wrought on his world, unrestrainedly presenting himself as "sobbing," "howling," "shrieking," "roaring," "burning," "aching," and "screaming" at his loss of Rog: "at this year's close I sobbed / and sobbed for us all" ("New Year's at Lawrence's Grave" [23]), "the sundering with its howl that never ends" ("Half Life" [17]), "I . . . / . . . shriek your name" ("Three Rings" [32]), "the smallest thing will trigger it . . . / . . . roar me back burning" ("The Losing Side" [38]), "me . . . / aching to find [you]" ("The Losing Side" [39]), "I wake with the scream / in my blood it never never goes . . . / . . . my life has suffered an irreversible stroke" ("Dreaming of You" [56]).

These vivid, aggressive, and blunt features of *Love Alone*'s content are powerfully confronting in themselves. But the quality that makes *Love Alone* the fullest and finest example so far of immersive AIDS writing is each poem's seemingly chaotic form, in which Monette consciously disrupts all traditional notions of focus, sequence, tone, and structure. All the poems in *Love Alone* are long and impossible to present fully here. Let me take some moments from "Three Rings," already mentioned above, as examples of Monette's disruptive approach throughout the book. The title of this five-page-long poem refers to a ring Rog's father gave him and to two mourning rings Paul buys after Rog's death, one of which he eventually buries at Rog's grave. The first passage consists of the opening lines. The second presents Paul in Taos, where he has bought the mourning rings, jade and gold for himself and a Zuni jet and silver for Rog's grave. In the third Paul is back in Los Angeles, at the cemetery, where he had begun to moan spontaneously as he buried the ring; now he realizes he was echoing Rog's dying sound, which had been a call to him in Rog's last minutes. In the fourth passage, the final lines, Paul has orbited himself into space in answer to Rog's call and nears a tenuous meeting with him (in what may be a metaphor for a reunion he foresees after his own death or simply a moment of imagined transcendence and unity that has chiefly emotional value for him).

> before I left you I slipped off the ring
> the nurse had taped to your finger so it
> wouldn't get lost the last day you think I'd
> forget I forget nothing was there the day
> Dad gave it to you Chestnut St a continent
> ago there when you said in the bathtub ten
> years later sobbed really *If something happens*   (29)

. . . .

> fingers after the lid's shut all the same
> it fit me perfect and what's a Visa for
> if not to go a little mad think of
> the cabfare one is saving staying home
> for the rest of time so the Zuni went into
> my pocket I flexed the Jade hand clever
> as a showgirl baubled by a sheik of course
> I knew right along it wouldn't touch the pain
> it was just a game but one hungers so
> for ritual that's portable you can't walk out
> with tapers burning not to the 7-Eleven you want
>   (30–31)

. . . .

> saw it all in a blaze YOU WERE CALLING ME
> my sailor brother oh I didn't know Death
> had reached your lips muscles gone words dispersed
> still you moaned my name so ancient wild and

lonely it took ten weeks to reach me now
I hear each melancholy wail a roar like
fallen lions holding on by your fingertips
till I arrived for how many drowning hours
to say *Goodbye I love you* all in my name
all by the howl that knows that after love
is nowhere who the fuck cares if we reassemble
as vermilion birds and fields of violets now   (32)

. . . .

no wonder I'm always packing till the moan
became my weather and compass my heart had
no place to go it followed the law and stayed
put but how did they think they could hold us
to one ground we met on a journey that is
why the world though stopped like a car wreck keeps
doubling back robbed of you as I am promising
shortcuts whispering of a Northwest Passage
I nearly lost my mind last week screaming
too late down an empty road but there you are
we're full of the same agony you for an hour
I for the rest the nameless dark hasn't
spared us a pang my love but give us this
if ever either of us lands we are one
cry one dream tight as a black gold ring   (33)

Here, as in all of *Love Alone*, Monette matches his harrowing content
with a harrowing style by upsetting every conventional expectation of order an audience might bring to the text. Though each poem has a predomi-
nant situation and/or concern, Monette typically adds a variety of other
content as well, abruptly shifting reference and focus and jumping back
and forth in time. Here Chestnut St, sheiks, 7-Elevens, and the Northwest
Passage are evoked in the same long breath as emaciation, death moans,
howls, and losing one's mind; the settings shift from Los Angeles to Cambridge to Taos back to Los Angeles, and from hospital to graveyard to outer
space; and we lunge from present to immediate past to distant past to present to future. The tone of each poem varies in a parallel way. Here, for
example, in the course of one work it shifts from toughness ("I forget nothing") to camp humor ("what's a Visa for," "clever / as a showgirl") to
heartfelt pathos ("oh I didn't know Death / had reached your lips") to
fierce anger ("who the fuck cares") to piercing despair ("I nearly lost my
mind last week screaming") to unashamed lovingness and fervent desire
("my love," "we are one / cry one dream"). The same spirit of apparent

derangement also governs each poem's structure, which Monette strips of all customary stabilizing markers. As evident here, no poem contains stanza breaks; each moves from first word to last in one single long block. Each poem, moreover, lacks punctuation and extra spacing between sentences, and, except in the cases of proper names and the occasional phrase set in italics or complete uppercase for emphasis, no capitals are used at all. Similarly, the overwhelming majority of lines are run-on rather than end-stopped.

At the stage of the AIDS epidemic recorded in *Love Alone*, Rog, Paul, and their affected gay male community are in a state of unrelieved and compound shock. Shattered by the physical horrors of AIDS alone, they are further maddened by society's complete abandonment of them to the disease and by the lonely struggle thus forced upon them. To use his language in "Three Rings," in *Love Alone* Monette incarnates this total "wrecking" of his world in a thoroughly "wrecked" form, designed to subject his readers to an immersive "wrecking" in turn—i.e., by throwing them into a completely fractured, unmarked, and destabilizing text and requiring them to make what sense of it they can entirely on their own, he tries to force upon his readers an imaginative version of the shock and isolation that he, Rog, and other affected gay men have had to face. Embodying his devastating content, where the horrors of AIDS are relentlessly thrust in the reader's face, in an equally devastating style, where secure ground is relentlessly taken out from under the reader's feet, Monette hopes to jolt his audience out of its denial of AIDS and to urge on it a sense of emergency that he and his community already know too well.

So great is that denial in the larger culture, Monette implies, that his effort to undo it in *Love Alone* must even circumscribe his other, compassionate concern in the book. As mentioned, immersive AIDS writing tends to have two assumed audiences—the denying reader I just discussed, and the audience harrowed by AIDS whom it wants to assure and hearten. For Monette in *Love Alone* this second readership is chiefly his fellow gay men, partly because at the time they seemed to be the only group devastated by AIDS, and partly because as traditionally untouchable and unspeakable they will see their suffering go largely unheeded unless one of their own bears witness for them. The strain between Monette's two commitments in *Love Alone*—to that suffering audience and to his attack on denial—is most pointed in the book's profoundly moving last poem, "Brother of the Mount of Olives," which depicts a spontaneous visit Paul and Rog made to a Benedictine monastery on Mount Olivet while on a 1983 vacation, before

AIDS had, to their knowledge, entered their personal lives and indeed before it seemed to have much relevance to them at all.[6]

Throughout *Love Alone* Monette is understandably conscious of the malice directed at the gay community even before AIDS, as indicated by his emphasis on gay oppression in many of the poems and by his implicit attack on homosexual stereotype in the book as a whole—e.g., his prominent mentions of Mormons who "for chrissakes want us dead" ("Black Xmas" [19]) and of the "cool indifferent genocide" of "the Feds" ("Manifesto" [41–42]), and his defiant emphasis on love in the title of the book, which challenges the popular image of gay men as obsessed with genital sex only and doomed to loveless and lonely lives. In "Brother of the Mount of Olives" Monette offers a carefully constructed series of achieved emotional connections designed to offset the potentially corrosive effects of such hatred and defamation, especially to counteract the isolation that can easily befall gay men under oppression and whose threat is compounded now by the onslaught of AIDS. The first of these occurs between Paul and Rog and the old monk who shows them through the monastery, "our particular brother John" of the title (60). From his delighted and utter attention to them, especially his constant touching ("grips us by the biceps," "clutching my hand"), they conclude that John too, must be gay—"I'm certain now / that he likes touching us that we are a world / inside him whether he knows or not . . . / . . . a blind and ancient hunger not unspeakable / unsayable" (61–62). Their next surprise connection is forged with gay history, for they discover among the cloister's frescoes a portrait of a "bare-clad Jesus [with] love-glazed eyes" by the homosexual Italian Renaissance painter nicknamed Il Sodoma (62). This exhilarating discovery raises the even more sustaining possibility that most of the monks may be gay—"JUST WHAT KIND OF MEN ARE WE TALKING ABOUT / are we the heirs of them or they our secret / fathers and how many of our kind lie beneath / the cypress alley crowning the hill" (62).

Each of these moments seems clearly meant to assure Monette's beleaguered gay male readers that they are not the ephemeral, solitary, and eccentric figures depicted by oppression. Here, in contrast, homosexual identity is something profound ("a world / inside him"), universal ("our kind"), and perennial (an "ancient hunger"). Through the first half of the poem, these points are conveyed by connections Paul and Rog achieve with outside figures or with increasingly broad external frameworks (an individual monk, perhaps an entire monastery, gay history as a whole). In the next incident, the culminating event of the visit, Monette shifts to an intimate emphasis. Brother John takes a "sudden noon photograph" of Paul and Rog with their own camera, a photograph that Monette later celebrates as their "wedding portrait," in which they are "joined / . . . [in] a ritual not in the book," and that, in an inescapable indication of its significance to him, he reproduces on the cover of the collection (62, 64). Focusing now on a solid, joyful, and close homosexuality in the present, with this "wedding" Monette gives his audience "joinings" on every level of the poem and across several dimensions of experience. Besieged by AIDS, his gay male readers can still have historical, public, and private occasions to take heart.

With the rest of "Brother of the Mount of Olives," however, Monette restricts these points, while not negating them. The moments of achieved connection just described are in fact framed by representations of loss and discord in the poem as a whole. While still the central event of the poem, Paul and Rog's visit to the monastery is actually described in retrospect. "Brother of the Mount of Olives" starts not with it, but with a bereft Paul in the present, desperately "combing the attic for anything extra / missed or missing evidence of us" and in that way discovering the roll of undeveloped film that yields the "wedding" photograph (60). Furthermore, the poem ends by returning to a still-suffering and near-disconsolate Paul in the present, where endurance "doesn't get easier," where even an "intrusion / of promise" from the natural world is "dark," and where the happy "evidence" of his and Rog's monastery "wedding" feels "all but lost":

> it doesn't get easier Rog
> even now the night jasmine is pouring
> its white delirium in the dark and I
> will not have it if you can't I shut all
> windows . . . oh help be somewhere near
> so I can endure this dark intrusion
> of promise where is the walled place where we
> can walk untouched or must I be content
> with a wedding I almost didn't witness
> the evidence all but lost no oath no ring   (64)

Monette thus sustains Love Alone's overall note of wreckage even in the book's most "solidifying" poem. While not renouncing his desire to hearten his audience of suffering comrades—his other chief purpose in the poems—Monette implies that under current conditions immersiveness must take precedence. Though support and joy can (and indeed must) be found amid the ruins of AIDS, he seems to say, we are still so wracked by the physical and emotional suffering of the disease, and still so resisted by a majority audience that would deny the urgency of the epidemic, that our foremost duty now in our speech about AIDS is to wrack that audience in turn by relentlessly immersing it in the disease's devastation. The same point and outcome were of course implied in the general style of "Brother of the Mount of Olives," since even the stirring moments of connection in the center of the poem are conveyed in the same seemingly chaotic form as the rest of the collection.

III

While immersive writing piercingly and insistently documents the havoc of AIDS, it has so far not appeared in AIDS literature as frequently as counterimmersive AIDS writing. A model of counterimmersive writing is a 1986 short story by Andrew Holleran, "Friends at Evening," which appeared in the first *Men on Men: Best New Gay Fiction* anthology;[7] several other works of gay male fiction about AIDS share basic traits with Holleran's story. One of the most praised of contemporary American homosexual writers, Holleran helped spur the growing movement of frank fiction by younger, openly gay American men with his landmark 1978 novel *Dancer from the Dance*, which he followed in 1983 with the similarly revealing *Nights in Aruba*.[8] Since then Holleran has devoted himself as much to nonfiction, contributing essays regularly to the New York gay magazine *Christopher Street*. Several of the pieces in his most recent book, the nonfiction collection *Ground Zero* (1988), first appeared in that journal, and AIDS is a recurrent topic in them.

"Friends at Evening" follows four gay male friends in New York as they collect each other to attend the funeral of a fifth friend who died from AIDS. These are the unnamed narrator, who remains chiefly a background figure; a character called simply Mister Lark, a "wise queen" figure who dominates the opening of the story; Ned, who has moved away from New York but returned for the funeral; and Curtis. "Friends at Evening" consists chiefly of recollections and remarks by the last three characters about their dead friend and about their romantic and erotic lives in New York before and after the advent of AIDS. The story has three main settings: Mister Lark's room in a Chelsea welfare hotel, where the narrator has gone to pick him up and where they are joined by Ned; a cab the three men share uptown; and Curtis's east side apartment. The narrative ends as the four go down to the street and hail a cab to take them to the funeral.

The four friends, and the man who died, come from a "fast-lane" sector of New York gay male life dominated by the conventions of "camp." For example, the story refers frequently and familiarly to Fire Island Pines, bathhouses, discotheques, and cruising at the McBurney Y on 23rd Street; and two of the characters have secondary camp nicknames— Mister Lark calls Curtis "He Who Gets Slapped," and Curtis calls Mister Lark (whose name might already seem camp) "La Giaconda." The dead friend, Louis, is portrayed similarly. We are told that when dying Louis took a hospital towel from the bottom of his bed, laid it across his forehead, and asked Mister Lark "Don't you think I look like Mother Teresa?"; and Mister Lark remarks that Louis "was always at the newest nightclub, in the newest pants, doing the newest dance! Sometimes I think he died just because he did everything *first*" (101, 94).

"Friends at Evening" contains some blunt and vivid evocations of the devastation of AIDS. For example, Mister Lark refers to the epidemic as "this nightmare" and "this horror," and, commenting on Louis's callous treatment in the hospital (e.g., the private-duty nurse who called Louis's brother in the middle of the night and in one breath announced that Louis was dead and that she could not find her check), he rightly remarks that "The heartlessness of people is incredible!" At another point he adopts Gloucester's famous line from *King Lear* to the situation, proclaiming "We are to the gods as flies to wanton boys" (105, 110, 93, 94). Sometimes Curtis also speaks in the same catastrophic and unnerving terms. Exclaiming "These are hideous times!", he describes everyone in their world as either "sick, or sick with fear"; later he characterizes the four friends as "terrified" and compares their situation to "living in Beirut" (107, 108, 111). In addition, the emphasis on "evening" in the story's title conveys a sense of melancholy, in suggesting that AIDS has finished the men's "party" culture.[9]

However, in "Friends at Evening" any such unsettling moments or claims are not sustained for long. In the basic pattern of counterimmersive AIDS writing, they are ultimately framed in some kind of protective way that distances their fearfulness. For instance, the characters typically accompany or follow any reference to AIDS with a witty camp comment that, in deflecting the subject's horrors, works to deny the nightmare they have just acknowledged. A capsule example of this process is of course Mister Lark's remark above about Louis's dying "just because he did everything *first*," and its stages are graphically detailed in the structure of a conversation Mister Lark and Ned have about the epidemic as they prepare to leave his room. Here mentions of "no," "nothing," and "all" accumulate until their tension apparently becomes unbearable and must be skirted by an arch remark. In a perfect, if perhaps unintended, metaphor for the "smoothing" of fear that seems to be the passage's ultimate concern, Mister Lark is applying face cream as he speaks:

> "Do you think it's going to stop?" said Ned.
> "No," said Mister Lark. "I think we're all going to die."
> There was a silence. . . .
> "Do you really," said Ned in a soft voice.
> "Yes," said Mr. Lark. "Think of how many people we know who are already dead. . . ."
> "So you think nothing will ever, ever be the same?" said Ned.
> "Nothing," said Mister Lark, screwing the cap on his jar of face cream.
> "We're all going, in sequence, at different times. And will the last person please turn out the lights?"   (94)

Main characters who exercise related kinds of denial are a staple of counterimmersive AIDS writing. While Mister Lark's diversionary remark above still has a trace of the deathly subject it also works to obscure, i.e., by evoking "lights going out," even more blunt examples occur elsewhere in this category. For instance, B. J., the "worried well" former clone who narrates David B. Feinberg's *Eighty-Sixed* (1989), is an emotionally constricted figure in general, a fact he seems almost proud of at times—"I haven't had an emotion in the past fifteen years!" he proclaims at one point (245).[10] Consequently, B. J. is repelled and inept when pressured into helping a person with AIDS, a secondary character with whom he once had a brief sexual encounter:

> I've always hated hospitals. . . . The fact that the rooms are full of the sick and dying. . . . I don't want to commit myself to playing Mother Teresa twice a week. . . . Half a year ago I barely knew Bob. . . . I feel the burden to comfort Bob, play the adult, say the right thing, and I haven't a clue. . . . I call Bob every day. . . . I dread the phone calls. . . . I don't want to touch Bob. Suppose he sweats? . . . Sometimes the bed smells, and the sheets need to be changed. . . . I usually leave when this happens.   (235, 257, 258)

Mark, the protagonist of Edmund White's story "Palace Days" (1987),[11] is only somewhat less blatantly evasive about the disease. At the story's start, he is characterized as someone who prefers "light opinion rather than heavy information" (133), and we are told that he "couldn't face" an old roommate who came down with AIDS (132). Consequently, when Mark's closest friend Joshua contracts the disease and Mark tells his lover

Ned the news, we learn that "They stared at the truth only a few minutes. Soon Ned was hurrying off to his class and Mark was ironing a shirt for the evening" (160).

Even in the unusual instances when persons with AIDS themselves are the main characters in counterimmersive writing, they constrain any expression of disturbing feeling or are otherwise emotionally and socially detached. In Adam Mars-Jones's story "Slim" (1986), the self-restraint of the narrator, a homebound PWA, comes from what at first may seem a sense of decorum. Speaking of his relations with the buddy who visits him from an AIDS volunteer organization, he says, "I'm sure I haven't complained, I'm sure I haven't moaned," adding that "maybe a trouble shared is a trouble doubled" (9, 10). On the other hand, rage, envy, and alarm trigger the "clench" of the PWA narrator in Mars-Jones's tale "Remission" (1987). Angry at the pharmacist giving him instructions about his medication, he says, "I tried to make my voice campy. . . . If I'd had more . . . strength, perhaps I'd have said something really crushing," and, when he imagines the two helpful men who have been his platonic lovers since his diagnosis becoming lovers themselves, he admits to a "flinch" and a "terrible rattle of protest and warning," but experiences these "in spite of myself" and "behind clenched teeth" (110, 129). In Edmund White's story "Running on Empty" (1988), the denial of the protagonist Luke is directed toward other PWAs and stems at least in part from his prior denial of his homosexuality. We are told that, though Luke has always been attracted only to men, he "sought out . . . straight men, or close approximations of that ideal. . . . That was why he'd been surprised when he of all people had become ill. It was a gay disease and he scarcely thought [he] counted as gay" (216–17). Relatedly, we learn that though Luke aggressively pursued information and treatment after his diagnosis, "the one thing he couldn't bring himself to do was meet with other people who were ill" (221).

Besides focusing on characters who are in denial about AIDS, counterimmersive AIDS writing usually sustains that denial through the end of the work or at least does not significantly reverse it. In the final moments of "Friends at Evening," for example, Holleran creates an impression of change in his characters that he then retracts. While Mister Lark and Curtis hunt for a taxi, Ned and the narrator discuss Ned's reasons for leaving New York. Ned's explanation seems to reject a "romanticism" that, he implies, put him and his friends in the path of AIDS. "No one should live in this city unless he's in a state of extreme romantic excitement. I'm no longer in a state of romantic excitement," he says. When the narrator asks

"Why not?", Ned answers, "nodding south," "I can't romanticize this."
We immediately learn, however, that Ned has simply transferred his ide-
alizing rather than abandoned it and that, in objective terms, he may be as
liable as ever to AIDS risk behavior, only in a different locale. When the
narrator continues, "What can you romanticize?", Ned replies with no apparent sense of contradiction, "Budapest . . . in a light snow. Having
wine in a café, with a pale, handsome waiter with very bony hands." Then,
in the story's last words, the narrator, too, evokes the idea of romantic "excitement," seeming to embrace the same evasive spirit. Racing to reach
the cab the other men have caught, he says, "My heart was pound-
ing, . . . either from the run or that never-failing feeling of excitement
that accompanies the entrance of any cab in New York City; as if one renews one's life each time a meter switches on" (113).

Clearly, then, the personae in counterimmersive AIDS writing are typically the opposite of those in immersive AIDS writing. Paul Monette
works relentlessly to voice the "wreckage" of AIDS. Counterimmersive
characters or narrators imply at least some understanding of the same devastation and at times state it directly, but then they typically work to muffle
the jarring point they may have just made. More crucially, counterimmersive AIDS writing does not press its audience to experience the subject in
any way that significantly differs from its characters' stance. Of course, it
is possible that counterimmersive authors mean to satirize their denying
characters. For example, Holleran may want the "as if" above to have an
ironic weight heavier than its scant two words would suggest, and there are
a few moments in "Friends at Evening" that seem almost to advertise the
characters' defensive strategies—e.g., the face cream incident described
above and the cab conversation I shall discuss momentarily. But any critique of character in counterimmersive AIDS writing ordinarily does not
go beyond muted implication, and counterimmersive writing typically
does not include in its texts any forceful alternative to its characters'
detachment.

Thus, the relation of counterimmersiveness to its materials and audience can be understood in the same terms as its characters' ultimate
stance toward their unnerving perceptions: just as its characters persistently cushion themselves against the epidemic's fearfulness, and remain distanced from it, counterimmersiveness finally exempts its audience from too close a contact with the horrors of AIDS and makes no
compelling demands on the denying reader to change. The characteristic
way AIDS is handled in counterimmersive writing is nicely captured by
language from an earlier conversation in "Friends at Evening," though the

scene does not literally pertain to the subject of AIDS. Driving through Central Park in a cab on the way to Curtis's apartment, apparently remembering some earlier passionate encounters there, Mister Lark "murmurs" to Ned and the narrator (expropriating, without attribution, a line from Stevens's "Sunday Morning"), "The park is so lovely at night in this kind of weather. Gusty emotions on wet roads on autumn nights!"[12] Then, the narrator reports, "He put his hand between his teeth and bit it to repress the urge to shriek" (100). Counterimmersive AIDS writing acknowledges on some level the "gusty emotions" that AIDS inevitably provokes and implies that their most natural expression would indeed be a "shriek" (as it characteristically is in immersive AIDS writing). However, it ultimately puts a firm "bite" on the degree of outburst and disruption it will allow in its texts and into its audience's experience, imprinting a "repression" on its presentations and its readers. By restricting its narrative to the perspectives of denying characters, a counterimmersive text ultimately "allows" its audience the "escape" from the terrors of AIDS that immersive writing refuses to provide (to use Monette's terms from the preface to *Love Alone*), finally doing nothing to dislodge whatever impulse its readers may have to deny the disease.

IV

The prevalence of counterimmersiveness in AIDS literature by gay men may seem puzzling. Under heterosexual cultural domination, homosexuals are inevitably out of social and cultural order—i.e., their non-biologically-procreative love between "sames" makes them unavoidably anomalous next to the traditional emphasis in heterosexuality on love as a relationship between "differents" and as validated by biological procreation. Such a situation requires homosexuals to be radically self-inventing—they have to develop a new and appropriate order (i.e., forms and terms) for themselves entirely on their own. Conditioned to this fundamental disordering and reordering before—and separate from—the emergence of AIDS, gay male writers would seem to be naturally inclined toward, and skilled at, the basic task of immersive AIDS writing—e.g., directly addressing the "disorder" of AIDS and replicating it both on the page and in their readers' imaginations.[13]

The fact that some gay male authors would nevertheless write counterimmersively about AIDS seems to be rooted in a lingering depression about homosexuality and in stereotyped understandings of it. Andrew Holleran, for instance, is obviously deeply committed to homosexuality as a central subject, and his fiction has been justly praised for its compelling style. But in content Holleran's work chiefly falls into what I call the concessive and ironic modes of gay male literature. Its concessiveness is clearly seen in its frequently despairing, stereotypic statements about same-sex love, i.e., statements that seem to concede to the dominant culture by repeating its most negative conceptions and terms for homosexuality, often in the language of the most homophobic postwar psychology textbooks. The announced and recurrent subject of *Dancer from the Dance*[14] is "the doomed queen" (15); Malone, the novel's hero, asks "Do you sometimes not loathe being—gay?" (17); and the novel's narrator reports that "hopeless romanticism" (104) is "the great homosexual disease" (80). Similarly, the narrator of *Nights in Aruba* states that he "considered homosexual love affairs as likely to survive as a kamikaze pilot" and toward the end of the novel announces his "ceasing to believe in general in romantic love between two men"; at another point in the book gay men and lesbians are described without demur as "the wounded of their sex."[15]

When not being baldly concessive, Holleran's presentation of homosexuality is often restrictively ironic. Gay male literature's ironic mode is defined by a seemingly unintended contradiction. Rather than despairingly echo homosexual stereotype, ironic gay male writing seems to celebrate it. Yet this apparent rebelliousness still has an inescapable complicity with the dominant culture—it typically requires the presence and power of that culture for its force and success, since its enterprise often involves simply inverting the majority audience's norms and terms for "shock value." This unwitting irony takes several forms in gay male writing. One is the "homosexual criminal" tradition we see, for instance, in Verlaine, Rimbaud, Genet, and Burroughs. In Holleran's work it appears as the frequent championing of camp "nonseriousness," as "Friends at Evening" suggests.

The chief spokesperson in Holleran's fiction for this stance is Sutherland, the "doomed queen" who directs Malone's gay "education" in *Dancer from the Dance*—e.g., he tells a young man who is just coming out into the gay world, "Oh darling, . . . don't take it so seriously!", and when Malone later says "I'd like to be serious. . . . For a while," Sutherland answers "I think I should change clothes if we're going to be serious" (97, 51, 140). Furthermore, this "antiseriousness" is a rule and necessity in the novel's entire world, and not just the eccentricity of one key character. The narrator declares that "No one was allowed to be serious, except about the importance of music, the glory of faces seen in the crowd," and Malone is described as having "that necessary ability, acquired over the years, to eschew the serious and return to the blithe, to move, literally, from funeral to party" (114, 221–22).[16] In seeming to be chiefly a point-by-point inversion of bourgeois graveness, Holleran's presentation here ironically ends up both depending on the majority culture it seems to reject and needing its continued existence, for without that culture's presumably earnest official outlook his contrasting "frivolous" vision would have no significance.

The degree of depression about homosexuality implied in concessive gay male writing could disable anyone faced with the subject of AIDS. Already apparently despondent over male homosexual life, he would probably want to flee an issue that implied a further and large-scale "disorder" within it. Elsewhere in his work Holleran suggests that he was indeed driven from the topic in this way at times. In an essay in *Ground Zero*, he discusses an early novel about AIDS called *Facing It* and admits, "That was just what I didn't want to do; at least in literary terms."[17] Furthermore, AIDS would finally be an unencompassable subject for anyone conditioned to the "eschewing of the serious" that is basic to the kind of ironic gay male vision portrayed in *Dancer from the Dance*. Writing about AIDS need not bar "the blithe," as Monette's occasional campiness in *Love Alone* shows. But (as the difficulties of the characters in counterimmersive writing indicate) AIDS is clearly not a subject that can be ultimately cast in "party" terms, since it recurrently forces an awareness of the "funereal" on us. Fundamentally, however, immersive writing about AIDS would be impossible for authors caught in concessive and ironic visions of homosexuality because of the significant degree of obedience to the dominant culture that both modes entail—concessive writing blatantly, ironic writing more subtly. As we saw in Monette, at the heart of immersive AIDS writing lies a willingness to defy the dominant culture completely, in this case by totally assaulting its denial of AIDS, and that kind of thorough cultural dissent seems ultimately beyond the powers of concessive and ironic outlooks about homosexuality.[18]

Whatever other reasons there may be for the frequency of counterimmersiveness in gay male literature about AIDS, I want to stress in closing that both counterimmersive and immersive AIDS writing have merits and risks. For example, one benefit of counterimmersiveness is that it may effect a kind of bridge to the denying reader. As noted, counterimmersiveness does include some forthright statements about the havoc of AIDS, though ultimately framing them so that they do not cause much upset or pain. This pattern may somewhat loosen the defenses of the denying reader so that some frank recognition of the horrors of AIDS may be insinuated through them. However, because of the strict limits counterimmersiveness puts on unsettling portrayals, any potential in it to halt denial could only be realized through accumulation as suggested—i.e., only after reading a quantity of counterimmersive AIDS writing might the denying audience stop its sidestepping of the subject. At the same time, one limitation of counterimmersiveness is that it apparently writes only, or chiefly to that denying audience. The second, suffering audience that is as pronounced a concern in immersive AIDS writing seems rarely to figure in the considerations of counterimmersive authors, whom it would be impossible to imagine writing a work like Monette's "Brother of the Mount of Olives."

The chief problem of counterimmersiveness, however, is the one I sketched earlier. By doing nothing to dislodge its characters' and audience's skirting of AIDS, a counterimmersive work runs the risk of ultimately collaborating with the larger cultural denial of the disease. Counterimmersive writing's vulnerability to this collusion is illustrated perhaps most blatantly by the frequent absence of the word *AIDS* itself from its texts. The narrator of Mars-Jones's "Slim," for instance, announces at the start that "I don't use that word. I've heard it enough. So I've taken it out of circulation, just here, just at home"; instead he substitutes the title word, the colloquial African term for AIDS whose implication of mere dieting blurs the ruinous realities of the disease (1). Relatedly, Holleran uses the word *AIDS* only sparingly in *Ground Zero*, instead referring to the disease most often as the capitalized "It" and secondarily as "the plague."

In another cultural context, this omission might be understood differently—e.g., as a PWA's attempt not to be "reduced" to the status of being "only a disease," or as a writer's effort to universalize the AIDS crisis. But this non-naming certainly clashes with emphases in recent cultural analyses of illness—witness Susan Sontag's critique in *Illness as Metaphor* of the refusal to say the words *tuberculosis* and *cancer* to patients.[19] More to the immediate point, it also ignores the prevailing practice of evasion in our dominant culture. For instance, when we recall the still-common custom of lying about the cause of death in AIDS obituaries, it is hard to see how the deliberate omission of the word *AIDS* from an already muffled text about the disease cannot help but cooperate with the larger cultural interest in denial, no matter what else the author may intend.

Immersive writing's risk is that its raw embodiment of the wreckage of AIDS could defeat its chief purpose. Its blunt harrowings and wrenchings may so unnerve the denying reader that he or she will bolt its texts, and it will be left speaking "only" to its audience of fellow AIDS sufferers. On the other hand, immersive AIDS writing has at least two resounding merits: its willingness to defy the dominant culture directly and fully and its faithfulness to the emotional and social anguish of people affected by AIDS, especially to the catastrophic texture of gay men's experience under the double denial directed at them during the crisis. Immersive AIDS writing's deliberately chaotic form aptly captures the feelings of intense assault, neglect, and bewilderment gay men experienced in the early days of the epidemic and that they might still be enduring had AIDS not begun to be perceived as also a threat to groups more traditionally "touchable" and "speakable" than they. Similarly, its heightened pitch perfectly expresses the loudness gay men had to maintain to get a denying world to hear earlier in the crisis and that they still have to voice wherever AIDS is fundamentally perceived as "only a gay disease." As the pioneering gay film historian and AIDS activist Vito Russo declared on a panel on "Psychological Perspectives on the AIDS Epidemic" at the fall 1988 conference of the Lesbian and Gay Studies Center at Yale (two years before he himself died of the disease), "Those of us who are left behind see this as an emergency and not as a problem."[20]

NOTES

Parts of this essay were first delivered in papers at the annual conventions of the Society for Health and Human Values and the Modern Language Association and in a lecture in the History of Medicine Lecture Series at the Albert Einstein College of Medicine. I am grateful to those organizations, to Steven C. Martin, M.D., of Einstein for inviting me to speak, and to audience members on those occasions for useful comments. Thanks also to Joseph Wittreich for his encouragement at an early stage of this effort, to John Woodcock for valuable suggestions during revision, and to the students in my "AIDS and Its Literature" seminars at the University of Rochester Medical School for discussions that spurred me to refine my ideas about this material.

1. According to Centers for Disease Control statistics, as of May 1991 (the date of this essay's final revision) gay/bisexual men made up 64.5 percent of the diagnosed AIDS cases in the United States. This includes the CDC categories of gay/bisexual male only (58%) and gay/bisexual males who are also IV drug users (6.5%). In contrast, nongay IV drug users were 22 percent of the national total, and heterosexual contact cases unrelated to IV drug use were 5.4 percent. However, the latter two groups showed a greater proportionate rise in new cases. When compared with the figures for August 1990, the largest jump was in the heterosexual contact category, with a 23.87 percent increase in new cases, and, within that, a 24.64 percent rise among heterosexual women. Next was the "Undetermined Adult" category, with a 21.52 percent increase. This was closely followed by nongay IV drug users, with a 20.19 percent rise in new cases. Children of a mother with, or at risk for, AIDS had the next largest increase, 19.64 percent. Gay/bisexual men, in contrast, had a 16.86 percent rise in new cases. Calculations by the author based on personal communication with the CDC.

2. To my knowledge, the earliest written statements of these stigmas in the postclassical West appeared in the eleventh and twelfth centuries, in Peter Damian's *The Book of Gomorrah* (c. 1051) and Peter Cantor's "On Sodomy" (exact date unknown, Cantor d.

1192). The best-known modern echo of them is probably Lord Alfred Douglas's designation of homosexuality as "the love that dare not speak its name" in his poem "Two Loves," first published in the Oxford undergraduate literary magazine *The Chameleon* in December 1894. For more on homosexuality's history as uniquely "untouchable" and "unspeakable," see my "Teaching Homosexual Literature as a 'Subversive' Act," *Journal of Homosexuality* (in press).

3. Paul Monette, *Love Alone: Eighteen Elegies for Rog* (New York: St. Martin's, 1988). Where subsequent references to this work are contextually clear, page numbers will be cited in the text.

4. The jump in social and medical attention to AIDS in the United States later in the 1980s occurred only after the disease began to be viewed as also a threat to heterosexuals; had AIDS somehow remained only a "gay disease," the same sweeping denial might still be directed at it today. Widespread social and medical attention to AIDS started in the U.S. in early 1985, with the first newspaper stories about AIDS among female prostitutes, who could spread the disease to heterosexual men, who in turn could infect their wives, children, and female lovers. For a documentation of that shift, see Randy Shilts, *And the Band Played On: Politics, People, and the AIDS Epidemic* (New York: St. Martin's, 1987), pp. 508–13.

5. Kafka, from a letter to Oskar Pollak, quoted by Anne Sexton in the epigraph to her second book, *All My Pretty Ones* (Boston: Houghton Mifflin, 1961), p. vii; Tillie Olsen, *Tell Me a Riddle* (1961; reprint, New York: Dell/Delta, 1989), p. 61—the statement occurs in the story "O Yes."

6. At the start of *Borrowed Time*, Monette describes reading aloud to Rog in February 1982 an article from *The Advocate* about a disturbing new "gay cancer" (the word "AIDS" was not coined until July 1982). He reflects that "my first baseline response was to feel safe. It was *them* [to which this was happening]—by which I meant the fast-lane Fire Island crowd, the Sutro Baths, the world of [gay male] High Eros. . . . Not us" (*Borrowed Time: An AIDS Memoir* [New York: Harcourt Brace Jovanovich, 1988], p. 3).

7. Andrew Holleran, "Friends at Evening," in George Stambolian, ed., *Men on Men: Best New Gay Fiction* (New York: New American Library/Plume, 1986). Where subsequent references to this work are contextually clear, page numbers will be cited in the text.

8. In "Out of the Closet, Onto the Bookshelf," his essay on post-Stonewall gay literature in the June 16, 1991, *New York Times Magazine*, Edmund White credits Holleran, along with the novelist, playwright, and essayist Larry Kramer, with launching "the new [postliberation] gay novel" (22).

9. The title of Holleran's short story comes from a line Mister Lark attributes to Whitman. Raising a teacup to the gathered friends, he says, "I am reminded of a line from the perhaps over-rated, but occasionally divine, Walt Whitman, which I shall use to toast you. 'It is enough to be with friends at evening'" (92).

10. David B. Feinberg, *Eighty-Sixed* (New York: Viking, 1989). Where subsequent references to this work are contextually clear, page numbers will be cited in the text.

11. Edmund White, "Palace Days," in Edmund White & Adam Mars-Jones, *The Darker Proof: Stories from a Crisis* (New York: New American Library/Plume, 1988). Where subsequent references from White and Mars-Jones are to this work, page numbers will be cited in the text.

12. In part 2 of "Sunday Morning," Stevens mentions "gusty / Emotions on wet roads on autumn nights" among the "passions" that are now "the measures destined for" the protagonist's "soul" (Wallace Stevens, *The Palm at the End of the Mind: Selected Poems*

and a Play, Holly Stevens, ed. [New York: Knopf, 1971], p. 5). I am grateful to Claude J. Summers for reminding me of this line.

13. For more on this "disorderedness" and "self-invention" as features of gay consciousness and literature, see my "Not Happy in the Capitol: Homosexuality and the *Calamus* Poems," *American Studies* 19, no. 2 (1978):5–22.

14. Andrew Holleran, *Dancer from the Dance* (New York: Morrow, 1978). When subsequent references to this work are contextually clear, page numbers will be cited in the text.

15. Andrew Holleran, *Nights in Aruba* (1983; reprint, New York: New American Library/Plume, 1984), pp. 182, 202, 212. Holleran sometimes seems bothered by the concessiveness of his work and tries to retract it. For instance, late in *Dancer from the Dance* the narrator says, "It was [Malone's] joy that there were men who loved other men" (230), and in the letter to his friend that ends the novel he adds, "We are not doomed because we are homosexual, my dear, we are doomed only if we live in despair because of it" (249). But despairing generalizations about homosexuality still dominate the first, longer part of the novel, and these later statements only intensify the conflicted quality of the book as a whole.

16. Holleran does bring Sutherland to a seemingly "serious" end—he dies of a drug overdose at the end of one of his lavish Fire Island parties. Characteristically, however, Holleran works to rid the event of any painful meaning and effect. He rejects any suggestion of suicide ("Sutherland had little use for suicide and less for suicide notes") and casts an air of "equanimity" over Sutherland's fatal last act: "He had taken so many drugs that evening, mixing them in his bloodstream with the equanimity of a chemist in a research lab, and not even remembering what he had taken, half-asleep, he reached for another pill" (233).

17. Andrew Holleran, "Reading and Writing," in *Ground Zero* (New York: Morrow, 1988), p. 13.

18. In fairness, it should be noted that counterimmersive writing about AIDS has not been restricted to gay men. In fact, its "pioneer" text may have been Susan Sontag's widely praised story "The Way We Live Now," the first fiction about AIDS published in *The New Yorker* (November 24, 1986, pp. 42–51) and later selected to appear in *The Best American Short Stories, 1987* (Boston: Houghton Mifflin, 1987). "The Way We Live Now" has all the counterimmersive hallmarks I discuss here, but often in bolder relief—e.g., a focus on the reactions within a PWA's large circle of friends and not on the person with AIDS himself, who is never named but instead remains a faceless "he"; a detached and cool narrator whose account of the PWA typically consists of remarks like "he's reported to have said"; an avoidance of the word *AIDS* itself in favor of terms like *that* and *it*. Since Sontag's presentation in the story clashes so strongly with her nonfiction commentaries about disease (see the *Illness as Metaphor* passage I mention below), informed readers might be inclined to see "The Way We Live Now" as a biting satire of its characters. But, like the other counterimmersive authors I have discussed here, Sontag offers no forceful alternative to the characters' perspective in her text, and denying readers could still finish the story with their defenses largely intact.

19. Sontag, *Illness as Metaphor and AIDS and Its Metaphors* (1978, 1989; reprint, New York: Doubleday/Anchor, 1990), pp. 6–8.

20. Personal notation by the author at the conference.

Dante on Fire Island: Reinventing Heaven in the AIDS Elegy

James Miller

Vedrassi l'avarizia e la viltate di quei che guarda
l'isola del foco. . .
—Dante

I   The Anastatic Moment

Heaven is much harder to imagine than hell, especially if you don't believe in either. Without a faith to limit apocalyptic fantasy, hell hardly differs from history as constructed on the nightly news. It is a rain of fire on a bombed-out bunker where loudspeakers proclaim a "New World Order" to crowds groaning under fallen concrete slabs. It is a dead-end street in a spraypainted ghetto where enraged cops take turns beating a "suspect" into a state beyond submission. It is a network of deceit where a suave anchorman, caught off guard by voices shouting "Fight AIDS, not Arabs," cuts to a commercial and returns with apologies to his viewers for the disruptive tactics of certain "rude people."[1]

The blessed state never gets the same intense coverage, though now and then it is presented as a simple heightening of bodily pleasures. But a heaven that vibrates in the memory, that raises hope in the midst of deepening pain, must do more than address the aching needs of the body: it should also "emparadise the mind" (as Dante put it) with the fantastic prospect of transcendence.[2] Not transcendence of the body, of course, for only the dullest Platonist or dourest puritan would think of an abstract life of pure spirit as the height of bliss. Instead, if heaven is to transcend the hellish vistas of history, it must restore health in a dance without gravity and recreate culture as the "Newness of Life."

The elegy has traditionally been an emparadising stimulus for minds paralyzed during times of personal or cultural crisis, and so it is now, in the AIDS crisis, functioning as a kind of poetic therapy, although the old consoling promises of heavenly deliverance newly articulated by the poets of the epidemic are being met with determined theoretical resistance on the part of some radical activists. Douglas Crimp, for instance, has argued that the activist art practices developed to combat oppression and save lives in the AIDS crisis are fundamentally opposed to the transcendentalist impulses of traditional elegiac art. The elegist conventionally elevates the dead to the fantasy status of blessed spirits or raises undying artistic monuments to their memory in order to console (and thereby pacify) the outraged survivors with vague intimations of immorality. By contrast, the cultural activist counters all such falsely consoling discourses with texts and images designed to channel community outrage into radical social change in the here and now.[3]

Crimp himself, however, has recently questioned the need to separate militant political action from community mourning rites, and I shall follow him here in criticizing his original opposition of elegiac and activist responses to the AIDS crisis by examining the revitalized role of the elegy as a vehicle for radical social criticism.[4] Though I shall be concerned primarily with the AIDS elegy as a poetic form, a reinvention of the medieval *ubi sunt* lyric, my defense of this kind of radically poetic (as distinct from radically political) vision of the epidemic will also consider the challenging consolations of the anastatic moment in other modes of AIDS representation.

By "anastatic moment" I mean the illuminative climax of the personal or public struggles of the bereaved to make sense of death, and what they have lost to it, in opposition to the easy consolations provided by the dominant institutions in their culture. In ancient Greek, *anastasis* literally meant "standing up as at an awakening, taking a stand after being laid low, rising up, rebuilding"; in theological Greek, it signified the resurrection of Christ on Easter Day and of all the dead on Judgment Day. Elegies with anastatic moments may refer to either of these biblical events directly, like Milton's "Lycidas," or indirectly, through symbolic analogues, like Whitman's "When Lilacs Last in the Dooryard Bloom'd." In AIDS elegies anastasis comes as a blessed moment of recovery when the dead rise from the mass graves dug for them by the fatalistic discourse of public health and join forces with the living against the World, the Flesh, and the Virus.

Far from serving as religious opiates, anastatic moments deliver us from evil through a sudden imaginative breakthrough into the blessed state (however it is defined or experienced), which in turn opens new critical perspectives on the here and now. Heaven, the ultimate locus of social security, where the highest ideals of a culture are eternally realized, is not necessarily a theological given in elegiac art: rather, as the telos of all poetic allegorizations of death and rebirth, it has been reinvented time and again by poets seeking to ground their personal experiences of loss on a foundation of public hope for recovery.

Such reinventions challenge prevailing notions of moral purity, sexual destiny, and political order by breaking through the phobic constraints of conventional human wisdom—now commonly called "family values." Dante's word for this constructive breakthrough was *trasumanar*, which meant not only to exceed the limits of human experience, but also, more important, to carry human experience over into Paradise. Words were an ineffective vehicle for transhumanization, he warned, but they sufficed, at least to get the process started, when the visionary experience itself was lacking in a person's life.[5] As an elegist in both an erotic and ascetic tradition, he commemorated his own death to the World, his violent repudiation of the cupidinous Florentine *mondo*, while setting out to recover his lost love in a better world beyond the flames of lust. In the process he invented a brave new Paradise that still shocks the unimparadised mind with its extraordinary suffusion of the erotic life into the intensely erotophobic domain of Catholic morality. The souls of the lustful are purged on his fiery island not of their sexual identities per se but of their excessive and misguided passions in order to enter heaven as perfected lovers, saintly activists in the continuing drama of social reform.

Using Dante's anastatic vision of the lustful as a timely analogue to our own era's agonized contemplations of erotic guilt and lost innocence, I shall compare the reinvention of heaven in a number of elegies dealing with sex and death in the Age of AIDS; then, extending my discussion of elegiac activism beyond the confines of lyric poetry, I shall consider the paradisal reconstruction of social life in various other works that address the end of the epidemic in apocalyptic terms. But first a blast of fire and brimstone: heaven, or at least the need for heaven, is easier to see when its infernal opposite is located on the current map of AIDS fantasies.

II   Save the Males

Having placed New York at ground zero on the AIDS map—rather as medieval cartographers once placed Jerusalem at the devastated center of the Fallen World—Andrew Holleran came close to nuking all prospects of escape from AIDS hell for himself and Gay America. He was saved from despair, however, by a friend's dauntlessly queeny one-liner: "There has to be a beach at the end of this."[6]

Not the beach on Fire Island, of course, for that's still easy enough to get to even in the midst of the epidemic: just take the usual ferry from Long Island to Cherry Grove or The Pines, where you'll still see thousands of Speedoed men each summer day disembarking at the dock like the expectant shades stepping off the *vasello snelletto* onto the shore of Purgatory.[7] Since at least the 1940s, gay colonists have turned the national seashore of Fire Island into a margin of their own mythology. Its very name (like Dante's *isola del foco*) has a quaintly allegorical ring to it, a suggestion of flamboyant sinners and burning lusts, with a hint of searing yet purifying pain. It was an erotic literary locus, a theological hotspot, long before the advent of AIDS.

The "beach at the end of this" must surely be some imaginary version of Fire Island: an otherworldly resort lost in the heavy seas of nostalgia like The Pines evoked in Holleran's pre-AIDS novel *Dancer from the Dance*. For Malone, the novel's romantic lead, Fire Island was a pilgrimage site hallowed by the sacrilegious imagination of countless "circuit-queens"; and for Sutherland, Malone's Virgil, a doomed poet of drag who "seemed to have been alive, like the Primum Mobile, forever," it was a temporal substitute for heaven itself, a heaven made in hell's despite by the immortal longings of its decadent revelers.[8]

If there ever was a gay Eden, lost long ago by the sons of Adam who followed the demon of lust into the urban underworld of the Mineshaft, it was regained, miraculously, at The Pines, where disco stars like Malone were gracefully transformed into cosmic dancers whirled by the Primum Mobile. There the immortal Sutherland could reign as Queen of Heaven despite his suicidal addiction to speed and Speedos. In the mythic tale of Malone's creation and fall at the hands of Sutherland, Holleran provided the Fire Islanders with their own no-girls-allowed version of Genesis. The Pines was their *paradiso terrestre* and *selva oscura* rolled into one and rented by the share. As Malone in a rare mood of anagogic reverie observed to Sutherland on one of their many swoony summer visits to Fire Island, surveying from a terrace a crowd of gorgeous young men inhaling poppers and strutting their stuff on the dancefloor below: "It's all *we'll* ever see of the Beatific Vision!"[9]

If this was indeed the vision of heaven entertained by such men before the days of HIV-antibody tests, it has been mercilessly extinguished by the popular chroniclers of the AIDS crisis. Now Fire Island is commonly imagined as a zone of apocalyptic despair, a nuked prospect of desolate dunes, windswept beachgrass, and bare ruined pines where late the sweet boys cruised. It is the last resort of the Gay Man of Sorrows.

That's how Randy Shilts pictured it, anyway, in "The Gathering Darkness," an ominous early chapter in his unconsoling history *And The Band Played On*, which bills itself as a wholly nonfictional account of the first five years of the epidemic. [10] Weather conditions at the seaside are usually hard to predict, but since the beach on Fire Island is really a state of mind for Shilts, the mid-Atlantic skies cloud over with exquisite regard for pathetic fallacy (keeping "their steely cast") whenever a decadent reveler steels himself to walk the strand.

In April 1982, a darkness obligingly gathered around that ironic icon of American virility, the Marlboro Man, also known as Paul Popham, a legendary Fire Islander who had the unhappy task of casting the ashes of his dead lover into the sea. "What a fucking nightmare," Shilts imagines him thinking (140). Thought not being Popham's usual activity on the beach— he's not Prince Hamlet, nor was meant to be—the simplicity of his brief meditations on mortality may be forgiven, as may their telepathic reportage. (Shilts grants himself the divine power to read the minds of his fallen idols.) Popham did not have to be on poppers to realize that he and his kind had crossed the dire threshold of AIDS Awareness, a nightmare world of psychomachic consciousness in which sexual sin is literally embodied in their scattered ashes and figuratively enacted in the grim coition of the elements. "The cold white fingers of the sea stroked the indifferent sand," Shilts mourns in a curiously poetic fit of nonfiction (140). Earth, it seems, is indifferent to foreplay. Water's wickedly cold and grasping. Fire's out. All the elements are accounted for in this mocking pageant of the gay old days, except for Air. Not to worry, though, for Popham is subsequently described as gazing "out to where the leaden sky met the gray Atlantic" and wondering "where it would all end" (140). The horizon of his maritime cemetery seems to recede into the medieval past, where damnation and salvation were at the end of things as we poor mortals know them.

What did it all amount to in the end, all the hot stroking and poking on the beach? Nothing but guilt amid the garbage: so the beautiful Popham (soon to be diagnosed himself) must have felt that day as he scattered the cremains of his beloved Jack over the sand—which of course was already symbolically "littered by a winter's worth of misshapen flotsam" (140). The nightmare sea in this miniallegory of damnation did not just stroke the sand this time; its cruel "fingers reached to grab Jack's ashes and pull them into the brine" (140) as if it were the Devil himself dragging another well-tanned sodomite into the Abyss. The moral of this tale must have been obvious even to Popham: Don't pick up trash on the beach.

If Fire Island had been renamed "Brimstone Beach" for the Age of AIDS, it would hardly have increased its infernal mystique. As a mad mysterion where the Collective Cock of the Stonewallers was gleefully thrust into Hellmouth, it was already so well established in New York gay porn by the mid-1970s that Larry Kramer could send his gay antihero Fred Lemish there high on damnation discourse to revel in the homoerotic abandon of the "Meat Rack" (an infamous stretch of wooded dunes between Cherry Grove and The Pines) without having to explain to his readers why a little sandbar in the cold Atlantic should happen to be hot, hot, hot in a satanic sense.

What made Kramer's novel *Faggots* so controversial, at least in New York, was not its thunderous revelation that Fire Island was really hell— everyone in the know was perversely proud of that back then—but rather his Old Testament moralizations on fucking the trash on the beach and fisting the meat on the rack. Consciences were pricked. Pricks were exposed to the anaphrodisiac strokes of conscience (colder by far than the fingers of the sea). No televangelist in the service of the Heterosexist Panopticon could have poured a colder shower on the boys in the sand than an informed source like Kramer—a dancer from their own dance. Much to their embarrassed surprise, he was utterly serious in his condemnation of their "Beatific Vision" as a glamorous illusion, a trashing of the high ideals of Gay Culture in a Gehenna of lost souls.

Has there ever been a wandering tribe eager to hear jeremiads on the dire consequences of sexual sin? Craftily, Kramer lures his tribe to within hearing range of his ascetic homily by setting the finale of his novel at a fist-fucking scene on the beach at Fire Island.[11] A painful end indeed, and to read it now, with the guilty hindsight of a Paul Popham or a Randy Shilts, is to translate poor Fred's relentless sermonizing on the Cock of Ages into a prophetic book for the Age of AIDS. In Shilts's world, where Kramer emerges as the brightest culture hero in the gathering darkness, *Faggots* hardly qualifies as a work of fiction anymore: its hellfire fantasies read like tabloid truths.

Sexual sin is also the theme of Kramer's play *The Normal Heart*, a gay Lamentations in which the prophet looks back in anger at his fall from grace and exodus from the Gay Men's Health Crisis. "Shortly after Larry Kramer co-founded the Gay Men's Health Crisis," Holleran recalls in his introduction to the play, "he came out to Fire Island one sunny Saturday and set up a stand by the harbor to collect donations." The cause was not ecological but oncological—save the males by giving to the Gay Cancer Fund—which at the time seemed "so esoteric that when Larry appeared in the *New York Native* soon after this with an article on the epidemic (1,112 And Counting), a reader promptly wrote in to accuse him of peddling a gospel that the wages of sin are death."[12] Kramer's gospel, however, was simpler than that. Death was the wages of sex, or as Ned Weeks put it in the play: "Being defined by our cocks is literally killing us."[13] The "us" in question did not include all the males on earth who needed saving, but rather "all the kids on Christopher Street and Fire Island" who discovered their killer cocks after Stonewall. "We were a group of funny-looking fellows who grew up in sheer misery," Ned's friend Micky explains, "and one day we fell into the orgy rooms and we thought we'd found heaven."[14]

Gays don't have a heaven, of course, except for high cultural havens (such as the Sistine Chapel and the Glad Day Bookshop) constructed for homoerotic illumination here on earth. Such is Kramer's cock-transcending revelation. The voice of him that crieth in the Meat Rack no longer goes unheeded by Mickey and his brethren: Kramer's works are now required reading for Fire Islanders as they gloomily recline on what Shilts has called "the Beaches of the Dispossessed" to contemplate their fate under the obligatory leaden skies.[15]

III   Did the Lovers Burn?

If Holleran's Fall myth and Shilts's Chronicles are added to Kramer's Lamentations, we have the makings of a fundamentalist canon of plague scriptures for which there is no precedent in secular literature: a Gay Old Testament. All it would need to complete its dire design is a book of psalms, and that's what New York poet Michael Klein has supplied with his anthology *Poets for Life*, which reveals how "seventy-six poets respond to AIDS" by ignoring Crimp's activist scruples about elegiac art. Presented as a "Baedeker of the spirit for the dark travels that lie ahead," this resolutely inspirational volume is not really for first-time tourists to Fire Island. It's for the tribe already there, the sexual exiles who survived the straight captivity by journeying long ago to The Pines (literally or figuratively, it doesn't much matter) to celebrate "The mysterious quality of gay and lesbian love."

The preface to *Poets for Life*[16] was written by no less a divine than Paul Moore, the Episcopalian bishop of New York, to whom gay and lesbian love must be rather less mysterious than it is to his Roman Catholic counterparts. To Fire Islanders who have wandered far from the promised land,

Bishop Moore addresses his words of hope in the incongruous style of a black Baptist preacher—incongruous, that is, for someone speaking on behalf of men and women traditionally damned for their sexual identities by the establishment churches. "I have heard a Sister speak to me of the presence of the Kingdom of Love amongst the patients . . . in the AIDS ward of St Luke's Hospital," he declares in a ringing voice that carries through the ward all the way to the Beaches of the Dispossessed, "And I have sensed the strange shores of an alien land as I embraced the thin, disappearing body of a person with AIDS in peace and love."[17]

Before the requisite Hallelujah springs to our lips, we may well wonder who would give up the here and now for a ticket to such shores. Must the Hereafter be so vague? What Moore may have been sensing in his not-quite-Catholic way was death's other kingdom, the alien shores of Purgatory, where another Christian trembled in a spirit of love and tried long ago to embrace the thin, disappearing body of a shade. The doubter was Dante, and the shade his friend and fellow poet Casella.[18] If Moore fails to transhumanize in this Dantean situation, it's not for lack of soul. Perhaps the Age of AIDS is just too "post" in spirit—too postmodern, too post-Christian—to admit as genuine consolation a postmortem vision of an alien land without an unwelcome shudder of self-consciousness. Even with a Baedeker to guide it, the plague-weary spirit shrinks from sailing across Dante's *gran mar de l'essere* in search of never-never land.[19]

Pious sentimentality of this sort, however earnestly mobilized for the sake of AIDS Awareness, actually prevents the anastatic moment from taking off, from breaking through, by retreating without a fight into the realm of conventional religious discourse, with its reflexive allegories of otherworldly travel. The Church's kingdom of love, it's safe to say, is not what the males beached on Fire Island had in mind when they bought their ferry tickets and headed home to haven in sunny Cherry Grove.

Credit must be given to most of the seventy-six Poets for Life for refusing to accept Bishop Moore's painfully sincere transcendentalism. David Groff, for one, counters it unblushingly in his carnal reverie of the way things were on the familiar shores of the kingdom of lust. The opening lines of his elegy "A Scene of the Crime" literally suck one into a voyeuristic complicity with the lovers in the gay old days:

> Going home near dawn from the last great party
> Of the '78 season, where Miss Fire Island
> Got a long drugged kiss from a Perry Ellis model,
> He hears behind a slatted wooden fence
> The suction of two men fucking.[20]

The unnamed eavesdropper, wishing to be sucked into this scene, feels a change in the air—a strange transmutation of the elements—as the lovers recklessly exchange bodily fluids. They are heedless of the elemental signs as their "sweat seems to moisten the dry air." Little do they realize that night sweats will be their destiny! Equally unwary, the silent listener perceives their fluid exchanges as an echo of the amorous undulations of Dante's "great sea of being": "The ocean mutters, the men mutter / And laugh" (82). At what? Their metamorphosis into Fire Island Sirens? Adding a touch of drag-queen trashiness to the mysterious quality of gay love,

> a rhinestone bracelet
> Sails gleaming toward the stars
> Like a falling star until it sinks
> With a careless plop into the pool.   (82)

Careless it may seem to the uninitiated eye, but to voyeurs used to scanning the allegorical air of Fire Island, the fall of such a trinket must be construed as ominous. Falling stars presage the death of kings—and falling rhinestones . . . well, you guessed it.

But can you guess the identity of the eavesdropper? At first glance he might be taken for Miss Fire Island's shadow, a clone of Malone, for only such an alienated soul seeking the Beatific Vision would stand there "transfixed, lonely, high" (82) (in a druggy sense, no doubt, though the line has a Miltonic ring to it),

> Unable to force himself away,
> Smoking one, two, three cigarettes, awaiting
> The usual, shrill, orgasmic cry.   (82)

Orgasm comes on cue, but the Beatific Vision doesn't. The love that moves the sun and the other stars fails to move the smoking eavesdropper, though something like it induces the unseen lovers to dive into the water. Like laughing Rhinemaidens, their rhinestone counterparts don't head for the briny deep: they fall cupidinously into the "braceleted" pool.

It would take more than a long drugged kiss from a Perry Ellis model to keep one transfixed by such a banal scene of poolside hedonism, but Groff is high on nostalgia here, and its golden waves close round the lovers with a single splash that causes their eavesdropper "to love the whole idea of love." So intoxicated is he by this exciting idea that he accidentally drops his cigarette and forgets to scratch it out. Unaware of the dire consequences of his incendiary idealism, he heads back to his rented bed, where he "falls asleep, glad for the flaming island" (82).

If Fire Island Psalms are meant to laud and lament the human face of AIDS, as Episcopalian divines would put it, Groff's postexilic elegy does so in a grotesquely allegorical way by identifying the eavesdropper with Patient Zero and his unsnuffed smoke with the mythical AIDS virus.[21] If only Patient Zero had smoked in bed that night, and not outdoors! Then he would only have destroyed himself and perhaps his rented bed but not the entire island—which because of "the slyest kind of arson" will go up in flames. Literally: "An ember awakes to find itself a flame / And flames surprise themselves into a fire" (83). No wonder they're surprised—the cigarette has been smoldering there for three or four years, long enough to get us into the Reagan era. But since nothing in the tropological atmosphere of Fire Island can stay literal for long, the ember ignites an allegory of calamitous desire that Reagan himself and his Christian voters would surely have applauded: "Above the brush the boardwalk bursts / Into hunger so fierce it seems years in the making" (83). Dante would have called this hunger *cupidità*, the insatiable craving of voluptuous worldlings for all the World and the Flesh have to offer in the Devil's playground. To medieval theologians it would indeed have seemed "years in the making," since it began with a bang in Eden. No wonder the lusty blaze of cupidity has the power to burn not only the boys in the sand but the sand itself. It's a marvel of demonic pyrotechnics:

> It gobbles the dune to the door, unsated, until
> The house is a swift-collapsing pile of smoke
> And microscopic sparks dance from roof to roof.   (83)

since the sparks are really the replicated virus free at last to glitter and be gay in the cosmic revels of Miss Fire Island.

But the old dance of elemental order ends here, engulfed by the new viral version of apocatastasis or "world-conflagration."[22] The classical myth of the elements represented the conflagration as a cyclical disaster, the periodic triumph of hate over love, but this time it is truly volcanic in its chaotic energies, rivaling the fabled flames of Dante's *isola del foco*. On the Dantean world map Fire Island was Sicily, with Mount Etna at its heart, where the philosopher Empedocles (who invented the fatalistic dance of the elements) supposedly met his end in a suicidal leap into the smoking crater. Yet Etna was not half so destructive as the AIDS cigarette. Because of one unchecked ember, "Men who are seasoned but unprepared for fire / Scuttle from house after house that burns and burns," (83) giving new meaning, one can only conclude, to the old image of the flaming queer.

Floating on black billows of irony over this odd Twilight-of-the-Gays scene are the strains of "Gloria," a golden oldie from the High Disco era. *Sic transit*, and all that. If Groff had not trumpeted the moralistic theme of his psalm in this portentous way, one might be inclined to laugh off "A Scene of the Crime" as a camp parody of all the fire-and-brimstone rhetoric directed at gay men since the start of the crisis by Jesse Helms and company. But camp itself, in the person of Miss Fire Island, is lost in the fire, extinguished by the poet's earnest indignation at the merely accidental origin of the catastrophe. Yet if AIDS was an accident waiting to happen, why would he compare it to a cruelly premeditated and willfully executed act like arson? Why, indeed, unless deep down he actually regarded the lovers' flaming passion as some sort of erotic crime: the evil outcome of his own unsatisfied desire.

A plague on all their houses ("the usual comparison to AIDS that sweeps his island like a fire") at length draws the unwitting arsonist to the burnt-out house where the lovers of yore laughed in their innocence: "He breathes in hard and feels in his lungs / The stink of fire." No mere nostaglia trip, this. It's an acrid foretaste of damnation, a flash-forward to Hell, for at the moment of recognizing the house

> He recalls his smoke and chokes with guilt—
> But he considers how many years have passed
> Since the night he thought he fell in love with love.   (83)

What the poet seems to have fallen in love with is death, or at least the morbidly romantic fantasy of dying in sexual ecstasy like the lovers who disappear into the nocturnal pool after uttering their orgasmic cry. If AIDS were the denouement of a nineteenth-century opera, the fire-in-water exit of the Rhinestone Maidens would make some kind of dull aesthetic sense. But only a Wagnerian opera queen on the edge of hysteria would find serious consolation in the *Liebestod* motif these days.

Though Groff meditates on the old pastoral theme of love-in-death and struggles to evoke the contemplative mood of pastoral elegy, his erotic aestheticization of death prevents the anastatic moment from clearing away all vain surmises and bittersweet memories so that something more real than the reality of suffering can break through the darkness of loss under the illuminating influence of what Dante called *alta fantasia*.[23] The *Liebestod* is not a high fantasy: it only perpetuates the low-spirited suspicion that sex means death for all who indulge in it, however noble their characters or extensive their beachfront properties. Ending the imaginary arson story on a *Liebestod* note only confuses the serious ethical issues of sexual responsibility and social intervention raised by the elegist at his symbolic "scene of the crime." Like the arsonist, Groff himself should choke with guilt for suggesting that any one person was morally responsible for the epidemic, or that the plague itself in the absurd guise of a criminal should experience the very real and therefore agonizing sexual guilt of the survivors.

The arsonist's helpless response to this ethical confusion is to light another AIDS cigarette and wonder, as he stares at the ash-filled "crater" of the lover's pool, their unlikely Etna, whether they survived the erotic eruption. His final question—"Did the lovers burn?" (83)—admits of only one answer under the apocalyptic circumstances. Of course they did, and still do, for his own damnation discourse has condemned them to the eternal flames.

IV The Middle of the Burning Road

If Dante had come out (in a literal sense) on Groff's flaming island, he would surely have asked Virgil whether their trip through the earth had been worth it. They must have taken a wrong turn en route to Purgatory. Were they not still in Hell? Indeed, the surface temperature of Miss Fire Island's domain hardly differs by more than a guilty degree or two from the scorching Seventh Circle of the Inferno.

In the third ring of that circle, Dante witnessed a scene of volcanic torment similar to the conflagration in "A Scene of the Crime." Sparks rained down on a demonic dancefloor. Sand burned on a ravaged plain. Stinking ash fell over a desert ringed with boiling blood, a nightmarish current of corrupted bodily fluid. Troops of naked men scuttled here and there to avoid the flames. Lovers burned. Holding himself aloof from their agonies, like the voyeur still in love with the idea of love, Dante could not help sympathizing with these lost souls as they danced beneath the infernal roof, their singed arms forever flailing in a vain effort to brush away the fiery flakes landing on their skin.

Future contenders for the title of Miss Fire Island would do well to read cantos 15 and 16 of the *Inferno* if they wish to find out what's in store for them in the Circle of the Sodomites,[24] for sodomy, rather than arson, is the flagrant crime of which such flaming islands are the scene. Groff may have had this infernal circle in mind when he wrote his AIDS elegy, but if it was far from his thoughts when he literalized the fire in Fire Island, then one can only reflect on how long the medieval fantasy of damnation can lie dormant, emberlike, in the dry leaves of a literary tradition before bursting

into flames around the guilty (that is, sexually active) "carriers" of homosexuality.

Sodomy is certainly not what it used to be. Now, in the clinical Age of
AIDS, it is medically conceived as death through "unprotected" anal sex;
as such, ironically, it is once again morally synonymous with the seventh-
circle crimes of homicide and suicide. Retentively criminalized in many
parts of the "Free World," including some twenty-five American states, it
is now securely rimmed with all the taboos of tainted blood that Dante once
channeled into the crimson circle of the river Phlegethon. Though sodomy
has an unappealingly narrow legal sense in the rhetoric of televangelical
moralism—it is used to conjure up censored images of anal intercourse
between men—it was construed by Dante in the much broader terms of
scholastic theology as a willful attack on certain cherished assumptions
about Nature.

Strange as it may seem to the champions of sanctified monogamy in the
Age of AIDS, Dante, the West's great advocate of the "one man, one woman for life" policy, did not damn the Sodomites for any specific erotic perversion or practice. If he had, they would have been swept away quite un-
happily with Paolo and Francesca into the whirlwind of the *lussuriosi* in the
Second Circle.[25] Instead of damning them for homosexuality (a modern
psychopathological concept he blessedly did not entertain) Dante plunged
them five circles lower for the crime of *malizia,* or violence. They're
doomed to disco for ever on the sterile sands for defying the Prime Mover
whose charitable energies were transmitted to the cosmos through the
fructifying revolutions of the *Primum Mobile*.

Like the Late Antique Platonists, whose notions of natural virtue and
social harmony were championed by Dante's Florentine mentor, Brunetto
Latini, the Sodomites preferred real men to mythical gods as intellectual
soulmates. That Brunetto should also have preferred men in another sense
would only have been regarded as an outward extension of his inwardly
defiant orientation away from divine to human authority. So Dante appears
to have regarded his teacher's humanistic proclivities, for Ser Brunetto
turns up in blackface with the rest of the boys on the fire-and-brimstone
circuit. Instead of cruising his old student when they meet, which is what
one might expect from an old academic sod with eternal tenure, he engages Dante in philosophical conversation—the *other* vice of the Platonists. He was a sodomite in spirit, it seems, if not in flagrante.[26]

Modern Fire Islanders (with the possible exception of Larry Kramer)
may scoff at the notion of spiritual sodomy, but that's more or less what
Brunetto and his kind get scorched for in their waste of shame. In the ther-

apeutic idiom of Groff's contemporaries, these old-school Sodomites didn't have an identity crisis. They had an attitude problem.

So does the guilty survivor in "A Scene of the Crime." Pondering the demise of the poolside lovers along with the "salty come-togethers" (82) of thousands of other men, he reflexively strikes two infernolike poses in the hellish aftermath of the epidemic: first, in public, a blasphemous ACT UP stance of perpetual outrage at all government authorities who would rather fight Arabs than AIDS; then, beneath this, in private, an inflexible attitude of self-loathing for still being part of the whole damned Fire Island scene. While the first attitude may be politically correct, it's likely to land him in jail if he goes with it, which he doesn't. And though the second is morally edifying, it spells the end of Gay Liberation as a fight for personal dignity through community affirmation.

The result of Groff's *Liebestod* meditation is not a consoling call to AIDS activism but an idyll of vain *otium*. No personal or social progress is made in the splenetic closure of the poem, or can be made within its paralyzing terms, for hell (as poor Brunetto found out to his platonic chagrin) is not a progressive state. The dead cannot be enlisted here as martyrs to any cause or raised as loving spirits in a seance with the living. Even survival in such a state is damnation. The downside of spiritual sodomy is getting stuck in elegiac attitudes of guilt and alienation that leave the spiritual sodomite a victim to his own self-contemning sense of otherness. "Cui bono?," as Dante would have asked. Why suffer all the frustrations of radical indignation, plus all the pangs of Catholic conscience, without getting to the good stuff about deliverance from evil?

No one can blame Groff for not being Dante. The *Divine Comedy* is a hard act to follow—especially if you're gay. But there are a few acts in Dante's allegory that are worth following very closely if you are an AIDS elegist (gay or straight) looking for a communal exit from sexual despair or chronic survivor guilt. Look, for instance, at this ardent passage on the purgation of the Lustful:

> 'God of supreme mercy' in the heart
> > of the great burning was the song I heard then,
> > which made me no less eager to turn;
> And I saw spirits going through the fire.   (*Purgatorio* 25:121–23)

The fire here is no less miraculous than the arsonist's blaze on Groff's version of the *isola del foco*. It, too, burns on a fantasy island verged with sand and crowned with pines (though one rather more mountainous than Fire Island). It, too, seems years in the making, harking back in its apotropaic function to "the flaming sword which turned every way" outside the garden of Eden after the Fall. [27]

Eden, as Dante will discover a few cantos later, lies just beyond this great burning, which issues from the mountain wall in a horizontal sheet of flame covering all but a small walkway around the perilous circumference of the Terrace of the Lustful. At the terrace brink the flames are constantly blown backward and upward by the powerful winds buffeting the mountain. Like Groff's blaze, Dante's crackles with the collective lust and guilt of the crowds of former pleasure-seekers swimming through its *seno*, the gulf or heart of the *gran ardore*. It, too, appears to consume the diseased, those whose fleshly defenses were fatally weakened by the corrupting power of an invisible destroyer.

This merely literary comparison would be socially and theologically irrelevant to the Age of AIDS if Dante's fire did not also embrace (to the pilgrim's avowed surprise) a sizable number of men who love men. They are not among the first crowd of lovers he meets, however, for these are moving through the flames in his direction (to the right, as penitent straights are wont to do) alternately singing the praises of the God of mercy and lamenting the foul lust of Pasiphae for her bull. Dante is on the point of identifying himself to a member of this company when his eyes are struck by an *altra novità*, the appearance of a distinctive group of erotic Others moving leftward around the terrace toward him:

> For through the middle of the burning road,
>> came people with their faces opposite to these,
>> which made me gaze in wonder and suspense.
> There on each side I see all the shades
>> making haste and kissing one another,
>> without resting, content with a brief holiday
>> welcome:
> Thus within their dark band
>> one ant touches muzzles with another
>> perhaps to spy out their way and their fortune.
> As soon as they end their friendly greeting
>> before the first step there goes forth,
>> each one tries to shout the loudest:
> The new people cry out "Sodom and Gomorrah!"   (*Purgatorio* 26:28–40)

What does one call these newcomers who have no name for themselves? Despite their Old Testament exclamation, which is part of their ritual humiliation or *contrapasso* reminding them of what they once were like and might have been forever, they are not Sodomites—either *carnaliter* in the biblical sense, or *spiritaliter* in the moral sense that Brunetto so painfully embodied on the burning plain. Besides, there's nothing in the verses to suggest an all-male cast for this unprecedented scene. One can easily imagine the women in their company objecting strenuously to the collective label of "Sodomite," though "Gomorran" is hardly a better term for their identity.

John Boswell, normally a meticulous reader of the erotic implications of medieval nomenclature, thought they were called "hermaphrodites," since Guido Guinizzelli, a spirit Dante converses with on the burning road, uses this term in the same canto (26:82). Though Boswell rightly notes that the term hermaphrodite was loosely applied to all sorts of sexual deviants in the Middle Ages, he has misread its unusual usage here as a synonym for "homosexual."[28] For one thing, *ermafrodito* clearly signifies a purgeable sin in Guido's erotic vocabulary—not a permanent sexual identity or orientation. For another, Guido applies the term to himself and his companions, the rightward-turning spirits of the first company, and they're as straight as the poet who travels with them. Their sin, like Pasiphae's, was to join male and female (represented by Hermes and Aphrodite) in a bestial coupling contrary to "human law." For those who joined male to male or female to female in a bestial coupling contrary, presumably, to divine law, Guido also has a classical name. "The people who do not come with us," he informs Dante,

> "offended in that for which Caesar, triumphing,
> once heard "Queen" [*regina*] cried out against him"
> (*Purgatorio* 26:76–78)

which, besides testifying to the longevity of sexual slang and camp political humor in the Sutherland style, provides a classical precedent for the current practice of "outing."

Since no queen in the second company speaks to Dante directly, we have no way of knowing whether Guido's classical term was paralleled in their vocabulary. Dante simply called them *la nova gente*, the new people, and they were new to him, perhaps, not just because they happened to arrive after Guido's group but, more important, because their identity as a people, a tribe, an out-in-the-open movement, was an altogether novel concept even for an Ovidian poet at the racy end of the Middle Ages.

If modern Fire Islanders were to meet them racing along the burning boardwalk to the beach at the end of all this, the temptation to hail the new people as "Gays and Lesbians" or simply as "Gay People" would be hard to resist. Likewise, the intellectual resistance it would take (for a rigorous constructivist at least) to perceive them as culturally unrelated and spiritually alien to the lusty throngs who wouldn't dream of calling themselves "queens" after Stonewall would perhaps not be quite enough to overcome the same kind of rapport, the same strong sense of instinctive community bonding, that Dante reflexively felt for Guido and his kind.

In order to imagine his own redemption as a love poet, Dante seems to have demanded of his God the hitherto unimaginable redemption of all lovers, regardless of what we would now call their sexual identities, provided that their identity as Christians was strong enough to induce repentance before death. The repentance of the new people is for their intemperate lusts, not for their choice of sexual object, and it has accordingly put them on a moral plane equal to that of the penitent lechers from Guido's society. Down in Hell the unrepentant Sodomites not only danced to a different drummer but burnt up a different dancefloor at a considerable remove from the likes of Paolo and Francesca. Now, in Purgatory, all amorous types are raised to the same vertiginous heights—or lowered, as the metaphor of the ants suggests, to the same level of uncertain vision and humbling interdependence. Everyone must nuzzle up to one another at their meeting place on the burning road to find out where the two troops, forming a single "dark band," are headed, and whether they're likely to get there. Only their direction and their exclamation distinguish the second group of lovers from the first. Their social segregation is effectively over, though their integration within the City of God will not be perfected until all have "come out" as saints.

While Groff leaves his Fire Island ego in suspended alienation from both gay and straight society, a casualty to the new puritanism of AIDS Awareness, Dante defies the homophobic puritanism of his own day by daring to imagine a blessed end to the fiery isolation of the same-sex lover. The Terrace of the Lustful would seem the least likely spot to imagine such a salvation—especially if your imagination was conditioned by the rigorous morality of the late medieval Church. In the thirteenth century, as John Boswell has forcefully argued, the Church's traditionally ascetic resistance to the Flesh had hardened into an especially intolerant and exclusionary system of erotophobic doctrines privileging virginity and celibacy above even the time-hallowed state of matrimonial chastity. Its champions were the pervasively influential inquisitors of the Cistercian Reformation.[29] By the early fourteenth century, when Dante was at work on his *sacro poema*, no one considering a sexual relationship of any sort in Catholic Europe would have made our comforting public-health distinction between high-risk and low-risk activities. All sex was presented as mortally dangerous to the soul.

Yet carved into the stone wall of the seventh terrace of Purgatory is a way out of this sexual death trap, an escape route for anyone at odds with the ferocious intolerance of Cistercian-style piety. Veiled by the flames is a narrow *via* leading directly up from the burning road to the cool shades of the Edenic pine forest, and through this passageway all the spirits on the seventh terrace will eventually pass en route to heavenly bliss. It might take several centuries of purgative jogging around the summit to get the lustful in shape for this last ascent, but they are all assured of making it through the flames.

The immediate goal of their moral aerobics is not a reduction but a re-direction of their erotic energies, leading to an eventual restoration of Golden Age *amore*. If this sounds like safer sex in its ideal state, Dante should perhaps be given credit for foreshadowing the reformist erotics of the Latex Age.

Though all the hugs and kisses at the end of Christian purgation may come as a surprise to proabstinence crusaders, penitent lechers will no doubt be relieved to learn of the spiritual benefits of heated carnal activity. For what the lustful are burning out of their souls up here is not erotic desire in itself (which Dante, like Augustine, regarded as essentially good because it was divinely implanted in the prelapsarian soul) but rather the postlapsarian inclination to transform their erotic energy into fleshly *cupidità*. When they make it to the top, their raging lust will disappear like smoke, leaving their amorous nature in a glowing state of continent refine-ment. As anyone who's ever taken a strenuous exercise class will tell you, rhythmic physical motion does not exhaust sexual energy. If anything, it stokes the fire. Where muscle queens on Fire Island see brain chemistry behind their postworkout erotic glow, Dante sees the ascendent operations of the Holy Spirit.

Whatever spirit it was that moved Dante toward this little passageway in the seventh terrace, his *via erotica* must figure in the history of sexuality as a tremendous threshold of social enlightenment. Here was invented, if not the idea of sexual identity itself, then surely the notion of diverse sex-ualities working together toward a common goal of social integration. Here, in a supremely unecclesiastical exercise of charity, Dante dared to translate the paralyzing and isolating discourse of "unnatural lust" (which his scholastic authorities had inherited from the Latin Fathers) into the socially mobilizing terms of what we would recognize today as a theory of "sexual orientation." Though he could not articulate such a theory within the terms of medieval faculty psychology, he could, as an allegorist, work out its social and moral implications visually in the symbolic choreogra-phy of the flaming island. The two companies literally dance out their sex-ual differences by orienting themselves in opposing revolutions about the summit; yet their dynamic opposition proves to be only an apparent conflict, a temporary separation, for it periodically leads them all back into a brief but harmonious moment of communion across the sexualities, a tentative but mutually fortifying embrace.

This moment must happen twice a revolution, at two opposing points along the circumference of the terrace, just as the balancing equinoxes are created when the sun crosses the celestial equator in the spring and the fall. Following this old cosmic model, Dante has presented both sexual orientations as part of the Divine Plan, with the morally surprising but necessary result that the ludicrous patristic distinction between natural and unnatural lovers is literally blown away by the Love that moves the sun and the other stars.

It is one thing to place the two companies on the same plane. It is quite another to imagine them hugging and kissing at the same *festa*, which is the word Dante uses to describe the welcome moment of holiday camaraderie breaking up their workouts on the burning road. Such a moment had never been imagined before in Western literature, either classical or Christian, and it would take some six and a half centuries after Dante's death before it would be seriously imagined again by poets striving to transhumanize sex by reconciling *amore* with *carità*. The kiss of peace and the hug of loving kindness were traditionally depicted in tableaux of Christian rebirth as gestures of reawakened charity: at the bottom of Botticelli's *Mystic Nativity,* for instance, three angels dutifully embrace a trio of men (still held at arm's length) to signify the loving outreach of the Spirit toward the Flesh. But Dante's mystic proclivity was to enact this scene between fleshly sinners whose embraces could never be wholly spiritual. No angels were needed—just goodwill toward men.

The life-affirming festival of goodwill at the top of the mountain effectively reverses the fatal experience of Empedocles on Etna: where the philosopher fled the vileness and cupidity of human society and hurled himself in despair into the volcanic flames, Dante finds a celebration of social renewal at a dance where love keeps lifting him higher and higher. His rebirth on the fire-crowned summit has the ascendent momentum of all the erotically liberated souls behind it.

It's fair to suppose, however, that not all the straights in Guido's company were benevolently disposed at first to embrace their counterparts on the *regina* side, and vice versa, for Purgatory was doctrinally rather remote from Harvey Milk's San Francisco. But it was still a place where sinners could be conditioned to act charitably in the body, the erotic body, while their spirits were learning to catch up with the saints.

Their moment of transcendence would appear to be reached individu-

ally whenever any completely purged soul breaks out of the burning circuit and steps through the doorway into Eden, as Dante himself will do in
spite of his quite reasonable fear of being burned alive as a heretic for love:

> As soon as I was within it I would have hurled myself
>   into molten glass to cool myself off,
>   so without measure was the burning there.   (*Purgatorio* 27:49–51)

For proposing that same-sex lovers could follow his steps there, Dante
must have anticipated intense heat from the Catholic authorities—who
did in fact hurl progressive thinkers into the flames from time to time. That
no fire came from the guardians of public morality probably indicates that
they were quite unable to understand the novel doctrinal implications of
this momentous passage. Or did they simply fail to notice the moment of
collective illumination that precedes it and in a sense permits the individual's ascent from the flames?

For surely the guiltless embrace, the festive nuzzle-up, is the great
breakthrough for the spirits of the lustful, even if they do not recognize it
as such until they've performed it several thousand times in the middle of
the burning road! For Dante the pilgrim, a single glimpse of this unfore-
seen *festa* is enough to convince him that amorous humanity is at heart not
opposed to divine charity but rather embraced by it and embraceable
through it, and it is this refreshing sight that in turn strengthens his spirit
for the daunting passage through the heat. Thus does he die to the world by
committing his old erotic self to the flames so that he can become, like the
new people, *un altra novità* himself: an "other" in the newness of life. Not
by eliminating sexual otherness, then, but by recognizing and celebrating
it in the midst of the fire does Dante the poet transhumanize his own desire
for the Other and reach the anastatic moment, the Glad Day awakening,
when Paradise can be reinvented to contain his joy.

V   Savior Sex

It needn't take a Last Judgment to bring a new heaven down to earth in the
age of AIDS. Sometimes a snap judgment on the propriety of a PWA's
death, or the impropriety of his funeral outfit, is enough to provoke the
anastatic moment in all its illuminative urgency.

For Mark Doty, whose elegy "Tiara" sparkles in the funereal gloom of
the *Poets for Life* anthology, the anastatic moment comes at a wake, when
resurrection is the last thing on his mind. To re-create his unexpected experience of illumination, he sets up a traditional Christian contrast between worldly and otherworldly crowns in his poem and then subverts it

with a gay reading of the self-coronation of a new saint for the AIDS Empyrean. Like Donne's "Corona" sonnets and Marvell's "The Coronet," Doty's meditation on sanctity owes much to the metaphysical conceit of the crown of concord elaborated in Dante's *Paradiso*.[30]

"Tiara" takes off where Malone's campy line about the Beatific Vision left us—on the Terrace of the Lustful, looking down at the erotic dance instead of up. Doty's dead friend was a Sutherland-style queen named Peter, who could marvel at Bette Davis as Queen Elizabeth one moment and replay her death scene the next (for real), complete with wig and diadem as dictated by the *ars moriendi* tradition. The old art of dying was, for the new saint, simply an extension of his theatrical art of living.

Though a drag queen would hardly seem a promising subject for beatific meditations, Doty has celebrated Peter's *toujours gai* spirit in an imparadising ode to joy that addresses the same overwhelming question Dante struggled with all through his pilgrimage: Do those who love life, especially life in the body, deserve to die? This was also the question Groff asked in "A Scene of the Crime," but in "Tiara" there is no ethical confusion or *Liebestod* nostalgia to stop the elegist from getting to an erotic answer. Like Dante, Doty is fully prepared to transhumanize the erotic life without transcending the body, to practice savior sex as if his afterlife depended on it.

The prosodic structure of "Tiara"—its fifteen stanzas are composed in a kind of terza rima without the rhymes—invites a Dantean reading of its anastatic design. For Doty, as for Dante, anastasis is not an eternal state of mind dimly apprehended after death but an erotic defiance of death clearly prompted by an awakening to life. The social cue for this awakening in "Tiara" is the sight of Peter's casket, mysteriously closed, round which his friends are gossiping about his funeral attire:

> Peter died in a paper tiara cut
> from a book of princess paper dolls;
> he loved royalty, sashes
> and jewels. *I don't know,*
> he said, when he woke in the hospice,
> *I was watching the Bette Davis film festival*
>
> *on Channel 57 and then—*
> At the wake the tension broke
> when someone guessed
>
> the casket closed because
> "he was in there in a big wig
> and heels," and someone said,

"You know he was always late,
he probably wasn't there yet—
He's still fixing his makeup."[31]

The transgression of social pieties in an excruciating effort to keep up social appearances is one definition of camp, and it seems to have kept Peter's defiant act going strong even "in the hospice," that theater of pre-
scribed resignation. A grand actress to the last, even to the point of making
his own paper crown for the grand finale, Peter would not be upstaged by
anything so vulgar as death. His flamboyant costume defies the standard
media image of the passive AIDS victim, etherealized by suffering into a
thin, frail, disappearing ghost. To preserve this spectral image, that reflexively consoles straight society (and its gay assimilationists) by preserving the insidious decorum of the Invisible Minority, the casket must be
politely, politically closed.

   No matter how outrageously "out" you are in life, in death, it seems, you
must be closeted up again to preserve the illusion of gay resignation to the
dominance of decent society. Doty blows his lid off when he hears a mali-
cious mourner drawing the moral distinction (so common in decent society) between guilty and innocent AIDS victims: "And someone said he
asked for it, / *Asked* for it—," (66) which in turn blows the lid off Peter's
casket. Like an explosion of *alta fantasia*, a fantasy much higher than Peter's tabloid dreams of royal glamour, all his erotic yearnings, memories,
pleasures, communions as a Fire Islander come rushing out in his
defense. For all he did

> was go down into the salt tide
>
> of wanting as much as he wanted,
> giving himself over so drunk,
> or stoned it almost didn't matter who,
>
> though they were beautiful,
> stampeding into him in the simple,
> ravishing music of their hurry.   (66)

If the poem ended here, with an orgasmic crescendo of Peter's seaside
pleasures accelerated to ramming speed, it would have run aground on the
Beaches of the Dispossessed and littered the page with the flotsam of
nostalgic reveries such as Shilts might have dourly recorded, and Groff
dimly contemplated, under fallaciously pathetic skies. But Doty refuses to
allegorize Peter's sex life: his wet dream of horses stampeding on the beach
(a fragment of which surfaces here) does not carry the poet in a demonic

funk to the Circle of the Sodomites or in a drugged trance to the Perry Elli-
sian fields.

Rather, like the salt tide of yearning that carried the shades to Purgatory, it raises his thoughts above the sensual world with an anagogic momentum that soars into outer gayspace and apotheosizes the dead queen
and all his lovers:

> I think heaven is perfect stasis,
> poised over the realms of desire,
> where dreaming and waking men lie.   (67)

Though Doty's privileging of stasis over dynamic change is Platonism of a
fairly primitive sort, his liberationist vision of male desire presided over
(but not policed) by heaven is ethically complex and theologically provocative. Dante saw this "perfect stasis" as the still point of the Divine Presence round which creation danced.

But did Peter see it as such as he lay among the waking and dreaming
men on Fire Island? Is perfect stasis what the *nova gente* sought as they
raced around the burning road looking for an erotic redemption that would
preserve their collective identity? As gay people, would we wish to lie with
Regina Peter looking heavenward

> on the grass while wet blue horses
> roam among them, huge fragments
> of the music we die into
>
> in the body's paradise   (67)

if the body's paradise had to be left behind, abandoned on the shore along
with our wigs and paper crowns, in order for us to make it into heaven?
Presumably the answer to this lies in our understanding of "the music we
die into": if it were simply the hot soundtrack of the Fire Island golden
age—the Gloria in Excelsis disco bellowing ironically over Sutherland's
dancefloor of the damned—it would hardly raise Peter from the dead or
unbridle a troop of wet horses in anyone's fantasy of seaside sex. On the
other hand, if it were simply a repeat of the old angelic music resounding
through Dante's Paradise, then it would hardly break the gay sound barrier
and shatter into "huge fragments" synesthestically translated into blue
horses, an ultrabaroque image of erotic passion in the key of Neptune.

Surely the sort of music we would die "into" if we had the choice would
be a uniquely gay synthesis of the sexual and the spiritual: some kind of
anagogic disco hit to accompany the apotheosis of a drag queen. The kind
of salvation gays would ask for if we believed in Peter's deliverance from

evil, Doty suggests, is attainable only through sex—not in spite of it—for
the closest we come to perfect stasis in our earthly lives is at the hurried
moment of erotic death, the ejaculatory release. Or maybe it is a bit later,
in the dreamlike but not disquieting period of unknowing after the music of
our hurry dies:

> Sometimes we wake not knowing
> how we came to lie here,
>
> or who has crowned us with these temporary,
> precious stones.   (67)

Doty's empathetic identification of himself and his generation with the
drag queen's indomitably erotic spirit reaches its climax here, so that "we"
may experience an almost telepathic communion with the AIDS saint in
his dual role as laid-out corpse and laid-back Corybant. We lie "here," in
the casket, wearing Peter's paper tiara with its temporary precious stones,
while we also wake up in the grass over there, in the fantastic realms of
desire beneath Gay Heaven, where Peter will wear a crown of immortal life
with eternal jewels.

   In the end Peter becomes a genius of the Fire Island shore, an erotic
tutelary spirit whose campy death provokes an *apologia pro vita nostra*, a
collective defense of our stampeding life in the body:

> given
> the world's perfectly turned shoulders,
>
> the deep hollows blued by longing,
> given the irreplaceable silk
> of horses rippling
>
> in orchards, fruits thundering
> and chiming down, given salt
> and a tongue to long for it
> and gravity, what could he do,
> what could any of us ever do
> but ask for it.   (67)

This "it" may refer to death, sex, or heaven. If we all asked for it in the
hubristic sense that we tempted fate in our long stampede down the
beaches of sexual liberation in the 1970s and received the death sentence
of AIDS as a divine punishment, then there can be no distinction between
deserving and undeserving victims of the gay plague. All the dreaming
and waking men in the grass deserved to get it—as the prophets of the New

Right, speaking for the God of the Old Testament, vengefully maintained in the 1980s.

Yet why did only some of the men (like Peter) get it, and not others who were equally "deserving"? Either the divine justice department is manifestly unjust in its arbitrary selection of sinners to punish in this uniquely brutal way, or it works in mysterious ways. And if it works in mysterious ways, then those who believe in it must acknowledge, as Doty implicitly does, that all people with AIDS are innocent regardless of their sexual experiences on Fire Island or in any other realm of desire.

Beyond this stirring ACT UP moral, however, Doty has a few radical points to make about heaven as constructed from a gay viewpoint. If we all ask for "it"—the rush of sensual and sensory pleasures evoked at the end of the elegy—then for a while, like Peter, we may get what we want in our temporary realms of desire, and whatever we love in the body's paradise cannot be evil, since it provides us with a dynamic image of the heavenly beauty poised over it like a crown. And if we all ask for "it"—a heaven that does not exclude the desires of gay people from the crowning circuit of beatitude—then we may see it in permanent form eventually (as we may imagine Peter seeing it now, even in his closed casket) through the opened eyes of the *nova gente*. Doty's camp appropriation of the *corona beata* motif from the Christian apocalyptic tradition is not sacrilegious in the end. It's sanctifying.

While heaven is isolated (without being insulated) from the realms of desire in Doty's apocalypse, the two worlds are mystically conflated in the poetry of Michael Lynch. In 1989 Lynch, a professor of American literature at the University of Toronto and a leading activist in the city's lesbian and gay community, published ten AIDS elegies under the sonorous Whitmanesque title *These Waves of Dying Friends*. Opening on a quiet note with the Fire Island monody "Sand," it culminates in a choral crescendo with the cheers of AIDS activists outside the American Supreme Court in "Yellow Kitchen Gloves": a lyrical modulation from individual sorrow to collective defiance that effectively counters Crimp's simplistic opposition of elegiac and activist responses to the crisis. For Lynch, the social consolations of activism can only grow out of the personal consolations of elegiac meditation.[32]

In "Sand" a lonely survivor (the poet himself as a seropositive breaker of silences) defeats the paralyzing romantic impulse to lament his own losses by celebrating the resistant cohesiveness and continuity of his culture. In "Yellow Kitchen Gloves" a crowd of protesters resist the ideological tendency to devalue individual experience by inscribing the names of

dead PWAs on the gloves they have donned in mocking imitation of the
AIDS-phobic Washington police. Like the individual steps and choral
turns on Dante's Purgatory, movements on Lynch's redemptive map of
America may seem to go in opposite directions, but they all converge on an
imaginary dancefloor where death can have no dominion. Thus the private
retreat to Fire Island in "Sand" prepares Lynch the elegist, even as it prepares his readers, for opposing the policers of desire in public demonstrations like the Washington march commemorated in "Yellow Kitchen
Gloves." But looking back at the pastoral world of the first poem from the
political vantage point of the last, we can also see that the fighting spirit of
the Washington demonstrators (recollected in anything but tranquillity!)
prevents Lynch the activist from slipping into romantic melancholia on
Fire Island. He makes a heaven in hell's despite on the very sandbar where
"everything not music" inevitably disintegrates. Miraculously, it seems,
tragic dissolution is turned into divine comedy.

Like Doty, whose Fire Island Paradiso is a rather noisy place with
stampeding horses and chiming fruits, Lynch implicitly equates silence
with death by explicitly equating sound with life. Hence the allegorical
soundtrack of "Sand":

> I always hear the silence on this island
> not only thumping woofers others
> hear, not the oceanic roar
> or the contrapuntal crickets who now before
> the hurricane make like violins tuning
> and trilling at triple speed as if to get all in
> for the rest of the yellow season before the
> storm.   (stanza 3)

Counterpointing this cacophony of cheerful beach noises with the mournful silence created on the island, or within its collective consciousness, by
the loss of so many islanders to the epidemic, Lynch gives the muted dead
a sound again, a slight acoustic trace, in the commemorative creaking of
the planks on the boardwalk. Over these familiar planks he passes in a
painful effort to pull himself together again—as a separate self, a resolute
survivor, a living islander—after disembarking on the strangely un-
familiar shore, which threatens at any moment to become the Beaches of
the Dispossessed with its stormy skies and human flotsam:

> Arriving today hardly together at all—
> a dissolving crystal immersed in another man
> or (my state required two metaphors, like

light) the flotsam of a shattered craft
in the aftermath of the hurricane to come—
I walked it off on the boardwalks, walked them
in, rather, since each board gave me back a loss.   (stanza 3)

Resisting the Shiltsian temptation to infernalize the shorescape of loss,
Lynch manages to walk off the despair that overcame his predecessors on
this allegorical strand. Unlike the stricken Marlboro Man, he does not
give in to the paralyzing thought that he too will become trash on the beach
but strives instead to find significant patterns amid the shattered remains
on the sand and even in the tiny movements of ants across a wall:

On the cedar that planks the wall
ants crisscross paths
the set eye turns to netting
until they find and crawl back into
the slits between the planks.
All lines between sleep and wake dissolve.
One's self is runny on this island.   (stanza 4)

Like the souls on the Terrace of the Lustful, Lynch must see life close up
from the humble perspective of the ants in order to perceive the grand
pattern—the "netting"—that binds even the tiniest motions in the realms
of desire together with the most calamitous changes into the cycles of the
cosmic dance.

Though the self threatens to dissolve on a sandbar where "everything
tends towards sand," it also has the capacity to integrate itself with the
chorus of lovers dancing to the music of time. Lynch mischievously but
marvelously replays this old Dantean music, the divine symphony
prompting the *regressus mentis ad Deum*, over the sound system of a Fire
Island boom-boom room:

My friends who rarely boogie never know
the telling mark of the great DJs, the sense
of everlastingness, of music without end,
of seamless mixes and 8 a.m. conclusions that
don't conclude but do go round again
one more time. When I last left
I knew when I'd return I'd have the sense
of nothing ended, nothing altered, nothing new
in the only life I count as true: the dancefloor.   (stanza 5)

With this new realization of the everlasting truth and presence of a gay
communal identity, or rather with the return of this realization from his lost

Fire Island past, comes the blessed moment of recovery. The dead return
to boogie with the living on Sutherland's old dancefloor, a truly beatific
vision now, without the in-crowd ironies or outsider angsts:

> Last night I danced as we did two years ago,
> alive with love, with Larry, Vito,
> Ray and a dozen unnamed others
> the virus thinks it has taken from the floor.   (stanza 5)

These unnamed others find their names again on the yellow kitchen
gloves held high by the activists on the steps of the Supreme Court, and to
this reclaimed gayspace on the threshold of an ideal democracy, a paradisal threshold yet to be crossed but nevertheless open to us if we only dare
to cross it, the survivors summon the AIDS saints to rally with them on
behalf of gay people everywhere and to triumph in victorious dance o'er
heterosexist folly and intolerance:

> We want you all beside us on these steps,
> this other dancefloor, gloved fists in the air
> defying the empowered who deny
> our lives and deaths, our fucking, and our hate.
> ("Yellow Kitchen Gloves," stanza 7)

The virus cannot take us from either floor, Lynch proclaims, whether
we are rallying for justice against those who deny our hate or dancing for
joy among those who affirm our love. In the ideal democracy toward which
both movements, the elegiac disco and the activist demo, impel us with the
momentum of purgatorial zeal, there will be no tension between gay activism and gay estheticism. The one will lose its melancholy languor as it
marches down the road of fire, and the other its hateful anger as it rises into
the dance of love. Where both movements converge, there will be only one
dancefloor.

VI   Cloister Cases

In harmony with ACT UP's radically utopian orthodoxy, which happens to
coincide with traditional Christian trumpetings on the sonic boom of the
blessed life, Doty and Lynch exclude the silence of death from their resto-
rations of heaven. Sound = Life is their radically poetic answer to the radically political slogan Silence = Death. So tune out the sounding brass and
tinkling cymbals: the elegists of the epidemic are hymning the Dantean
theme of *caritas* to the accompaniment of chiming fruits, trilling crickets,

creaking boardwalks, blaring woofers, and anything else on Fire Island that will fill the viral void.

But in their efforts to compose the new song of the gay afterlife, do these unlikely successors to Dante go so far as to include the voices of straights on the celestial soundtrack? Can the shades who would have cried "Pasiphae" on the Terrace of the Lustful make a joyful noise unto the Lord with Peter and Vito and all the other members of the Sodom and Gomorrah chorus whom "the virus thinks it has taken from the dancefloor"?

Apparently not. Straights simply do not figure in the resurrection of the dead imagined by the Fire Island psalmists. Yet like Dante, who met with no gay saints in *Paradiso* though he prepared a way for them thither in *Purgatorio,* Doty and Lynch call no straight souls (male or female) to their transfigured isle, though they'd probably be the last to post a "Gay Men Only" sign over the gates to paradise. Just as anyone can hop a ferry to Fire Island in its untransfigured state, so any soul who wants a place in the eternal sun (and a perpetual holiday from Helmsian bigotry) can ride out the waves of dying friends and land safely on the purgatorial sandbar. There are many rooms, after all, in the Father's beachhouse.

Swept away by the happy thought of an eschatology that celebrates sexual diversity, one might suppose that no gay poet who had lost lovers and friends to AIDS would entertain the notion of a gays-only heaven except as an escapist fantasy—a dalliance with false surmise, as Milton put it, "so to interpose a little ease."[33] Not so. Such a fantasy is religiously entertained by Paul Monette in "Brother of the Mount of Olives," the pastoral finale of his song-cycle *Love Alone: Eighteen Elegies for Rog.*[34]

Roger Horwitz, the poet's lover, died of AIDS in 1986. In 1983, a few months before his diagnosis, he and Monette visited a monastery in the Sienese hills where they were photographed by a certain Brother John. As monks go, their "rapturous guide" (61) was definitely on the worldly side: despite the language barrier, he quickly ascertained that his guests were gay men in love with "youth and laughter and beautiful things" (61). John was promptly scanned by Rog and Paul in return and positively identified as a brother of their gay aesthetic order. Gaydar evidently works even in the Catholic cloister.

Meditating on John's snapshot of them, which in mournful retrospect becomes their wedding portrait, the poet is temporarily consoled by the romantic thought (springing, perhaps, from Boswell's history of cloister cases in the Middle Ages) that his "pagan" union with Rog had been covertly blessed by the Church. Not by the fag-hating official Church, of course, but by its fun-loving underground homophile association, which has miraculously sustained the Golden Age tradition of hedonistic gay eros even in the chillingly straight atmosphere of monastic piety. To the founder of Brother John's official order is assigned the role of fatal silencer:

> Benedict having commanded *shh*
> along with his gaunt motto *ora et labora*
> pray work   (60)

as if he were the early medieval counterpart of Cardinal O'Connor. ACT UP would surely approve of Monette's subsequent characterization of Pope John Paul II as a "Polack joke" who "wants his fags quiet." By contrast, the rapturous guide seriously announces the Sound = Life theme:

> our particular brother John
> couldn't stop chattering not from the moment
> he met us grinning at the cloister door   (60)

a door that leads inward to a paradise of all-male delights, an abode of chattering church-queen otium in the midst of all that silent Benedictine labor.

The experience might be called "coming in." As an initiate admitted to inner gayspace, Monette can with high aesthetic impunity worship a peeling fresco by (who else?) Sodoma. Membership has its privileges, it seems, and not even the reformist zeal of Douglas Crimp and all the brethren of ACT UP can dampen the idolatrous cryptopapist enthusiasms of the oblates in Brother John's secret order. "Are we the heirs of them?" cries the unwitting groom in an enthusiastic moment more out of Henry James than John Boswell,

> or they our secret
> fathers and how many of our kind lie beneath
> the cypress alley crowning the hill beyond.   (62)

Heaven has literally gone underground here. And if an underground heaven sounds like a paradox, something the Devil would think up to keep the Sodomites and the Sodoma-worshippers on their toes in the burning sands, don't be perplexed: it only exists on the anticlerical brink of AIDS fury reached by Monette with the spiritual counterpart of the "Spartacus Guide."

Like every pastoral elegy since "Lycidas," Monette's bittersweet idyll interposes easeful recollections of the lost beloved with diseaseful blasts of anticlerical satire. Milton, one suspects, would have written pamphlets

condemning the eschatological apologetics of the Fire Island Psalter, but
as a good puritan he would certainly have applauded the verve of Monette's
pope-bashing polemics. So for that matter would Dante, who consigned a
fair number of popes to Hell in order to promote the heavenly mission of
the Church. He also consigned the Blasphemers to the same burning
sands as the Sodomites for denying God's role in salvation history. Monette, also denying that role, goes one step further than Dante or Milton by
damning anyone who thinks the Church (Catholic or Protestant) has any
sort of heavenly mission. "Far brother" begins his bitter invitation to any
straight Christian inclined to empathize with the gay brothers whom the
virus has taken from the cloister,

> if you should pass beneath our cypresses
> you who are a praying man your god
> can go to hell   (65)

which sounds like the kind of fist-shaking blasphemy that would earn him
merit points with ACT UP. But in the jasmine-scented verses of his final
hedonistic prayer the blasphemer turns out to be a softlife aesthete instead
of a diehard activist:

> pray that my friend and I be still together
> just like this at the Mount of Olives blessed
> by the last of an ancient race who loved
> youth and laughter and beautiful things so much
> they couldn't stop singing and we were the song.   (65)

The song "we" turn out to be is no ACT UP chant or Ice Palace gloria or
purgative holler of "Sodom and Gomorrah": it's an eerie epithalamion
sung sotto voce by secretive shades cloistered from the stormy blasts and
early frosts of the epidemic. Monette's underground heaven is as exclusionary as any dreamed up by the Cistercians in Dante's day or the Calvi-
nists in Milton's. Singing the praises of gay love beneath swaying Tuscan
cypresses is nice work if you can get it, but for most laborers in the vine-
yard perhaps a little too much ease is interposed here to ring true in the
void.

The deep appeal of pastoral fantasy for gay men in determined aesthetic
retreat from the burning road of AIDS activism has been wisely satirized
by Robert Ferro in his surprisingly upbeat final novel *Second Son*. In a
chatty letter to the novel's ailing hero, Mark Valerian, Matthew Black, a
fortyish writer who lives secluded from the world in his dotty mum's Florida homestead, reports that he'd recently got a strange letter

from a gay group in Austin that is raising funds for a private space program, to find a livable planet to colonize. A gay planet, darling. Like the Pines I guess only bigger and not so hard to get to.[35]

The "planet Mary," as he first jokingly calls it, or "Splendora," as its Texan colonists solemnly christen it, ceases to be a joke for him after a while: so strong is his desire to escape plague-darkened America for some bright realm of perpetual gaiety that he seriously begins to believe that it's easier to reach the Dog Star than to get a share at The Pines (which has no more reality for him in his current panic than a dream of the gay old days). Splendora becomes his Fire Island in the sky, the ultimate homeland for his tribe, a long-lost paradiso attainable at last through the miracle of American space technology.

Though Matthew tries to persuade Mark and his lover Bill to leave "it" all behind and join the expedition to outer gayspace, they resist the lure of the anagogic ascent. Bill simply concludes that Matthew has gone off his rocker, victimized more by America's AIDS phobia than by Austin's scam artists. Mark, though equally skeptical, nevertheless remains sympathetic to his friend's heavenly aspirations. "We all have our fantasies," he jokes in a letter to Matthew,

> Mine is being a blond, while you seek the planet Mary . . . [Bill] wants it to be true. He wants you to go. I suppose he would even like us to go. But that's not because he believes it is really possible—the Fusion, the spaceship, the destination—but only because he knows what it represents, as an idea. (170)

And what is the idea behind it? Ferro, who came out of (and out in) the Catholic force field of an Italo-American family, knew very well what was represented by a place like The Pines "only bigger":

> Salvation. A better place. Something after. Play orchestra play. But darling if only believing could make it so. Then buggers like you and me would ride. (170)

Play orchestra play, indeed, for in the symphony of beatitude there are no rests for death to silence the saved. Once again Sound = Life, a Big Band Sound for the Dantean *festa* on high.

However much he may have identified himself with Mark Valerian, Ferro was not one to dally long with false surmises: he had evidently settled his own crisis of faith (if he ever had one) in favor of genteel skepticism. Yet his vision of Mark's transformation from a tremulous second son into a triumphant lover despite the infernal ravages of AIDS proves to be comic in the end—divinely comic. Though Mark does not visit Fire Island in the aftermath of his diagnosis, he does find a beach of sorts at the end of all this, together with Bill, at a Splendora-like cottage twinkling with thousands of fairy lights on a peaceful lake in the North Woods.

VII   The Post-Mortem Bar

Must the immortal longings activated by AIDS Awareness always find satisfaction in the prospect of an exclusively gay zone in the afterlife? Ferro suggests not, though his pair of plague-struck lovers opt for pastoral retirement from the world instead of political engagement with it or palliative care beyond it. Heaven remains just a quaint idea for them, like salvation, so it is put aside with other childish things as they pace out the rest of their days on their private beach. For a radically poetic AIDS apocalypse along Dantean lines, with Fire Island translated into a paradise where gays and straights can hug each other on the same stretch of beach and dance for joy at the same prospect of deliverance, you have to go to the movies.

Consider, for instance, the final scene of *Longtime Companion* (1990). Against the blue-gray backdrop of an overcast Atlantic sky two men and a woman walk the bitter strand, grim-faced, barefoot like pilgrims, their weary eyes searching the horizon for some sign of where it will all end. No sign comes—except the monotonous fall of the breakers. Have the Beaches of the Dispossessed ever looked so bleak? The waves of dying friends have receded into the Gathering Darkness, leaving nothing behind but these friends of dying waves.

The two men are hard to recognize at first as the film's gay heroes Willy (Campbell Scott) and his lover Fuzzy (Stephen Caffrey), since one has grown a moustache and the other shaved his beard. Completing the solemn trio is Fuzzy's married sister Lisa (Mary-Louise Parker), who also sports an older-but-wiser hairdo. Their altered looks are a clue to their sea-changed roles: where previously they had acted like ordinary people caught up in the film's relentlessly docudramatic plotting of the epidemic as a threat to the upscale good life of the American middle class, now—the scene is dated "July 19, 1989"—they seem oddly removed from the settings and strategies of social realism. They assume an oracular role outside the historical limits of their social and sexual identities as the chorus of Fire Island Fates.

Fuzzy sports an ACT UP T-shirt with the semiotic injunction "Read My Lips" printed across a picture of two military men kissing—as if their prophetic discourse had broken the heterosexist sound barrier and could only be read by the antigay "enemy" as defiantly visible action on the hyper-allegorical stage of the AIDS Apocalypse. Though the trio may look and sound like ACT UP recruiters, their mission here is really to announce the founding of the Gay Salvation Army.

"Seems inconceivable, doesn't it?" muses Willy, "that there was ever a time before all this when we didn't wake up every day wondering who's sick now, who else is gone." Inconceivable? Hardly. Writer Craig Lucas and director Norman René conceived a vividly prelapsarian "time before all this" for us in the early scenes of the film. As the opening credits flashed by to the carefree strains of "The Tide is High," we saw Willy as a kind of gay Adam innocently skinnydipping on a remarkably clean, un-crowded beach. We saw him lap up the good life under the watchful eye of the Father, an independently wealthy gaytriarch named David (Bruce Davison), whose beach house proves to have many rooms. We saw Willy fall for the doggedly loyal Fuzzy—no Eve he—amid the swaying beach-grass and whispering pines of the gay old days before Kramer turned the Meat Rack into the Waste of Shame. Back then the beach meant freedom from shame. Licentiousness was liberty. So the boys discovered one night as they strolled along the beach, their ears still ringing with "Casta Diva" (David's preferred beach music): fleetingly, by the light of Norma's en-chanted moon, they glimpsed a chorus of white-clad youths merrily chased into the Gathering Darkness by an old circuit-queen dressed up in chiffon robes like the Statue of Liberty.

The Edenic evocation of Fire Island in its golden age culminated in an idyllic moment when Willy and party boy John Deacon (Dermot Mulroney) came upon a couple of innocent deer grazing amid the dunes: so you thought there'd be beached males humping in the hollows! John and Willy preferred brotherly nature walks to sodomy in the sands when the tide in the affairs of men was high.

The tide is definitely low in the final scene. The before-and-after medi-tation begun by Willy is taken up by Fuzzy, whose monogamous fidelity throughout the film has apparently saved them both from the plague waves that took away John and David and David's not-so-monogamous lover Sean (Mark Lamos). "Do you ever wonder," asks the second gay Fate, "if they do find a cure if people would go back to sleeping around?" People would, we know, if there was a chance of going back; but here, in the final scene, as we contemplate the dark backward and abysm of time from the atemporal viewpoint of the monogamous saved, our thoughts are directed away from sex altogether—since sex is more or less equated with the history of the Fallen World in the theological subtext of the film.

On the surface, however, the film does its liberal damnedest not to preach about sexual cupidity. "I'm sick of hearing people pontificate about it," Willy declares, to which Lisa sardonically replies: "Except us." She's right, of course. As the straight Fate, she has an important role in voicing Middle America's pressing need to find a moral for the gay plague story, its urgent demand for closure in a crisis narrative that threatens to go on and on, world without end. Like Beatrice, whose tough-love tactics prevent Dante from sliding from mushy nostalgia into desperate apostasy, Lisa knows when to smile sweetly at her boys as they try to philosophize about love and death and when to upbraid them for failing to get to the religious point: divine intervention is the *only* way out of their morally indeterminate, mortally inescapable story.

"Except us . . . exactly," admits the chastened Willy, ready now at the howling brink of defeated liberalism (and liberationism) to grit his teeth, squint his eyes, imagine a miraculous denouement for the realist fable, and hurl himself into eternity on a politically incorrect but poetically triumphant leap of faith. But where is the doctor-ex-machina to perform the miracle? Heaven hides him behind its leaden skies.

"I just wanna be there," Willy pleads with the Absent Presence, "if they ever do find a cure." Realizing that a collective activation of the divinely inspired poetic imagination (Dante's *alta fantasia*) is more likely to pull this miracle off than all the activist political rallies announced on his Read My Lips T-shirt, Fuzzy invites his lover and his sister to hope for a miracle by joining him in an anagogic flash-forward: "Can you imagine what it would be like?" Lisa, moved by the imaginative prospect of Love Triumphant, mainstreams the high fantasy by likening it to "the end of World War Two": not to the spiritually devastating end of the Holocaust, presumably, for that would drag in Larry Kramer's tragic reckoning with human depravity in a godless existential universe; but rather to the V-Day celebrations in Times Square when everyone thanked heaven it was all over and kissed and hugged and had a big party and lived happily ever after through the beach-movie 1950s.

A moment of silence ensues. It cannot be the fatal silence of apathy shouted down by activists, for the AIDS Fates have paid choral lip service to the Silence = Death campaign at the start of the scene by proclaiming their intention to get arrested in an impending ACT UP demonstration. Nor can it be the silence of the grave into which so many music-loving revelers in the film have slipped, starting with John, whom we last saw (from an eerie overhead angle, as if we were hovering over him with the Angel of Death) sweating feverishly in his hospital bed, isolated by

ominous medical machinery, his mouth stopped up by intubation appara-
tus. Rather, like the respectful hush at a Memorial Day ceremony before
the veterans' band strikes up the national anthem, the pause swells with
the trio's shared expectations until it becomes a stretto demanding religious resolution in the orchestration of their shared griefs.

So there is much more to the present silence than meets the ear. It
marks the passing of conventional documentary realism in the screenplay
and of fashionable post-Christian skepticism in the discursive foreground
of the dialogue: we have reached the littoral end of the film's literal narration of the epidemic as social history.

From here on out, the film will be reborn as an apocalyptic vision of the
Fire Island afterlife as an escape from the grim historical realities of
the New York epidemic. The silence on the shore proclaims the futility of
the ACT UP Reformation even as it heralds the blessed end of activist art
practices—for who needs any activists in Heaven? Through the miracle of
allegorical special effects we are transported to a moment of Dantean transcendence when the survivors cast off their tragic guise as the chorus of
Fates and greet the Glad Day as the trio of the Christian Virtues. Forsaking
his old role as an exercise instructor plagued with AIDS-phobic doubts
about Life and Love, Willy now embodies Faith. Fuzzy, always an optimist
even when facing the desperate intransigence of the system in his worldly
role as gay advocate, now takes on the otherworldly role of Hope. And
Charity, of course, is his loving sister, the token Female Other who manages to transcend the déclassé role of fag-hag by mothering the boys of
summer through the winter of the plague.

Lisa smiles at one point during their solemn conversation, and like
Beatrice's enlightening *riso de l'universo,* her brief acknowledgment of the
divine comedy they're enacting has a miraculous effect on what might otherwise have been another depressing stroll down the Beaches of the Dispossessed.[36] It breaks the purgatorial tension of the stretto, and at once
the anastatic moment breaks through with the appearance of a large crowd
(mostly men but some women) sprinting over a boardwalk bridge toward
the sea.

The dead have risen for a *festa* on the sand. As they race leftward across
the screen toward the contemplative spectators, who at first do not recognize John and David and Sean and all the other Fire Islanders silenced by
death, the clamorous AIDS shades resemble the anonymous throng of jogging spirits on the seventh terrace of Purgatory whom Dante called the new
people. Instead of shouting "Sodom and Gomorrah," however, they exchange private greetings in the anal-erotic idiom of old beach buddies:

WILLY: You fuckin' son of a bitch!

JOHN: You asshole!

Then, like the companies of the lustful, they ritually convert their abundant sexual energies (which in the gay old days would have led to burning orgies in the Meat Rack) into chaste hugs and kisses—the public enactment of perfected charity.

All losses are restored and sorrows end in an extemporaneous party scene that recaptures the joie de vivre of the Fire Island revels at the beginning of the film, minus, of course, the poppers and booze and virus. It's a party that even Nancy Reagan could have approved if she had ever set foot on the island. True to the allegorical formula Sound = Life, the booming soundtrack enlivens the Glad Day get-together with an anthem celebrating resurrection:

> We'll go down to the post-mortem bar
>> and catch up on the years that've passed between
>> us and we'll tell our sto-o-ries

just like Guido Guinizzelli and the many other shades who told Dante their stories when they met in the afterlife. This version of the new song sounds like beach blanket pop from the early 1960s with nostalgic overtones of folk and blues, but its lyrics take us back even further—back to the *musica divina* resounding through Dante's Paradise, back to the *Hilariter* hymns chanted in Dark Age monasteries to evoke the luminous revels of the saints, way back to the "Gloria in excelsis" flooding the garden of Eden when the world was still innocent:

> Do you remember when the world was just like
>> a carnival openin' up?
> If I could have one day with you the way
>> it used to be,
> All the things I should have said
>> would pour outta me

just like the divinely inspired psalms that poured out of David when he walked through the valley of the shadow of death. Dante walked through that shadowy place too, and now so does the singer of "The Post-Mortem Bar" (Zane Campbell) in a recapitulation of the *selva oscura* theme:

> I took a walk—I didn't know which way
>> I was goin'—
> But somehow or other I ended up here
>> whe-re

We said we'd meet again, an' I guess
    I was hopin'—
But the place was closed down awhile—
    it was all dark in there.

Now it's all light and love again as we meet our lost friends in the place that was closed down awhile. But just as swiftly as "there" became "here" at the anastatic moment, "here" loses its apocalyptic immediacy and reverts to "there," the vanishing point on the horizon of the soul's high fantasy, leaving Willy to reiterate the anastatic wish of the faithful: "I just wanna be there."

Though Craig Lucas and Norman René were criticized by conservative and radical reviewers alike for confusing the end of the epidemic with the End of the World, they were not theologically confused about what they were doing in this controversial scene. Nor were they merely selling out to bourgeois salvation fantasies or fairy-tale happy endings for the sake of the bottom line, as they were of course suspected of doing by the dissenting preachers of the ACT UP Reformation. They had made a clearly liberal decision about the kind of pop-cultural heaven needed to sustain public hope in the wake of individual losses to the plague. If the movie was ever to have a socially constructive impact beyond the Fire Island circuit, it would have to raise the AIDS shades in an intermediary realm of desire that mainstream audiences wouldn't mind paying their admission prices to glimpse and maybe enter. That was a tall order. To pull it off, the film had to build a bridge of sympathy between the gay coterie on the island and the straight world on the mainland, which it effectively did through the Beatrice-like intercessions of Lisa.

Her participation in the final scene saves it from falling into the hokey revivalism of Bishop Moore's kingdom of love on the one hand, and the bitter separatism of Paul Monette's cloister of gaiety on the other. Lisa's charitable mediation between the boys in the sand and the boys on the ward earns her the right to hug them all again at the postmortem bar. She deserves a hug in return (and gets it from David) for resisting the fundamentalist separation of the gay goats from the straight sheep, and the liberationist exaltation of the gay sheep over the straight goats, even though she's the most likely character in the cast to give way to either apocalyptic extreme. Raised as a southern belle, she ought to shrink in Helmsian horror from the very thought of involvement with the gay men's health crisis. But instead she becomes the first character in the film to volunteer for telephone duty at the Gay Men's Health Crisis. She is also the first to enunci-

ate Michael Lynch's radically poetic argument that AIDS activism may be
our best long-term consolation during the crisis, short of faith in the General Resurrection, an elegiac insight she casually shares over lunch with
her brother one day when she notices that grief and fear have paralyzed his
normally energetic spirit.

Yet even as an unlikely proselytizer for ACT UP, she does not immolate
herself in the flames of radical utopian outrage depicted on their protest
posters. Her life as a straight woman in the big city goes on. She runs her
antique shop. She vacations at David's beach house. She gets married. She
attends memorial services and benefit concerns. She plans to get arrested
at a demonstration. She is no token presence at the gay anastasis, therefore, but a socially encouraging reason for hoping that someday the gulf
between gays and straights that the epidemic has perilously widened will
be narrowed by a universal smile, so that we may all dance for joy and get a
hug on the Beaches of the Repossessed.

NOTES

This essay is dedicated to the memory of Michael Lynch, who died in July 1991.

Translated, the epigraph reads "It [namely the Book of Life opened before the Throne of God in Revelation, 20:12] will show the avarice and the baseness of him who keeps watch over the Isle of Fire"
(*Paradiso* 19:130–31). Dante refers here to Sicily under the unhappy reign of Frederick II. All quotations from Dante in this essay are from the Italian text of the *Commedia* (Giorgio Petrocchi, ed., 1966–
68) reprinted in *The Divine Comedy*, Charles S. Singleton, trans. (Princeton: Princeton University
Press, 1970–75). All English translations of Dante in this essay are my own, though they owe much to
Singleton's translations and annotations.

1. "There were some rude people here," Dan Rather testily observed after the "CBS
Evening News" was zapped by a band of media guerillas from ACT UP on January 22,
1991. Presumably he would not have been so ruffled if the invaders of his studio had expressed their outrage against American action in the Gulf (as inaction against AIDS) in
more polite terms, e.g., "Please, sir, would you mind terribly if we just interrupted your
broadcast for a moment to point out the imperialist, racist, and heterosexist biases of your
bourgeois reportage?" Ironically, when Rather broke for a commercial to censor the protes-
tors, the screen simply went blank: the zap succeeded in exposing the complete inability of
the news-gathering medium to deal with news actually breaking out within its sanctified
domain of civilized (read: controlled) behavior. For an account of this incident, footage of
which was cheerily recycled on "Entertainment Tonight" the next evening, see *Toronto
Star*, January 23, 1991, p. F2.

2. "*Quella [Beatrice] che 'emparadisa la mia mente*" *Paradiso* 28:3.

3. Douglas Crimp, "AIDS: Cultural Analysis/Cultural Activism," in Douglas Crimp, ed., *AIDS: Cultural Analysis/Cultural Activism*, (Cambridge, Mass.: MIT Press, 1988), pp. 4–14.

4. Douglas Crimp, "Mourning and Militancy," *October* 51 (1989):3–18.

5. *Paradiso* 1:70–72.

6. Andrew Holleran, "Oceans," in *Ground Zero* (New York: New American Library, 1988), p. 219.

7. *Purgatorio* 2:35–51. After receiving the sign of the cross from the angelic steersman, the shades "all flung themselves upon the beach" (49–50).

8. Andrew Holleran, *Dancer from the Dance* (1978; reprint, New York; New American Library, 1986), p. 49.

9. Ibid., p. 227.

10. Randy Shilts, *And the Band Played On: Politics, People, and the AIDS Epidemic* (New York: St. Martin's, 1987). "This book is a work of journalism," Shilts disingenuously declares in his notes on sources (607). "There has been no fictionalization." Where subsequent references to this work are contextually clear, page numbers will be cited in the text.

11. Larry Kramer, *Faggots* (1978; reprint, New York: New American Library, 1987), pp. 268ff.

12. Andrew Holleran, introduction to Larry Kramer's *The Normal Heart* (New York: New American Library, 1985), p. 23.

13. Kramer, *The Normal Heart*, p. 115.

14. Ibid., pp. 61, 103.

15. Shilts, *And the Band Played On*, pp. 25–33.

16. Rt. Rev. Paul Moore, Jr., preface to Michael Klein, ed., *Poets for Life: Seventy-Six Poets Respond to AIDS*, (New York: Crown, 1989), pp. 1–2.

17. Ibid., p. 1.

18. "Three times I clasped my hands behind him [the shade of Casella] and as often brought them to my breast." *Paradiso* 2:80–81.

19. "The great sea of being" *Paradiso* 1:113.

20. David Groff, "A Scene of the Crime," in *Poets for Life*, pp. 82–83.

21. On "Patient Zero" (Gaetan Dugas), see Shilts, *And the Band Played On*, pp. 23, 147, 156–157, 258, 438, 460.

22. On the pre-Socratic origins and Stoic elaborations of the theme of the world conflagration, see James Miller, *Measures of Wisdom: The Cosmic Dance in Classical and Christian Antiquity* (Toronto: University of Toronto Press, 1986), pp. 366, 403, 414, 443, 478, 555.

23. *Paradiso* 33:142.

24. For a description of the sodomites on the burning plain, see *Inferno* 15:16–42 and 16:1–6.

25. The epithet *lussuriosa* is specifically applied to Cleopatra in *Inferno* 5:63, though its double meaning ("luxury-loving" as well as "lustful") pertains to all the other shades named in the second circle.

26. On the medieval concept of spiritual sodomy, see Elio Costa, "From *locus amoris* to Infernal Pentacost: The Sin of Brunetto Latini" in *Quadereni d'Italianistica* 10 (1989):109–32.

27. Genesis 3:24: "He drove out the man; and at the east of the garden of Eden he

placed the cherubim, and a flaming sword which turned every way, to guard the way to the tree of life."

28. John Boswell, *Christianity, Social Tolerance, and Homosexuality* (Chicago: University of Chicago Press, 1980), p. 375 n. 50.

29. On later medieval intolerance toward "unnatural" love and lovers, see Boswell, *Christianity, Social Tolerance, and Homosexuality*, pp. 269ff.

30. For a spectacular version of the crown of concord, see *Paradiso* 10–12, which probably influenced Botticelli's depiction of it in the heavens above the manger in the *Mystic Nativity*.

31. Mark Doty, "Tiara," in *Poets for Life*, pp. 66–67.

32. Michael Lynch, *These Waves of Dying Friends* (New York: Contact II Publications, 1989), pp. 2–8 for "Sand"; 86–92 for "Yellow Kitchen Gloves." See also the note on the historical background of the latter poem on the unnumbered page following it. Where subsequent references to this work are contextually clear, stanzas will be cited in the text.

33. John Milton, "Lycidas," pp. 152–153.

34. Paul Monette, *Love Alone: Eighteen Elegies for Rog* (New York: St. Martin's, 1988). See pp. 60–65 for "Brother of the Mount of Olives." The Catholic religiosity of this elegy is rendered somewhat ironic by the fact that Rog was Jewish.

35. Robert Ferro, *Second Son* (New York: Crown, 1988), p. 81. Where subsequent references to this work are contextually clear, page numbers will be cited in the text.

36. *Paradiso* 27:4–5.

Testimony

Timothy F. Murphy

Words are for those with promises to keep.
—W. H. Auden

I

The writing about the experience of sickness and death in the AIDS epidemic, much of it by and about gay men, comes on the heels of the rise of noteworthy gay literature in the United States. Richard Hall has drawn attention to some of the ways that literature has changed considerably since World War II. What was once a literature of secrecy, guilt, and apology has become a literature of defiance and celebration of sexual difference, offering characters who are gay without complaint: "No more slashed wrists and leaps into the sea."[1] Such characters are no longer typically enmeshed in psychiatric and moral quagmires by reason of their homoerotic lives; they have escaped definition by social stigmas, and they resist the distortions of their private truths by public mythology.

Gay and lesbian literature now charts instead the familiar problems of looking for love, of finding a family, of determining the worth of career and power in the order of things.[2] In moving to discussions of relationships and families, such a literature has had to move beyond coming-out stories in order to address the trials of ordinary human life, love gone wrong, and the aging and death of parents, among others. And because of events beyond anyone's choosing, it has also had to countenance the AIDS/HIV epidemic and grapple with the meaning of unexpected illness and death.

This writing has taken various forms in fiction, poetry, auto/biography, and obituaries. Obituaries are now as much a standard feature of the pages of the *Windy City Times*, the *Advocate*, and the *New York Native* as their inevitable phone-sex ads. In obituary form or not, much of this writing has taken as its task the blessing of the dead. It is not, of course, only gay men who have written about their experiences and losses in the epidemic. Other people close to the devastations of AIDS and its antecedents in HIV infection have also set out their encounters with illness, dying, loss, and fear. Yet there are precious few encomiums penned to poor, drug-using men and women who have died with AIDS. Gay men, either as authors or subjects, dominate the written word in the literature of the epidemic. Their publications and booksellers are the epicenters of writing about AIDS.

Douglas Crimp has said: *"Anything said or done about AIDS that does not give precedence to the knowledge, the needs, and the demands of people living with AIDS must be condemned."*[3] Taken literally, this position would condemn the worth of writing about those dead with AIDS unless that writing also served in a utilitarian way the cause of those with AIDS who remained behind. But this would be a stern requirement imposed on those who want, among whatever else, to testify to the worth and value of those who have died. Writing about the dead may or may not offer explicit activist dimensions—some writing does certainly involve explicit and implicit political critique—but it is not clear that such writing is worthwhile only insofar as it advances a political or medical reformation. On the contrary, such writing seems to have a moral integrity of its own, and Crimp himself has come to conjoin rather than detach mourning and militancy.[4] This is not to say that elegiac writing says all that needs to be said in the epidemic or that elegiac writing isn't sometimes a poor substitute for informed and effective political discourse. But it is to say that it is better to write something than to say nothing and thereby let death, in its extinguishing finality, arrogate to itself all privilege in deciding the fate and worth of human life. Elegy, or testimony as I prefer to call it, belongs to the continuum of moral and political conscience that fuels activism in the epidemic and has as an important function the protection of the individual.[5] Such testimony also offers the opportunity to resist the infantilizing of the dying that often occurs in the context of their health care. That continuity and insistence on the primacy of the individual may be seen by considering representative examples from the literature of testimony.

II

Barbara Peabody was among the first to chronicle in journal form her experiences in caring for her son sick and dying with AIDS. In *The Screaming Room*, she describes how her gay son, Peter VonLehn, aspired to a career in opera and theater but worked mostly as a waiter in New York. After being diagnosed with AIDS in December 1983, Peter returned from New York to live with his mother in San Diego. Peabody tells of tending her son on the good days and the bad. In that account, small events loom large against the confines and constraints of Peter's illness; the account therefore has much in common with slow, oppressive accounts of prison life. There were sleepless nights and intractable diarrhea, reclusive behavior and loss of memory, endless trips to doctors and hospitals, spinal taps and drug regimens, the loss of sight, and finally, the watch at the deathbed. There is pain and suffering on every page of this book. At Peter's death there is nothing left for Peabody but tears: "And I am just another mother who has lost her child, who holds his empty, wasted body in her arms and mourns, grieves, cries for loss of part of her own body and soul" (248).[6]

But for all the suffering, for all the costs she paid in caring for him, the book remains nevertheless a memorial to Peter and to her love of him. She remembers him as bright, inquisitive, musical, introspective, intellectual, imaginative, humorous, and independent. And despite the suffering they both endured, she never hoped for his death.

Andrew Holleran's novel *Dancer from the Dance* appeared in the late 1970s and told the tale of drag queen Sutherland and his handsome protégé Malone as they spent their lives looking for love in Manhattan's nights, discos, parks, and bathhouses, at summer parties in the Pines, in drugs, in any pair of eyes, really, that offered a promise of repose. After the stories about long nights, extravagant parties, and the art of cruising that were integral to his *Dancer* and the later *Nights in Aruba*,[7] Holleran now writes mostly about the consequences of the HIV epidemic, about hospitals and funerals, about the deeply felt loss of friends, about how the period he described in his haunting first novel appears to be gone forever, felled by the most archaic form of life—if even alive at all—a virus. Nostalgia permeates the essays that appear in *Christopher Street*, nostalgia for the forms of intimacy and belonging that the epidemic has closed off to gay men.

There is reflection, too, on the many in his circle who have died. There is a remembrance of Cosmo, nicknamed for his worldly air.[8] He and Holleran became friends in Philadelphia. Cosmo had a mania for puns as well as a wicked sense of humor. "He seemed, on his ten-speed with his knapsack, utterly independent, as if all he needed in life was a combination lock, a Penguin paperback, and a can of V-8 juice" (7). After a separation of a few years, Holleran dialed Cosmo's number only to be told that Cosmo was dead with AIDS. "Cosmo was not like everyone else," Holleran says, "Cosmo was special. . . . Cosmo loved life, treasured his body, was only thirty-five, succeeded in his career, and had much to look forward to" (7). Holleran is grieved to observe that, despite the death of a person so much to be treasured, New York and the world at large could proceed as if Cosmo were utterly dispensable. The *New York Times* would continue to make its daily report, and Chernobyl's radioactive cloud would spread westward across Europe as if there had never been a Cosmo. Though he had already experienced other deaths with AIDS and knew as well as anyone that everyone will die, still Holleran is shattered by the inexplicable death: "Cosmo's death horrified. What a waste! What an insult!" No theory could make sense of the death as a moral judgment, as the consequence of self-hate, the inability to love, or even shame at being gay. "His death does not illuminate anything that leaves us morally edified, or superior, or enlightened—it was just part of the vast human waste that is occurring; just mean and nasty" (10).

Holleran also remembers Ernie Mickler, author of the well-known *White Trash Cooking*. Holleran points out that Ernie was funny, had high spirits, nerve, wit, style, and stories to tell. Mickler planned the details of his funeral down to the menu to be served at the luncheon afterward, and Holleran finds himself feeling helpless at not being able to thank his friend for this last kindness. He finds the world emptier without Ernie even as the world seems to bespeak his presence: "The day is hazy and warm, the river flat and still, the woods soft and empty, and the whole afternoon, somehow, like the lunch itself, part of Ernie."[9] There is also, in *Ground Zero*, a remembrance of Eddie, whose life Holleran found essential to the vitality of New York. Eddie lived nocturnally, was in the clubs almost every night, knew the details of New York, knew where to get a Shiatsu massage, knew where to buy cowboy boots, knew where to see a strip show near Times Square. Eddie unfailingly enjoyed everything new in the city: nightclubs, phone systems, winter coats. Holleran says that he had the impression that Eddie got AIDS only because he was, ironically, the first to do everything. After his death, Holleran finds, the city is less vital. But it remains true nevertheless, in Holleran's view, that Eddie remains present in spite of his death (201–9).[10] This refrain recurs in much writing about people dead with AIDS: death does not extinguish personal presence. On the contrary, ironically, death and absence may confirm its very existence.

Holleran writes about many more deaths in *Ground Zero*. There was the death of Charles Ludlam, the founder of the Ridiculous Theater Company. Holleran is lavish in his praise here: Ludlam was an actor, playwright, adored genius, smoldering anarchist, madman. He was loony as Rasputin and funny beyond accounting (91–99). There is also a reflection on O., sick with AIDS, less known to the world but worldly nevertheless, especially as a host par excellence. In facing O.'s likely death, how is it possible to thank him, Holleran wonders, for the many years of wit, wine, conversation, laughter, happiness? How is it possible to make sense of so substantial a man laid waste by this disease (73–80)? There is the account of Michael, who came from a good family, went to Cornell, kept a garden, was a talented architect, and was, before the sickness, concupiscent and lascivious. What, Holleran wonders, did the germs need with him (29–36)? And the dying is not over yet; one supposes that Holleran will offer more memorial reflections as more death comes day after day, name after name, without end in sight.

Such portraits put a face on the epidemic and offer a counterliterature to the discourse both of medical journals, in which PWAs are described as patients or cases, and of the media, where PWAs are still described and represented as victims and predators. They certainly give the lie to the notion that PWAs are beyond the moral community—are both unloving and unloved. Such portraits may not always "analyze" the broad cultural assumptions by which the epidemic is approached, but they do identify those in whose name analysis and activism go forward. One could not, after all, find Peter VonLehm or Eddie Mickler when looking at the numbers in the latest edition of the *HIV/AIDS Surveillance Report* from the Centers for Disease Control. As a mere assortment of diagnoses and treatments their medical charts would also be unrevealing. If there is a counter-discourse to the stereotyping and stigmatizing uses of *AIDS*, it is to be found in the names and lives of those who have borne the burden of the epidemic.

III

It is not surprising, then, that a considerable body of writing about people in the epidemic takes a testimonial form. Such writing first creates a record of the lives of the dead, sharing details beyond the name, age, and residence. It describes these persons then and now still, to the extent that words can provide a verbal equivalent of their presence. And yet, writing is no substitute for the dead themselves. These are losses that cannot be recompensed, so Holleran is left looking for answers about the meaning of the epidemic, of life itself: What can it all mean that these men suffer and die? What can all the beauty and intimacy of men be for if not to live and love in the ways they can? What can all the virtue and accomplishment of life mean if they die nevertheless?[11] If finally, as Holleran's writing seems to suggest, the world itself does not care about the dead, still, there are those who do care when they write, and those who do when they read what has been written. Thus is this writing also a protest of what happens to mortal beings.

This is not to say that these pieces have been written only as eulogy. Most of the people writing these accounts say that they have written for other reasons as well: as a way to make sense of events. Peabody said she wrote to fend off grief: "I gradually found my way out of my screaming room by sorting out and writing down all that happened to us" (253). Elizabeth Cox says that she wrote *Thanksgiving*, recounting her husband's death with AIDS, to create something that would help her remember, that would help make sense of the unexplainable, that would give her a place to put the anger she felt at the cruelty of life.[12] Andrew Holleran has said, too, that writing offers a way of coping with adversity, even if only to probe the questions forced by unexpected death.[13] Paul Monette, in *Borrowed Time*, offers the same motive too: writing offers a small measure of power over the nightmare (227).[14] Much of the writing about those with HIV-related conditions also details the considerable efforts exerted by family and friends to secure help and comfort for the sick and the dying.[15]

Whatever else it cannot offer, testimonial writing seems able to offer some measure of healing—not an inconsequential good. Such writing is not typically, however, mired in its own solipsistic needs. Writers like Peabody and Holleran and the others frequently express the hope that others will not have to go through this, that the epidemic will be brought to an end. Although they may begin with private grief, many of them consciously aim beyond the limits of personal anguish and, in articulating the need for the conquest of the epidemic, do not mistake profound sorrow as any substitute for education and social action. Without judging the extent to which she may have been successful in this regard, Elizabeth Cox says, for example, that she wrote to help overcome social ignorance of and indifference to AIDS (225). Even if testimonial writing begins as so much flailing at unbearable emotions, it nevertheless can heal and can make it easier for others to talk about AIDS—easier for others, whatever their political, sexual, and cultural agenda, to care about the epidemic.

The most accomplished memoir to appear in English thus far for someone who has died with AIDS is *Borrowed Time*, in which Paul Monette discusses the life and loss of his friend and lover, Roger Horwitz. (Monette has also written about their relationship, and the place of AIDS in it, in a collection of poems, *Love Alone*.[16]) Paul and Roger met at a party on Boston's Beacon Hill and were lovers for more than twelve years, not without difficulties, not either without sex outside the relationship. Roger was diagnosed with AIDS in March of 1985 and died in October of the following year. Monette himself has an HIV infection: "The virus ticks in me" (1).

Roger's illness began as minor frets—the loss of a few pounds, minor coughing, short periods of fever, nothing really that made either of them think of AIDS—and ended in a broad array of debilitating disorders: bouts of *Pneumocystis carinii* pneumonia, thrush, herpes, kidney disorder, blindness, shingles, and more. Like Peabody before him, Monette tells about shuttling Roger to doctors, about experimental drugs, about all the kinds of care Roger needs, about the worries and concerns of friends and family, about watching others in their circle of friends fall ill and die after diagnoses of AIDS. Monette protects Roger in the ways that he can: providing the right food, dousing him with vitamins, steering him clear of dirt, cautioning against strain, berating neighbors for the overflow of their septic tank.

There is unreserved high praise for Roger throughout the memoir:

How do I speak of the person who was my life's best reason? The most completely unpretentious man I ever met, modest and decent to such a degree that he seemed to release what was most real in everyone he knew. It was always a relief to be with Roger, not to have to play any games at all. By a safe mile he was the least flashy of all our bright circle of friends, but he spoke about books and the wide world he had journeyed with huge conviction and a hunger to know everything. (9–10)

Monette, moreover, even characterizes Roger as a paradigm of the classical Greek ideal of virtue, *sophrosyne:* the whole of virtue characterized by a harmony of soul acting according to right reason. He lavishes praise and celebrates Roger's native intellect, his commitment and devotion in their relationship, and his endurance throughout the nineteen-month course of illness. When Monette's own disturbingly low T-cell counts come rolling in, Roger was there, he says, with loyalty and concern (151). Monette credits Roger with always looking on the bright side, even in the worst throes of his illness (251). He is hard-pressed to understand why Roger does not cry out against his blindness (161). It is, Monette thinks, as if Roger had an instinct to make others feel better (161).

Monette is not trying to resurrect Roger with this memoir; neither does he mistake writing for taxidermy. It is not Roger's life that Monette is trying to hold on to here; it is his *goodness*. And the incentive for that effort is nothing more than the finitude of human life resisted by the counsels of human love. "Loss teaches you very fast," Monette says, "what you cannot go without saying" (252). Disease and death may kill, but they cannot always diminish the importance of a single human life, cannot always silence the voice of tribute. The line between praise of the dead and protest against death is a slim one indeed.

Narratives about those dead with AIDS typically praise the worth of the dead, citing variously their interests and their contributions. They speak of love of travel and cooking, attachment to friends and family, affection for pets, passion in politics, and accomplishments of intellect. In this regard, obituaries in the gay press are often more indulgent than those in mass-circulation papers. In some detail, such obituaries may describe the persons who have died with AIDS and their influence on the circle of people who loved them. Any one chosen at random from, say, the *PWA Newsline*, shows considerable effort at sympathetic portraiture. For example, in describing John B. Hettwer, an artist and dancer, his lover Stephen describes him as "a striking vision of compact muscular power and physical beauty with crystal blue eyes and a golden halo of hair. He was the most generous and kind person I have ever known. His smile spoke of a warm heart, a great sense of humor, [a] sexy and confident young man of strong opinion and honest conscience."[17]

Such writing does not necessarily blink away individual failing either. Barbara Peabody was aware of certain failings of her son, seeing in his character the weakness that put him in the path of HIV infection; she thought him impetuous and self-destructive and inattentive to his native gifts (7). In *Borrowed Time*, Monette likewise expresses his anger at Roger for getting sick: "My anger was growing more and more unmanageable. But I thought I understood the difference—then, anyway—between being mad at him and being mad at AIDS" (88). Elizabeth Cox also reports a great deal of anger toward her husband when she discovered his relationships with men.[18] Yet in the end, anger was either a luxury made impossible by the needs of caring for the sick, or it was beside the point.

It may be surprising that so many sins are forgiven and vices forgotten in writing about the dead. Of the living we often judge unsparingly. Why do the dead escape our harsh judgments when they can no longer exert any form of resistance or revenge? Why does vice wither away without a trace in the grave? In the end, for example, Elizabeth Cox does not dwell on the way her husband may have put her and their son at risk of HIV infection. There are no angry remonstrances in *Borrowed Time* about whose sexual liaisons might have been responsible for whose infection. Perhaps such forgiveness is itself an act of compassion, a way of making amends for the evil suffered in death. Silence about vices is perhaps a way of saying that no evil deserves the consequence of death or that in death there is already what punishment any possible theory of retribution could require.

In their spoken and unspoken meanings, obituaries and other first-person accounts of the dead have much in common with the appliqué panels of the Names Project.[19] However else they might be interpreted, the panels can be seen as soft-sculpture tombstones whose display, for example, on the Capitol Mall in the District of Columbia, evokes a cemetery in visual expanse and moral purpose. The panels themselves are sometimes beautiful, witty, poignant, and funny. Even when they are simple and artless, they are motivated by a desire to name and preserve the significance of the person who has died and to honor, if not assuage, the loss felt by those left behind. Letters often accompany these panels as they come into the headquarters of the Names Project. Often simple and always sad, these letters written by lovers, friends, mothers, fathers, sisters, brothers, and even strangers explain how they have come to make the panel they are submitting. They describe the persons with AIDS known to them with a catalogue of virtues: talented, special, courageous, compassionate, loyal, dedicated, encouraging, original, honest, kind, helpful, warm, gentle, motivating, confident, assured, artistic, funny, intelligent. The letters and panels make it clear that what these people want to do is to preserve the memory of a life that has touched them, that deserves something better than silence.

This attempt at pointing out individual virtues is a continuous refrain of writing about the dead. Indeed, in the writing about and memorials to persons dead with AIDS, assertions of love, of worth, and of loss are universal. Some descriptions raise the religious belief of an afterlife as hope that the dead will go on living, their virtues intact for all eternity. And it is interesting that the chief value perceived in that afterlife is not typically union with god and the glory of that experience but the chance to see human friends and loved ones again, which says as much about the origin of heaven as any other account. A hope of this kind is an assertion that one cannot be alone in the universe, that there must be something at the center of being that impels human lives toward their happiness, that people cannot live with others and love them only to have them turn to dust. Not all persons, of course, share such a religious belief, and for those who do not, death is that much more a tragedy without recompense. But what consolations there may be are nevertheless found and asserted: in the time shared together, in the hope that one's struggle with AIDS will help spare others in the future or that a life's influence will continue to be felt even long after death.

This writing almost always protests that the dead with AIDS have died too early, that they have died too young with too many things left undone. Implicit in such a view is the notion that death is less an atrocity if it comes later when we are old. Perhaps aging is after all a consolation in the way it prepares us for death by withering our bodies, minds, and even our hopes. But perhaps this is the rationalization of inevitability. If senescence were something inflicted on us involuntarily by another person or caused by a communicable virus, it would be intolerable: we would condemn it outright as an immorality of the first order. Perhaps, then, we need to wonder if aging and the death associated with it are any less an atrocity because they come from nature. Perhaps we need to wonder if illness, death, and grief teach us anything that we do not already know many times over. Could it be that all death—and not only death with AIDS—is always an atrocity, and are the origins of medicine to be found here? Barring any breakthrough that could stave off aging and death, we are left of course to countenance the lives we must have. Under the circumstances in which we live the years are precious enough, writers about the unexpected dead seem to say, that not even one can be spared.

IV

For all the good intentions at work in memorializing, writing about the dead sometimes risks being sentimental self-indulgence. It is, after all, easy to find in others' death evidence of one's own good fortune and moral nobility. The effort exerted on behalf of writing may seem, moreover, ill-justified when printed pages do not take anyone out of a hospital bed. In "Reading and Writing," for example, Holleran says that he cannot imagine that anyone could read books about AIDS with pleasure. The only thing people want to read, he suggests, is the headline: CURE FOUND (12). How can one write, after all, when the suffering is so real? When all that matters is taking care of friends, starting support services, and carrying out the lab work that can bring all the misery to a hasty conclusion?

Writing is helpless, he says, because it cannot produce a cure, it cannot heal, and it cannot explain. The best writing, he predicts in *Ground Zero*, may likely turn out to be a lament that we are as flies to wanton gods killing us for their sport or a simple list of names—those who behaved well, those who behaved badly in the epidemic (11–18). Yet for all that, he acknowledges, one must continue to write if only to relieve anxiety and depression.

But there are other good reasons as well. And thus are explained the many AIDS volumes and articles on cultural criticism, social policy, legal analysis, and medical research, and all the others yet to come. This wealth of motives and forms of narrative about the sick and the dead makes it clear that writing is not always an idle extravagance. On the contrary— such writing amounts to an assurance that if death cannot be staved off, lives nevertheless may be "saved" another way. French philosopher Gabriel Marcel offered an account of testimony that is revealing here and relevant to the descriptions offered in so much writing about AIDS.[20] Testimony, in his analysis, is always subjective, bearing on an event that is unique and irrevocable: testimony always comes after. If events or lives could be reconstructed, testimony would be superfluous. But events and lives are lost, and testimony is the only way possible to preserve a sense of the worth and merit of persons: "To witness is to act as guarantor."

Thus construed, testimony is even morally obligatory inasmuch as it is an essential part of our relationships with one another, as much as honesty or fidelity. Grief and mourning are not therefore only psychological states serving cathartic resolution of pain or anguish. The open affirmation and willingness to face disbelief that define testimony are part of morality itself. Testimony is thus a judgment of worth, an estimate of loss, an acknowledgment of limitations, and, for those who remain behind, an opportunity for intimacy.[21] Testimony for the dead is not driven by a desire to overcome death, but to prevent it from eroding the meaningfulness of life. Testimony, not death, is the last word.

The capacity and worth of writing and speaking in protest or lament are not, therefore, to be undervalued; they are something, after all, other than tears writ large. It is certainly true that writing about AIDS for pleasure would be ghoulish, yet it would be worse, by several orders of magnitude, if there were no writing at all about the epidemic or the dead. The narratives about the dead with AIDS may not by themselves directly generate lab space or produce educational programs, but they have their place in the order of human needs. They have their place, whether in the form of eulogy or written narrative, in representing and interpreting the meaning of a person's presence, a presence that can remain even after death. It is not surprising therefore that these narratives typically focus on the way a person dead with AIDS held a unique role in the narrator's life (as son, friend, lover, husband), and on what those qualities were that did not deserve the end to which they came. This is why those narratives that try to summarize a person by demographics of race, occupation, and residence fail to be interesting or convincing. A testimony is something other than demographics. Neither does testimony attempt to substitute words for persons; that would be mere fetishism. Testimony is witness in front of an indifferent world about the worth and merit of persons. And thus one writes, for the world unconvinced, that someone was here and that, death notwithstanding, a presence remains.

It is not surprising that personal names loom large in all testimony of this kind, because we understand names as symbols of persons, not as summaries—so there is the emphasis to ensure that names endure, names like Peter VonLehn, Roger Horwitz, Eddie Mickler, and all the others. A memorial in the names of the dead suggests that these persons, after all, are acknowledged as a continuing presence. And thus do memorials, whatever form they take, typically insist on the primacy of names; thus is there the horror attached to mass graves. In the years following World War II, the Imperial War Graves Commission listed in page after page of the seven volumes of the *Civilian War Dead in the United Kingdom, 1939–1945* the names of civilians killed in the course of the war, many of whom were killed by bombs falling on their homes. Inside the west door of Westminster Abbey in London one of these volumes is open to display the names of some of those who died: "George Alfred Yeomans. Age 46; of 10 Troutbeck Road. Husband of Laura Rose Yeomans. 2 August 1944 at 10 Troutbeck Road." Or again, "Beryl June Yeomans. Age 15; of 10 Troutbeck Road. Daughter of George Alfred Yeomans. 2 August 1944 at 10 Troutbeck Road." Like this register of persons, the Vietnam Memorial in Washington is finally remarkable not because of its materials, form, or design but because it found room for the name of every person who died during that divisive conflict and is thus a reminder that these testimonials are not finally about art but about persons.

Jeff Nunokawa has pointed out that there is a deep cultural presumption associating male homosexuality with death, associating gay men with certain extinction.[22] A cultural tradition that defines death as an essential attribute of gay men, of course, places unique demands on writing about those who have died with AIDS. Some persons so want to distance their dead from the tradition of "deadly homosexuality" that they take pains in their memorials, even on panels in the Names Project, to state the route of infection so that it will not be assumed that the deceased was homosexually inclined. This kind of cemeterial apartheid, of course, extends the cultural presumption that some people with AIDS are and some are not "innocent" victims: there are those who develop AIDS following a blood transfusion, artificial insemination, or robust heterosexual promiscuity, as in the case of Earvin "Magic" Johnson, and then there are gay men.

It is a challenge, of course, to memorialize men who are supposed to be responsible for their own death because of their actions. It is also difficult to memorialize gay men without also invoking and reinforcing the view that homosexuality leads ineluctably to death, especially when other views of the lives of gay men are pervasively and systematically absent from the media of entertainment and education. This challenge has been met in many of the writers discussed, inasmuch as they create what Nunokawa has called alternative obituaries.[23] First-person narratives and obituaries are the primary venue for writing about those who have died with AIDS, though some experiences may have been fictionalized. This writing remains primarily the province of gay authors and readers, if only because gay authors and readers find obstacles in venues outside their control. Some newspapers, for example, will not list gay lovers in obituaries even if the relationship existed for years, even if the biological family was long since geographically and emotionally absent.[24] Gay newspapers, by contrast, routinely name surviving partners and often use the word *lover* in place of the usage preferred by some mainstream papers, *companion*. They will often mention the number of years the men spent together, and along with blood relatives, the gay newspapers may also cite the friends who from day to day became a gay man's family. By themselves, of course, testimonials written for gay men will not rectify larger cultural views that gay identity is necessarily doomed, but they do offer the opportunity for gay men to speak with their own voice about the meaning, their meaning of their lives and death.

While struggle about public representations of gay men continues even in regard to their obituaries, it is characteristic nevertheless of all obituaries, regardless of their policies about survivors, to find what kind word there is to say of the dead, whether he or she is the chairman of a university academic department, a Roman Catholic priest, a bartender, or a librarian. As a matter of preserving the meaning of lives, testimony in fiction, eulogy, and monument is a moral act. It is the moral heart of writing about the epidemic. It is the essence of the deeply personal Names Project. It is an essential part of any moral analysis of the epidemic. It is an important way to challenge the public mythology about promiscuous, fast-track, unloving gay men. The grief of the epidemic and the incentive to memorialize are no mere biological reflexes—they are an assertion against the leveling effect of death that persons are not replaceable, that death does not nullify presence. They can also be important, if less commonly used, vehicles of moral wisdom and social criticism.

In *Borrowed Time*, the metaphor Monette invokes to represent the experience of AIDS is that of living on the moon. But it is clear that Monette does not intend the moon as the faithful, consoling light of the night sky, the Roman patroness of the hunt. He invokes the moon as a barren and lifeless expanse inhospitable to human hope and love (69, 83, 72). Only those who know the epidemic firsthand can know what this desolation is like, Monette says; those who live in the lush expanse of good health cannot appreciate what hopes and fears are necessary there, cannot appreciate the rarity of abundant health. It is no wonder, then, that Monette finally blurts out to a friend: "I'm not going to be around long myself, and I don't want to talk to people without AIDS anymore" (312).

But in their writings, Monette and all the others mentioned here *do* talk to people without AIDS. Indeed, they will be talking to people with and without AIDS so long as their writing endures. They do so because the failure to testify would amount to betrayal, would be continuous in meaning with the absurdity of the epidemic. The personal narratives of those dead and dying of AIDS may have ultimate designs on social reformation and medical advance, but they all begin as the story of an individual life, an individual person. This kind of narrative is nothing so much as a will to preserve in ink and paper the virtues of persons who are lost in the more evanescent medium of flesh. It is what way there is to resist the absurdity of suffering and death. To be sure, it is not the only form of discourse required to speak against the absurdities of suffering and death whose origins belong ultimately in political and social judgments, but it is a necessary voice and one that has moral import even where it reveals only the homely truths that we deserve better than we get, that we mourn more than the world can know, that we are each other's only refuge.

NOTES

Epigraph from W. H. Auden, "Their Lonely Betters," in Edward Mendelson, ed., *Collected Poems* (New York: Random House, 1976), p. 209.

1. Richard Hall, "Gay Fiction Comes Home," *New York Times Book Review*, June 19, 1988, p. 1. For a leap into the sea, see Fritz Peters, *Finistère* (New York: New American Library, 1985).

2. See David Leavitt, *Family Dancing* (New York: Knopf, 1984); *The Lost Language of Cranes* (New York: Knopf, 1986); *Equal Affections* (New York: Weidenfeld and Nicolson,

1989); Robert Ferro, *The Family of Max Desir* (New York: Dutton, 1983); Armistead Maupin, *Babycakes* (New York: Harper & Row, 1984); *Significant Others* (New York: Perennial, 1987); and Stephen McCauley, *Object of My Affection* (New York: Simon and Schuster, 1987).

3. Douglas Crimp, "How to Have Promiscuity in an Epidemic," in Douglas Crimp, ed., *AIDS: Cultural Analysis/Cultural Activism* (Cambridge, Mass: MIT Press, 1988), p. 240; emphasis in the original.

4. See Douglas Crimp, "Mourning and Militancy," *October* 51 (1989):3–18.

5. See Richard Mohr, "Text(ile): Reading The Names Project Quilt," in *Gay Ideas: Outing and Other Controversies* (Boston: Beacon, forthcoming).

6. Barbara Peabody, *The Screaming Room* (San Diego: Oak Tree Publications, 1986). Where subsequent references to this work are contextually clear, page numbers will be cited in the text.

7. Andrew Holleran, *Dancer from the Dance* (New York: Morrow, 1978); see also Andrew Holleran, *Nights in Aruba* (New York: New American Library, 1983).

8. Andrew Holleran, "Circles," *Christopher Street* no. 103 (1986):7–10.

9. Andrew Holleran, "Ernie's Funeral," *Christopher Street* no. 108 (1988):7–11.

10. Andrew Holleran, *Ground Zero* (New York: Morrow, 1989). Where subsequent references to this work are contextually clear, page numbers will be cited in the text.

11. Holleran, *Ground Zero*, pp. 29–36.

12. Elizabeth Cox, *Thanksgiving* (New York: Harper & Row, 1990).

13. Andrew Holleran, "Reading and Writing," *Christopher Street*, 115 (1987):5–7.

14. Paul Monette, *Borrowed Time* (New York: Harcourt Brace Jovanovich, 1988). Where subsequent references to this work are contextually clear, page numbers will be cited in the text.

15. Ines Rider and Patricia Ruppelt, eds., *AIDS: The Women* (San Francisco: Cleis, 1988), pp. 31–35.

16. Paul Monette, *Love Alone: Eighteen Elegies for Rog* (New York: St. Martin's, 1988).

17. "In Loving Memory of Jon B. Hettwer," *PWA Coalition Newsline* 67 (July 1991): 47.

18. Cox, *Thanksgiving*, p. 76.

19. Cindy Ruskin, Matt Herron, and Deborah Zemke, *The Quilt: Stories from the Names Project* (New York: Pocket Books, 1988).

20. Gabriel Marcel, *The Philosophy of Existentialism* (Secaucus, N.J.: Citadel Press, 1956), pp. 91–103.

21. See Robert C. Solomon, *The Passions* (Notre Dame, Ind.: University of Notre Dame Press, 1976), pp. 359–60.

22. Jeff Nunokawa, "'All the Sad Young Men': AIDS and the Work of Mourning," *Yale Journal of Criticism* 4 (1991):1–13.

23. Ibid., p. 9.

24. Though it refused to do so for a very long time, the *New York Times* will now name lovers in obituaries. At the death of Enno Poersch, a cofounder of the Gay Men's Health Crisis, the newspaper reported, for example, "He is survived by his parents, Herbert and Ingeborg Poersch, and a brother, Ranier, all of Portland, Oregon. His companion was Michael Hatoff of Manhattan." See "Enno Poersch, 45, Dies; AIDS Group Founder," *New York Times*, May 10, 1990, p. B11.

Annotated Bibliography of AIDS Literature, 1982–91

Franklin Brooks and Timothy F. Murphy

Fiction

Barnett, Allen. *The Body and Its Dangers*. New York: St. Martin's, 1990. Some stories, including "Philostorgy, Now Obscure" and "The Time as It Knows Us," follow persons with AIDS, friends, and family through their experiences.

Barrow, John. "Killing the Pope." *Christopher Street* no. 110 (1987):51–57. A visitor to the Vatican wonders whether he should kill the pope, who sees homosexuality as a sin and AIDS as its consequence.

Barrus, Tim. *Genocide: The Anthology*. Stamford, Conn.: Knights Press, 1989. A futuristic consideration of repressive responses to the epidemic.

——. "Life Sucks, or Ernest Hemingway Never Slept Here." In George Stambolian, ed., *Men on Men 2*, pp. 255–274. New York: New American Library, 1988. A story set in Key West: "This is the place where many of my friends are dying. Not gracefully. None of them are going gently into that good night."

Beard, J. "The Hospital Journal." *James White Review* 3 (1986):11–13. A narrative in the first person about the miseries of a hospital stay and the consolations taken in the man in the next bed and in the nurse who offers a back rub.

Beattie, Ann. "Second Question." *The New Yorker*, June 10, 1991, pp. 38–44. A straight woman tells of her life with Richard, who is dying with AIDS, and Richard's former lover, who has never been tested for HIV.

Bishop, Michael. *Unicorn Mountain*. New York: Arbor House, 1988. A ranch in the mountains of Colorado shelters a herd of unicorns afflicted with a mysterious, fatal disease and human beings threatened by AIDS (*Lambda Rising*).

Borgman, C. F. *River Road*. New York: Plume, 1988. Writer/performance artist Eugene Goessler experiences himself shunned because of the epidemic, but in an expression of love submits to unprotected sex with his lover.

Bram, Christopher. *In Memory of Angel Clare*. New York: Fine, 1988. An ably told novel about a circle of friends coping with the unlikable lover of their friend Angel Clare, who died with AIDS a year earlier.

Bryan, Jed A. *A Cry in the Desert*. Austin, Tex.: Banned Books, 1987. "Follows the beginnings of an effort to control the spread of AIDS by quarantining a Nevada town" (*Publishers Weekly*).

Bryant, Dorothy. *A Day in San Francisco*. Berkeley: Ata Books, 1982. The occurrence of sexually transmitted diseases in the gay male community destroys a mother's confidence in her son's life-style on Gay Pride Day, 1980. A presage of the epidemic.

Buck, Charles H. *The Master Cure*. New York: Jove, 1989. A futuristic depiction of a society beset by another epidemic, as a figure for AIDS.

Burrell, Walter Rico. "The Scarlet Letter Revisited; A Very Different AIDS Story." *James White Review* 7 (1990):3–6. A black man tells in diary form about his relations with his physician and his father.

Calhoun, Jackie. *Lifestyles*. New York: Naiad, 1990. This novel tells the story of Kate, Kate's brother, and Kate's lesbian lover. It recounts both the coming out of recently divorced Kate, her reconciliation with her gay brother Gordie, and her attendance as he dies with AIDS.

Cameron, Lindsley. *The Prospect of Detachment*. New York: St. Martin's, 1990. Short stories. "The Angel of Death" details a dispute over the fate of a statue sculpted by a woman whose husband has died with AIDS. In "Gospel for a Proud Sunday," "Jesus" cures one waiter of AIDS but is decked by an angry companion for letting all the others suffer and die.

Cashorali, Paul. "The Ride Home." In George Stambolian, ed., *Men on Men 3*, pp. 298–314. New York: Plume, 1990. Two Latinos seek enlightenment in *Santeria*, *orishas*, and Catholic saints. Their Anglo partners share only a prospect of death and their alienation in this culture. One couple's self-destructiveness proves unworthy of *Santeria*; the second finds strength in mutual faithfulness.

Champagne, John. *The Blue Lady's Hands*. Secaucus, N.J.: Stuart, 1988. *Booklist* says this is "the first gay novel that is truly post-AIDS in consciousness." Its characters explore the growth and meaning of love between two men now that AIDS is an established, inevitable reality.

Chappell, Helen. *Acts of Love*. New York: Pocket Books, 1989. "A failed screenwriter dying of AIDS intends to commit suicide at a twentieth college reunion, reminiscent of *The Big Chill*" (*Publishers Weekly*).

Chiodo, Andrew. "Autumn Chill." *Christopher Street*, no. 116 (1987):54–59. Manhattan's nights, drugs, and men now appear, in the epidemic, as dangers, not thrills.

———. "Blaze." *Christopher Street*, no. 103 (1986):42–46. Twelve-year-old Justin learns of the death of his neighbor, Blaze, when Jack comes to make arrangements for the funeral.

Cohen, Elizabeth. "Poison." *Christopher Street*, no. 155 (1991):35–36. A woman finds that her boyfriend insists on an HIV test.

Cohen, Jaffe. "Just Got Off the Phone with Charlie." *James White Review* 7 (1990):14, 15, 7. [Yes, this is correct.] A friend copes with Charlie's diagnosis of AIDS, first writing in a diary, then after Charlie's death by writing diary entries as if they were letters to him.

Cook, Robin. *Godplayer*. New York: Putnam's Sons, 1983. Gay men, including one with AIDS, are among the victims of a murderous physician in a Boston teaching hospital.

Curzon, Daniel. *The World Can Break Your Heart*. Stamford, Conn.: Knights, 1984. Ben grows up and marries in a blue-collar, straight world. Beside being a story of his coming out, this novel is charged with the bitter irony of AIDS.

D'Allesandro, Sam. "Nothing Every Just Disappears." In George Stambolian, ed., *Men on Men*, pp. 126–32. New York: New American Library, 1986. A story about the beginning of a relationship and the loss of a lover to AIDS.

Davis, Christopher. *The Boys in the Bars*. Stamford, Conn.: Knights, 1989. A collection of short stories, many of them previously printed elsewhere, in which AIDS makes its influence felt in relationships on Fire Island, New York, in a period from the late 1970s to "beyond the present."

——. *Valley of the Shadow*. New York: St Martin's, 1988. A young man with AIDS remembers his sentimental and sexual education in the New York City of the 1970s and 1980s and a lover who has died.

Dedrick, Lucas. "The Beach." *James White Review* 7 (1990):14. A friend sneaks Armand, dying with AIDS, out of the hospital for an excursion to the beach.

Define, M. A. "You Can Say What You Want I'm Not Walking Out." *Christopher Street*, no. 113 (1987):56–59. Friends in Greenwich Village on a winter Tuesday evening feel the effects of the epidemic in their relationships and life choices.

Delany, Samuel R. "The Tales of Plagues and Carnivals." In *Flight from Neveryon*. New York: Bantam, 1985. AIDS-inspired science fiction chronicles the apocalypse in a city like New York.

Diamon, N. A. *Castro Street Memories*. San Francisco: Persona, 1988. This novel follows the changes in the life of George Pappas at the same time that it traces the transformation from the social innocence of the 1970s to the sobering realities of the 1980s.

Dunne, Dominick. *People Like Us*. New York: Crown, 1988. In what is perhaps the most melodramatic scene in all of AIDS fiction, a Park Avenue mother rejects her AIDS-stricken son. Later he and his lover take a suitable revenge.

Duplechan, Larry. *Tangled up in Blue*. New York: St Martin's, 1989. California is the setting for this story of a pregnant woman, her bisexual husband, and his lover—their best friend—who has ARC.

Exander, Max. *Lovesex*. Boston: Alyson, 1986. An effort to represent the erotic possibilities in "safe sex."

——. *Safestud*. Boston: Alyson, 1985. The diary of a man first resisting then discovering the rewards of safe sex.

Fast, Howard. *Dinner Party*. New York: Houghton Mifflin, 1987. AIDS is the unexpected guest when a senator entertains the secretary of state and the senator's son and his black lover come home from Harvard Law School.

Feinberg, David B. "The Age of Anxiety." In George Stambolian, ed., *Men on Men 2*, pp. 322–37. New York: New American Library, 1988. An "existentialist" copes when his lover with AIDS plans to move to San Francisco.

——. "Egg Paranoia." *James White Review* 4 (1987):12–13. Gay urban professional sex takes place as if the partners were between glass.

——. *Eighty-sixed*. New York: Viking/Penguin, 1989. This first novel by a New York mathematician records the changes in gay life-styles precipitated by AIDS in monthly diarylike reports between 1980 and 1986.

Ferrell, Anderson, "Why People Get Cancer." In George Stambolian, ed., *Men on Men 2*, pp. 211–23. New York: Plume, 1988. Two men visit hospitals to explain to patients that disease is divine punishment for sin.

Ferro, Robert. *Second Son*. New York: Crown, 1988; Plume, 1989. Death and financial collapse destroy an affluent Philadelphia family's security while its second son faces the fact that he and a new lover have AIDS.

Fox, John. "Choice." In George Stambolian, ed., *Men on Men*, pp. 19–36. New York: New

American Library, 1986. The risk of AIDS is part of a gay son's life that is un-acknowledged by his family and that drives him away from relationships.

Graham, Clayton R. *Tweeds*. New York: Knights, 1987. Loving someone with AIDS forces a young man to come out and accept responsibility in their relationship.

Groff, David. "Labor Day." *Christopher Street*, no. 119 (1988):36–43. A father cares for his son with AIDS, a son whom he says he doesn't love.

Hall, Brian. *The Dreamers*. New York: Harper and Row, 1988. In Vienna an HIV-positive American graduate student "becomes involved in a raunchily sexual and tempestuous relationship" with a "demanding and suicidal" woman (*Publishers Weekly*).

Hall, Richard. "Avery Milbanke Day." *James White Review* 6 (1989):12–15. Author Avery Milbanke is honored by small Midlothian College while his lover, Coleman, is dying.

———. "A Faustian Bargain." *James White Review* 3 (1986):11–13. In the throes of choosing between marriage and men, a thirty-year-old musician encounters the rituals of safe sex and the difficulty of making love to the surface of a body.

Hallasy, Paul. *New York Trilogy*. New York: Downtown, 1990. AIDS, or the narrator's awareness of it, is an undercurrent in all these stories, but its unavoidable, ominous presence most fully permeates "Love and Sex."

Hansen, Joseph. *Early Graves*. New York: Mysterious, 1987. David Brandstetter, Hansen's gay Los Angeles insurance investigator, tackles the murder of a crooked bisexual land developer whose death seems to be the latest in a series involving men with AIDS.

Haule, Robert. "Blond Dog." In George Stambolian, ed., *Men on Men 3*, pp. 48–70. New York: Plume, 1990. The *axis mundi* in a San Francisco flower bed reunites three friends with their totemic selves, the forest, and the desert. A PWA who dies with a brain tumor is the satyr, a foul-mouthed mimic, tap dancer, beautician, and decorator. His artifices loosen the present world's grip on their spirits.

Hayes, Mary-Rose. *Amethyst*. New York: Dutton, 1989. *Publishers Weekly* calls this an "altogether standard potboiler." Its motifs are commonplaces of AIDS fiction: an unfaithful husband who is homosexual, a "manipulative bisexual," and a "gratuitous, moralistic use of AIDS," in a "sordid ending."

Hoctel, Patrick. "Slave of Babylon." *James White Review* 4 (1986):12–13. A discovery of an obituary reporting the death of a former lover.

Hoffman, Alice. *At Risk*. New York: Putnam's Sons, 1988. Amanda is an eleven-year-old gymnast dying of AIDS, contracted from a blood transfusion; this novel focuses on her family's helplessness in a storybook Cape Anne town.

Holleran, Andrew. "Friends at Evening." In George Stambolian, ed., *Men on Men*, pp. 88–113. New York: New American Library, 1986. In one of the most finely crafted stories about the experience of AIDS, a group of friends discusses the meaning of the epidemic while en route to a funeral.

———. "Homosexuality, Part Two." *Christopher Street*, no. 119 (1988):4–7. A door-to-door salesman pitches pills that control the loneliness that has followed both the epidemic and the coming of age.

———. "A House Divided." In Michael Denneny, Charles Ortleb, and Thomas Steele, eds., *First Love/Last Love*, pp. 216–26. New York: Putnam's Sons, 1985. Sarah takes on the role of conscience for her gay friends.

———. "How to Cruise Outer Space." *Christopher Street*, no. 100 (1986):13–16. Permanently destined to orbit the earth, Homosexual 1,346,794 corresponds with a companion across the galaxies, telling about the coming of the epidemic and the expulsion of hated groups from Earth.

———. "The Last Train from Cold Spring, NY." *Christopher Street*, no. 106 (1986):6–10. An ironic tour of an institute that teaches courses in safe sex.

———. "Lights in the Valley." In George Stambolian, ed., *Men on Men 3*, pp. 321–39. New York: Plume, 1990. An Ohio landscape of hills, valleys, chasms, and ravines depicts the disintegration of one man's life. AIDS-related deaths, a father's stroke, a mother's broken spine, accident victims, and paralysis divide his world into the sick and the well, who care and grieve. The syllables of "together" fall apart in a stutter.

———. *Nights in Aruba*. New York: Morrow, 1983. A forty-year-old New Yorker, with aging parents and friends threatened by AIDS, remembers his childhood, adolescence, and military service in Germany.

———. "Ties." In Michael Denneny, Charles Ortleb, and Thomas Steele, eds., *First Love/Last Love*, pp. 206–15. New York: Putnam's Sons, 1985. At a cafe after a funeral, one man grasps the ties of his friends, as if to hold them all together.

Houston, Bo. "This is Not That." *Christopher Street*, no. 155 (1991):29–33. Though her son has come home with AIDS, a mother still finds in him more to admire than in her conventional daughter.

Humphries, Scott. "Tinky." In Charles Jurrist, ed., *Shadows of Love*, pp. 99–110. Boston: Alyson, 1988. A woman scatters the ashes of her friend after his death.

Indiana, Gary. *Horse Crazy*. New York: Grove, 1989. "No work of fiction has treated sexual relationships in the era of AIDS more satisfyingly and authentically than *Horse Crazy*, poet and journalist Gary Indiana's first novel. It portrays a New York writer's growing obsession with a beautiful and paranoid ex-heroin addict seven years younger than himself" (*Dare*).

Innaurato, Albert. "Solidarity." In George Stambolian, ed., *Men on Men 2*, pp. 87–118. New York: New American Library, 1988. Fat New York opera queens, rejected by both gays and straights, show more compassion than anyone else to people with AIDS in this retelling of the Good Samaritan story.

Jennings, Bud. "Eric Back in Boston." *Christopher Street*, no. 129 (1988):22–36. Roommates Murdoc and Stan take Eric into their apartment after his diagnosis with AIDS.

Johnson, Toby. *Plague: A Novel about Healing*. Boston: Alyson, 1987. This novel considers AIDS in the context of a government plot, a religious crusade, a detective story, and a spiritual quest, linking the lives of four men and a woman.

Kerr, M. E. *Night Kites*. New York: Harper and Row, 1986. This young adult novel concerns a boy, his brother who has AIDS, and their family's reaction to the disease.

Klass, Perri. *Other Women's Children*. New York: Random House, 1990. In this story, a young physician tends a child with AIDS through his hospital care, family difficulties, and eventual death.

Lawrence, Sean. "The New York Chronicle." *Christopher Street*, no. 123 (1988):48–51. A young gay man's brother covers the AIDS epidemic for a major New York paper.

LaPierre, Dominique. *Beyond Love*. New York: Warner Books, 1991. "The epic story of doctors and scientists, sisters and patients, heroes and dreamers, fighting the greatest plague of our time: AIDS" (*Lambda Book Report*).

Leavitt, David. *Equal Affections*. New York: Harper and Row, 1989. Though not a novel about experiences with AIDS, this story of a family is remarkable in that its gay characters can "cheat" on one another through a computer communication network, practicing the safest sex of all.

———. *A Place I've Never Been*. New York: Viking, 1990. The story "Dedicated" brings us Celia and Nathan, who look back at their lives in light of the epidemic. In "Gravity" a mother confronts the sorrow she feels caring for a son with AIDS.

Lemon, Brendan. "Female Trouble." *Christopher Street*, no. 116 (1987):48–52. Because of the dangers of AIDS, a gay man attempts to date women.

———. "Positive Results." *Christopher Street*, no. 114 (1987):22–24. Fred dies quickly with AIDS, leaving behind a daughter and friend.

Mains, Geoff. *Gentle Warriors*. Stamford, Conn.: Knights Press, 1989. A group of gay men plot the assassination of the president in retaliation for government inaction against the AIDS epidemic.

Mars-Jones, Adam. See Edmund White.

Martin, Herbert Woodward. "The Last Days of William Short." *James White Review* 6 (1988):8–9. Willie Short, in the hospital following a gunshot wound, is diagnosed as having an HIV infection.

Martin, Kenneth. *Billy's Brother*. London: GMP Publishers, 1989. His brother goes to San Francisco to investigate Billy's death and looks for clues in the AIDS support and activist groups.

Maso, Carole. *The Art Lover*. San Francisco: North Point, 1990. Caroline returns to New York and renews an old, close friendship with Steven, who is dying with AIDS. Imposed on this story is Maso's own first-person account of the loss of her own friend.

Matousek, Mark. "The Last Song." *Christopher Street*, no. 112 (1987):30–34. On a plane to Rome, where he must tell his lover that he has AIDS, an attorney talks with an elderly woman.

Maupin, Armistead. *Sure of You*. New York: Harper and Row, 1989. Michael sums up the San Francisco AIDS experience this way: "My mother gave me a new address book last Christmas. I haven't written in it yet, because I can't make myself leave out the people who are dead. I can't even cross out their names. There's one on every page. All the H's are gone except you."

Mayes, Sharon. *Immune*. New York: New Rivers, 1987. Not even a woman's research in immunology and infectious disease can protect her from AIDS or prevent her from spreading it when drugs and group sex destroy her self-control.

McBain, Ed. *The House That Jack Built*. New York: Holt, 1988. This Matthew Hope mystery features the murder of Jonathan Parrish, a gay man with AIDS, in the Florida Keys.

McFarland, Dennis. "Nothing to Ask For." *The New Yorker* (September 25, 1989):55–62. A straight friend takes care of Mack (and his lover Lester) in the way Mack once helped him with his alcoholism.

McGehee, Peter. *Boys Like Us*. New York: St. Martin's, 1991. The narrator traces the effects of the epidemic on his circle of friends and family.

———. "Never Be Famous." *James White Review* 5 (1988):11. A reflection on seeing a familiar face in a *Newsweek* photo spread of persons dead with AIDS.

———. "Sex and Love." *James White Review* 4 (1987):6–7. How the epidemic affects sex and love in Canada.

McKague, Thomas R. "Testimony." *James White Review* 4 (1987):6. From his hospital bed, a twenty-six-year-old man silently looks at visitors and the stars.

Micklowitz, Gloria D. *Good-bye, Tomorrow*. New York: Delacorte, 1987. A novel for adolescents that explores the emotions of a high school senior who develops ARC after a blood transfusion.

Mitchell, Larry. *My Life as a Mole*. New York: Calamus, 1988. "White Walls" follows the story of Mark's death in Atlanta with his family living in Maine.

Moffett, Judith. "Tiny Tango." *Isaac Asimov: Science Fiction* (February 1989):16–65. A biologist with AIDS chronicles the years from 1985 to beyond 2000 and reaffirms her life with the help of her research in Mendelian genetics, mutants, virus-immune plants, nuclear disaster ETs, and a boy named Eric.

Monette, Paul. *Afterlife*. New York: Crown, 1990. A circle of AIDS widowers come to grips with sickness, death, grief, anger, and the possibility of commitment in the aftermath of AIDS.

———. *Halfway Home*. New York: Crown, 1991. Tom Shaheen, aka "Miss Jesus," is an antireligious performance artist and PWA who unexpectedly saves his brother and family from violent criminals. Rebirth and reconciliation dissipate several generations of hatred and anger, and California grants them all a new life of their choice.

Moore, Patrick. *This Every Night*. New York: Amethyst, 1990. Written by a member of ACT UP, this story covers the life of a young man in New York and his moral transformation from hedonist to activist.

Mordden, Ethan. "The Dinner Party." *Christopher Street*, no. 104 (1986):10–16. Cliff, who has AIDS, sees his summer with friends at the Pines as punctuation to the sentence Stonewall began and wonders who will remain to remember it all.

———. *Everyone Loves You: Further Adventures in Gay Manhattan*. New York: St. Martin's, 1988. AIDS is part of the life in Manhattan, Woodstock, Fire Island, and London evoked in these stories narrated by middle-aged Bud.

Murphy, Haughton. *Murder Keeps a Secret*. New York: Simon and Schuster, 1989. "In this fourth and latest in a mystery series featuring Reuben Frost, the 77-year-old head of a Wall Street firm, the crucial clue is provided by the victim's assistant, who is dying of AIDS" (*Dare*).

Musto, Michael. *Manhattan on the Rocks*. New York: Holt, 1989. New York and its clubs are the background against which the effects of AIDS are presented.

Neval, Lucia. "Close." *The New Yorker* (November 7, 1988):36–39. Flying to her gay brother's funeral in their Indiana hometown, a New York social worker, specializing in teenage suicide, weighs the demands of family and her brother's love affair and death with AIDS.

Persky, Stan. *Buddy's: Meditations on Desire*. Vancouver: New Star Books, 1989. Centered on the life of a bar, this volume offers a view on how the plague has and has not changed the nature of desire.

Platt, Richard and Orah. *Letting Blood*. New York: St. Martin's, 1989. The husband-and-wife detective team in this medical mystery are physicians, as are the book's authors. The murders are traced to a Philadelphia hospital and to its blood supply, which is contaminated with HIV (*Publishers Weekly*).

Preston, John, ed. *Hot Living: Erotic Stories About Safer Sex*. Boston: Alyson, 1985. A collection of sixteen stories in which safer sex is practiced.

Puccia, Joseph. *The Holy Spirit Dance Club*. New York; Liberty, 1988. A novel that follows the beginning of the epidemic in the dance and drug culture of Manhattan.

Puckett, Andrew. *Bloodstains*. Garden City, N.Y.: Doubleday/Crime Club, 1989. An inquiry into crimes at an English blood transfusion center is complicated by the fact that the investigator's hemophiliac brother has AIDS.

Purdy, James. *Garments the Living Wear*. San Francisco: City Light Books, 1989. In this "transvestite-transsexual comedy of gay mannerism," AIDS is "the Pest" that complicates the life of its New York characters, united in theatricals and Pentecostal evangelism (*New York Times*).

Real, Philip. "Stronger and Stronger." *James White Review* 5 (1988):1. A narrative in the first person describing the puzzlement, public perception, and experience of AIDS.

Redon, Joel. *Bloodstream*. Stamford, Conn.: Knights, 1988. The *New York Times* calls this "a semi-autobiographical four-month slice of life as experienced by a young AIDS victim," paying particular attention to drug treatments and the love he seeks with family and another person with AIDS.

Reed, Paul. *Facing It: A Novel of AIDS*. San Francisco: Gay Sunshine, 1984. This novel chronicles the last four seasons of a man with AIDS and covers the early days of public awareness and medical research concerning the disease.

——. *Longing*. Berkeley: Celestial Arts, 1988. A coming-out novel set in San Francisco in the early 1980s when AIDS became a fact of life.

Rees, David. *Letters to Dorothy*. Exeter: Third House, 1991. Short stories and essays about having AIDS, the loss of friends, and the burdens of the epidemic.

——. *The Wrong Apple*. Stamford, Conn.: Knights, 1988. The protagonist wonders whether to get tested, what the test means, and what to do when the results aren't the ones you want. *Lambda Rising Book Report* calls this novel "an all too realistic account of such a fear-inspiring ordeal."

Rickets, Wendell. "Wasps." *James White Review* 7 (1989):14–15. Along with mugging, cancer, diabetes, aging, and the summer heat, AIDS is discussed in a long, rambling conversation.

Rosario, John. "Lovers Anonymous." *James White Review* 7 (1989):8–9. Christopher joins a support group to overcome his "addiction" to lust and refuses to cruise or linger at a sex bar.

Royle, Dave. *Pleasing the Punters*. Exeter: Third House, 1990. Stories about the "risk of relationships at a time when Aids is more than four letters on a poster," when candles used in romance are left over from AIDS vigils.

Rubin, Martin. *The Boiled Frog Syndrome*. Boston: Alyson, 1987. This leather-sex novel exploits the Inquisition, the Spanish Civil War, the Third Reich, the Holocaust, and AIDS to give plausibility to its tale of a fascist, homophobic America in the near future.

Rudy, Sam. "Sheet Music." *James White Review* 6 (1989):8–9. Harlan Miller falls in love with Ricky Hoover who, with AIDS, has moved back to his hometown from New York City.

Rule, Jane. *Memory Board*. New York: Naiad, 1987. A novel of the reunion of David with his twin sister, Diana, from whom he had been estranged by reason of his wife's disapproval of her lesbianism. After the wife's death, Diana becomes involved with the care of a young man with AIDS.

Schulman, Sarah. *People in Trouble*. New York: Dutton, 1990. Kate, married to Peter, finds herself involved in a sexual relationship with Molly. The drama of these relationships is set against a backdrop of the social problems (especially homelessness and AIDS) that exist even as American society continues its blind pursuit of wealth.

Sontag, Susan. "The Way We Live Now." *The New Yorker* (November 24, 1986):42–51. A man dying of AIDS is at the center of all the talk that is the fabric of this experimental narrative, some of the finest writing yet done about reaction to the disease.

Spinrad, Norman. "Journals of the Plague Years." In Lou Aronica and Shawna McCarthy, eds., *Full Spectrum*. (New York: Bantam Spectra, 1988), pp. 324–99. Spinrad's short story in this science fiction anthology is "rude, erotic." (*Publisher's Weekly*)

Stephens, Jack. *Triangulation*. New York: Crown, 1989. In this novel, AIDS structures the relationships of a Baltimore physician.

Turnbull, Peter. *Two Way Cut*. New York: St. Martin's, 1988. A woman dying of AIDS is one element in this murder mystery set in Glasgow featuring the law enforcers of the P. Division.

Uyemoto, Holly. *Rebel without a Clue*. New York: Crown, 1989. AIDS is presented in this novel against the backdrop of Hollywood money, sex, and drugs.

Veigner, Matias. "Twilights of the Gods." In George Stambolian, ed., *Men on Men 3*, pp. 237–47. New York: Plume, 1990. In this farcical meetings of minds, Rock Hudson, Michel Foucault, and a penniless Roy Cohn spend their last days together in a Paris clinic. Beauty and truth's mutual attraction and Frenchmen and Americans' fascination with each other make an outsider of Cohn. Finally compassion grants all wishes, even his.

Verghese, Abraham. "Lilacs." *The New Yorker* (October 14, 1991):53–58. A PWA considers the nature of his life and death.

Warburton, Richard. "Disappearances." *Christopher Street* no. 132 (1989):35–42. Mrs. Millweed warns the apartment building manager, Becky, that a gay tenant has been playing with Becky's son, and the man might, you know, have AIDS.

Warmbold, Jean. *June Mail*. Sag Harbor, N.Y.: Permanent, 1986; New York: Berkeley Publishing Group (Jove), 1988. *Publishers Weekly* calls this "a mystery novel dealing with the origin and epidemiology of the AIDS virus and its possible link to genetic engineering and biological research."

Weir, John. *The Irreversible Decline of Eddie Socket*. New York: Harper and Row, 1989. How the AIDS crisis has affected the lives and loves of two very different generations of gay men.

Weltner, Peter. "Beachside Entries." *James White Review* 6 (1988):11. What if desire could resurrect each name? "Russell has just stepped off the bus or Steve barged in dripping from the shower. Alex stands there eagerly knocking on the door."

White, Edmund. "An Oracle." In George Stambolian, ed., *Men on Men*, pp. 331–69. New York: New American Library, 1986. After his lover's death, Ray travels to Greece, where he takes up with a young hustler who counsels him in surprising words.

White, Edmund and Adam Mars-Jones. *The Darker Proof: Stories from a Crisis*. New York: NAL/Plume, 1988. Four stories by Mars-Jones and three by White in which the toll of AIDS is measured.

Wiley, Christopher. "Slippers." *James White Review* 7 (1987):12. An employee of the National Museum of American History steals Judy Garland's *Wizard of Oz* ruby slippers to show to his friend who is hospitalized with AIDS.

Wolfe, Tom. *The Bonfire of the Vanities*. New York: Farrar Straus Giroux, 1987; Bantam, 1988. In a central episode of Wolfe's novel, Lord Buffing, an English poet dying of AIDS, tells the story of "The Masque of the Red Death" to bewildered, overfed guests at a lavish New York dinner party.

Poetry

Baysans, Greg. "All I Dare Say, or: Another AIDS Poem." *James White Review* 3 (1986):10. An alarum on the ways the threats of AIDS increase without any obvious way to contain them.

Boucheron, Robert. *Epitaphs for the Plague Dead*. New York: Ursus, 1985. Poetry about many aspects of the epidemic.

——. "Pavane pour les bains défunts." *James White Review* 3 (1986):9. Wondering what the future holds now that the past has been denied.

Butkie, Joseph. "With AIDS." *James White Review* 5 (1987):10. AIDS as the work of voodoo.

Cunningham, Tom. "The Third Disaster." *James White Review* 6 (1989):11. An AIDS death as the last of the disasters that always seem to come in threes.

Curtis, Rex. "Puzzle of Foreclosure." *James White Review* 7 (1990):13. A study in the epidemic as if it were the onslaught of an enemy campaign.

Gunn, Thom. "Lament." *Christopher Street*, no. 109 (1987):53–55. A description of the sickness, hospitalization, and death of a friend.

Hadas, Rachel. *Unending Dialogue: Voices from an AIDS Poetry Workshop.* New York: Faber and Faber, 1991. This volume reports the experiences of people affected by AIDS as expressed in poetry.

Hershey, Christopher. "While We Waited in the Free World." *James White Review* 7 (1989):10. A consideration, from the point of view of the uninsured, of the costs of AIDS care.

Kelly, Thomas. "A Letter to the Boys in the 24th Century." *Christopher Street*, no. 109 (1987):63. A mocking tribute to the cleansing effects of AIDS.

Kirby, Jeff. "Untitled." *James White Review* 4 (1987):9. A sardonic account of how AIDS began.

Klein, Michael. "Naming the Elements." *James White Review* 5 (1988):10. The names of the AIDS dead take their place among the elements.

Klein, Michael, ed. *Poets for Life: Seventy-six Poets Respond to AIDS.* New York: Crown, 1989. Conceived as a verbal equivalent of the Names Project Quilt, this volume collects poetry that represents the experiences of the epidemic.

Koestenbaum, Wayne. "Dog Bite." *Ontario Review* (1987–88):83–88. A dog bite functions as a figure for AIDS and sexual infection.

Lassell, Michael. "Surviving." *James White Review* 7 (1989):10. A friend's death with AIDS is seen against the backdrop of other trials of urban life.

Lawrence, Sean. "The Truth about AIDS." *Christopher Street*, no. 107 (1987):59. Boiling blood as a metaphor for anger against the "official truths" about AIDS.

Liu, John. "My Resolution with AIDS by a PWA." *Christopher Street*, no. 114 (1987):25. Rhyming verse ranging across a breadth of emotions in the wake of AIDS.

Lynch, Michael. *These Waves of Dying Friends.* New York: Contact II Publications, 1989. Ten poems that memorialize and celebrate friends: "by turns elegiac, witty, celebratory, but always precisely beautiful in image and intonation" (Richard Hall).

Merritt, James W. "The Suddenness of Symptoms." *James White Review* 6 (1989):11. A characterization of fear in the epidemic.

Meyer, Douglas. "The Test." *James White Review* 6 (1989):1. A pondering of the HIV antibody test.

Mills, Stephen R. "Rending of AIDS." *James White Review* 3, 4 (1986):9. A witnessing of the agonies of AIDS.

Monette, Paul. *Love Alone: Eighteen Elegies for Rog.* New York: St. Martin's, 1988. Poetry that recounts Monette's relation with Rog Horwitz and the devastation of the epidemic.

Morse, Carl. "Couplets and Envoi for Those who Think that Death is a Gay Disease." *Christopher Street*, no. 118 (1987):60. Taunting the fearful about how they might catch gay disease.

Mycue, Edward. "Stick It Against." *James White Review* 3 (1986):5. A recognition of the epidemic's impact on sex.

Saint, Assotto. *Saints.* Galiens, 1989. In "The Memory of Suffering" lovers receive the results of an HIV test. In "De Profundis" a dead neighbor is recalled. "The Quilt" reacts to policies, accusations, and loss. "Heaven in Hill" is a memorial poem to a "blue-eyed booted brute."

Schreiber, Ron. *John*. Brooklyn, N.Y.: Hanging Loose, 1988. Poems witnessing the sickness and death of a lover.

Sherrill, Jan-Mitchell. "Citizen of Sodom." *James White Review* 5 (1987):12. A witness speaks of the destruction of Sodom but does not see its destruction as any victory over him.

———. "Courtship in the Plague Years." *James White Review* 6 (1988):8. A hermit's pleasures have become the order of the day.

Steinberg, David. "After James' Death." *James White Review* 6 (1989):11. A revulsion toward fish and meat after the death of friends.

———. "Spring, San Francisco, 1987." *James White Review* 4 (1987):4. In February trees bloom oblivious to the epidemic.

Tierney, Karl. "Sot." *James White Review* 7 (1990):9. The deaths from AIDS are interpreted as victory by an ancient moralist.

White, Edmund. "Michael Grumley." *Christopher Street*, no. 124 (1988):48–49. A short memoir and poem.

Young, Tom. "Crutches on the Sun." *James White Review* 6 (1989):8. A poem ranging across the sickness and death of the epidemic.

———. "Tubs 2." *James White Review* 5 (1988):5. A lament about the change evident in the bathhouses: the heat is down, and it costs more than ever.

Drama

Bumbalo, Victor. *Adam and the Experts*. New York: Broadway Play, 1989. "*Adam* provides a tragicomic dose of medicine, the bandage of a smile on the fatalistic situations produced by AIDS. Bumbalo uses dry humor to vanquish a formidable enemy" (*Lambda Book Report*). An excerpt in which Adam discovers that his best friend, Eddie, has Kaposi's sarcoma, appears in *Christopher Street*, no. 139 (1989):12–16.

Cady, Joseph. "AIDS on the National Stage." *Medical Humanities Review* 6 (1992):20–26. Cady lists many of the published and unpublished plays with AIDS themes. In this useful review, he discusses, for example, Larry Kramer's *Just Say No*, William Finn's *Falsettoland*, Jean-Claude van Itallie's *Ancient Boys*, and Wendy Wasserstein's *The Heidi Chronicles*.

Chesley, Robert. *Hard Plays/Stiff Parts: The Homoerotic Plays of Robert Chesley*. San Francisco: Alamo Square, 1990. Plays that look at various aspects of the epidemic.

Fierstein, Harvey. *Harvey Fierstein's Safe Sex*. New York: Atheneum, 1987. Three plays— *Manny and Jake*, *Safe Sex*, and *On Tidy Endings*—that raise a range of issues related to the experiences and loss in the epidemic.

Hoffman, William. *As Is*. New York: Vintage, 1985. In conversations between Rich (who has AIDS) and his former lover Saul, this play raises the importance of the epidemic for all.

Kramer, Larry. *The Normal Heart*. New York: New American Library, 1985. A portrayal of the indifference of politicians, newspapers, and even gay men themselves to the emergence of the AIDS epidemic.

Osborn, M. Elizabeth. *The Way We Live Now: American Plays & The AIDS Crisis*. Introduction by Michael Feingold. New York: Theatre Communication Group, 1990. An anthology of scenes from ten plays, including *Andre's Mother, A Poster of the Cosmos, Angels in America, Zero Positive, Athens in Ruins, As Is, Seeking Wild,* and *Jack*.

Temerson, Catherine, and Françoise Kourilsky, eds. *Gay Plays: An International Anthology*. New York: Ubu Repertory Theater Publications, 1989. Includes Copi's *Grand Finale*, in "gala black farce style (somewhere between Joe Orton and Chris Durang) about the last hours of a camp queen dying of AIDS, whose demise is attended by rollicking cartoon-style figures Dionysiacally drugging and dramatizing his end" (Robert Patrick). Also includes a play by Jean-Claude Van Itallie that "uses shifting time and space and focus to tell about another PWA, a considerably grimmer, indeed melancholy, set-designer already pretty depressed by his own erotic alienation before he got ill" (Robert Patrick).

Biography and Autobiography

Barbo, Beverly. *The Walking Wounded*. Lindsborg, Kans.: Carlsons, 1987. A mother's firsthand report on her experience with two sons with AIDS.

Callen, Michael. *Surviving AIDS*. New York: Harper/Collins, 1990. An account of one of the longest survivors of AIDS and his involvement in the politics of AIDS, as well as some practical counsel.

Clark, J. Michael. *Diary of a Southern Queen*. Dallas: Monument, 1990. A complex journal intermingling thoughts on promiscuity, religious spirituality, friendship, social intolerance, and Levi and leather clubs, as these have all been put in relief by the epidemic.

Clark, Tom, and Dick Kleiner. *Rock Hudson, Friend of Mine*. New York: Pharos, 1989. Written by a longtime confidant and friend, this book reminisces about Hudson's interactions with Hollywood celebrities as well as his illness and death.

Cox, Elizabeth. *Thanksgiving, An AIDS Journal*. New York: Harper and Row, 1990. A woman tells the story of her early married life, her musician husband's diagnosis with AIDS, the discovery of his hidden sexual past, and her involvement in his assisted suicide.

Dreuilhe, Emmanuel. *Mortal Embrace: Living with AIDS*. New York: Hill and Wang, 1988. Military imagery abounds in this collection of essays that recount the ways in which Dreuilhe approaches his illness.

Glaser, Elizabeth, and Laura Palmer. *In the Absence of Angels: A Hollywood Family's Courageous Story*. New York: G. P. Putnam, 1991. The personal story of a woman who contracted HIV through blood transfusion and who went on to commit herself to pediatric AIDS groups.

Guibert, Hervé. *To the Friend Who Did Not Save My Life*. New York: Atheneum, 1991. A fictive autobiography that recounts the effects of HIV on the narrator and those around him.

Hendrikson, Peter A. *Alive & Well: A Path for Living in a Time of HIV*. New York: Irvington, 1991. This account offers guidelines for living in ways to promote health and acquire skills for living with HIV.

Hudson, Rock, and Sara Davison. *Rock Hudson: His Story*. New York: Morrow, 1986. An account of the famous actor's life and death with AIDS: his trips to clinics in Paris, the last days, the cremation, Marc Christian, and the press.

Josephs, Larry. "The Harrowing Plunge." *New York Times Magazine* (November 11, 1990):38–46. A personal account of Josephs's experience with pneumonia, hopelessness, and religion: "In the last few months I have come to accept the fact that AIDS is going to kill me."

Kelly, Kevin. *One Singular Sensation: The Michael Bennett Story*. New York: Kensington, 1990. The biography of the creator of long-running Broadway musicals who was among the first to use AZT in his struggle against AIDS.

Kramer, Larry. *Reports from the Holocaust*. New York: St. Martin's, 1989. Essays from one of the earliest, most outspoken activists, who recounts his own increasing political and personal involvement in the fight against AIDS as well as the indifference and obstacles he has found.

Kübler-Ross, Elisabeth. *AIDS: The Ultimate Challenge*. New York: Macmillan, 1987. A study in caring for a broad array of persons with AIDS from the woman who pioneered the study of dying.

McCarroll, Tolbert. *Morning Glory Babies: Children with AIDS and the Celebration of Life*. New York: St. Martin's, 1988. The book follows the story of three babies who were taken in by a small, lay Catholic community and covers the year that the babies lived with them in their farm home.

Monette, Paul. *Borrowed Time*. San Diego: Harcourt Brace Jovanovich, 1988. The eloquent and acclaimed memoir of Monette's life with Roger Horwitz, who died with AIDS.

Money, J. W. *To All The Girls I've Loved Before: An AIDS Diary*. Boston: Alyson, 1987. Warm, humorous, and incisive pieces, written in 1986, ranging over life, Edith Sitwell, lovers, and the importance of friends.

Moore, Jonathan. *Perry Ellis: A Biography*. New York: St. Martin's, 1988. A biography of the eminent fashion designer who at age 46 died with AIDS. His last words: "Never enough!"

Nassaney, Louie, and Glenn Kolb. *I Am Not a Victim*. Santa Monica, Calif.: Hay House, 1990. The personal account of a man who has survived eight years after a diagnosis of AIDS: "I used to be a victim of aids, but I am no longer a victim, and I'm thriving."

Nungesser, Lon G. *Epidemic of Courage*. New York: St. Martin's, 1986. Persons with AIDS and others who have faced the epidemic talk about their experiences, faith, sickness, and the path to acceptance.

Owen, Bob. *Roger's Recovery*. Malibu, Calif.: DAVAR, 1987. The account of a physician treating a person with AIDS.

Peavey, Fran. *A Shallow Pool of Time*. Philadelphia: New Society Publishers, 1990. A woman living in San Francisco tells about her own experience with AIDS.

Petrow, Steven. *Dancing in the Darkness*. Lexington, Mass.: Lexington Books, 1990. A broad range of interviews with people with AIDS, accounts of women and family members hit by the epidemic, and the story of a journalist reporting his own illness.

Preston, John. *Personal Dispatches*. New York: St. Martin's, 1989. Stories and personal accounts of people in the epidemic. Includes work by Allan Troxler, Andrew Holleran, Edmund White, and others.

Reed, Paul. *The Q Journal*. Berkeley: Celestial Arts, 1991. A journal reporting on the author's involvement with an experimental drug, Compound Q.

Rider, Ines, and Patricia Ruppelt, eds. *AIDS: The Women*. San Francisco: Cleis, 1988. Essays about and by women as they have cared for people with AIDS or experienced it themselves.

Thorson, Scott, and Alex Thorliefson. *Behind the Candelabra: My Life with Liberace*. New York: Knightsbridge, 1990. An "inside look" at Liberace's life with the author, detailing the denials and final truth about Liberace's sickness and death.

Weitz, Rose. *Life with AIDS*. New Brunswick, N.J.: Rutgers University Press, 1991. A medical sociologist interviews thirty-one people with HIV and reports how HIV has changed their lives.

White, Ryan, and Ann Marie Cunningham. *Ryan White: My Own Story*. New York: Dial Books, 1991. The story of a teenage hemophiliac whose exclusion from an Indiana school brought national attention to his life and death.

Whitmore, George. *Someone Was Here: Profiles in the AIDS Epidemic*. New York: New American Library, 1988. Reports on gay men with AIDS and their case buddies, the mother of a drifter son with AIDS, hospital workers who daily face the trials of caring for people with AIDS, and the cemetery workers who bury babies dead with AIDS in paupers' graves.

Wojnarowicz, David. *Close to the Knives: A Memoir of Disintegration*. New York: Vintage, 1991. "There may be more polished accounts of HIV-related illness in fiction and non-fiction but there can be few so curiously brilliant" (*Lambda Book Report*). An angry account from someone whose artwork sparked national debate about censorship, pornography, and public funding of the arts.

Essays, Criticism, and Analysis

The ACT UP New York Women and AIDS Book Group. *Women, AIDS, and Activism*. Boston, Mass.: South End, 1990. A compendium of facts, numbers, routes of transmission, and interpretations of the significance of AIDS for women, as well as autobiographical essays, cultural criticism, lesbian perspectives, and political and advocacy recommendations.

Altman, Dennis. *AIDS in the Mind of America: The Social, Political, and Psychological Impact of a New Epidemic*. New York: Doubleday, 1986. This political and social commentary describes how sex and politics have been viewed since the advent of the AIDS epidemic.

Bateson, Catherine, and Richard Goldsby. *Thinking AIDS*. Reading, Mass.: Addison-Wesley, 1988. An easy introduction to the nature of HIV-related disease as well as sympathetic and insightful reflections on testing, blame, and social reactions.

Bayer, Ronald. *Private Acts, Social Consequences: AIDS and the Politics of Public Health*. New York: Free, 1989. An account of the beginning of public policy regarding AIDS in the United States.

Black, David. *The Plague Years: A Chronicle of AIDS, the Epidemic of Our Time*. New York: Simon and Schuster, 1985. A reporter looks at images of AIDS and his own emotions in the early years of the epidemic.

Boffin, Tessa, and Sunil Gupta, eds. *Ecstatic Antibodies: Resisting the AIDS Mythology*. London: Rivers Oram, 1990. "Nineteen essays by cultural theorists and activists on the politics of representation that characterize government campaigns and mainstream media coverage of the AIDS epidemic (for example, "the in/visibility of certain communities—Black people, lesbians, and gay men)" (*Women and Language*).

Cady, Joseph, and Kathryn Montgomery Hunter. "Making Contact: The AIDS Plays." In Eric T. Juengst and Barbara A. Koenig, eds., *The Meaning of AIDS*, pp. 42–49. New York: Praeger, 1989. A consideration of some of the thematic content and techniques in some of the early plays about AIDS.

Carter, Albert H., III, and Lois LaCivita Nixon. "To Embrace the Messenger: Connections in Three Plays about AIDS." *AIDS Education and Prevention* 1 (1989):126–33. The educational efforts of two plays and a TV drama are considered in order to argue that the messengers of AIDS should not be shot for the news they bear.

Carter, Erica, and Simon Watney, eds. *Taking Liberties: AIDS and Cultural Politics*. London: Serpent's Tail and ICA, 1989. Essays from a conference at which journalists, activists, academics, and others analyzed the way AIDS has been seen as "fundamentally challenging the meanings, values, and practices in which our experiences of sexuality, love, the body, life, death and physical processes are grounded." Other essays explore the meanings of AIDS, feminism, and sexual politics, and the construction of the terms *volunteer* and *expert*.

Corless, Inge B., and Mary Pittman-Lindeman, eds. *AIDS: Principles, Practices and Politics*. Cambridge, N.Y.: Hemisphere, 1988. A broad-ranging collection of essays treating analysis of the language used in the epidemic, social responsibility, and aspects of public policy.

Crimp, Douglas. *AIDS Demo Graphics*. Seattle: Bay, 1990. Photographs and reflections on images used to confront social resistance to the epidemic.

——. "Portraits of People with AIDS." In Cary Nelson, Lawrence Grossberg, and Paula A. Treichler, eds., *Cultural Studies Now and in the Future*. New York: Routledge, forthcoming. "An analysis of photographic and video representations of people with AIDS, contrasting examples of memorializing portraits in a formalist/minimalist tradition with activist work that seeks to challenge and disrupt the distancing and apolitical assumptions of formalism" (*Women and Literature*).

——, ed. *AIDS: Cultural Analysis, Cultural Activism*. Cambridge, Mass.: MIT Press, 1988. Now-classic essays on language, representation, historical precedents, portraiture, promiscuity, and cultural responses to the AIDS epidemic.

Denneny, Michael. "A Quilt of Many Colors: AIDS Writing and the Creation of Culture." *Christopher Street*, no. 141 (1988):15–21. An essay on how AIDS, for all its ills, has mobilized many gay men spiritually and politically.

Fee, Elizabeth, and Daniel M. Fox, eds. *AIDS: The Burdens of History*. Berkeley and Los Angeles: University of California Press, 1988. Essays that show the ways in which the AIDS epidemic and its interpretation are framed by past events and cultural presumptions.

Ferlinghetti, Lawrence, and Nancy J. Peters, eds. "AIDS, Cultural Life and the Arts: A Forum," *City Lights Review #2*. San Francisco: City Lights Books, 1988. A collection of poems, memoirs, essays, artwork, and cartoons from twenty-six contributors.

Fitzgerald, Frances. *Cities on a Hill*. New York: Simon and Schuster, 1986. A reporter looks at the effects of the AIDS epidemic in the Castro section of San Francisco and its hysteria-producing effect on the tantric sex practices of the Baghwan Rashneesh's northwestern U.S. enclave.

Gostin, Lawrence O., ed. *AIDS and the Health Care System*. New Haven, Conn.: Yale University Press, 1990. A collection of articles about legal and ethical aspects of health care delivery and responsibility.

Greenly, Mike. *Chronicle: The Human Side of AIDS*. New York: Irvington, 1986. The story of becoming involved with AIDS and the interviews and observations that followed.

Grover, Jan Zita. "AIDS, Keywords and Culture." In Cary Nelson, Lawrence Grossberg, and Paula A. Treichler, eds., *Cultural Studies Now and in the Future*. (New York: Routledge, forthcoming). "Grover draws on Raymond Williams' accounts of language and culture to examine the evolution of AIDS discourse, gay and lesbian activism, and the role of the academy" (*Women and Language*).

———, ed. *AIDS: The Artists' Response*. Columbus: The Ohio State University, 1989. "This handsome and informative catalogue, prepared for an exhibition of art, photography, and video addressing the AIDS epidemic, provides an excellent introduction to a range of artists' responses to AIDS and to debates over representation within the art and activist communities" (*Women and Language*).

Harris, Daniel. "AIDS & Theory." *Lingua franca* (June 1991): 1, 16–19. An argument that "critical theorists" have trivialized and reduced "the engagement theory of AIDS" to innocuous realities.

Helmken, Charles M. *AIDS: Images for Survival*. Washington, D.C.: Shosin Society, 1989. A collection of AIDS posters produced in the U.S. and Korea, ranging from images promoting fear of AIDS to images urging compassion for PWAs.

Hippler, Mike. *So Little Time: Essays on Gay Life*. Berkeley: Celestial Arts, 1990. Funny, smart, and serious essays collected from a columnist for the *Bay Area Reporter*. There are belated valentines and reflections on the obituaries but no apologies for gay sex.

Holleran, Andrew. "Anniversary." *Christopher Street*, no. 121 (1988):4–13. On the occasion of the tenth anniversary of *Christopher Street*, Holleran looks back at the way in which, amid all the other issues, AIDS cast its pall over gay life.

———. "Blood Work." *Christopher Street*, no. 158 (1991):6–8. A review of *The Q Journal* by Paul Reed, and a reflection on the relationship between the experience of AIDS and authorship.

———. "Changes." *Christopher Street*, no. 125 (1988):7–10. Encounters with strangers once offered the prospect of warmth and touch, but they are now overlaid with questions about AIDS and desire.

———. "Circles." *Christopher Street*, no. 103 (1986):7–9. Wondering what the virus needed with Cosmo, who seemed "on his ten-speed with his knapsack, utterly independent, as if all he needed in life was a combination lock, a Penguin paperback, and a can of V-8 juice.

———. "Cleaning My Bedroom." *Christopher Street*, no. 105 (1986):6–9. Thoughts of the Titanic after cleaning a Manhattan bedroom and finding a picture of friends, who have died, at the beach.

———. "Fragments." *Christopher Street*, no. 155 (1991):6–8. A reflection on the nature and attraction of one war over another.

———. "Friends." *Christopher Street*, no. 138 (1989):3–5. A reflection on the nature of friendship and how the epidemic provoked the question, "Who would care for me if I got sick?"

———. "Giving Up." *Christopher Street*, no. 148 (1990):5–7. Reflecting on the dismal news coming out of the 1990 International AIDS conference and the continuing evidence of the epidemic around him, Holleran notes the importance of a cure.

———. *Ground Zero*. New York: William Morrow, 1988. Essays collected mostly from *Christopher Street* that mourn lives lost and that document how the transformation of sex into something feared affects gay thinking today.

———. "I Want to Take Off Your Glasses." *Christopher Street*, no. 128 (1988):3–5. A discussion of how uncertainty about the communicability of the epidemic has changed sexual practices/desires, and what has been lost as a result.

———. "Linoleum City." *Christopher Street*, no. 147 (1990):4–7. A consideration of the way the epidemic has masked other issues important to gay life in the United States.

———. "Little Boats." *Christopher Street*, no. 104 (1986):7–9. A visit to the museum offers a respite from the world of AIDS, newspaper headlines, doctor's offices, and vials of blood.

———. "More Life." *Christopher Street*, no. 142 (1990):6–9. In a visit to New York, Holleran finds the city with all its attractions in place, hears about deaths that would "draw tears from a stone," and finds the city still in the grips of the claustrophobia of the epidemic.

———. "Notes on Celibacy." *Christopher Street*, no. 110 (1987):8–10. A number of observations on celibacy, including: "Celibacy is easier in the country than in town."

———. "Notes on Promiscuity." *Christopher Street*, no. 114 (1987):5–8. A number of observations on promiscuity, including: "When asked why he was moving from New York City to San Francisco in 1978, a friend of mine said with an ironic smile: 'To improve the quality of my promiscuity.'"

———. "Reading and Writing." *Christopher Street*, no. 115 (1987):5–7. Amid the proliferation of writing on AIDS, there is only one thing people want to read: "CURE FOUND."

———. "Roofers." *Christopher Street*, no. 108 (1987):7–9. With the roofers working on his house, Holleran thinks back to the summers spent on Manhattan roofs and how the epidemic has brought a "beady-eyed realism" to relations between men.

———. "The Room." *Christopher Street*, no. 123 (1988):4–8. Visiting a hospital room, watching helicopters come and go outside the window, and wondering how much longer before a treatment comes.

———. "Talking to O." *Christopher Street*, no. 109 (1987):6–8. What it's like to discover that a friend has AIDS.

———. "Trust." *Christopher Street*, no. 117 (1987):4–8. A reflection on the way the epidemic has transformed this postmodern world into an era posttrust as well.

———. "The Way We Live Now." *Christopher Street*, no. 134 (1989):3–5. An essay in which Holleran wonders why AIDS has suddenly fallen from the conversational urgency it once held, why the immediacy of this "shark attack" has become banal.

Howard, Billy. *Epitaphs for the Living: Words and Images in the Time of AIDS*. Dallas, Tex.: Southern Methodist University Press, 1989. Photographic portraits of people with AIDS and their reflections on their lives.

Illingworth, Patricia. *AIDS and the Good Society*. London: Routledge, 1990. A moral argument that insofar as society is responsible for the adverse choices of gay men and needle users, that same society owes them compensation in the epidemic.

Institute of Medicine, National Academy of Science. *Mobilizing against AIDS*, rev. ed. Cambridge, Mass.: Harvard University Press, 1989. A discussion of the scope of the epidemic, its disease manifestations, and recommendations for public-health policy.

Juengst, Eric, and Barbara Koenig, eds. *The Meaning of AIDS: Implications for Medical Science, Clinical Practice and Public Health Policy*. New York: Praeger, 1989. Essays on naming the virus, language and responsibility, decisions in health care relations, and the foundations of restrictions on and against people with HIV.

Kinsella, James. *Covering the Plague*. New Brunswick, N.J.: Rutgers, 1989. An account and criticism of the coverage of the AIDS epidemic in the United States media.

Lauritsen, John. "Saying No to HIV: An Interview with Professor Peter Duesberg." *Christopher Street*, no. 118 (1987):17–34. An interview with a biochemist who disputes the role of HIV in causing the diseases attributed to it.

McKenzie, Nancy F., ed. *The AIDS Reader: Social, Political, and Ethical Issues*. New York: Meridian, 1991. Essays by Larry Kramer, George Whitmore, June E. Osborne, and others are included here.

Miller, James, ed. *Fluid Exchanges: Artists and Critics in the AIDS Crisis*. Toronto: University of Toronto Press, 1992. A collection of essays that analyze representations of AIDS.

Murphy, Timothy F. "No Time for an AIDS Backlash." *Hastings Center Report*

(March/April 1991):7–11. A consideration of the argument that AIDS has already received its fair share of public attention and funds.

——. "Philosophy in the Bedroom." *Christopher Street*, no. 96 (1986): 33–37. A reflection on the coming of AIDS and a call for compassion for those with it.

Nelson, Emmanuel S. *AIDS: The Literary Response*. Boston: Twayne, forthcoming). A collection of critical essays that look at a wide range of issues in writing about AIDS.

Nixon, Nicholas and Bebe. *People with AIDS*. New York: David R. Godine, 1991. "A collection of biographical sketches accompanied by photographs of fourteen people with AIDS: a brave and honest portrayal of death and dying" (*Lambda Rising News*).

Nunokawa, Jeff. "'All the Sad Men': AIDS and the Work of Mourning." *Yale Journal of Criticism* 4 (1991):1–2. A study in how the representations of people with AIDS are continuous with historical representations of suffering gay men.

Nussbaum, Bruce. *Good Intentions: How Big Business and the Medical Establishment Are Corrupting the Fight Against AIDS*. New York: Atlantic 1990. A study of the "personalities" of the epidemic and harsh judgments on the way personality and policy impede advances against the epidemic.

O'Malley, Padraig, ed. *The AIDS Epidemic*. Boston: Beacon, 1989. Over thirty-six essays consider various aspects of the epidemic: the clinical spectrum of disease, vaccine development, HIV testing, ethics in research, costs, education, and literature.

Ortleb, Charles L. "Scientist Zero." *Christopher Street*, no. 133 (1989):8–14. In considering Randy Shilts's *And the Band Played On*, Ortleb points out a number of persons and policies that he thinks controlled the representation of the epidemic, permitted expansion of the epidemic, and impede its control.

Panem, Sandra. *The AIDS Bureaucracy*. Cambridge, Mass.: Harvard University Press, 1988. An examination of the advent of AIDS and its reception by institutions charged with the care of public health.

Pastore, Judith. *Literary AIDS: The Responsibilities of Representation*. Urbana: University of Illinois Press, forthcoming. A collection of critical essays, fiction, poetry, and teaching guides.

Patton, Cindy. *Sex and Germs*. Boston: South End, 1985. An analysis of the extent to which sex has been linked with disease and death in the epidemic.

——. *Inventing AIDS*. New York: Routledge, Chapman, and Hall, 1990. Patton, an early member of the AIDS Action Committee, considers various representations of AIDS in media and science, examines the cultural assumptions behind institutional processes, and offers ideas on teaching about AIDS.

Pierce, Christine, and Donald VanDeVeer, eds. *AIDS: Ethics and Public Policy*. Belmont, Calif.: Wadsworth, 1988. A collection, useful for classrooms, of essays on the concepts used to understand AIDS, justifications and proposals regarding the restriction of liberty, and sexual identity and autonomy.

Rist, Darrell Yates. "AIDS as Apocalypse: The Deadly Costs of an Obsession." *Christopher Street*, no. 131 (1989):11–14. Originally published in *The Nation* (February 13, 1989), this essay points out the ways in which the exclusive focus on the epidemic has impeded gay advances and invention elsewhere.

Ruskin, Cindy. Photography by Matt Herron. *The Quilt: Stories from the Names Project*. New York: Pocket Books, 1988. An account of the origin of "the quilt" and photographs of the individual panels.

Saint-Phalle, Niki. *AIDS: You Can't Catch It Holding Hands*. San Francisco: Lapis, 1987. A colorful picture book with some broad messages about self-protection and distinguishing between disease and PWAs.

Satuloff, Bob. "Suspension of Disbelief." *Christopher Street*, no. 155 (1991):12–14. An expression of dissatisfaction with the way an essay by Andrew Sullivan in *The New Republic* swallows the "official line" about the epidemic.

Schecter, Stephen. *The AIDS Notebooks*. Albany: State University of New York Press, 1990. A notebook-style discussion on the language and import of AIDS, by a cultural sociologist.

Shilts, Randy. *And the Band Played On*. New York: St. Martin's, 1987. Beginning with a death in Denmark, journalist Shilts traces the discovery of a new viral syndrome and its reception by gay men, the media, government, science, and the public in the United States.

Social Research 55 (1988). A volume of essays devoted to an analysis of the epidemic, including essays by Charles Rosenberg, Sander Gilman, Lewis Thomas, Richard Poirier, and Allan M. Brandt.

Sontag, Susan. *AIDS and its Metaphors*. New York: Farrar Straus Giroux, 1989. A critical consideration of the conception and language of disease; argues in particular against certain AIDS metaphors and their presumptions.

Spender, Stephen, ed. *Hockney's Alphabet*. New York: Random House, 1991. Alphabet drawings by David Hockney are paired in this volume with short texts on moral, medical and sexual matters by, for example, Erica Jong, Susan Sontag, Norman Mailer, and Martin Amis.

Sullivan, Andrew. "Gay Life, Gay Death: The Siege of a Subculture." *New Republic*, December 17, 1990, pp. 19–25. A consideration of the way the epidemic has divided gay men and activist groups against themselves even in the personal ads.

Trent, Robert. "Love and Death." *Christopher Street*, no. 116 (1987):26–31. A witty essay on the ways "sex today requires invention, clever substitution, and an emphasis on the visual."

Video Data Bank. *Video Against AIDS*. New York: The Bank, 1989. Three videocassettes that feature a variety of narratives, interviews, and images on PWA power, discrimination, women, resistance, mourning, education, analysis, and activism.

Ward, Michael. "HIV: 'Deadly AIDS Virus,' or One More Watergate?" *Christopher Street*, no. 154 (1990):15–20. An essay advancing the view that HIV and its putative treatment are fraudulent inventions of a fascist, death-oriented medical system.

Watney, Simon. *Policing Desire: Pornography, AIDS, and the Media*. Minneapolis: University of Minnesota Press, 1987. Incisive consideration of the way media representations of the epidemic are framed by moral imperatives, and how the struggle against AIDS requires a rethinking of language, media, and representation.

Contributors

Emily Apter is associate professor of French in the Department of French and Italian at the University of California, Davis. She is the author of *Feminizing the Fetish: Psychoanalysis and Narrative Obsession in Turn-of-the-Century France* (Cornell University Press, 1991) and *André Gide and the Codes of Homotexuality* (Stanford French and Italian Studies, 1987). She is currently working on a study of colonial realism in France and North Africa, 1870–1940.

Peter M. Bowen, a doctoral candidate at Rutgers University, is finishing a dissertation on the markings of Colonial American space as a field of penal reform.

Franklin Brooks is associate professor and director of graduate studies of French and Italian at Vanderbilt University. His principal research is in seventeenth-century French literature and society. His interest in plague literature, past and present, is a response to the AIDS crisis. He has served as the graduate school's representative on the Vanderbilt AIDS Project.

Joseph Cady teaches literature and medicine in the Division of the Medical Humanities at the University of Rochester Medical School and gay and lesbian literature at the New School for Social Research.

John Clum is professor of the Practice of Theater and professor of English at Duke University. He is the author of *Acting Gay: Male Homosexuality in Modern Drama* (Columbia, 1992), and coeditor of *Displacing Homophobia: Gay Male Perspectives in Literature and Culture* (Duke, 1989). He has written widely on twentieth-century British and American drama and on gay male literature.

Richard Dellamora teaches in the Departments of English and Cultural Studies at Trent University in Peterborough, Ontario. He is the author of *Masculine*

Desire: The Sexual Politics of Victorian Aestheticism (University of North Carolina Press, 1990) as well as of "Traversing the Feminine in Oscar Wilde's *Salomé*," in Thaïs Morgan, ed., *Victorian Sages and Cultural Discourse: Renegotiating Gender and Power* (Rutgers University Press, 1990). He is currently writing a series of essays about sexual politics and the sense of an ending in late nineteenth- and twentieth-century writing.

Lee Edelman, associate professor of English at Tufts University, is the author of *Transmemberment of Song: Hart Crane's Anatomies of Rhetoric and Desire* (Stanford, 1987). He has published widely on modern poetry, literary theory, and gay studies, and his recently completed volume, *Homographesis: Essays in Gay Literary and Cultural Theory,* is forthcoming from Routledge.

Sander L. Gilman is the Goldwin Smith Professor of Humane Studies at Cornell University and professor of the History of Psychiatry at the Cornell Medical College. For the 1990–91 academic year he was the Visiting Historical Scholar at the National Library of Medicine. He is an intellectual and cultural historian who has been a member of the Cornell faculty since 1969. He is the author or editor of over twenty-seven books, the most recent—*Sexuality: An Illustrated History*—having been published in 1989 by John Wiley and Sons.

Phillip B. Harper is assistant professor at Harvard University, where he teaches in the departments of English and Afro-American Studies, He is currently at work on a book on social division in African-American culture.

James W. Jones is assistant professor of German at Central Michigan University. He is the author of *"We the Third Sex:" Literary Representations of Homosexuality in Wilhelmine Germany* (Peter Lang, 1990), "Discourses on and of AIDS in West Germany, 1986–1990," in the *Journal of the History of Sexuality* (2, no. 1 [1991]), as well as articles on gay and lesbian literature and on literary theory. He received his Ph.D. from the University of Wisconsin.

James Miller taught English at Harvard from 1979 to 1985 and is currently Faculty of Arts Professor at the University of Western Ontario. In 1988 he organized Canada's first interdisciplinary seminar on AIDS and the Arts and curated "Visual AIDS," a traveling exhibition of AIDS posters from around the world. He has also edited an anthology of essays on AIDS and culture, *Fluid Exchanges: Artists and Critics in the AIDS Crisis* (University of Toronto Press, 1992). He plans to visit Fire Island in this life.

Timothy F. Murphy is assistant professor, Medical Humanities Program, Department of Medical Education, University of Illinois College of Medicine at Chicago. He holds a Ph.D. in philosophy from Boston College, has written on

AIDS for a number of academic journals, and is at work on a book on ethical dimensions of sexual orientation therapy and research.

Suzanne Poirier is associate professor of Literature and Medicine, Medical Humanities Program, Department of Medical Education, University of Illinois College of Medicine at Chicago and is the author of a forthcoming history of the Chicago Syphilis Control Program, 1936–40.

Michael S. Sherry, professor of History at Northwestern University, is the author of *The Rise of American Air Power: The Creation of Armageddon* (Yale University Press, 1987) and teaches military history, gay and lesbian history, and modern American history.

Paula A. Treichler is associate professor at the University of Illinois College of Medicine at Urbana and teaches in the College of Medicine, the Institute of Communications Research, and the Women's Studies Program. She is coauthor of *A Feminist Dictionary* (Pandora, 1985) and *Language, Gender and Professional Writing: Theoretical Approaches and Guidelines for Nonsexist Usage* (Modern Language Association, 1989) and coeditor of *For Alma Mater: Theory and Practice in Feminist Scholarship* (University of Illinois Press, 1985) and *Cultural Studies* (Routledge, 1992). She has published widely on feminist theory, medical discourse, and the AIDS epidemic. Her Ph.D. is in linguistics.

Index